Th
Book

From the Six
to the Twelve

KEESING'S PUBLICATIONS

Other titles currently available in the Keesing's International Studies series (all published by Longman Group UK Limited):-

China and the Soviet Union 1949–84, compiled by Peter Jones and Sian Kevill (1985)

Conflict in Central America, by Helen Schooley (1987)

The Keesing's Reference Publications (KRP) series (all published by Longman Group UK Limited) includes the following currently available titles:-

Border and Territorial Disputes, edited by Alan J. Day (1982); a second edition is to be published in late 1987

Political Dissent: An International Guide to Dissident, Extra-Parliamentary, Guerrilla and Illegal Political Movements, compiled by Henry W. Degenhardt (1983); a revised and updated version, *Revolutionary and Dissident Movements*, is to be published in late 1987

Political Parties of the World (2nd edition), edited by Alan J. Day & Henry W. Degenhardt (1984)

State Economic Agencies of the World, edited by Alan J. Day (1985)

Maritime Affairs: A World Handbook, compiled by Henry W. Degenhardt (1985)

Latin American Political Movements, compiled by Ciarán Ó Maoláin (1985)

Communist and Marxist Parties of the World, compiled by Charles Hobday (1986)

OPEC, Its Member States and the World Energy Market, compiled by John Evans (1986)

Treaties and Alliances of the World (4th edition), compiled by Henry W. Degenhardt (1986)

Peace Movements of the World: An International Directory, edited by Alan J. Day (1986)

Keesing's Record of World Events (formerly *Keesing's Contemporary Archives*), the monthly worldwide news reference service with an unrivalled reputation for accuracy and impartiality, has appeared continuously since 1931. Published by Longman Group UK Limited on annual subscription; back volumes are also available.

From the Six to the Twelve:

the enlargement of the European Communities

KEESING'S INTERNATIONAL STUDIES

By Frances Nicholson and Roger East

Longman

FROM THE SIX TO THE TWELVE:

THE ENLARGEMENT OF THE EUROPEAN COMMUNITIES

Published by **Longman Group UK Limited**, Longman House,
Burnt Mill, Harlow, Essex CM20 2JE, UK

Distributed exclusively in the United States and
Canada by St. James Press, 425 North Michigan
Avenue, Chicago, Illinois 60611, USA
Telephone: (312) 329 0806.

ISBN 0-582-90276-2   (Longman)
ISBN 0 912289 74 0 (St. James)

First published 1987

British Library Cataloguing in Publication Data

Nicholson, Frances—
    From the six to the twelve: the enlargement of the
European Communities.—(Keesing's international studies)
    1. European Economic Community
I. Title   II. East, Roger, *1952–*
III. Series
337.1'42   HC241.2

ISBN 0–582–90276–2

Typeset in 10/11 Linotron Times
by The Word Factory, Rossendale, Lancashire

Printed in Great Britain by Robert Hartnoll (1985) Ltd, Bodmin

CONTENTS

INTRODUCTION

The European Communities, created in the 1950s as the European Coal and Steel Community, the European Economic Community and Euratom, had grown by 1986 from the original group of Six to a much more heterogeneous and wider group of Twelve.

As the original Six—Belgium, France, the Federal Republic of Germany, Italy, Luxembourg and the Netherlands—began to establish common external tariffs and common policies on coal, steel, agriculture or social affairs, other West European countries saw a need to discuss involvement in the integration process. The United Kingdom, Denmark and Ireland applied for membership in mid-1961, as did Norway in May 1962, but de Gaulle's veto of the UK approach in January 1963 effectively blocked any extension of the Community experiment until his departure from the political scene in 1969.

At the Hague summit in December of that year the Six agreed on new initiatives to strengthen the Communities, looking forward to the first enlargement. The Six became the Nine in 1973 with the accession of the UK, Denmark and Ireland, while the Norwegian people in a referendum in September 1972 voted not to join. The impetus towards integration, however, was set back by the economic shock of the oil crisis in 1973–74, and by uncertainty about the UK commitment to membership, at least until the renegotiation of terms by the new UK Labour government had been approved in a referendum in June 1975.

The latter part of the 1970s saw the opening of the Communities towards the south of Europe, where democratic governments had succeeded the dictatorships in Greece, Spain and Portugal. Greek accession went ahead in January 1981, the Nine becoming the Ten, but the Spanish and Portuguese applications were delayed, in part because of internal Community problems, such as the level of UK budget contributions and attempts to control agricultural overproduction. It was not until January 1986 that the Ten became the Twelve, after the temporary resolution of key problems in Fontainebleau in June 1984 had made it possible for the "relaunched" Communities to conclude negotiations with the two Iberian applicants.

By this time the political balance of the European Communities had shifted away from the industrialized countries of northern Europe towards the less-developed and more agricultural Mediterranean member states. This shift in balance placed new demands on the Community machinery to reduce the wide economic disparities between north and south. Seeking more effective mechanisms to meet these challenges, the Twelve have formulated a Single European Act, designed to strengthen Community decision-making and to provide for closer co-operation in various policy areas. Whether such new initiatives can hold the Communities together remains to be seen.

From the Six to the Twelve details the course of the successive enlargements, with coverage also of Turkey as a prospective thirteenth applicant, and the 1985 withdrawal of Greenland. The book uses an easily accessible reference-style format designed to give a clear account of events, using contemporary reports, documents and speeches without entering the realms of comment or analysis.

The main chronology at the start of the book and the individual chronologies at the beginning of each chapter are designed to provide an overview of events and to help locate and highlight specific key developments. The appendices give details of institutional and other changes resulting from the successive enlargements and also provide summaries of the Treaties of Paris and of Rome, which established the ECSC and the EEC and Euratom.

The book draws heavily on material originally published in Keesing's Record of World Events (formerly Keesing's Contemporary Archives), and like Keesing's it aspires to high standards of objectivity and thoroughness. Special thanks go to the members of Keesing's staff and to Kit Nicholson for their help in compiling the book. Grateful acknowledgments are also due to Carpress International Press Agency for the maps on pages xii and xvii and to Eurostat, the Statistical Office of the EC, for the diagrams on pages xx and xxi.

GENERAL CHRONOLOGY

April 18, 1951	ECSC treaty signed in Paris
July 25, 1952	ECSC comes into operation
Oct. 23, 1954	WEU treaty signed
Dec. 21, 1954	Association agreement signed between Britain and ECSC
June 2–4, 1955	Messina Conference on further European integration
Feb. 7, 1957	British proposal for establishment of EFTA
March 25, 1957	Treaty of Rome signed to establish EEC and Euratom
Jan. 1, 1958	EEC and Euratom come into operation
Feb. 4, 1959	Co-operation agreement signed between Britain and Euratom
Dec. 29, 1959– Jan. 4, 1960	EFTA Convention signed in Stockholm
May 3, 1960	EFTA comes into operation
Feb. 10–11, 1961	Paris summit of Six on development of union which "could be expanded in the near future"
July 18, 1961	Bonn Declaration by Six on political union
July 9, 1961	Agreement on Greek associate membership of EEC signed
July 31, 1961	Ireland applies for membership of Communities
Aug. 3, 1961	UK House of Commons supports government decision to seek negotiations aiming at membership of Communities
Aug. 10, 1961	UK and Denmark request negotiations aiming at membership of Communities
Oct. 10, 1961	UK negotiations with EEC begin
Oct. 23, 1961	Irish negotiations begin
Oct. 26, 1961	Danish negotiations begin
March 2 and 5, 1962	UK applies for membership of ECSC and Euratom
May 2, 1962	Norway requests negotiations
July 4, 1962	Negotiations with Norway begin
Sept. 10–19, 1962	Commonwealth Conference in London
Nov. 1, 1962	Agreement on Greek associate membership of EEC takes effect

Jan. 14, 1963	De Gaulle's "non" at press conference in Paris
Jan. 22, 1963	Signature in Paris of Franco-German Treaty of Co-operation
Jan. 29, 1963	UK negotiations broken off
July 20, 1963	Yaoundé Convention signed
Sept. 1, 1963	Agreement on Turkish associate membership of EEC signed
Dec. 1, 1964	Agreement on Turkish associate membership takes effect
April 3, 1965	Treaty concluded to establish unified Council and Commission of Communities
May 11 and July 24, 1966	CAP agreed
Nov. 10, 1966	British government decides on "new high-level approach"
January–March 1967	Wilson and Brown visit EEC capitals
April 21, 1967	Military coup in Greece
May 10–11, 1967	UK, Denmark and Ireland formally apply for membership of EEC, ECSC and Euratom
July 1, 1967	Unified Council and Commission implemented
July 24, 1967	Norway formally applies
Sept. 29, 1967	Commission delivers Preliminary Opinion
Dec. 18–19, 1967	Deadlock in Council of Ministers on negotiations with UK after French insistence that resumption must be conditional on improvement in UK economy
April 2, 1968	Commission submits Opinion on transitional arrangements
July 1, 1968	Removal of EEC internal customs duties and establishment of common external tariff
Feb. 4, 1969	UK–Euratom co-operation extended for 2 years
July 10, 1969	Pompidou (having succeeded de Gaulle who resigned in April) declares that he does not oppose UK entry in principle
Oct. 2, 1969	Commission submits updated Opinion
Dec. 1–2, 1969	Hague summit agrees on principle of enlargement
December 1969	End of Community's transition period: future finance regulations drawn up
June 29, 1970	Preferential trade agreement between Communities and Spain signed

June 30, 1970	Opening of negotiations with UK, Denmark, Ireland and Norway
Oct. 1, 1970	Preferential trade agreement between Communities and Spain comes into effect
June 23, 1971	Agreement with UK at ministerial level on main issues
July 7, 1971	UK White Paper recommending entry
Oct. 28, 1971	UK parliamentary vote for entry after so-called "Great Debate"
Dec. 3, 1971	Opening of bilateral negotiations between Communities and six non-applicant EFTA countries
Jan. 22, 1972	Conclusion of negotiations and signature of Treaty of Accession by UK, Denmark, Ireland and Norway in Paris
May 10, 1972	Irish referendum "yes"
July 22, 1972	Conclusion of Special Relations Agreement between Communities and EFTA countries
Sept. 24–25, 1972	Norwegian referendum "no"
Oct. 2, 1972	Danish referendum "yes"
Oct. 17, 1972	Royal assent in UK for European Communities Act
Oct. 19–20, 1972	Paris heads of government summit of Nine sets guidelines for future Community development
Dec. 31, 1972	UK and Denmark leave EFTA
Jan. 1, 1973	Portuguese and other EFTA countries' special relations and preferential trade agreements with Communities come into effect
Jan. 1, 1973	Accession of UK, Denmark and Ireland to Communities
Feb. 1, 1973	Agreement on accession to CAP and on 5-year transition
May 14, 1973	Signature of trade agreement with Norway
December 1973	Copenhagen summit declaration on European identity
April 1, 1974	UK Labour government presents demands for renegotiation of accession terms
April 25, 1974	Portuguese revolution
June 4, 1974	Callaghan statement at Council of Ministers giving details of UK renegotiation requirements
July 1974	Restoration of democratic rule in Greece
Dec. 9–10, 1974	First meeting of European Council
March 10–11, 1975	Conclusion of UK renegotiations at Dublin European Council meeting

June 5, 1975	UK referendum on continued Community membership
June 12, 1975	Greek application for membership
Oct. 6, 1975	Negotiations on new trade agreement with Spain broken off
Nov. 20, 1975	Death of Franco and return to democracy in Spain
Jan. 20, 1976	Agreement on resumption of negotiations with Spain on new trade agreement
July 27, 1976	Formal opening of negotiations on Greek accession to EC
March 28, 1977	Portuguese application for EC membership
July 28, 1977	Spanish application for EC membership
Oct. 17, 1978	Opening of formal accession negotiations with Portugal
Dec. 7, 1978	Multilateral free trade agreement initialled between Spain and EFTA
Feb. 5, 1979	Opening of accession negotiations with Spain
March 13, 1979	Establishment of European Monetary System
May 28, 1979	Signature of Accession Treaty with Greece
June 7–10, 1979	First direct elections to European Parliament
June 21–22, 1979	Mrs Thatcher's request for reduced budget contributions at Strasbourg European Council
Jan. 1, 1981	Accession of Greece to EC
Feb. 23, 1981	Attempted coup in Madrid
Oct. 18, 1981	Greek elections to European Parliament
Oct. 21, 1981	Dr Papandreou to power in Greece
Feb. 23, 1982	Greenland referendum in favour of withdrawal from EC
March 1982	Presentation of Greek memorandum
June 30, 1982	Agreement on declaration on revised budgetary procedures
Oct. 17–18, 1983	Community agreement on organization of fruit, vegetable and olive oil markets
Jan. 1, 1984	EEC–EFTA free trade area established
March 13, 1984	Signature of agreement on withdrawal of Greenland from EC
June 25–26, 1984	Fontainebleau Council meeting. Agreement on annual correction mechanism from 1985 for UK rebate, on increase in Community resources from January 1986
Dec. 4, 1984	Community agreement on budgetary discipline and on curbing wine production at European Council, Dublin
Feb. 1, 1985	Withdrawal of Greenland from EC

March 29, 1985	Conclusion of enlargement negotiations with Spain and Portugal
March 29–30, 1985	European Council meeting in Brussels. Agreement on Integrated Mediterranean Programmes
April 29–30, 1985	Conclusion of bilateral agreement between Spain and Portugal
June 12, 1985	Signature of Spanish and Portuguese Accession Treaties
Dec. 2–3, 1985	Luxembourg summit agreement on provisional texts for Treaty of Rome amendments
Dec. 16, 1985	Foreign Ministers' agreement on reforms to Treaty of Rome
Jan. 1, 1986	Accession of Spain and Portugal to Communities
Feb. 17, 1986	Signature of reforms by nine Community member countries
Feb. 27, 1986	Danish referendum approving reforms
Feb. 28, 1986	Signature of reforms by Denmark, Greece and Italy
Dec. 31, 1986	All member countries except Ireland ratify Single European Act

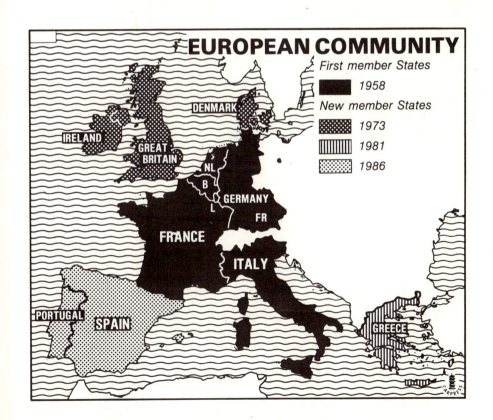

Table of western European countries' membership of key organizations

	Belgium	Denmark	France	West Germany	Greece	Ireland	Italy	Luxembourg	Netherlands
EEC[1]	*	*	*	*	*	*	*	*	*
ECSC[1]	*	*	*	*	*	*	*	*	*
Euratom[1]	*	*	*	*	*	*	*	*	*
Council of Europe	*	*	*	*	*	*	*	*	*
EFTA									
NATO[2]	*	*	*	*	*		*	*	*
WEU[3]	*		*	*			*	*	*
Nordic Council		*							
Special Relations Agreement with EC									
Benelux	*							*	*
CERN[4]	*	*	*	*	*		*		*
Eureka programme[5]	*	*	*	*	*	*	*	*	*
European Space Agency[6]	*	*	*	*			*	*	*

Notes to Table:
[1] The institutions of the EEC (established by the Treaty of Rome signed in 1957 and effective from Jan. 1, 1958), the ECSC (established by the Treaty of Paris signed in 1951 and effective from July 25, 1952), and the Euratom (established by a treaty also signed in Rome in 1957) were merged as from July 1, 1967.

[2] NATO: France withdrew from NATO's integrated military structure in 1966/67. Spain, a member of NATO only since May 1982, is not formally part of the integrated military structure, in that Spanish forces are not placed under the direct command of foreign NATO officers, although Spain participates fully in the Atlantic Council and all the various military, defence and nuclear planning committees. Iceland, having no military forces, does not participate in NATO's integrated military structure. The USA and Canada are full members of NATO.

Portugal	Spain	United Kingdom	Austria	Cyprus	Finland	Iceland	Liechtenstein	Malta	Norway	Sweden	Switzerland	Turkey
*	*	*										
*	*	*										
*	*	*										
*	*	*	*	*		*	*	*	*	*	*	*
			*		*	*			*	*	*	
*	*	*				*			*			*
			*									
					*	*			*	*		
			*		*	*	*		*	*	*	
*	*	*	*						*	*	*	
*	*	*	*		*	*			*	*	*	*
	*		*		*				*	*	*	

[3] WEU: The Portuguese government applied to join the WEU in October 1984 and Spain issued a declaration of intent to do so at that time.

[4] CERN: Poland, Turkey and Yugoslavia have observer status.

[5] Eureka: Canada and Argentina are also involved in Eureka projects.

[6] ESA: Finland became an associate member from January 1987. Canada has observer status.

Gross domestic product per head (EUR 12 = 100 in purchasing power parities, 1984)

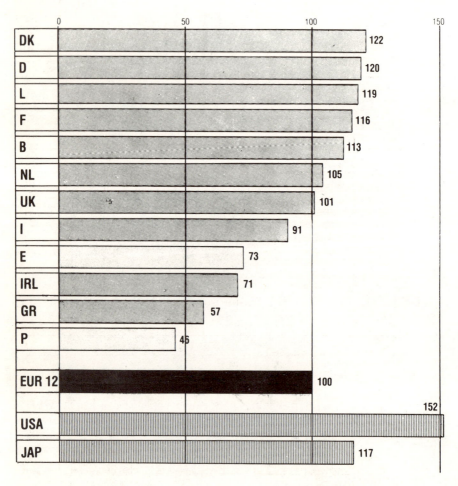

Source: Eurostat.

Note:
    Purchasing power parities are designed to allow for comparison of standards be-
tween countries without the distorting influence of market exchange rates and are used
by the UN International Comparison Project. They are calculated on the basis of data
on prices of an agreed list of products, each of which gives rise to a price ratio such that
if one unit of the product costs 2 marks in West Germany, 4 francs in France and 600
lire in Italy, then for this product 2 marks are equivalent to 4 francs and to 600 lire.
Price relatives for the aggregates up to gross domestic product are then obtained as
suitably weighted averages of these price ratios.

Density (inhabitants per sq. km, 1983)

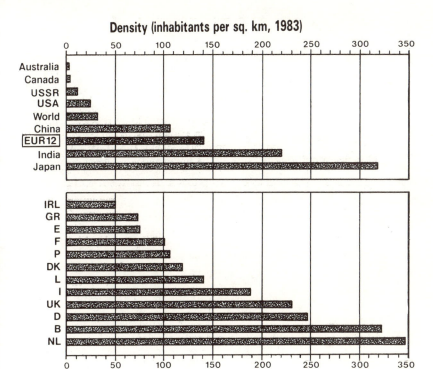

Source: Eurostat.

Share of world imports[1]   ## Share of world exports[1]

[1] 1984, as %. Intra-Community trade not included.

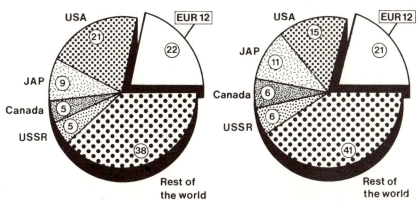

Source: Eurostat.

LIST OF KEY ABBREVIATIONS USED

ACP	African, Caribbean and Pacific countries party to the Lomé Convention
Benelux	Benelux Economic Union (of BElgium, the NEtherlands and LUXembourg)
CAP	Common agricultural policy
CERN	European Organization for Nuclear Research/Comité européen pour les recherches nucléaires
EAGGF	European Agricultural Guidance and Guarantee Fund (commonly also known by its French acronym FEOGA)
EC	European Communities
ECOSOC	Economic and Social Committee
ECSC	European Coal and Steel Community
ECU	European currency unit
EEC	European Economic Community
EFTA	European Free Trade Association
EIB	European Investment Bank
ERDF	European Regional Development Fund
ESF	European Social Fund
Esprit	European strategic programme for research and development in information technology
EUA	European unit of account, the forerunner of the ECU
Euratom	European Atomic Energy Community
GATT	General Agreement on Tariffs and Trade
IMF	International Monetary Fund
IMP	Integrated Mediterranean Programmes
NATO	North Atlantic Treaty Organization
NCI	New Community Instrument
u.a.	unit of account
UN	United Nations
UNCTAD	United Nations Conference on Trade and Development
VAT	Value Added Tax
WEU	Western European Union

1: FIRST UK APPLICATION

1.1 Chronology of events

July 25, 1952	ECSC comes into operation involving the Six
Oct. 23, 1954	WEU treaty signed involving the Six and the UK
Dec. 21, 1954	Association agreement signed between Britain and ECSC
Sept. 23, 1955	Entry into force of UK–ECSC Association Agreement
Feb. 7, 1957	British proposal to OEEC for establishment of European free trade area
March 25, 1957	Treaty of Rome signed by the Six to establish EEC and Euratom
Jan. 1, 1958	EEC and Euratom come into operation
Feb. 4, 1959	Co-operation agreement signed between Britain and Euratom
Dec. 29, 1959– Jan. 4, 1960	EFTA Convention signed in Stockholm by the "other Seven" including UK
May 3, 1960	EFTA comes into operation
Feb. 10–11, 1961	Paris summit of Six on development of union which "could be expanded in the near future"
July 18, 1961	Bonn Declaration by Six on political union
July 31, 1961	Macmillan's announcement in UK House of Commons of government decision to seek negotiations aiming at full membership of EEC
Aug. 3, 1961	UK House of Commons supports government decision
Aug. 10, 1961	UK lodges formal application with EEC Council of Ministers requesting negotiations aiming at membership of Communities
Sept. 12–14, 1961	Meeting in Accra of Commonwealth Consultative Council to discuss implications for Commonwealth of UK entry into EEC
Oct. 10, 1961	Meeting between Heath and ministers of the Six
Nov. 8, 1961	UK negotiations with EEC begin formally at first of 17 ministerial sessions
March 2 and 5, 1962	UK applies for membership of ECSC and Euratom
Sept. 10–19, 1962	Commonwealth Prime Ministers' Conference in London
Dec. 15, 1962	Macmillan–de Gaulle meeting at Rambouillet

Dec. 18–21, 1962	Macmillan–Kennedy meeting in Nassau and agreement on Polaris nuclear missiles
Jan. 14, 1963	De Gaulle's "non" at press conference in Paris
Jan. 22, 1963	Signature in Paris of Franco-German Treaty of Co-operation
Jan. 29, 1963	UK negotiations broken off
July 11, 1963	EEC agreement to hold regular WEU meetings including discussion of EEC–UK economic co-operation issues

1.2 Announcement of UK application

The UK application for full membership of the EEC under Article 237 of the Treaty of Rome was announced on July 31, 1961, by the Conservative government of Harold Macmillan and formally lodged with the EEC Council of Ministers on Aug. 10. Edward Heath (the UK Lord Privy Seal in charge of European affairs) met with ministers of the "Six" on Oct. 10, setting out the details of the UK approach in a lengthy opening statement, and negotiations opened on Nov. 8 at ministerial level.

Heath's Oct. 10 opening statement also set out the UK's intention of applying for membership of the European Coal and Steel Community (ECSC) and the European Atomic Energy Community (Euratom). (The EEC Council of Ministers had laid down, on receipt of the UK application, various principles to be observed in the negotiations, including that "for political and economic reasons a country's accession to the EEC would also involve its accession to the ECSC and Euratom".) The relevant applications were sent on March 2 and March 5, 1962.

The UK had from 1952 sought a close relationship with the ECSC (which was set up under the Treaty of Paris signed by the Six on April 18, 1951, and which entered into effect on July 25, 1952). Negotiations in London in 1954 had resulted in an Agreement of Association being signed on Dec. 21, 1954, and entering into force on Sept. 23, 1955. With regard to Euratom (set up together with the EEC under the Treaties of Rome and entering into effect on Jan. 1, 1958), a co-operation agreement had been signed by the UK on Feb. 4, 1959.

The UK application was received at a time of increasing discussion among EEC member countries on the issue of the development of political union in Europe.

1.3 The "political union" issue (February–July 1961)—The Paris summit and the Bonn Declaration

The heads of government of the Six (in the case of France, Gen. de Gaulle the head of state), together with their Foreign Ministers, had a two-day meeting in Paris on Feb. 10–11, 1961. Dr Konrad Adenauer, the West German Federal Chancellor, had arrived a day earlier for private talks with President de Gaulle at the Elysée, on which no statement was issued. De Gaulle had also had private and secret talks at Rambouillet on Jan. 28–29 with Harold Macmillan, the UK Prime Minister (who met with Adenauer shortly after the Paris meeting, in London on Feb. 22–23).

The heads of state or government taking part in the Paris meeting were de Gaulle, Dr Adenauer, Amintore Fanfani (Italy), Dr Jan de Quay (Netherlands), Gaston Eyskens (Belgium) and Pierre Werner (Luxembourg). The meeting, which was presided over by de Gaulle, ended with the publication of the following communiqué:

". . . . The six countries are already linked by special ties on the economic level, and these have been reinforced by the entry into force of the Treaties of Paris and Rome. The six governments are desirous, in a spirit of goodwill and friendship, of seeking agreements aimed at maintaining and developing exchanges with the other European countries, in particular with Great Britain, as well as with the other countries of the world. They will strive, in this spirit, to find solutions to the problems arising from the existence of two economic groupings in Europe [i.e. the EEC and EFTA—see below].

"The conference had for its object the seeking of the right means of organizing closer political co-operation . . . [in order] to lay the foundations of a union which would develop progressively. This union, limited for the moment to the member states of the European Economic Community, could be expanded in the near future.

"It was noted that the establishment of a new type of relationship in Europe—based on the development of a single market through the abolition of all customs barriers, harmonization of economies, and political co-operation in a spirit of friendship, confidence and equality —constitutes one of the major facts of our time. In the midst of the crises and unrest now disturbing the world, Western Europe . . . must become a zone of entente, liberty, and progress. Thereby Europe's action will make itself better felt in the world to the advantage of all free countries, especially in the development of co-operation with the United States.

"It has been decided to set up a committee, consisting of representatives of all the six countries, to submit to the next meeting concrete proposals concerning meetings of heads of state or government and of Foreign Ministers, as well as any other meetings that may appear desirable. The committee will also study other problems concerning European co-operation, notably those dealing with the Communities. The second meeting will take place on May 19, 1961, in Bonn."

Although not stated in the communiqué, it was understood that the Netherlands had strongly opposed any move towards closer European political union which excluded the United Kingdom, and had insisted that British participation was essential for the success of any such union.

Speaking in The Hague on Feb. 22, the Netherlands Foreign Minister Dr Joseph Luns said that while his government welcomed all moves towards closer European integration, he personally did not think that de Gaulle's plan for a political confederation—agreed with Dr Adenauer on the eve of the Paris conference —would further this aim. He suggested that the type of political co-operation envisaged by the French President could best be achieved within the framework of the Western European Union, which included Britain among its members.

The Bonn Declaration on political union in Europe was issued in the final communiqué of the summit meeting of the Six held in the West German capital on July 18, 1961. The declaration placed the emphasis on the European Communities framework for the development of European union; while "wishing for the adhesion to the European Communities of other European states", it stated explicitly that such states should be "ready to assume in all spheres the same responsibilities and the same obligations".

The Six declared themselves to be "desirous of affirming the spiritual values and political traditions which form their common heritage; united in the awareness of the great tasks which Europe is called upon to fulfil within the community of free peoples in order to safeguard liberty and peace in the world; anxious to strengthen the political, economic, social and cultural ties which exist between their peoples, especially in the framework of the European Communities, and to advance towards the union of Europe; convinced that only a united Europe, allied to the United States of America and to other free peoples, is in a position to face the dangers which menace the existence of Europe and of the whole free world, and that it is important to unite the energies, capabilities, and resources of all those for whom liberty is an inalienable possession; [and] resolved to develop their political co-operation with a view to the union of Europe and to continue at the same time the work already undertaken in the European Communities".

The Six accordingly decided:

"(1) To give shape to the will for political union already implicit in the Treaties establishing the European Communities, and for this purpose to organize their co-operation, to provide for its development and to secure for it the regularity which will progressively create the conditions for a common policy and will ultimately make it possible to embody in institutions the work undertaken.

"(2) To hold, at regular intervals, meetings whose aim will be to compare their views, to concert their policies and to reach common positions in order to further the political union of Europe, thereby strengthening the Atlantic Alliance. The necessary practical measures will be taken to prepare these meetings. In addition, the continuation of active co-operation among the Foreign Ministers will contribute to the continuity of the action undertaken in common. The co-operation of the Six must go beyond the political field as such, and will in particular be extended to the sphere of education, of culture and of research, where it will be ensured by periodical meetings of the ministers concerned.

(3) To instruct their committee to submit to them proposals on the means which will as soon as possible enable a statutory character to be given to the union of their peoples."

A major factor in the discussion of European union was the Franco-German rapprochement. On a state visit to France in July 1962 Dr Adenauer had a series of meetings with de Gaulle, a joint communiqué issued on July 5 expressing the hope "that the negotiations now in progress in Brussels will resolve the problems arising from the request of Great Britain to join the European Communities, in order to strengthen the building of Europe"; it also recorded the desire of the two leaders "to conclude as soon as possible, and in agreement with their partners, talks on the creation of a political union which will consolidate the work already accomplished in the political field". When de Gaulle paid a state visit to West Germany in September 1962, no further statements were added on the subject of the UK application, the occasion being devoted to the theme of the reconciliation and European partnership of France and West Germany (which led to the signature in January 1963 of the Franco-German Treaty of Co-operation).

1.4 Background to the UK application: (i) The position within EFTA

The UK had stood apart from the process of formation of the EEC under the 1957 Treaties of Rome, primarily through opposition to the concept of "supranationality" and because of the belief that relationships within the Commonwealth [see 1.5] would not be compatible with a European customs union. However, a policy reappraisal beginning as early as 1956 (i.e. even before the Six had signed the Treaty of Rome) had led to an unsuccessful British initiative for a wider European free trade area (excluding agriculture), to come into effect at the same time as the EEC in 1958. This formula was proposed to the OEEC (the forerunner of the OECD) in a memorandum published as a White Paper (Cmnd. 72) in February 1957, and was the subject of detailed negotiations over a period of more than two years. The lack of prospects for fruitful negotiations with the Six, after the French government had in November 1958 stated that a free trade area was impracticable without a common external tariff, eventually led the UK, Austria, Denmark, Norway, Sweden and Switzerland to discuss the formation of their own more limited free trade area. By mid-July 1959 these six countries and Portugal (consequently becoming known as the "Seven") had agreed a draft plan which became the November 1959 Stockholm Convention (Cmnd. 906), establishing the European Free Trade Association (EFTA) which came into being on May 3, 1960.

Almost from EFTA's inception, however, the possibility of EFTA member countries joining the EEC had been under consideration. At the fifth EFTA ministerial meeting, held in Geneva on July 28, 1961, a communiqué (the "Geneva Declaration") was issued on July 31 following the announcement by the British and Danish governments the same day that they were applying for membership of the EEC. After recalling "the repeated statements by members of the EEC of their willingness to accept other countries as members or in an associated status", the communiqué went on to say that the British and Danish decisions provided "an opportunity to find an appropriate solution for all EFTA countries and thus to promote the solidarity and cohesion of Europe". In order not to miss "this new opportunity", all the EFTA member states would "examine with the EEC the ways and means by which all members of EFTA could take part together in a single market embracing some 300,000,000 people". The EFTA Council would consider what further action should be taken in the light of these developments.

1.5 Background to the UK application: (ii) The Commonwealth

Harold Macmillan on July 31, 1961, announcing the UK application for EEC membership, gave an assurance that the Commonwealth would be consulted "at every point" of the negotiations and that if it was "thought desirable to have a meeting of Commonwealth Prime Ministers, probably when negotiations have reached a certain stage, I would be the first to welcome such a meeting".

The implications of Britain's entry into the European Community were first discussed at Commonwealth level at a meeting of the Commonwealth Economic Consultative Council in Accra on Sept. 12–14. Concern that it might weaken Commonwealth ties was expressed by many, including Australian and Canadian ministers.

The communiqué issued at the end of the Accra meeting contained the following section on the question of Britain's application for membership of the EEC:

"The Council meeting provided the first opportunity for a general discussion amongst Commonwealth countries of the situation resulting from the decision of the UK government to apply for . . . membership in the EEC.

"Representatives of the United Kingdom reviewed the various reasons that had led them to make the application.

"All other Commonwealth representatives expressed grave apprehension and concern regarding the possible results of the initiative taken by the United Kingdom. They reaffirmed the value and importance they attach to traditional Commonwealth trading arrangements under which most foodstuffs, raw materials, and manufactures enter the UK free of duty from Commonwealth countries with, in most cases, preferential advantages, and other Commonwealth countries make reciprocal tariff concessions. The benefits of these arrangements accrue to the United Kingdom as well as to other Commonwealth countries.

"Most Commonwealth countries questioned whether the UK, with its other international and domestic obligations, could possibly secure in the proposed negotiations an agreement which would protect Commonwealth interests adequately and effectively. It was generally agreed that any impairment of these interests would damage some or all Commonwealth countries and could have adverse effects on particular industries and areas. Several representatives stressed the danger that if the UK succeeded in negotiating special benefits in the EEC for only certain Commonwealth countries, the result could be damaging to Commonwealth solidarity.

"Certain countries pointed out that major changes in the present Commonwealth trading arrangements would inevitably force realignment of their trading patterns and could lead to the emergence of further trading blocs. Such a development would undermine traditional multilateral trading arrangements to which all Commonwealth countries had given their support.

"Because of the inseparable nature of economic and political relationships with the Commonwealth, and because of the political and institutional objectives of the EEC and the terms of the Treaty of Rome, it was feared by the other Commonwealth countries that UK membership in the EEC would fundamentally alter the relationship between the United Kingdom and Commonwealth countries. Indeed, this relationship might be so imperilled as to weaken the cohesion of the Commonwealth as a whole and thus reduce its effectiveness as a world instrument for understanding, prosperity, and peace.

"The UK delegation made it clear that, in their view, until the proposed negotiations took place it was not possible to ascertain whether satisfactory arrangements could be made to safeguard the essential interests of Commonwealth countries. It was emphasized by the UK delegation that there would be continuing and close consultation with all Commonwealth governments at all stages in the negotiations."

The meeting of Commonwealth Prime Ministers on the EEC issue was in fact not held until Sept. 10, 1962, in London, by which time the entry negotiations between the UK and the EEC member states had been under way for nearly a year [see below].

Immediately before the meeting, the issue was discussed in London on Sept. 8–9 by leaders of the British and overseas Commonwealth Labour parties (those of Great Britain, Canada, Australia, New Zealand, Singapore, Tanganyika, and several territories in the West Indies). At the conclusion of these talks the Commonwealth Labour leaders unanimously approved a communiqué which stated that "if Britain were to enter the Common Market on the basis of what has so far been agreed [in the Brussels negotiations], great damage would inevitably be done to many countries in the Commonwealth and therefore to the unity of the Commonwealth itself". After declaring that Britain should not enter the EEC "until the present vague promises and assurances have been converted into satisfactory agreements", the Commonwealth Labour leaders urged that "no final decision be taken by Britain until a further meeting of Commonwealth Prime Ministers has been held to consider a more precise and satisfactory programme".

Hugh Gaitskell made the following statement after the meeting on the attitude of the British Labour Party towards Britain's projected entry into the EEC: "We have always recognized that, while the economic arguments are evenly balanced, there are important political considerations which can be said to favour entry. But we have also insisted that we could not go in until certain conditions were fulfilled. . . . If the government propose to go into the Common Market on terms which the Labour Party regard as wholly unacceptable . . . then undoubtedly in my view we should ask for a general election."

At the beginning of the Prime Ministers' meeting on Sept. 10, two lengthy speeches were made by Macmillan and Heath (who gave a detailed account of his negotiations in Brussels during recent months).

Rejecting the view that Britain was faced with a choice between Europe and the Commonwealth, Macmillan emphasized that the Commonwealth remained a system and an association of cardinal importance and great value for its members and for the world as a whole. On the economic side, the United Kingdom's value to the Commonwealth lay in the market and the capital which it provided; but Britain could increase her market only by increasing her wealth, and there were better prospects of doing this if she were inside the EEC than if she remained outside.

Moreover, there would be "great and manifest" political advantages if Britain were to join Europe; had Britain been more closely involved in the European political scene in 1914 or even in 1939, two world wars might have been avoided. The British government therefore welcomed the political reconciliation which was taking place in Europe, wished to help in consolidating it, and believed that British partnership in Europe could be an important element in shaping its evolution. In short, "a new opportunity has opened up for Britain to contribute to the economic progress of all peoples and all continents, and an opportunity to play her part in bringing nearer a world order towards which mankind must move or perish".

Statements on the attitude of the Commonwealth countries were made by all the Commonwealth representatives at plenary sessions on Sept. 11 and 12, and again on Sept. 17 before the ending of the conference. Despite the ovation given to Macmillan and Heath after their opening speeches, nearly all the Commonwealth Prime Ministers expressed concern at the economic or political implications for the Commonwealth of Britain's entry into Europe. While recognizing that the final decision was Britain's, and Britain's alone, only two of the Commonwealth Premiers expressed unreserved support for the United Kingdom's entry into the EEC — Dr Williams, the Prime Minister of Trinidad, and President Makarios of Cyprus.

While the Commonwealth Conference was in progress, President Ayub Khan of Pakistan visited Paris on Sept. 16 for a meeting with de Gaulle. Before leaving London for Paris, President Ayub had aroused much interest by a suggestion for a conference between the EEC countries and the Commonwealth countries—"the Six and the Sixteen"—to discuss some form of economic relationship between the Commonwealth and the European Community. He emphasized, however, that this was "just an idea in my mind which I suggested to one or two friends at the [London] conference", and that the main purpose of his Paris visit was "to pay my respects to a great man".

In a statement before leaving for Paris, President Ayub said: "As I see it, the Common Market is the germ of something bigger emerging in the world. The United Nations has ceased to be the effective organ the world wanted it to be. Would it not be better to take this opportunity to enlarge the scope of the Common Market, not necessarily politically, but in the economic field? This is a crucial moment in human history. Something greater and grander can emerge if there is foresight."

Summing up the discussions at the London conference on Sept. 17 at the final plenary session, Macmillan said that, in his view, four points of general agreement had emerged from the discussions:

(1) The need to work for an expansion of world trade.

(2) The need to improve the organization of the world market in primary foodstuffs, e.g., a fresh approach to the negotiation of international commodity agreements.

(3) The need for recognition by the developed countries that increased chances for trade were no less important than financial help for the developing nations; and

(4) The need to regulate the disposal of any agricultural surplus to meet the needs of those people in the world who were in want.

He made it clear that the United Kingdom would bear all these points in mind, as well as the many more detailed points which had been raised during the conference, when negotiations were resumed with the EEC. He hoped that means would be found to enable Britain to enter the Common Market on terms consistent with these broad objectives.

In a general review of the present position, he said that it was no longer true that Britain could, by herself, hold the balance of power in the world to form an effective counterweight, "as perhaps had been possible in the days long ago when America had been scarcely heard of and Russia hardly developed". Dealing with the economic side, he spoke of major changes which had occurred in the pattern of Commonwealth trade since the time of the Ottawa Agreement. The broad concept that raw materials were to be exchanged for processed goods had become outdated, and all the Commonwealth countries were increasingly making their own goods and trying to export them. He could not see how Britain could maintain alone her free-entry system when a tariff structure was being built up against it in many parts of the Commonwealth, with protection for home industries.

The final communiqué of the London conference, issued on Sept. 19, contained the following passages on the EEC issue:

"British ministers set out the broad political and economic considerations which had led the British government to initiate the negotiations in Brussels. They emphasized that, in the view of the British government, Britain's accession to the Community on satisfactory terms would have the result of strengthening the position of Britain, the Commonwealth, and Europe. They explained in detail the position so far reached in the negotiations in Brussels, and emphasized the principal points among the many provisional arrangements which had been worked out. In the first place, an offer of association on advantageous economic terms was open to Commonwealth countries in Africa and the Caribbean and the majority of British dependent territories. Should certain of the countries not become associated, the provisional agreement reached in Brussels offered further discussion . . . with a view to the possible conclusion of other arrangements.

"Secondly, the Community were prepared to negotiate as soon as possible trade agreements with India, Pakistan, and Ceylon which would have the declared objective of developing mutual trade to maintain and, as much as possible, to increase the level of their foreign currency receipts and in general facilitate the implementation of their development plans.

"Thirdly, as regards temperate products, the enlarged Community would make, at the time of British accession, two important declarations. One would express their intention to initiate discussions on international commodity agreements for temperate foodstuffs on a world-wide basis. It would recognize the greatly increased responsibilities of the enlarged Community by reason of its predominant position among world importers.

"The second declaration would relate to the price policy of the Community. While taking appropriate measures to raise the individual earnings of those engaged in agriculture in the Community, the Community would do its utmost to contribute to a harmonious development of world trade providing for a satisfactory level of trade between the Community and third countries, including Commonwealth countries. British ministers considered that the policy which the enlarged Community intended to pursue would offer reasonable opportunities in its markets for exports of temperate agricultural products.

"The representatives of other Commonwealth governments welcomed this opportunity for personal consultation on this issue and for supplementing the exchanges of information and consultation which had already taken place between ministers and officials.

"They took note of the considerations which had influenced the British government in deciding to accede to the EEC if satisfactory terms could be secured. They recognized that, after full and continuing consultation with the other countries of the Commonwealth and in the light of the further negotiations to be held with the members of the Community, the responsibility for the final decision would rest with the British government.

"The representatives of the Commonwealth countries freely acknowledged the strenuous efforts which the British government have made to ensure on the part of the Six a full understanding of the safeguards required if Britain's entry into the Common Market is not to be on such terms and conditions as to impair their vital interests.

"They expressed their hope that the members of the EEC will wish to preserve and encourage a strong and growing Commonwealth, in furtherance of their own ideals of an expanding and peaceful world order.

"At the same time the representatives of various Commonwealth governments expressed anxieties about the possible effects of Britain's entry into the EEC. They trusted that, should there be closer association between Britain and Europe, it would not be allowed, as it developed, to weaken the cohesion of the Commonwealth or its influence for peace and progress in the world. They drew attention to the difficulties to which these developments could give rise in relation to their trade both with Britain and with other countries. They explained the economic points of special concern to their respective countries and the extent to which their interests had not so far been met in the Brussels negotiations.

"Some independent African countries considered that association with the Community under Part IV of the Treaty of Rome would not be acceptable to them. On the other hand the government of Sierra Leone wished to consider further their attitude towards association, after consultation with other African territories which are not members of the Commonwealth. In the Caribbean, Trinidad and Tobago will be willing to accept association, and Jamaica will wish to consider her attitude further. The Prime Ministers were informed that the Federation of Rhodesia and Nyasaland is willing to accept association. They were also informed that, after appropriate consultations, it seemed likely that the majority of the British dependent territories eligible for association would wish to accept it.

"The representatives of India, Pakistan, and Ceylon urged that, if Britain entered the Community, the trade agreements which the enlarged Community had offered to negotiate with their governments should be concluded as soon as possible and that, meanwhile, no change should be made in their existing trade arrangements with Britain. They expressed their apprehension that if the treatment of their products in the United Kingdom was altered before wider trading arrangements had been worked out for the enlarged Community, their foreign exchange earnings and investment in export industries would be adversely affected at a critical stage in the implementation of their development plans.

"Importance was attached to the need for securing adequate safeguards to protect the essential interests of Commonwealth producers of temperate foodstuffs and other agricultural products, including tropical products, as well as certain raw materials for which zero tariffs had been requested. The importance for some Commonwealth countries of trade in a broad range of manufactured and processed goods was also emphasized.

"The Prime Ministers took note that the negotiations in Brussels were incomplete and that a number of important questions had still to be negotiated. Only when the full terms were known would it be possible to form a final judgment."

In a broadcast on Sept. 20, Macmillan described the Commonwealth Prime Ministers' meeting as "perhaps the most important conference ever held in the Commonwealth". He spoke about "the discussions we have had on the immense question of Europe, Britain, and the Commonwealth", rejecting "the view that Britain is faced with the choice between the Commonwealth and Europe".

The Commonwealth, which itself had undergone great changes since 1945, had, he said "a kind of historic link", and he went on: "We are, I hope, outward-looking and not inward-looking. Not, I hope, selfish and narrow, but try to take the broad view. That is the link, and that is what makes the Commonwealth an instrument of real and increasing value in the world today.

"But if you contrast that with the Common Market of Europe, of course that is quite a different thing. At present it is a group of six countries in Western Europe. . . . They have made a customs union or Common Market, as it is called, and that means that after a transitional period of a few years—after the time for adjustment by 1970—these countries propose to make themselves into a single economic unit, without any tariffs or customs barriers between them. Just, in fact, like England, Scotland, and Wales are today.

"It has been a great success up to now. They form a great economic group. There is no direct political commitment in the Common Market, but of course it is one of the objects of the member countries to grow closer together politically; and naturally, as their economic growth comes together, so will their political.

"What we have been discussing with the Commonwealth is really this—how to reconcile the strong historical structure of the Commonwealth and the new developing structure on the continent of Europe. This isn't really essentially a new problem for us, because all through our history, combined with the immense outward growth of the British people all over the world, we have still been very much involved in Europe's affairs. . . .

"A year ago the British government decided—it was a great decision—to start to talk and negotiate with the European Community, to see whether we could deal with the situation by joining the Common Market ourselves on terms which would be both honourable and acceptable. We took this great decision for two reasons: one political, the other economic.

"Politically, because we were very glad to see the end of Europe's quarrels—quarrels in which we have been tragically involved thoughout history; twice in my lifetime. Because we wanted to strengthen the new unity of Europe. And also because we knew that if we were not in Europe our influence would begin to decline, and with the decline of our influence in Europe we should lose our influence in the world outside.

"With Britain and some other countries—Norway perhaps, and Denmark, and other countries now members of the European Free Trade Area to which we belong —if these all get together the European Community will become a community of between 220 and 230 million people—just as strong economically, and in every other way, as the Soviet Union or the United States.

"But supposing we aren't in it? Supposing we stand outside? Of course we shall go on, but we shall be relatively weak, and we shan't find the true strength that we have and ought to have. We shan't be able to exercise it in a world of giants. So that was the first reason—a political reason; a great historic reason—why we made this decision. To preserve the power and strength of Britain in the world.

"Then there is the economic argument. Economically these are the facts. In the newly developed countries in Asia and Africa and all the rest of the Commonwealth —if they are to have a really good chance, a fair chance—they must sell some at least of their manufactured goods to the advanced countries. And if we in Britain are to take these goods in sufficient quantities, we must be strong enough economically to make the necessary changes and adaptations in our own industrial life.

"British industry will have to concentrate more and more on the complicated, sophisticated, specialized goods. . . . And yet it is just these very industries which require immense investment of capital. . . . They need a big plant, and so, if you are to sell them at a competitive price, you need a very large market. . . .

"I know there are some people who talk as if there was an alternative system to the Common Market. The Commonwealth, they say, might form a close economic unit, vast in population and natural resources and able, on its own, to equal the great economies of America, Soviet Russia, or Europe. I don't think this idea has been a practical proposition for the Commonwealth in recent years, and I am quite certain that the Commonwealth countries realize this. None of the conditions exist which would allow a common Commonwealth, for these are countries with totally different backgrounds, different races, different stages of development, scattered all over the world. They simply do not make a compact grouping.

"Well, how have we got on so far? Where do we stand in Brussels in our negotiations? In the so-called temperate foodstuffs . . . we all of us . . . hope by world agreements to get a market on a fair basis, with price policies fair and reasonable to producers and consumers, and to provide access to markets for traditional suppliers. That is agreed. For New Zealand, everybody accepts that some special arrangements will have to be made to suit her very special circumstances.

"For the Asian countries we have got, on the whole, very good terms. For African and Caribbean countries we have got wonderful terms, if they choose to take them. . . .

"As I say, we have got a long way in Brussels, but there is a lot to be done before we can see exactly what arrangements we and the Six can make together to give fair entry for the Commonwealth and the right conditions for our own British agriculture. When we know the final position, then it will be for us here in Britain to decide what to do. All the Commonwealth have accepted that fact.

"So we want to preserve and strengthen the Commonwealth. We want also to play our part in Europe. Many of us, especially those who are young in heart or in years, are impatient of the old disputes; intolerant of obsolete conceptions; anxious that our country should take its part, and if possible a leading part, in all these new and hopeful movements.

"All over Western Europe people are looking to Britain to join them in this work of peace and progress. And given the right terms of entry, I am sure this is the right way ahead for us."

1.6 Background to the UK application: (iii) Attitudes within the Liberal, Labour and Conservative parties

The Liberal Party, which had won only six seats at the October 1959 general election, was the most enthusiastically pro-European and indeed the only one of the three parties which had a firm position at the time of the Macmillan government's decision to seek negotiations on EEC entry terms.

The two main parties, Conservative (365 out of 630 seats at the general election) and Labour (258), both contained groups disposed to support membership, and groups disposed to oppose it. By emphasizing that its negotiations were about possible entry terms, rather than about actual accession, the Macmillan government made it possible for the parties to delay the resolution of their positions; however, the process of negotiation during 1962 provoked considerable debate and was reflected in the importance of the EEC issue at the annual party conferences which followed the Commonwealth Prime Ministers' Conference in the autumn of 1962.

The first of the three conferences, held by the Liberals in late September, gave enthusiastic support for European "federalism".

The second, Labour's conference in Brighton in October, had been preceded by Gaitskell's meeting with Commonwealth Labour leaders [see 1.5]. At the conference itself, Gaitskell gave greater emphasis than hitherto to shortcomings in the terms being negotiated, and was regarded by some "pro-Marketeers" in the party as having departed from the spirit of a neutral statement drawn up by the national executive.

In May 1962 Gaitskell had said that to enter the EEC on good terms would be the best solution (this being supported by the "pro-Marketeers" associated in particular with Roy Jenkins), but that "history would not forgive us" for entering on bad terms. The Labour Party set out five conditions for assessment of the terms for entry; besides safeguarding the Commonwealth, the position of other EFTA countries and the position of British agriculture, such terms should ensure that Britain remained free to pursue an independent foreign policy, and that Britain retained the right to pursue national economic planning. These last two conditions reflected not only the concerns within the party about the level of integration already achieved in the EEC, but suspicion about the implications of future development, particularly in the area of political union. However, it was the growing awareness that the terms appeared unlikely to satisfy a number of Commonwealth members, allied to the perception that the Conservatives might make their own pro-membership stance an election issue, which strenghtened the position of the so-called "moderate anti-Marketeers", associated in particular with Douglas Jay, who tended to portray the government as failing to drive a sufficiently hard bargain in the Brussels negotiations.

The Conservative conference, held later in October in Llandudno, became the occasion for a strong endorsement of the government's pro-membership position, and a motion was passed welcoming the progress of the negotiations. The anti-EEC group on the right wing of the party, generally also associated with pro-Commonwealth sentiments, was apparently reduced to a small minority in the face of pro-EEC enthusiasm at this conference.

1.7 The UK application—Macmillan's announcement—Parliamentary debate—Formal application—Heath's opening statement on Oct. 10, 1961

The question of British membership had been discussed in the UK parliament on a number of occasions during the first part of 1961, forming in particular one of the major subjects of a foreign affairs debate in the House of Commons on May 17–18, 1961.

The announcement that the government had decided to make a formal application under Article 237 was made by Macmillan in the House of Commons on July 31, 1961.

"The future relations between the EEC, the UK, the Commonwealth, and the rest of Europe," said Macmillan, "are clearly matters of capital importance in the life of our country, and indeed of all the countries of the free world.

"This is a political as well as an economic issue. Although the Treaty of Rome is concerned with economic matters it has an important political objective—namely, to promote unity and stability in Europe, which is so essential a factor in the struggle for freedom and progress throughout the world. In this modern world the tendency towards larger groups of nations acting together in the common interest leads to greater unity, and thus adds to our strength in the struggle for freedom.

"I believe it is both our duty and our interest to contribute towards that strength by securing the closest possible unity within Europe. At the same time, if a closer relationship between the UK and the countries of the EEC were to disrupt the long-standing and historic ties between the UK and the other nations of the Commonwealth, the loss would be greater than the gain.

"The Commonwealth is a great source of stability and strength, both to Western Europe and to the world as a whole, and I am sure that its value is fully appreciated by the member governments of the EEC. I do not think that Britain's contribution to the Commonwealth will be reduced if Europe unites. On the contrary, I think its value will be enhanced.

"On the economic side, a community comprising, as members or in association, the countries of free Europe could have a very rapidly expanding economy supplying, as eventually it would, a single market of approaching 300,000,000 people. This rapidly expanding economy could in turn lead to an increased demand for products from other parts of the world, and so help to expand world trade and improve the prospects of the less developed areas of the world.

"No British government could join the EEC without prior negotiation with a view to meeting the needs of the Commonwealth countries, of our EFTA partners, and of British agriculture consistently with the broad principles and purpose which have inspired the concept of European unity and which are embodied in the Rome Treaty. . . .

"If, as I earnestly hope, our offer to enter into negotiations with the EEC is accepted, we shall spare no efforts to reach a satisfactory agreement. These negotiations must inevitably be of a detailed and technical character, covering a very large number of the most delicate and difficult matters. They may therefore be protracted and there can, of course, be no guarantee of success. . . ."

At the end of a two-day debate in the House of Commons on Aug. 2–3, 1961, a government motion was approved, by 313 votes to five, supporting the decision "to make formal application under Article 237 of the Treaty of Rome in order to initiate negotiations to see if satisfactory arrangements can be made to meet the special interests of the United Kingdom, of the Commonwealth, and of EFTA" and accepting the government's undertaking that "no agreement affecting these special interests or involving British sovereignty will be entered into until it has been approved by this House after full consultation with other Commonwealth countries, by whatever procedure they may generally agree". A similar motion was carried in the House of Lords without a vote.

The United Kingdom's application (dated Aug. 9, 1961) was officially lodged with the EEC Council of Ministers on Aug. 10.

The application stressed the UK government's need "to take account of the special Commonwealth relationship as well as of the essential interests of British agriculture and of the other members of EFTA". The government believed "that member governments will consider these problems sympathetically, and therefore have every confidence in a successful outcome to the negotiations. This would constitute an historic step towards that closer union among the European peoples which is the common aim of the UK and of the members of the Community".

The EEC Council of Ministers' formal acknowledgement was made on Aug. 14, 1961, by its president, Dr Ludwig Erhard, then West German Vice-Chancellor. Following a meeting of the Council of Ministers on Sept. 25–26 a further letter from Erhard was sent to the British government expressing the Council's unanimous decision that negotiations should be opened, and suggesting a preliminary meeting in Paris.

In this letter (dated Sept. 27) Erhard said that the governments of the Six had noted the British government's references to its obligations to the Commonwealth, British agriculture, and other EFTA members, and invited the British government to participate in a meeting to be held in Paris on Oct. 10, so that the governments of the Six might become "fully informed" concerning these problems and so that the negotiations might open "under the most favourable conditions".

As soon as the six governments had concluded their examination of the British government's views, they would, while reserving their right to request additional explanations, "concert with the UK government to fix a date for the opening of the negotiations proper," which could " be held in Brussels and commence in the first half of . . . November".

The British reply (dated Sept. 30) accepting the invitation was published on Oct. 2, 1961.

It had earlier been announced on Aug. 17, 1961, that Edward Heath would be the Minister in charge of the negotiations, while the further appointments were announced on Sept. 11 of Sir Pierson Dixon (Ambassador in Paris) as official head of the UK delegation and of Eric Roll, a Deputy Secretary in the Ministry of Agriculture, Fisheries, and Food, as his deputy.

In a subsequent report from the EEC Commission to the European Parliament "on the state of the negotiations with the UK," published on March 5, 1963, it was stated that as soon as the British government's application was received the EEC Council of Ministers had laid down certain principles to be observed in the negotiations, viz.:

(1) "That any application for accession to the Community would mean that the country concerned unreservedly accepted the rules and objectives of the Treaty of Rome; consequently negotiations for accession could only deal with the conditions of admission and the adaptations of the Treaty which these would involve.

(2) "That for political and economic reasons a country's accession to the EEC would also involve its accession to the European Coal and Steel Community and Euratom.

(3) "That these principles should be made known to the countries applying for membership to the EEC at the very first meeting."

It had also been laid down that since the negotiations were between the six Community states and the UK, "as far as at all possible the six Community states will present a joint point of view when dealing with Great Britain"; and that the EEC Commission should take part in the negotiations as adviser to the Six, with the right to speak.

The meeting on Oct. 10, 1961, was held in private and the full text of Heath's statement was at first classified as secret, although Heath gave accounts of the relevant portions to representatives of Commonwealth and EFTA countries separately on Oct. 11; an outline of it was also released to the press. Following press reports that the whole text had been "leaked", however, it was stated by the Foreign Office on Nov. 25, 1961, that copies of the whole text would be sent to the governments of Commonwealth and EFTA countries, while Heath announced in the House of Commons on Nov. 27 that as an agency tape had started publication of the full text it had been decided to publish it as a White Paper.

The major portions of the White Paper, which was published on Nov. 29, 1961, as Cmnd. 1565, are given below.

The Treaty of Rome. "HM Government are ready to subscribe fully to the aims which you have set yourselves. In particular, we accept without qualification the objectives laid down in Articles 2 and 3 of the Treaty of Rome, including the elimination of internal tariffs, a common customs tariff, a common commercial policy, and a common agricultural policy. We are ready to accept, and to play our full part in, the institutions established under Article 4 and other Articles of the Treaty.

"So far as we can judge at this stage, we see no need for any amendments to the text of the Treaty, except of course in those Articles where adaptations are plainly required consequent on the admission of a new member. We think it should be possible to deal with our special problems by means of protocols. This would be very much in line with the procedure adopted for dealing with the special problems of the original signatories when the Treaty was drafted.

"In addition to the major problems mentioned in our application, about which I will speak later, there will, of course, be other subjects arising from various Articles of the Treaty which we should like to discuss with you. Since the Treaty came into force decisions, recommendations, directives, and regulations have been adopted. How far these measures can be applied to the UK as they stand should, I suggest, be a matter for joint examination. In some cases, this could wait until after our accession to the Treaty. On other, more vital matters, either you or we would doubtless wish to have a measure of mutual understanding before our accession. . . . We should be happy, if that were your general wish, to arrange for technical discussions on these matters to take place with your experts simultaneously with the negotiations on the problems of Commonwealth trade and UK agriculture.

"Now I turn to a central feature of the EEC—the common external tariff. We are . . . ready—and I think this simple solution may be agreeable to all of you—to accept the structure of the present EEC tariff as the basis of the common tariff of the enlarged Community. In these circumstances we think that the necessary lowering of tariff levels might be achieved by making a linear cut in the common tariff as it stands today. . . . No doubt both you and we would wish to single out some items for special treatment. I can assure you that our own list will not be long.

"We are also ready, once we enter the Community, to make, in a single operation, the same cuts in tariffs on trade between member states as you will have yourself made by that date. In addition we are prepared to move our most-favoured-nation tariff towards the new common tariff by a step equivalent to that which you have already taken. This would be a considerable leap forward; but it is one which we are ready to make in the interests of the Community as a whole.

"So far I have spoken entirely about the European Economic Community. But we recognize that the unity of the Six goes beyond the EEC. I should like now to say something about our attitude towards the European Coal and Steel Community, Euratom, and the Bonn Declaration of July 18 [1961].

"As regards the ECSC and Euratom we shall be prepared . . . to enter into negotiations with you, at the appropriate moment, with a view to joining these two Communities when we join the EEC.

"We have followed with close interest your progress towards greater unity in fields other than those covered by the three existing Communities. The latest public statement of your position in these matters was the declaration issued by the heads of state and of government at their meeting in Bonn on July 18. We fully share the aims and objectives, political and otherwise, of those who drew up this declaration, and we shall be anxious, once we are members of the Community, to work with you in a positive spirit to reinforce the unity which you have already achieved. That indeed animates our whole approach. The more that we, the United Kingdom, can contribute to the unifying process of this great European Community, the more we shall feel that we are joining the historic enterprise which the genius of the European peoples has launched. . . .

Three major problems. "I will now turn to the three major problems posed by the particular circumstances of the United Kingdom . . . those of Commonwealth trade, of UK agriculture, and of the arrangements which could be made for our partners in EFTA.

"I wish to make it clear that we are not seeking a privileged position for the UK. We fully recognize that the solutions to be worked out must be compatible with, and not disruptive of, the Common Market.

The Commonwealth. "We believe that you share our view of the value of the Commonwealth, not only to the UK but also to yourselves and to the whole free world. . . . I should be misleading you if I failed to say how deeply the British people feel about this association. That, I am sure, is a sentiment which the members of the Community will fully understand.

"Commonwealth trade is one of the strongest elements in maintaining the Commonwealth association. It would be a tragedy if our entry into the Community forced other members of the Commonwealth to change their whole pattern of trade and consequently, perhaps, their political orientation. I do not think that such a development would be in your interest any more than in ours. Nor, looking at it from the point of view of a potential member of the Community, would any of us wish the Community to be met with the hostility which would flow from a large group of countries strung across the world if they were to feel that their interests had suffered at our hands.

"The economies of most Commonwealth countries have been built up on the basis of supplying the British market, which has traditionally imported their produce duty-free and often on preferential terms. In the last few decades the majority of them have sought to enlarge both the variety of their production and the range of their markets. But the British market is still of great importance to the economies of most Commonwealth countries.

"I am sure that you will understand that Britain could not join the EEC under conditions in which this trade connexion was cut, with grave loss and even ruin for some of the Commonwealth countries. For our remaining dependent territories we have a special and direct responsibility.

"The problem of Commonwealth trade has analogies in the problems which faced you when you were negotiating the Treaty of Rome. Your problems concerned a considerable number of countries which were in varying constitutional relationships with members of the Community. The total volume of trade affected was large. Your problems were dealt with, either in the Treaty or in its accompanying protocols, without damage to the interests of the countries concerned, and in some cases with considerable advantage to them. It is a striking fact, and very relevant to the Commonwealth problem, that in no case was a tariff imposed on trade where one had not been in force before the Treaty was signed. . . .

"On the assumption that there is general recognition of the need to devise satisfactory arrangements to protect vital interests of Commonwealth countries, and with this background in mind, I think it would be helpful to suggest in more detail how the problem might be split up into its different components, and how each of these might be treated.

"Apart from Cyprus, Malta, Gibraltar, and the Falkland Islands, [all the less-developed members of the Commonwealth and dependent territories] have tropical or sub-tropical climates. They nearly all produce tropical products and raw materials, many of which are also produced by the countries and territories at present associated with the Community under Part IV of the Treaty of Rome. Many of them are seeking to establish secondary industries in order to diversify their economies and reduce their very great dependence upon imports. India, Pakistan, and Hong Kong are also exporters of certain manufactured goods; and some others, such as Malta and the West Indies, hope to follow their example, though on a much lesser scale.

"All these countries and territories attach importance to the preferences and duty-free entry which they enjoy in the UK market. There are a few other special arrangements which are vital to certain of them. For some territories it is also of importance —in some cases of great importance—to be able to compete in the markets of the rest of Europe on equal terms with other exporters of similar products. They would certainly not understand if, as a result of becoming a member of the Community, the UK were obliged to discriminate against them in favour of other non-European countries. Another feature of many of these countries and territories is that their need to encourage industrial development and their unavoidable reliance on indirect taxation for revenue makes it necessary for them to put tariffs on imports of manufactured goods.

"We have studied with great interest the arrangements laid down in Part IV of the Treaty of Rome and in the related Convention for the Association with EEC of certain Overseas Countries and Territories with whom members of that Community previously had special relations. Some Commonwealth countries have expressed the opinion that the present arrangements for association are not appropriate for independent states. But this view may not apply to the new arrangements when it is known what they will be. In any case we should like to see the less-developed members of the Commonwealth and our Dependent Territories given the opportunity, if they so wish, to enter into association with the Community on the same terms as those which will in future be available to the present Associated Overseas Countries and Territories. . . .

"Association may, therefore, be a solution for the problems of many Commonwealth countries and territories. But for others it may not be possible. One way of dealing with the problems of those who are not associated would be to arrange for them to maintain unimpaired their rights of access to the UK market, in the same way as was done for Morocco's trade with France or for Surinam's trade with Benelux, under the relevant Protocol to the Rome Treaty. But we recognize that this solution would not be applicable in all cases. Another method of proceeding would be to consider the problems on a commodity-by-commodity basis. Perhaps it would be helpful if I were to say something at this point about the main groups of commodities —tropical products, materials, manufactures, and temperate foodstuffs.

Tropical products. "Difficulties will arise over tropical products if one or more of the less-developed countries or territories of the Commonwealth do not enter into an appropriate form of association with the Community. There does not appear to be any complete solution of such difficulties. But we see two alternative lines of approach. The first, which would be appropriate when not only equality of opportunity but also some measure of protection is essential, would be to grant free entry into the UK market alone for the Commonwealth country or territory which is not associated, and then to fix the common tariff of the enlarged Community at a level which would safeguard the interests both of that country and of the countries and territories associated with the Community. The second line of approach would be to fix a zero, or a very low, level for the common tariff. For a few important commodities we believe that it would be possible to do this without significant damage to the interests of the countries and territories associated with the Community. For example, tea is a commodity of great importance to India and Ceylon, and so is cocoa to Ghana. A zero common tariff would go a considerable way to meet the trade problem of those countries if they were not solved by association.

Materials. "Materials should not in general give rise to difficulties, as the common tariff on most of them is zero. There are, however, a few on which it is substantial. Five of them—aluminium, wood pulp, newsprint, lead, and zinc—are of great importance to certain Commonwealth countries: on these five materials we would wish to seek a zero tariff.

Manufactures. "Manufactures are, with a very few exceptions, imported duty-free into the United Kingdom both from the developed countries in the Commonwealth— Canada, Australia, and New Zealand—and from the less-developed Asian countries. Exporting industries in all these countries have been assisted in their development by free entry and the preferential position they have enjoyed in the United Kingdom. They would be seriously affected not only by loss of preferences in our market but also if their position were transformed into one in which the whole of their export trade was affected by reverse preferences in favour of the major industrial countries in Europe.

"Nevertheless we recognize that indefinite and unlimited continuation of free entry over the whole of this field may not be regarded as compatible with the development of the Common Market, and we are willing to discuss ways of reconciling these two considerations. I believe that the problem is of manageable proportions. The trade in question is important to the Commonwealth countries concerned, but it is not large in total in comparison with European trade.

"The problem arises in a special form for manufactures from the less-developed countries, the so-called low-cost manufactures. It occurs most acutely in relation to Asian Commonwealth countries and the colony of Hong Kong. There is increasing international recognition that developed countries have a duty to facilitate international trade in this field as much as they can. But what the nature of the solution should be in the context of our joining the EEC must depend on how far it can be dealt with under arrangements for a Part IV Association. You will probably agree that it would not be in the general interest that the UK should erect fresh tariff barriers to cut back such trade.

Temperate foodstuffs. "A major concern of the more fully developed members of the Commonwealth is their trade with us in temperate foodstuffs. Australia, New Zealand, and Canada, in particular, have vital interests in this field for which special arrangements must be made. . . .

"New Zealand's total exports in 1959 were valued at £290,000,000. Of these £170,000,000 worth, or about 60 per cent, were temperate foodstuffs; £131,000,000 worth out of the total of £170,000,000 came to the UK. The bulk of these exports to us consisted of mutton, lamb, butter, and cheese. If in the future New Zealand cannot, by one means or another, be assured of comparable outlets for them, her whole economy would be shattered. . . . Australia, even though she exports a much more varied range of products, relies on temperate foodstuffs for 35 per cent of her exports. The temperate foodstuffs she sends abroad are valued at £250,000,000: of these, £100,000,000 worth come to the United Kingdom. . . .

"To many Commonwealth countries the UK has brought moral and contractual obligations, on the basis of which they have planned the development of their economies. I will mention only the Commonwealth Sugar Agreement. . . . It provides an assured basis for sugar production, which is particularly important in the case of our dependent territories.

"The problem, therefore, is to reconcile our obligations to the Commonwealth with the common agricultural policy as it evolves. We believe that solutions can be found which will prove satisfactory. The Commission's proposals emphasize that trade policy in agricultural products should take into account not only internal agricultural considerations but also the need to maintain trade with third countries. This is a liberal approach and one with which we fully agree. . . .

UK agriculture. "I turn to the question of UK agriculture. Here, let me say at once, we started from common ground. The agricultural objectives of the Treaty of Rome are in line with the objectives of our own agricultural policy. We, like you, are fully committed to the maintenance of a stable, efficient, and prosperous agriculture. The Treaty of Rome aims at increasing agricultural productivity, a fair standard of living for the agricultural population, stable markets, regular supplies, and reasonable prices and supplies to consumers. These objectives command our wholehearted support. Moreover, we are prepared to take the major step of participating with you in a common agricultural policy and in developing a common organization of agricultural markets. We fully accept that the Common Market must extend to agriculture and trade in agricultural products.

"This, however, poses big problems for us. Our system of support, except for horticultural produce, relies mainly on Exchequer payments to ensure the maintenance of a satisfactory standard of living for our farmers. Our tariffs on foodstuffs are low and a large proportion of our supplies, particularly those from the Commonwealth, enter our market free of duty. We make very little use of import restrictions. Broadly speaking, we buy our food at world free market prices. Our people are therefore accustomed to low prices for food. Their tastes are related to a traditional pattern of food supplies.

"At the same time our farmers have guaranteed prices for all their principal products. These guarantees are provided by means of Exchequer payments which make up the difference between the average price realized by farmers on the market and the guaranteed price determined by the government. In addition, we make direct farming grants designed to encourage improved farming methods and to raise the general efficiency of the industry. The level of the guaranteed prices and of the direct farming grants is settled annually by the government after consultation with the producers' representatives. We have legislation which sets definite limits to the amount of the reductions which may be made from one year to the next both in the general level of support and in the guaranteed prices for individual commodities. The UK government have pledged themselves to make no change in the statutory limits during the lifetime of the present parliament, which can continue until October 1964.

"Our farmers are thus assured of reasonable stability of income. Furthermore, the annual review of the guarantees provides the opportunity for a careful examination of the economic condition and prospect of the industry. This annual review is a key feature of our system. It enables us to look not only at the prices of individual commodities but at all the main factors affecting the industry's prosperity. The review is conducted on the basis of statistics which have been discussed fully with the farmers' representatives. We assess the extent of changes in farmers' costs since the last review and make assumptions about the gain from increasing efficiency. In order to discount the effects of particular weather conditions, we look at the level of farmers' incomes not only as they have actually developed but as they would have done under normal weather conditions. We also study the trend of production of individual commodities, the likely movement of imports, the prospective course of demand, and the way in which market prices can be expected to develop in the coming year. We take account of all these factors, together with the cost of Exchequer support, in determining the level of guaranteed prices and direct farming grants. We are also able to take account of the effects of our policy on our trade relations with the Commonwealth and with other overseas suppliers. . . .

"The method of support which characterizes our present system is very different from the method to which you are accustomed. It has been developed to meet our particular situation, and it is one in which our farmers have come to place great faith. They value especially the stability it secures, the sound basis it provides for planning ahead, and the fact that the system of annual reviews ensures that changes are made gradually and with due regard to their effects on the level of farming incomes. I need not emphasize the advantage which the consumer enjoys under our system and which in turn helps the producer, since lower food prices encourage demand.

"In moving towards your method of support we should have to introduce great changes affecting both producers and consumers. But provided we can see that in future—with the new methods decided upon—we are able to maintain the stability and living standards that we have established for our farmers, I believe that the problems raised by the differences in our present methods are in no way insuperable. . . . We are encouraged by the recognition which the Treaty itself gives to the importance of ensuring that changes in agriculture are brought about gradually. If the necessary changes in the UK are to be introduced without harmful effects to our agricultural economy, or indeed to our economy as a whole, the period allowed must be long enough to give our farmers time to adjust to new conditions and to permit increases in food prices to the consumer to take place gradually. . . . The transitional arrangements for the UK could, where necessary, continue for a period of between 12 and 15 years from when we join. . . .

"We should be moving continuously in the direction of a common policy. However, the changes we shall need to bring about are of such fundamental character that it is impossible for us to judge what their effect will be on the standard of living of our farmers when we have reached the end of the transitional period. Consequently, we regard it as of the utmost importance that we should continue to be able to use such means as are necessary to safeguard our farmers' standards of living. . . .

"The UK government are also pledged to ensure for horticulture a measure of support equivalent to that given to the agricultural industry generally. In the UK we mainly rely on the tariff as the instrument of support for horticulture and not, as for agriculture generally, on direct Exchequer subvention. You will therefore appreciate that the adoption of a common policy for horticulture will face us with some particularly complex problems. The problem of the removal of our tariffs on imports from the Community countries cannot be considered in isolation from your own existing arrangements and from those which may be made for these producers in the common agricultural policy. We shall therefore need to devise, in consultation with you, arrangements for the different horticultural products which will enable the UK government to continue to implement its pledges to horticulture.

EFTA. "I should next like to consider the position of the countries associated with the UK in the European Free Trade Association. It has long been our view that the present division of Western Europe into two economic groups—a division which in our opinion has political as well as economic dangers—should be brought to an end. We believe that the other members of EFTA, including the neutral countries, have a significant part to play, and that it would be wrong from the political as well as the economic point of view if they were excluded. In recent months we and our EFTA partners have considered this problem very carefully. As you will know from the statement issued by the EFTA Council on July 31, we concluded that each member of EFTA should examine the possibility of entering into a direct relationship with the Community.

"The UK and Denmark have already applied for full membership. We were delighted to hear of your decision to open negotiations with the Danish government later this month. Some members of EFTA consider that for political reasons they cannot apply for full membership. We believe that this should not be allowed to prevent them finding an appropriate relationship with the Community.

"At the EFTA Council meeting in London last June we agreed with our EFTA partners to maintain the Association—and here I quote from the communiqué—'until satisfactory arrangements have been worked out . . . to meet the various legitimate interests of all members of EFTA and thus enable them all to participate from the same date in an integrated European market.' HM Government earnestly trust that, when the other EFTA countries have explained where they stand, it will be possible to agree on ways and means of meeting their legitimate interests. I am sure you will appreciate that, given our obligations to our EFTA partners, we should not ourselves be able to join the Community until this had been done.

"There may in the past have been some misunderstanding of our views about arrangements for the EFTA countries. At the risk of some repetition I would like to make them perfectly clear. We hope to see an enlarged Community, including ourselves and as many of our EFTA partners as may wish to become full members. As to the remainder of the EFTA countries, we should like to see an association between each of them and the enlarged Community. If satisfactory arrangements could be made on these lines, the wider trading area thus created would include not only the members of the enlarged Community but also the remaining members of EFTA and, of course, Greece. EFTA itself would disappear. Contrary to what some people seem to have thought, therefore, there is no question of the UK seeking to maintain for itself a trading relationship with its present partners in EFTA in any way different from that which would be enjoyed by all other members of the enlarged Community.

Finland. "I should like to say a special word about Finland, whose case does not present the same problems as that of the members of EFTA. Finland, although associated with EFTA, is not of course a full member. Given her difficult political position, it may not be possible for her to establish a formal relationship with the EEC. But I am sure we should all wish that something should be done, in due course, to enable her to preserve her commercial links with Western Europe.

Irish Republic. "There is one other European country I should like to mention, namely, the Irish Republic. We have special trading arrangements with the Irish, deriving from the days when they were part of the United Kingdom. I do not think it necessary to describe these in detail. I will limit myself to saying that we in the UK were pleased to see that the Republic had applied for membership of the Community. If their application succeeds—as we hope it will—our trading arrangements with them will be subsumed in the wider arrangements of the enlarged Community, and no special problems need arise.

Procedure. "I should like to say a word now about procedure. I do not, of course, expect you to comment on my statement in any detail at this opening meeting. . . . When the time for our next meeting comes, I hope that we shall be able to discuss the principles on which the negotiations should proceed and give our officials instructions which will enable them to get down to work at once.

Conclusion. "All of us here have come a long way in the brief span of time since the Second World War. The application which we have made for membership of the Community, if it raises the difficulties which I have dealt with at some length, presents us all with a great opportunity for new advances together. We in the UK will regard the successful conclusion of these negotiations as a point of departure, not as the end of the road. The present dangers which confront the free world generally, and Europe in particular, are an added spur to us in seeking a new step forward in European unity. On the one hand we have a situation in which—owing to the advent of so many new states—the old and experienced voices of Europe find themselves more and more in a minority in world councils. We also have the phenomenon of blocs and groupings forming amongst these new states for the purpose of furthering their interests and increasing their influence in the world. On the other hand, nearer home, we have the direct threat to the security and well-being of European peoples from Communist expansionism, and in particular the threat to Berlin which weighs so heavily upon us at the present time. Great European nations have heard themselves described as 'hostages.' I can imagine no better way of counteracting the anxieties to which these events give rise in all our countries than by making rapid and visible progress with the task which we are undertaking today. An early success in this would, I think, do more than anything else to restore confidence in the future. It would compel our adversaries to treat us all with new respect, and encourage all who believe in the future of free peoples. . . ."

In taking official note of Heath's statement, the Six indicated the following limits within which the negotiations could take place:

"We have been assured that the UK's accession will, apart from the necessary adaptations, not require any amendments to the Treaty establishing the EEC and that it will be possible to settle by means of additional protocols the problems which will arise in connexion with this accession. Nevertheless, we start from the principle that these protocols must not be allowed to modify the tenor and the spirit of the Treaty and must essentially concern transitional arrangements.

"In fact, however grave and important the problems facing the UK may be—and we willingly recognize that they are in many cases grave and important—they need to be settled without exceptions becoming the rule and vice versa. Exceptions made must not be of such scope and duration as to call into question the rules themselves or impair the possibilities of applying these rules within the Community. The accession of new members must take place in such a way that they may subsequently share fully in the working out of common decisions in a Community spirit."

1.8 Progress of the Brussels negotiations—Partial agreement on common external tariff—The Commonwealth, agriculture and EFTA problems

The negotiations themselves started at ministerial level in Brussels on Nov. 8–9, 1961, a total of 17 meetings being held. The chairmanship of the conference rotated among the different countries as follows: West Germany until the end of 1961; France from January–March 1962; Italy from April–June 1962; Luxembourg from July–September 1962; Netherlands from October–December 1962; and Belgium in January 1963.

As indicated in Heath's statement in Paris, the negotiations were concerned primarily with the level of the common customs tariff, Commonwealth trade, UK agriculture, and relations with other EFTA countries, although this last problem had been little discussed by the time the negotiations broke down in January 1963.

The main points discussed and agreements reached between the six EEC countries and the United Kingdom on these subjects are outlined below, based on statements made by Heath in the House of Commons, White Papers published from time to time by the British government, and reports issued by the European Economic Community.

Details of the negotiations and partial agreements on the level of the common external tariff and on British requests for nil tariffs on certain products were as follows:

General level of common external tariff. Heath had suggested in his statement of Oct. 10, 1961, that Britain would accept the structure of the existing EEC tariff as the basis of the common tariff of the enlarged Community, with a linear reduction of 20 per cent in the common tariff as it stood—i.e., there should be no need for a recalculation on an arithmetical basis of the average of the tariffs of all the member countries of the enlarged Community.

While welcoming this attitude, the EEC stressed that the "common external tariff" which Britain proposed to accept subject to a 20 per cent linear reduction would mean only the tariff as established at meetings of the EEC Council of Ministers in 1960, and not the tariff which would have already been reduced by 20 per cent as a result of negotiations under Article XXIV (6) of GATT.

The EEC further maintained that the common external tariff was compatible with GATT and disagreed with the British proposal that at the end of the negotiations the Six and the UK should "together examine whether the level of the tariff resulting from [the] negotiations was appropriate as a tariff for the enlarged Community or whether it still needed to be adjusted by complementary reductions which would not exceed the 20 per cent envisaged for the negotiations."

In a statement on the ministerial meeting in Brussels on May 11–12, 1962, which he made to the House of Commons on May 16, Heath said that there was "broad agreement" on the general level of the common external tariff but that the UK "reserved the right to propose a review of the position at the end of our negotiations".

Nil tariffs. The United Kingdom stated that in the case of certain products it would be unable to accept the rates laid down in the common external tariff; at the beginning of the negotiations the UK delegation listed 24 products for which it requested a nil tariff, a further two items being added in April 1962. In addition to a number of other minerals, the list included in particular aluminium, lead, and zinc, as well as wood-pulp, newsprint, petroleum products, casein, tanning extracts, and certain chemicals —representing about 16 per cent of the UK's industrial imports. While in most instances the British argument was based on the fact that a large proportion of the UK imports of the products in question came from Commonwealth countries and were admitted duty-free or given preferential treatment under the British customs tariff, in other cases the main reason was that prices might rise if the common external tariff were applied to imports of these items by the United Kingdom.

Other requests for changes in tariffs. During the negotiations the UK delegation requested changes in the rates laid down in the common external tariff for 10 manufactured products of interest to India, Pakistan and Ceylon; for 25 tropical products; and for 17 processed foodstuffs.

After preliminary discussions, the question of Commonwealth trade was considered under three main headings.

Canada, Australia, and New Zealand. *Industrial products.* The UK suggested that as British imports of manufactured goods from these countries represented only a very small proportion of the enlarged Community's imports, they should be the subject of a special protocol similar to that covering trade between East and West Germany. The EEC rejected this proposal on the grounds that such imports by the UK in fact amounted to 11 per cent of her non-agricultural imports in 1961 and that their entry duty-free would raise "insoluble problems".

As a concession, however, the EEC proposed that *décalage* [i.e. a slower than normal rate of alignment of tariffs] should operate for the alignment of British duties for manufactured goods from these three Commonwealth countries in relation to the common external tariff.

The EEC also expressed willingness to take part in multilateral negotiations aimed at reducing, on a reciprocal basis, customs duties on industrial products; and the enlarged Community would be prepared to examine in 1966 and 1969, in consultation with Canada, Australia, and New Zealand, the development of its trade with these countries and to take the appropriate measures in the light of all the circumstances and in conformity with the provisions of the Treaty of Rome.

Farm products. On the question of temperate foodstuffs, it was reported after the ministerial meeting of May 29–30, 1962, that the Six had found British requests for "comparable outlets" for temperate foodstuffs from the Commonwealth "difficult to accept" and "incompatible" with the EEC's common agricultural policy, since to accede to them would involve discrimination and might prejudice the possibility of concluding world-wide commodity arrangements.

Heath informed the House of Commons on July 2, 1962, however, that at the ministerial meeting of June 28–30 it had been envisaged that the enlarged Community should negotiate agreements for suitable commodities—cereals, meat, dairy produce, and sugar—"on a broad international basis"; at the same time it had been recognized that alternative arrangements should be made for commodities "where international agreements appeared impracticable or had not been concluded by the end of the transitional period."

At the meeting on Aug. 1–5, 1962, the Ministers outlined the points to be covered by such long-term international agreements. A framework was worked out at the same meeting for the treatment which could be applied during the transitional period to all individual commodities for which there would be an intra-Community preference; in the case of cereals, the Community would ensure that the operation of such a preference would "not lead to sudden and considerable alterations in trade patterns". If these were to occur, however, the Community would review the operation of the intra-Community preference in consultation with Commonwealth countries, a similar safeguard being offered for all products where there would be an intra-Community preference. It was also agreed that imports into the UK of cereals at present enjoying a tariff preference in Britain should benefit from an agreed application of the intra-Community preference; the precise application would be discussed later.

Finally, the ministers of the Six stated that they "recognized the particular difficulties affecting New Zealand because of its high degree of dependence on the UK market, and expressed their readiness to consider special provisions to deal with these difficulties".

Officials had agreed by November 1962 that a *décalage* similar to that for manufactured goods from Canada, Australia, and New Zealand [see above] should also apply to certain processed agricultural products in which Commonwealth trade was relatively small. At the Nov. 15–17 meeting, the Six made new proposals for the 29 items on which agreement had not been reached (out of about 80 originally submitted by the UK): in reply, Heath agreed that the more gradual *décalage* would be an adequate arrangement for some smaller items, but that Britain maintained her proposals for duty reductions and duty quotas on others.

India, Pakistan, Ceylon, and Hong Kong. By the time of the breakdown of the Brussels negotiations, detailed proposals on Hong Kong had been submitted only by the United Kingdom. The EEC Commission, in their report published on March 5, 1963, stated that they were "firmly of the opinion that the problem of relations with Hong Kong could in the long run have been solved only in the framework of the Community's common commercial policy".

In the case of India, Pakistan, and Ceylon, proposals were agreed at the Aug. 1–5, 1962, meeting on a number of exports from these three countries, the ministers recognizing that "in the definition of the future commercial policy of the enlarged Community account should be taken of the necessity for these countries to increase and to diversify their national production with a view to raising the standard of living of their populations". These proposals contained the following main details:

Comprehensive trade agreements. The enlarged Community would seek to negotiate comprehensive trade agreements with India, Pakistan, and Ceylon by the end of 1966 at the latest. The objective of these agreements would be to develop trade and thus maintain and increase the foreign currency earnings of these countries, and in general to facilitate the implementation of their development plans. The means by which this could be done would include tariff policy, quota policy, export policy, and measures to facilitate the promotion of private investment and the provision of technical assistance.

Cotton textiles. A special time-table would be laid down for the application of the common external tariff to cotton textiles from India and Pakistan. If, as a result of this progressive application of the common external tariff by the UK, cotton textile exports from India and Pakistan to the enlarged Community were to decline, the Community would "take steps to restore the situation", until the above-mentioned trade agreements had been concluded or until the end of 1966, whichever was the earlier date.

Other products. Tariffs would be reduced to nil in respect of tea and of sports goods and certain other minor industrial products; and duties would be suspended under Article 28 in the case of cashew nuts, handloom products, and some other goods. The common external tariff would be progressively applied to jute goods (other than heavy jute goods), the UK establishing a quota for such goods from other member states amounting initially to 3,000 tons and increasing annually by 700 tons; quantitative restrictions would be abolished not later than Jan. 1, 1970.

For most other manufactured goods and processed foodstuffs, a "soft *décalage*" would operate—viz., 15 per cent of the appropriate common external tariff rate on the UK's accession; 15 per cent on July 1, 1965; 20 per cent on Jan. 1, 1967; 20 per cent on July 1, 1968; and the final 30 per cent on Jan. 1, 1970.

At the Oct. 25–27, 1962, meeting, agreement was reached on the text of a declaration which would be made by Britain and the EEC stating their intention, if Britain became a member, to open negotiations with India and Pakistan within three months of the UK's accession. At the same meeting the Six stated that they were "not prepared to agree to any suspension in the application of the common external tariff on textiles which had been previously agreed in August".

In their report of March 5, 1963, the EEC Commission gave further details of tariff concessions which had been offered by the Six for Indian and Pakistani exports, viz.: (1) nil tariffs not only on tea and sports goods (polo sticks and cricket bats) but also on lemon grass oil, decolourized or bleached shellac, and handloom products; (2) suspension of duties—indefinite or otherwise—in respect of a number of spices, essential oils, and certain other tropical products, and of castor oil and dessicated coconut; and (3) partial suspension of the tariff on East India kips, hand-knotted carpets, heavy jute goods, and coir mats and matting—for all of which the UK had requested nil tariffs. In reply to these offers by the Six, the UK had in January 1963 abandoned its initial position on hand-knotted carpets, heavy jute goods, and coir mats and matting, but had requested tariff reductions which "went much farther than those contemplated by the Six". No proposals had been made on the question of Indian tobacco.

Association of other Commonwealth countries. This subject was first fully discussed at the meeting of Aug. 1–5, 1962, when the principal points of agreement were:

(1) That for most dependent territories of the Commonwealth, association under Part IV of the Treaty of Rome provided the most satisfactory arrangement and that such territories would be eligible for this form of association;

(2) That for Commonwealth countries in Africa and the Caribbean which were independent or would shortly become independent, and which so desired, association under the new Convention of Association (then being negotiated and subsequently initialled on Dec. 20, 1962, and signed on July 20, 1963) would be a suitable arrangement, and that "at the appropriate time there should be consultation between the member governments of the Community (after consultation with the states already associated) and the British government (after consultation with the governments of the Commonwealth countries concerned) with a view to the association of these countries";

(3) That if certain countries did not become associates, further consultations should be held between the UK and the member states of the EEC about possible alternative economic arrangements.

General provisions. At the meeting of Oct. 8, 1962, Heath gave a full account of the discussion on the Brussels negotiations which had taken place at the Commonwealth Prime Ministers' meeting; in particular he stated that some independent African countries had considered association under Part IV unacceptable to them: referring to the agreement reached at the beginning of August, he "emphasized the importance which must now be attached to finding solutions [for these countries] during these further consultations."

At the subsequent meeting on Nov. 15–17, 1962, it was agreed that the opportunity to associate with the Community should remain open to all the Commonwealth countries in question (the proposed new Convention of Association containing an article which would make provision for new associates). In addition, it was stated that the enlarged Community would work towards commodity stabilization agreements where practicable, and would declare its readiness to negotiate commercial agreements with any Commonwealth countries not choosing association which might so desire.

Further points of agreement reached at this meeting were (1) that *décalage* should operate in the application of the common external tariff by the UK to exports of Commonwealth countries and territories which decided not to avail themselves of the opportunity of association with the Community (the rate being the same as that to be applied to industrial products other than cotton textiles from India and Pakistan—see above); (2) that the possibility of association should be made available for Aden, with the addition of a protocol dealing with the export of petroleum products from Aden to the Community; and (3) that the common external tariff on tropical hardwoods (which were of particular importance to Ghana and Nigeria) should be reduced to nil.

Malaysia. It was agreed at the meeting of Dec. 10–11, 1962, that the Community would be "prepared to envisage negotiations with a view to concluding a trade agreement with Malaya and the territories which it is planned should constitute the Federation of Malaysia, if the latter so desired it". While 85 per cent of the proposed Federation's exports would continue to enjoy free entry into the Community, since the common external tariff on many of the products of principal importance to the Federation was already nil, Malaya and the other territories should benefit for other commodities from the same *décalage* in tariffs as had already been agreed for India, Pakistan, and Ceylon [see above].

Malta. The ministers agreed on Dec. 10–11, 1962, that in the case of Malta a special protocol might be necessary to cover that country's problems as an interim measure (possibly with an element of customs union with the Community as a whole, while maintaining continued free entry for Malta's exports to the UK). Heath stated at the Dec. 19–20, 1962, meeting that in the light of the Malta government's reactions the EEC's proposals were "acceptable to HM Government".

Cyprus. Cyprus applied on Dec. 19, 1962, for negotiations to be opened with a view to reaching an agreement for her association with the Community under Article 238—the type of association "embodying reciprocal rights and obligations, joint actions, and special procedures" and being the form of association entered into with Greece. The EEC Council of Ministers agreed on Jan. 24, 1963, to initiate the appropriate procedure for these negotiations.

High Commission Territories. It was agreed on Dec. 19–20, 1962, that a protocol should be drawn up covering the three High Commission Territories (Basutoland, Bechuanaland, and Swaziland) "ensuring the continuation of the present customs regime in the UK for exports from these territories". The UK government would take steps to ensure that exporters in other countries could not take advantage of these arrangements by sending their goods through any of the three territories to the UK.

Gibraltar. In the case of Gibraltar, the UK submitted a proposal whereby Gibraltar would have become in due course an integral part of the Community under Article 227 (4), which states that "the provisions of this Treaty shall apply to European territories for whose external relations a member state is responsible". The UK suggested, however, that there should be an interim period during which no change should be made in the customs treatment applied to imports of goods from Gibraltar.

African countries declining association. In its report of March 5, 1963, the EEC Commission stated that of the independent countries of the Commonwealth, Ghana, Nigeria, and Tanganyika had declared that association would not be an acceptable formula for them; that Nigeria and Tanganyika had suggested that the possibility of trade agreements with them should be considered; and that Kenya had reserved its position for the time being.

Others. No detailed discussions had been held on the Rhodesia and Nyasaland Federation by the time the negotiations broke down, nor had South Africa's problems been studied, although the South African government had submitted a memorandum to the Conference and its views had been stated to the Conference by Dr Diederichs (South African Minister of Economic Affairs) on Nov. 20, 1962.

The most serious difficulties during the negotiations arose over the harmonization of British and EEC agriculture.

British proposals. Heath outlined the British system of agricultural support in his statement of Oct. 10, 1961. Following the formulation of the EEC's common agricultural policy in January 1962, Heath repeated at the next meeting in Brussels on Feb. 22–23, 1962, that "the UK fully accepts that the Common Market must extend to agriculture and trade in agricultural products", and that Britain was "prepared to participate in a common agricultural policy". He added, however, that in the British view "some adaptation of the decisions already reached by the EEC would be necessary, because, for example, the accession of the UK and other countries would alter the supply and demand situation, and because it would be necessary for the smooth and progressive harmonization of the present UK food and agricultural system with the new system which would be established in an enlarged Community".

Christopher Soames (UK Minister of Agriculture, Fisheries and Food) stated at the same meeting that Britain would ask for a transitional period of not less than 12 years, i.e. the same length of time as would have elapsed between the establishment of the EEC on Jan. 1, 1958, and Jan. 1, 1970, when the common agricultural policy would be fully implemented.

Agreement on annual Community farm review. Agriculture was the main subject of discussion at the July 20–21, 1962, meeting, when an arrangement was worked out for the establishment of a comprehensive Community review incorporating the results of reviews undertaken by national governments. The Community accepted that, if the annual review showed that the remuneration in the agricultural industry did not ensure for the farmers of the Community or of particular areas of it a fair standard of living, the Commission would take up the question either on its own initiative or at the request of a member state. The Commission would submit to the Council of Ministers proposals to remedy the situation, and the Council would then take the necessary decisions. (The Six accepted the principle on July 28, 1962, of an annual comparison between farm-workers' incomes and those in other industries, on the basis of which Community assistance might be given to agriculture if this was found necessary.)

Duration and terms of transitional period. At the meeting of Oct. 25–27, 1962, Heath repeated the British view that while the UK "recognized that at the end of the transitional period the present British system of deficiency payments would have to be replaced by the arrangements agreed for the Community as a whole", the aim must be to make the transition as smooth as possible and adequate time should therefore be allowed for it. The UK's arrangements for commodity subsidies, he went on, should therefore be continued during the transitional period, but the level of British market prices should be progressively adjusted so that by the end of the period they would be harmonized with those of the Community as a whole. This, together with adjustments in the prices guaranteed to producers, would ensure that by the end of the period of transition the commodity subsidies would have disappeared.

The Community proposed that the system of guaranteed prices should be replaced, at the moment of Britain's accession to the Community, by a system of consumer subsidies when justified, or in exceptional cases by producer subsidies. These subsidies should themselves be phased out by the end of the transitional period which the Community had agreed for themselves—namely, by Dec. 31, 1969.

In the course of discussion at the Dec. 10–11, 1962, meeting, Heath clarified the British proposals for the gradual phasing-out of deficiency payments and on the length of the transitional period; offered assurances to the Community as to the way in which these proposals would be implemented; and "made it clear once again that the government fully accepted the common agricultural policy for the single market period".

It was then decided to establish a Ministerial Study Group—which would "not in any sense be a negotiating group"—comprising the Ministers of Agriculture of the six EEC countries and of Britain, under the chairmanship of Dr Sicco Mansholt (one of the Vice-Presidents of the European Commission) to "examine urgently the practical problems arising from the proposals made by both sides to deal with the transitional arrangements for British agriculture" on a commodity-by-commodity basis.

By the time of the next ministerial meeting on Dec. 19–20, 1962, the Study Group had considered cereals, pigmeat, and eggs. Its report (covering also poultry and the length of the transitional period) was completed on Jan. 15, 1963.

A statement by Heath at this ministerial meeting recognized the link between the length of the transitional period and the nature of the transitional arrangements, and agreed that the difficulties foreseen about the date mentioned for the conclusion of the transitional period would be eased if it were possible to find the right kind of arrangements for it; if such arrangements could be found, it might be possible to accept Dec. 31, 1969, as the end of the transitional period for the commodities covered by the Mansholt Report (i.e. excluding, inter alia, horticulture). Heath's statement was "warmly welcomed" by many of the ministers present, who considered that it "provided a good basis for further consideration of the transitional problems".

Financial provisions. As regards Regulation 25 on the financing of the common agricultural policy, which not only provides for the establishment of an Agricultural Guidance and Guarantee Fund but also contains provisions on how the levies charged on imports of farm products from non-member countries should be used, Heath had confirmed at the Aug. 1–5, 1962, meeting that the British government would accept the Regulation in full if the UK joined the Community, and that at the appropriate time they would be prepared to participate with other members of the Community in an examination of the relation of this Regulation to the financing of Community expenditure in the period from 1965–70 and in the Common Market period thereafter.

Further discussion on both the Regulation and the subject of agriculture generally were still being held when the negotiations were broken off on Jan. 29, 1963.

The question of Britain's obligations towards the other EFTA countries was not discussed at any length during the negotiations. Article 234 of the Treaty of Rome was, however, considered on Dec. 10–11, 1962. This Article lays down principally that "the rights and obligations resulting from conventions concluded prior to the entry into force of this Treaty between one or more member states on the one hand and one or more third countries on the other shall not be affected by the provisions of this Treaty", and that "in so far as such conventions are not compatible with this Treaty, the member states or states concerned shall take all appropriate steps to eliminate any incompatibility found to exist". The EEC ministers stated their view that this Article was not intended to apply to preferential agreements with third countries but was intended to cover non-preferential agreements such as GATT. Heath confirmed this view and said that Britain accepted that the common external tariff should apply towards all non-member countries, except where special agreements had been negotiated by the time of the UK's accession.

As regards other EFTA countries, the EEC ministers indicated that if the UK negotiations were successful there were "favourable prospects for a satisfactory outcome of negotiations which have already begun with Denmark and Norway", though "for practical reasons they foresaw difficulty in reaching a rapid conclusion with other EFTA countries". In reply, Heath explained Britain's obligations to her EFTA partners, pointed out that the other EFTA countries were "anxious to begin negotiations as soon as possible", and expressed the conviction that "once the conclusion of our negotiations and those with Denmark and Norway is clear, it should be possible to complete negotiations with the other EFTA partners, which would not raise so many problems as our own, within a reasonable time".

The other principal topics discussed during the negotiations were the UK's application to join the European Coal and Steel Community and Euratom, problems of economic union, financial questions, and institutions. Heath's opening statement on the application to the ECSC was delivered to the Community's Council of Ministers in Luxembourg on July 17, 1962, and discussions at ministerial level were held on Oct. 4 and Nov. 19, 1962. The British government's position on the application to Euratom was set out in a statement to the Council of Ministers on July 3, 1962, and the Council gave its reply on Nov. 14, 1962.

Economic union. At the May 29–30, 1962, meeting, Heath accepted the provisions of the Treaty of Rome concerned with economic union (e.g. free movement of goods, of labour, and of capital; rules of competition; freedom of establishment; wages policy; transport; and social security) together with the regulations, directives, decisions, and recommendations in force, "subject to a small number of adjustments on timing and administration". The EEC Commission's report of March 5, 1963, stated that these reservations were primarily (*a*) a more detailed study of the rules of competition applicable to agriculture; (*b*) the special position of Northern Ireland as regards the free movement of labour; and (*c*) the time-table for establishing equal pay for men and women in the UK. In addition, a working party had studied certain administrative difficulties which might arise because of the special features of the British social security system—particularly, possible distortions of competition due to the fact that while "in the six [EEC] countries social charges are very largely financed by employers' and workers' contributions proportionate to earnings", in the UK "the main burden is borne by the taxpayer".

The report commented that "it may be considered surprising that the Conference paid relatively little attention to the problems of economic union, at least in their general aspects"; it explained, however, that this was "mainly due to the fact that the UK delegation was intent above all on defining the points on which it had to ask for a modification or an exception to the Community law in force", whereas "in the field of economic union . . . most of the common policies have still to be established".

Financial questions. Britain suggested that she should contribute the same amount as France, West Germany, and Italy to the Community budget and the same amount as France and West Germany to the Social Fund—suggestions which were "favourably received" by the Six. No decision had been reached on the British contribution to the Overseas Development Fund or on the Financial Regulation [see above], while the question of the contribution to the European Investment Bank had not been raised by the end of January 1963.

Institutions. Heath stated at the Dec. 19–20, 1962, meeting (i) that the UK would expect to enjoy the same voting position as other member states of comparable size; (ii) that the scale of British participation in all the institutions of the Community should likewise be of the same order; (iii) that he assumed that English would be an official language of the Community; (iv) that the UK would accept the corresponding obligations under the Treaty, in particular in relation to contributions under Article 200; and (v) that the UK accepted that the broad principle of a two-thirds majority in decisions of the Council as reflected in Article 148 of the Treaty of Rome (except for decisions requiring unanimity) should be maintained.

At the next meeting on Jan. 14–18, 1963, Hendrik Fayat (Belgian Assistant Minister for Foreign Affairs and then Chairman of the Conference) said that the Six agreed to these proposals, subject to further discussions on certain aspects of the question of financial contributions.

Macmillan paid a visit to Rambouillet on Dec. 15, 1962, for talks with de Gaulle, who reportedly expressed doubts over Britain's readiness to make the adjustments in policy and attitude which he believed to be necessary for joining the European Community. Macmillan then held his scheduled meeting with President Kennedy of the United States on Dec. 18–21 in Nassau, Bahamas, accepting the withdrawal of US support for the Skybolt missile project and the Nassau agreement under which the UK accepted Polaris nuclear missiles instead, within the structure of a multinational NATO nuclear force, a defence orientation rejected for France by de Gaulle.

1.9 De Gaulle's "non" on UK membership

President de Gaulle, dealing with the question of Britain's application to join the Common Market in a press conference on Jan. 14, 1963, clearly implied that in the French government's view Britain was not at present willing to join

the EEC on any terms which would be acceptable to France, and also stated
that the entry of Britain and the other members of EFTA would "completely
change" the nature of the Community, which would ultimately become "a
colossal Atlantic Community under American domination".

Asked to "define explicitly France's position towards Britain's entry into
the Common Market and the political evolution of Europe", de Gaulle
replied:

"The Treaty of Rome was concluded between six continental states—states which
are, economically speaking, one may say, of the same nature. Indeed, whether it be a
matter of their industrial or agricultural production, their external exchanges, their
habits or their commercial clientele, their living or working conditions, there is
between them much more resemblance than difference. Moreover, they are adjacent,
they inter-penetrate, they are an extension of each other through their communications.

"The fact of grouping and linking them in such a way that what they have to
produce, buy, sell, and consume is produced, bought, sold, and consumed in preference among themselves is therefore in conformity with realities. Moreover, it must
be added that from the point of view of their economic development, their social
progress, their technical capacity, they are keeping pace. They are marching in similar
fashion.

"It so happens, too, that there is between them no kind of political grievance, no
frontier question, no rivalry in domination or power. On the contrary, they are joined
in solidarity, first of all because of the consciousness they have of together constituting
an important part of the sources of our civilization; and also as concerns their security,
because they are continentals and have before them one and the same menace from
one extremity to the other of their territorial entity (*ensemble*). Then, finally, they are
in solidarity through the fact that not one among them is bound abroad by any special
political or military agreement.

"Thus it was psychologically and materially possible to create an economic community of the Six, though not without difficulties. When the Treaty of Rome was
signed in 1957, it was after long discussions; and when it was concluded, it was
necessary—in order to achieve something—that we French put in order our economic,
financial, and monetary affairs . . . , and that was done in 1959. From that moment
the Community was in principle viable . . .

"However, this treaty, which was precise and complete enough concerning industry,
was not at all so on the subject of agriculture, and for our country this had to be
settled. Indeed, it is obvious that agriculture is an essential element in our national
activity as a whole. We cannot conceive of a Common Market in which French
agriculture would not find outlets in keeping with its production. And we agree further
that, of the Six, we are the country on which this necessity is imposed in the most
imperative manner.

"This is why when, last January, consideration was given to the setting in motion of
the second phase of the treaty—in other words a practical start in its application—we
were led to pose the entry of agriculture into the Common Market as a formal
condition. This was finally accepted by our partners, but very difficult and very
complex arrangements were needed and some rulings are still outstanding.

"Thereupon Great Britain posed her candidature to the Common Market. She did it
after having earlier refused to participate in the Communities which we were building,
as well as after creating a sort of Free Trade Area with six other states, and finally—I
may well say it as the negotiations held at such length on this subject will be recalled
—after having put some pressure on the Six to prevent a real beginning being made in
the application of the Common Market.

"England thus asked in turn to enter, but on her own conditions. This poses without
doubt to each of the six states, and poses to England, problems of a very great

dimension. England in effect is insular, she is maritime, she is linked through her exchanges, her markets, her supply lines to the most diverse and often the most distant countries; she pursues essentially industrial and commercial activities, and only slight agricultural ones. She has in all her doings very marked and very original habits and traditions. In short, the nature, the structure, the very situation that are England's differ profoundly from those of the continentals.

"What is to be done so that England, as she lives, produces, and trades, can be incorporated into the Common Market, as it has been conceived and as it functions? For example, the means by which the people of Great Britain are fed, and which are in fact the importation of foodstuffs bought cheaply in the two Americas and in the old Dominions while at the same time considerable subsidies are given to English farmers? These methods are obviously incompatible with the system which the Six have established quite naturally for themselves.

"The system of the Six consists of making a whole of the agricultural products of the entire Community, strictly fixing their prices, prohibiting subsidies, organizing their consumption between all the participants, and imposing on each participant the payment to the Community of any saving which they would achieve in fetching their food from outside instead of eating what the Common Market has to offer. Once again, what is to be done to bring England, as she is, into this system?

"One might sometimes have believed that our English friends, in posing their candidature to the Common Market, were agreeing to transform themselves to the point of applying all the conditions which are accepted and practised by the Six . . . But the question is to know whether Great Britain can now place herself, like the Continent and with it, inside a tariff which is genuinely common, to renounce all Commonwealth preferences, to cease any pretence that her agriculture be privileged, and, more than that, to treat her engagements with other countries of the Free Trade Area as null and void. That question is the whole question. It cannot be said that it is yet resolved. Will it be so one day? Obviously only England can answer.

"The question is even further complicated, since after England other states, which are linked to her through the Free Trade Area, would like or wish to enter the Common Market for the same reasons as Britain. It must be agreed that first the entry of Great Britain, and then of these states, will completely change the whole of the adjustments, the agreements, the compensation, the rules which have already been established between the Six, because all these states, like Britain, have very important peculiarities. It will then be another Common Market whose construction ought to be envisaged. But this Market, which would be increased to 11 and then 13 and then perhaps 18, would without any doubt no longer resemble the one which the Six built.

"Further, this Community, expanding in such fashion, would see itself faced with problems of economic relations with all kinds of other states, and first with the United States. It can be foreseen that the cohesion of its members, who would be very numerous and diverse, would not endure for long, and that finally it would appear as a colossal Atlantic community under American domination and direction which would quickly have absorbed the European Community. It is a hypothesis which in the eyes of some can be perfectly justified, but it is not at all what France wanted to do or is doing—and which is a properly European construction.

"Yet it is possible that one day England might be able to transform herself sufficiently to become part of the European Community, without restriction, without reserve, and in preference to anything else, and in that event the Six would open the door to her and France would raise no obstacle, although obviously the very fact of England's participation in the Community would considerably change its nature and its volume.

"It is possible, too, that England might not yet be so disposed, and this is certainly what seems to emanate from the long, long Brussels conversations. . . .

"Moreover, I repeat, even if the Brussels negotiations were shortly not to succeed, nothing would prevent the conclusion between the Common Market and Great Britain of an agreement of association designed to safeguard exchanges, and nothing would prevent close relations between England and France from being maintained, nor the pursuit and development of their direct co-operation in all kinds of fields, notably the scientific, technical, and industrial—as the two countries have just proved by deciding to build together the supersonic aircraft Concorde.

"Lastly, it is very possible that Britain's own evolution, and the evolution of the universe, might bring the English towards the Continent, whatever delays this achievement might demand. For my part, that is what I readily believe, and that is why, in my opinion, it will in any case have been a great honour for the British Prime Minister, my friend Harold Macmillan, and for his government, to have discerned that goal in good time, to have had enough political courage to have proclaimed it, and to have led their country the first steps along the path which one day, perhaps, will lead it to moor alongside the Continent."

1.10 Reactions to President de Gaulle's statement

Commenting on Jan. 15 on de Gaulle's attitude towards Britain's entry into the Common Market, a British Foreign Office spokesman stated only that "all we can say is that we are continuing to press on with our negotiations in Brussels". On the question of the Bahamas agreement, the spokesman said: "President de Gaulle was clearly referring to the Nassau agreement entirely from the French point of view. We ourselves regard the Nassau agreement as a constructive contribution to the indivisible defence of the Western Alliance, and we would hope that other members of the Alliance would so regard it. The NATO nuclear force is under discussion between all the NATO Allies, and we would hope that France herself would one day have second thoughts."

Strongly critical comments on the President's views were made by statesmen of the other Common Market countries, who expressed the firm hope that the negotiations for Britain's entry would be successfully concluded.

Dr Luns, the Dutch Foreign Minister, said on Jan. 14 that he could "not hide the feeling of disappointment" at President de Gaulle's statement and, while declining to comment on the President's suggestion of associated status for the United Kingdom, declared that "we are negotiating with Great Britain for her adherence to the Community as a full member".

Paul–Henri Spaak, the Belgian Foreign Minister, declared on Jan. 15 that "as far as the Belgian government is concerned, the approach of Great Britain as put forward at [the] Brussels negotiations is altogether different from the picture of it which the President of the French Republic has given". A "certain number" of the difficulties mentioned by de Gaulle had "already been surmounted," and while difficult problems remained, notably in the agricultural sphere, they were "no more insurmountable than the rest". The countries concerned "must continue to negotiate with even greater determination, and Belgium would "refuse to assume responsibility" for "a policy of intransigence which would lead the negotiations to failure".

The German delegation in Brussels, in a statement on behalf of the Foreign Minister, Dr Gerhard Schröder, declared on Jan. 15 that it was necessary on economic and political grounds for Britain to become a full member of the EEC; that de Gaulle's proposal for an association would not be a satisfactory solution; and that the delegation would do its best to bring the negotiations to a successful conclusion.

The Italian government announced on Jan. 15 that Italy would continue to give Britain "the strongest support" in the negotiations, while Ugo La Malfa, the Minister for the Budget, declared that "Italy and the other countries of the Common Market cannot be treated like colonies".

De Gaulle's views were also criticized by a number of French political personalities and commentators, notably by Jean Monnet, one of the founders of the movement for European unity, and president of the Action Committee for a United States of Europe.

Monnet said on Jan. 16 that "whatever General de Gaulle may say, I think that the negotiations for England's entry into the EEC could be rapidly concluded"; it was "necessary for world peace that England should unite with the Community and that a relationship as equal partners should be established between a United Europe, including England, and the United States."

De Gaulle, commenting on the reception given to his statement, said on Jan. 17 that "the British . . . will enter the Common Market one day, but no doubt I shall no longer be here"; when questioned about the critical attitude of the other five members of the EEC to his policy, he added: "They have signed a treaty, and so they must carry it out."

The latter part of the ministerial meeting in Brussels on Jan. 14–18, 1963, was taken up with a separate meeting of the ministers from the six EEC countries alone, at the end of which the following statement was agreed by these ministers, together with Heath: "The French delegation has requested that the negotiations with Great Britain should be suspended. The five other delegations of the EEC and the British delegation have opposed this. Discussion of this question will be continued in the course of the next session of the Conference which has been set for Jan. 28, 1963, in Brussels."

Macmillan expressed his views on de Gaulle's "non" in a speech in Liverpool on Jan. 21, 1963, to a Conservative rally.

"The movement for European unity was founded immediately after the war, with the help of many distinguished European figures, by the greatest English patriot of his or any other time, Sir Winston Churchill. It was supported in Britain by leading Labour figures like Ernest Bevin. It fitted the mood of Europe. It blossomed and developed. All these years Europe has been working by various institutions towards a solution of the problem of unity in diversity.

"A few years ago this movement took its most advanced shape so far, in the successful efforts of six European countries to bring about, through the Treaty of Rome, the European Economic Community. Its principle and its method have both been based on partnership, not on domination. It was in this spirit that, with the assent of parliament, the British government 18 months ago decided to open negotiations for our entry into the European Community. When after long months of negotiation this last round started a week ago it was recognized on all sides that the few outstanding problems were capable of solution.

"This was the general view—and for good reasons. We had made it abundantly clear that we accepted the Treaty of Rome and aligned ourselves with the political implications as well as the economic content of the treaty. In particular, we had accepted a common agricultural policy and the common tariff. We have reached agreed solutions over a very large part of the field; we still believe that given the will the remaining difficulties can be surmounted.

"What has happened has been a setback. I trust and pray not a fatal setback. It would be wrong at this moment not to pay tribute to the overwhelming demand that has been shown throughout Europe and the free world for the constructive settlement. And while recrimination is useless, it is, nevertheless, right that the truth should be known and that the record should be kept straight.

"When the Community accepted our application 18 months ago it was well known that complicated negotiations would follow to deal with the special problems of Britain making so great a change in her economic arrangements, affecting not only herself but also the Commonwealth. This is, indeed, precisely what the terms of the Treaty of Rome provided for. It was on this basis that negotiations started, and it is on this basis that negotiations have continued until now. If there was an objection in principle we should, surely, have been told so from the start. Indeed, at my meeting with him at Rambouillet, General de Gaulle himself reminded me that the length of the negotiations was inevitable in view of their complicated character.

"Similarly, it has been suggested that by making the Polaris arrangement with President Kennedy a few days after I had seen General de Gaulle himself at Rambouillet, I did not treat him with absolute sincerity. On the contrary, we discussed this question and I explained that if the Americans decided to abandon Skybolt as unlikely to prove satisfactory I would do my utmost at Nassau to obtain an effective alternative. I explained to him in some detail my view of the relation between interdependence and independence, and said that we must have a British deterrent available for independent use if need be. I am sure he fully understood our position. This impression was confirmed through diplomatic contacts after the Nassau agreement had been announced.

"I do not feel called upon to deal with some of the other rumours which I have seen quoted, rumours about new, secret undertakings given by me at Nassau and so forth. All these are false.

"I would only add one point. When we made our application to enter into negotiations with the European Community with a view to joining, this was accepted by all the Six, including, of course, the French. No point was made to the effect that our joining would alter the whole balance of the Community. Our size and our world-wide trading connexions were not held against us as a sort of reproach. The Channel was not regarded as an unbridgeable chasm. Now it seems things are different. I cannot believe that any of the six countries which accepted our application in principle can now reject it, not on any economic grounds, not because the negotiations have failed, but because in principle they prefer the Community without Britain.

"It has, of course, not been easy for us in this country readily to accept so marked a development in our historic policies as would be involved in our entering the European Community, and was even in a sense involved in our joining the NATO Alliance. It has been urged by some of our critics at home that we should stick to isolationism—'splendid isolation' was the phrase—which was our theme through the later part of the 19th century and the early part of the 20th century.

"I will only say in answer to this criticism that, through all our earlier history, these islands were always comparatively weak, both in wealth and in population, and so in those times we followed quite different policies. We worked in alliances and in coalitions which changed as the conditions changed. Nor was the 19th-century isolation, when we thought ourselves strong enough to indulge in it, so splendid after all.

"In other words, our aim is to make a true European unity. Then—and only then— will Europe be great and strong enough to build a more equal and worthy partnership with North America. The right relationship between friends and allies is the relationship of equal balance and co-operation, in which no partner seeks to dominate the others or dictate to the others.

"What did independence bring us in this present century? It brought us the frightful war of 1914–18 and the decimation and destruction of our youth on a scale never experienced in history. Again, what did the confusion of the Allies after 1918 bring? It brought the second war, longer and more terrible even than the first, and leading to the tragic division of Europe into free and Communist countries, and to the new terrors which today menace the world.

"It is because our people have felt something new was wanted, something more generous, more noble, and more up to date, more in time with the aspirations of youth as well as more long-sighted, that we have been able to get a general acceptance, first for the NATO policies, then for the policies of European unity generally, and now for our application to join the Economic Community. It is because we have seen all this movement that we have tried honestly and honourably to throw our lot in with it. And it is because they realize what we are trying to do that the Commonwealth countries show themselves so understanding both of our difficulties and of our aims.

"Of course, there is the material side as well as the ideal. We believe that the material wealth of Britain will be increased if she joins the Market in a move, with other countries, for the development of mutual prosperity. To make this prosperous society worthy of the ideals which we have set ourselves in the world it must be outward looking.

"That is our view of the new Europe, which must come, and we believe that it is the view also of the majority in the existing Community. We should not think of ourselves as a narrow and highly protected group having no regard to the interests of the outer world. We should try to look beyond our own back gardens. It is in this sense that a strengthened and forward-looking Western Europe can play a full part with the peoples of America, not only from the economic point of view in its trading relations, but . . . whether it is in defence, in political thought, or in aid to under-developed countries.

"Indeed, it is only if we in Europe join with America in playing this role that the competition between Communism and our way of life can proceed without war. It is only in this way that we shall be able to persuade all the world, the uncommitted and the unaligned, the new nations and the emerging nations, that this European movement to which we are anxious to give our adhesion is a movement not tainted with the memories of the past or the old ambitions and rivalries which have brought such misery to the world. It must be inspired by new thoughts, nobler emotions. It is these beliefs which have influenced those who were the founders of the European movement. And it is in their name that we have the right to claim that this great opportunity should not be lost to the world."

Macmillan's speech was made after the French Foreign Minister, Maurice Couve de Murville, had on Jan. 17 officially demanded the suspension of the Brussels negotiations for Britain's membership of the Common Market.

Further expressions of support for Britain's entry were made by various statesmen in the other EEC countries during the same week.

West Germany. Dr Schröder (West German Foreign Minister) said in a statement broadcast on Jan. 20—prior to the departure of himself, Dr Adenauer (then federal Chancellor), and other West German ministers for Paris for the signature of the Franco-German treaty of co-operation—that "for political and economic reasons, the entry of Britain into the EEC is necessary, urgent, and even very urgent", and that the federal government was "working with all its strength" to bring this about. Professor Erhard (then federal Minister of Economy) made a statement to the press on Jan. 23 emphasizing that "the negotiations with Britain must proceed. No one should retard or obstruct them. They are a test of the will of the European peoples to determine their fate in common." It was announced at the end of a West German Cabinet meeting on Jan. 25, following Adenauer's return from Paris on Jan. 23, that the Cabinet had agreed that the negotiations "can and should be continued with the aim of reaching a positive conclusion", and that the federal government "remains in consultation with the French government and the other partners in the EEC on this question".

Belgium. The Belgian Senate unanimously approved on Jan. 24 a motion "expressing anxiety at the disequilibrium which would be caused to the European Communities through the absence of Great Britain and the formation of a Franco-German bloc", and "hoping that the effort of the Belgian government and of the Executive Commission of the Common Market will result in the accession of Great Britain".

During the debate, Spaak (the Belgian Foreign Minister) said that France's change of mind had caused "stupefaction" among the other EEC and the British ministers then meeting in Brussels, and that "if the negotiations with England are suspended, it will be the end (*faillite*) of the Common Market, because it will be impossible to carry on or open negotiations with other countries".

Italy. In a debate in the Italian Chamber of Deputies on Jan. 27, Amintore Fanfani (then Prime Minister) gave a firm undertaking that Italian efforts would continue to be directed at ensuring British entry into the Common Market. He described the Franco-German treaty as damaging to the EEC, to the progress of European unity, and to the internal balance of NATO.

Netherlands. Dr Mansholt stated in a speech at the University of Louvain on Jan. 22 that it was "completely incorrect to say that the Brussels negotiations have reached a point where any positive solution is impossible . . .—[rather] the contrary is true". Solutions were in sight, although "admittedly they are not possible without important concessions on both sides"; these concessions, however, should not necessarily be to the detriment of the Treaty of Rome, but were concerned rather with the adaptations which the member states themselves had had to agree mutually when the Treaty was worked out. He hoped therefore that all who were interested in the decisions of the coming days understood that this decision concerned not only Great Britain, nor even only the Community, but essentially the whole of Europe and the Atlantic Alliance.

Meanwhile, Alain Peyrefitte (French Minister of Information) stated on Jan. 24, 1963, after a Cabinet meeting that the French government did not see how the Brussels negotiations could be resumed and that there was "no reason to go back on the decision taken last week". On the same day, in a division on the estimates of the Foreign Ministry in the National Assembly, the French government received a majority of 271 to 146, with 51 abstentions.

During the debate, Couve de Murville (the Foreign Minister) repeated President de Gaulle's arguments against Britain becoming a member of the EEC, notably the fact that if Britain, and then other countries, joined the Community, the EEC would become "much less homogeneous, much more loose, and consequently completely different". Nothing should be altered of "the essential, the edifice built by the founder-members, called the Treaty of Rome, with all its regulations".

He continued: "From the moment . . . that Great Britain asked not, as is generally believed, to adhere to the Treaty of Rome under the terms of Article 237, but to study with us the conditions under which she could envisage participation in the Common Market, we very clearly defined our position on this basis." The negotiations over the past 15 months, however, had been concerned not with the terms of adaptation but with the fundamentals—the one side wishing to maintain the Treaty and the other side to modify it.

After considering in particular the agricultural problems, Couve de Murville stressed that the door was not shut to Great Britain and that, if she had not yet arrived at the point where the "inevitable transformations" were acceptable, that moment would come. That was why the French government had proposed, as a temporary solution, that an agreement should be concluded between Britain and the EEC which, without going so far as formal accession, would permit the two parties to maintain and develop their trade and would let Britain proceed to the necessary changes until the decisive step could be taken. This idea had been immediately rejected, but "when calm returns" it was possible that it might finally be taken into consideration.

Later Couve de Murville said in reply to the debate that "if Great Britain accepts all the provisions of the Treaty of Rome, nothing could prevent her from entering the Common Market; but the burden of proof lies upon her and not upon us". The position of France's partners, he went on, was contradictory because they were for Europe, and for an integrated Europe, but at the same time for Britain's entry into the

Common Market, although everybody knew that this would substantially alter the data of the problem of integration and supranationality. Moreover, France was not concerned with whether Europe was "great" or "small" but whether it was European, and it was on that criterion that she would judge candidatures for entry into the Communities.

The final—17th—meeting in the negotiations was held on Jan. 28–29, 1963. On the first day Heath saw ministers from Belgium, West Germany, Italy, Luxembourg, and the Netherlands, and also Walter Hallstein (President of the EEC Commission), and after a number of separate meetings ministers from all six EEC countries met in the evening.

The following account of the 17th meeting was given by Heath to the House of Commons on Jan. 30:

". . . The Six met at about 7.15 p.m. on Jan. 28 and again at noon and in the early afternoon of Jan. 29. The ministers of Belgium, the Federal Republic of Germany, Italy, Luxembourg, and the Netherlands did all they could, during these meetings, to persuade the French delegation to agree on a basis for continuing the negotiations. As the House knows, their efforts were of no avail. I was, of course, kept fully informed throughout their discussions.

"At about 4.30 yesterday afternoon, the full Conference of the Seven met to consider the situation. I was accompanied at this meeting by . . . the Commonwealth Secretary [Duncan Sandys] and the Minister of Agriculture, Fisheries, and Food [Soames]. The chairman of the Conference, Fayat, opened the meeting by reading a statement, of which the following is a translation:

"'Following the decision taken by the seven governments on Jan. 18 last, the Six have resumed their discussions on the proposal of the French delegation to break off the negotiations between the member states of the EEC and the UK. The five other delegations of the EEC and the British delegation opposed this proposal at the time it was made. In the discussions held by the Six yesterday and today various compromise proposals have been examined. It has finally become apparent that the Belgian, the German, the Italian, the Luxembourg, and the Netherlands delegations agree to accept the following text. . . :

"'The European Commission is requested to draw up, during the next three weeks, a report on the present state of the negotiations for accession between Great Britain and the six states of the EEC; in this report the Commission will set out the results already obtained and the questions still in suspense, and will give its opinion on the latter. This report will be transmitted to each of the seven delegations comprising the Conference. The work of the Conference will be resumed not later than 10 days after the submission of this report. . . .

"'The French delegation has refused to accept this text because of a different view which they will explain in the course of this meeting.'

"After hearing this statement, ministers representing Belgium, the Netherlands, Germany, France, Italy, and Luxembourg then each spoke in turn. With the exception of the French Foreign Minister, each declared that it was his government's wish to continue the negotiations and his government's conviction that the outstanding problems could be resolved. Each one expressed deep regret at the situation which had arisen and anxiety as to its consequences.

"Professor Hallstein . . . also spoke. He said that the European Commission would seek to reduce to the minimum the harmful effects of these developments, both within the EEC and in its relations with other countries.

"M. Couve de Murville stated his government's reasons for having proposed a suspension of the negotiations. He argued that they had made no progress since October; that Britain had not been able to accept the disciplines of the Rome Treaty, notably the common agricultural policy; and that the entry of new members to a club which was not yet complete raised serious questions, notably for the founder-members.

"I [Heath continued] then said that, had the Six countries been able to agree on the draft terms of reference for a report by the European Commission which had been proposed by the five delegations, we should have been able to accept them, because they would have shown that the negotiations were being resumed in good faith. I recalled the reasons for our application to enter into negotiations with the Community.

"I completely repudiated the arguments advanced by the French delegation for advocating the suspension of negotiations; I said that we would not turn our backs on the Continent because of these events but would continue to work with all our friends in Europe for its future strength and unity.

"The Chairman of the Conference then said that, in the circumstances, he was forced to record the fact, with great regret, that the member states of the EEC were prevented from continuing the negotiations. He was convinced that this regret would be echoed throughout the world. M. Fayat then declared the meeting closed. . . ."

Heath and representatives of Belgium, West Germany, Italy, Luxembourg, and the Netherlands met immediately after the end of the conference to consider their future action.

Spokesmen for both the French and British delegations made statements to press correspondents in Brussels on Jan. 29.

Claude Lebel, spokesman for the French Foreign Ministry, said: "Whatever may have been said or written, [France] did not exercise a veto against Great Britain's entry into the Common Market. She stated—and the experience of the past months seems conclusive in this respect—that England, as a result of her situation and traditions, was not at present in a position to accept certain of the essential clauses of the Treaty of Rome. She deduced from this that, rather than continue down a dead- end, it was better to adjourn—I say adjourn and not break because, as has been said and repeated by the leading persons of responsibility in French politics, England has only to accept the clauses of the Treaty of Rome for her accession to pose no further questions."

Heath said in his statement: "We entered these negotiations 16 months ago in good faith and have endeavoured strenuously to reach a successful conclusion. Five countries and the Commission have said publicly that all remaining problems in the negotiations were capable of solution. I share that view. The Five governments and ourselves all wished to continue negotiations and bring them to a successful conclusion. The high hopes of so many have thus been thwarted for political reasons and the will of one man. The end of the negotiations is a blow to the cause of that wider European unity for which we have been striving."

A review of the Brussels negotiations was given by Prof. Hallstein at the beginning of a debate in the European Parliament on Feb. 5, 1963.

Summarizing the main points of discussion, Prof. Hallstein said that the negotiations fell into three main stages—one of "exploration, preparation, cautious reconnaissance of the other party's positions, and getting down to dealing with problems of substance", which had lasted from October 1961 until April 1962; one in which large parts of the problems raised by relations with the Commonwealth were solved, and which lasted until the beginning of August 1962; and the third, concentrating upon agricultural policy and nil tariffs, which continued until the breakdown.

Prof. Hallstein went on to explain the Commission's part in the negotiations. The Commission, he said, was still convinced that its own proposals for the procedure to be followed—namely that the negotiations should be organized on a bilateral basis between the Community, acting through a spokesman, and the United Kingdom — were "not only right in principle but would have been better in practice", as they would have "ensured a clear distinction between the taking of decisions within the Community and reaching agreement with our partner in the negotiations". While the negotiations were actually in progress, the Commission had "endeavoured to play the honest broker among the Six, for only as long as the Six were in agreement was there any chance of an arrangement with the British which could be transformed into a formal agreement"; at the same time the Commission's task had also been "to watch over the Treaty of Rome and the Community law based on it".

On the interruption of the negotiations, Prof. Hallstein stressed that, "without pre-judice . . . to the decision which is reserved to the individual countries as to whether they will sign an agreement bringing in a new member, membership is unquestionably also a Community matter, and a Community matter of fundamental importance". The manner in which "one member government took and communicated its decision to interrupt the negotiations" had therefore not been in harmony with the duties imposed by the Com-munity, since the results of an interruption affected the Community as a whole, and not just one member state. The opening of the negotiations had been decided unanimously by the six member governments at a session of the Council of Ministers and the negotiations had been going on for 15 months. In these circumstances, Prof. Hallstein declared, "one might at the very least have expected that the question of the future of the negotiations, if it had to be raised, would have been discussed fully and frankly amongst the members of the Community"; the fact that this had not happened had faced the Community with its "first real crisis".

The life of the Community depended on "everyone looking upon and treating Com-munity matters as matters of real joint responsibility", and this was only possible if the Community system and Community procedures were respected. The right of a veto was "subject to rules, and must be used with consideration". It was also "necessary to avoid creating the impression that the Community and its aims, the Community institutions, and the Community procedure are merely instruments of national diplomacy".

After stressing that the Commission must oppose any tendency to allow interruptions to occur in the proper functioning of the Community institutions, Prof. Hallstein con-cluded by pointing out that the negotiations had "made us more keenly aware than any academic considerations could have done how closely our Community is bound up with the circumstances, the difficulties, and the political realities of the whole world".

After debate two resolutions were carried unanimously by the European Parliament on Feb. 6, 1963, with the 13 French Union for the New Republic (UNR) deputies abstaining.

The first requested the European Commission to make a report within three weeks on the position reached on Jan. 29 in the negotiations between Britain and the six EEC countries, reviewing both the results achieved and the problems still pending and giving its opinions on the latter. The second resolution, after pointing out that "the ultimate aim of European integration is the creation of a United States of Europe, a supranational economic and political Community based on equality of rights among its member states and endowed with its own institutions independent of governments," and voicing "grave misgivings at the unilateral interruption of the negotiations . . . ," approved the statement made by Prof. Hallstein and requested the Council of Ministers to ensure that the Conference should continue regular discussions with the object of facilitating the accession of other countries, particularly the United Kingdom.

A third resolution presented in the name of the Socialist group in the Parliament, protesting against the method chosen by the French government to end the negotiations and affirming that the negotiations had been broken off for extraneous reasons, was lost on a tied vote of 38 for and 38 against.

The European Commission's report was published on March 5, 1963, and was debated in the European Parliament on March 27–29; a resolution was unanimously adopted which, inter alia, confirmed the Parliament's desire to see Britain and other countries join the European Communities, provided their accession did not prejudice the integration process or undermine the substantive rules or institutional structures of the Treaties of Rome and of Paris. The resolution also considered that notwithstanding the serious difficulties arising from the interruption of the negotiations, the Community must fulfil all the obligations laid upon it by the Treaty, both as regards action in the economic and social spheres and as regards relations with non-member countries.

The first definite step towards the resumption of contacts between the Six and Britain was taken on July 11, 1963, when the EEC Council of Ministers agreed: (1) that ministerial meetings of the Western European Union (comprising Belgium, France, West Germany, Italy, Luxembourg, the Netherlands, and the UK) should be held regularly every three months in each of the seven capitals in turn; (2) that the item "exchange of views on the European economic situation" should always appear on the agenda, in addition to the WEU's normal discussions of political matters; and (3) that the EEC Commission should take part in such economic discussions. (The possibility of using the WEU to "iron out" existing difficulties between the EEC and EFTA—through British membership of the WEU—had first been proposed by Dr Luns in February 1961.)

2: SECOND UK APPLICATION

2.1 Chronology of events

Nov. 10, 1966	Harold Wilson's announcement of British Labour government's decision to make "new high-level approach"
Nov. 16–17, 1966	House of Commons debate
Dec. 5, 1966 and April 28, 1967	Meeting with EFTA government representatives
January–March 1967	Wilson's and Brown's visits to EEC member states
May 2, 1967	Wilson's announcement of decision to apply for membership of EEC, ECSC and Euratom
May 8–10, 1967	House of Commons debate
May 10–11, 1967	Formal letter of application
May 16, 1967	de Gaulle's press conference on problems of British application
Sept. 29, 1967	Submission of Preliminary Opinion of the Commission on enlargement application
Nov. 27, 1967	de Gaulle's press conference on incompatibility of EEC with existing British economy
Dec. 18–19, 1967	Council meeting records failure to agree on steps to deal with enlargement application
February 1969	WEU crisis and French protest to UK over "Soames Affair"
Oct. 2, 1969	Commission's Revised Opinion
Oct. 17, 1969	French accept opinion that negotiations should begin
Dec. 1–2, 1969	Summit meeting of the Six at the Hague decides to open negotiations with applicant countries
Feb. 10, 1970	Publication in UK of White Paper on economic effects of membership
June 18, 1970	UK general election and return of Conservative government under Edward Heath
June 30, 1970	First formal stage of negotiations
Jan. 20–21, 1971	House of Commons debate on progress of negotiations

Jun. 21–23, 1971	Conclusion of main phase of negotiations
July 7, 1971	Publication of White Paper on negotiations
Oct. 21–28, 1971	Parliamentary approval in "Great Debate" of decision of principle to join the Communities
Dec. 12, 1971	Conclusion of negotiations on fisheries
Jan. 22, 1972	Signature in Brussels of Treaty of Accession
April 23, 1972	Approval of enlargement in French referendum
Oct. 17, 1972	Completion of passage of European Communities Bill
Oct. 19–20, 1972	First summit conference in Paris of "the Nine"
Jan. 1, 1973	Accession of UK, Ireland and Denmark as members of the European Communities
Feb. 1, 1973	Formal adoption of common agricultural policy to be implemented over five-year period

2.2 Announcement by Labour government in late 1966 of decision to make a "new high-level approach" on UK membership of the EEC

The prospects for a second British application began to appear more favourable some three years after the breakdown of the first set of negotiations. Britain's relationship wth the EEC was discussed at a number of meetings of the Western European Union during 1966.

At a meeting in London on March 15–16, Jean de Broglie (French Secretary of State for Foreign Affairs) was reported to have said that France would welcome Britain in the Community "in the spirit of the Treaty of Rome", while Michael Stewart (then UK Foreign Secretary) stated at a press conference on March 16 that the present situation seemed "healthier . . . than that which existed in 1963". George Thomson (then Chancellor of the Duchy of Lancaster with special responsibility for relations with other European countries), addressing the WEU Assembly in Paris on June 13, stressed that "the political will to join the EEC exists in Britain today" and that "the general debate on whether Britain should or should not join is finished". Discussion should now be concentrated on the conditions of membership, and Britain asked only for "the same basis of negotiations to safeguard essential interests that the six countries pursued in the long search for solution and compromise which led to the Treaty of Rome". At a press conference on Sept. 30, de Broglie called on Britain to make "concrete and precise" proposals on conditions for her entry into the EEC. Since the visit of Georges Pompidou, the French Prime Minister, to London in July, he said, the situation had been "clarified", but although France was not "doctrinally opposed to British entry", "numerous difficulties" remained; France maintained a position of "benevolent waiting" but was convinced that the matter could "not be resolved rapidly". Meanwhile it was not a question of bilateral negotiations between France and Great Britain but solely of concrete proposals by Great Britain to the Six.

Harold Wilson, Prime Minister at the head of successive Labour governments since 1964, announced in the House of Commons on Nov. 10 that the government had decided to make a "new high-level approach" to see whether conditions existed for fruitful negotiations on British membership.

"In recent weeks the government have conducted a deep and searching review of the whole problem of Britain's relations with the EEC, including our membership of EFTA and of the Commonwealth. Every aspect of the Treaty of Rome itself, of decisions taken subsequent to its signature, and all the implications and consequences which might be expected to flow from British entry, have been examined in depth.

"In the light of this review, the government have decided that a new high-level approach must now be made to see whether the conditions exist—or do not exist—for fruitful negotiations, and the basis on which such negotiations could take place.

"It is vital that we maintain the closest relations with our EFTA colleagues. HM Government therefore now propose to invite the heads of government of the EFTA countries to attend a conference in London in the next few weeks to discuss the problems involved in moves by EFTA countries to join the EEC.

"Following that conference the Foreign Secretary and I intend to engage in a series of discussions with each of the heads of government of the Six, for the purpose of establishing whether it appears likely that essential British and Commonwealth interests could be safeguarded if Britain were to accept the Treaty of Rome and join the EEC."

2.3 Major EEC developments since end of previous negotiations with applicant countries

In the three-and-a-half years since the suspension of the negotiations with applicant countries in January 1963, there had been major developments in the EEC with regard to external association; the Yaoundé Convention between the EEC and 17 African states and Madagascar (forerunner of the Lomé Convention) was signed on July 20, 1963. Internally, the organization of a market regime began to take effect during this period for most agricultural products, and the European Agricultural Guidance and Guarantee Fund began operating on July 1, 1964. However, the attempt by the EEC Commission President, Walter Hallstein, to solve the problem of financing the common agricultural policy, by giving the Community control over resources derived from the tariff revenue on imports from third countries, provoked a crisis within the Six over the development of "supranational" vis-à-vis collectively agreed national policies. Hallstein's plan, presented to the EEC Council of Ministers on March 31, 1965, was opposed by de Gaulle's government to the extent that France took no part in Community meetings during a seven-month "empty chair" period. French participation was resumed only by means of the "Luxembourg compromise" of Jan. 28–29, 1966, under which a member state could effectively exercise a veto over decisions on matters which it declared to be affecting its vital interests.

In a significant institutional development, the Six signed a treaty on April 8, 1965, providing for the merger of the three Councils of the three European Communities into a single Council, and the merger of the ECSC High Authority and the EEC and Euratom Commissions to form a single Commission of the European Communities. This treaty came into effect on July 1, 1967. (The Parliamentary Assembly and the Court of Justice had, from the entry into force of the Treaties of Rome in 1958, been common to all three Communities.)

2.4 Wilson's Guildhall speech

At the Lord Mayor's Guildhall banquet on Nov. 14, 1966, Wilson dealt at length with Britain's role in Europe.

"Britain has much to give but also much to gain," said Wilson, "provided our essential interests can be met, as those of the Common Market countries were met nine years ago [during the Treaty of Rome negotiations]. To join the EEC means joining the European Coal and Steel Community and Euratom, and few countries have more to contribute in the fields covered by these communities. In particular, Britain leads the world, barring none, in the peaceful application of atomic energy.

"But let us regard this process as what it is going to be, a dynamic process. Nothing is static. We have much to contribute to the European community, including change. It was never ordained from on high that there should be only three such European communities. I would like to see . . . a drive to create a new technological community to pool within Europe the enormous technological inventiveness of Britain and other European countries. . . .

"I hope that we are not, at every stage in the debates within this country on the government's decision, going to be dominated by the failures of the past. Many of the anxieties that some of us expressed three or four years ago are much less real because of developments within the Common Market and within EFTA."

At the same time, Wilson went on, it would be unrealistic to deny that further developments within the Six had created new problems—in particular the agricultural policy, which would in present circumstances add a heavy burden to Britain's balance of payments and, through the effect on the cost of living, on her competitive position.

Wilson concluded his speech by emphasising the importance of "an outwardly responsible community", asserting:

"There is no future for Britain in a Little England philosophy. There is no future, either, for anyone in a Little Europe philosophy. For we do not see this venture, any more than our friends in Europe do, as a self-sufficient rich man's club—the identification of the EEC with the development of so many African territories is a manifestation of this, as is the aid the countries of the EEC have given on a wider scale."

2.5 November 1966 House of Commons debate—EFTA consultations in December 1966 and April 1967

A two-day debate on Britain's approaches to the EEC was held in the House of Commons on Nov. 16–17. The debate did not follow strict party lines, since although the two front benches and the Liberal spokesman expressed support in principle for British membership of the Community on appropriate terms, backbenchers of both the Labour and Conservative Parties were divided, with a minority on both sides opposed to British entry on grounds of economic disadvantages, likely harm to Commonwealth trade, possible loss of political sovereignty, or—among some Labour members—the hardening of the division between Eastern and Western Europe.

George Brown, who had succeeded Michael Stewart as Foreign Secretary, opened the debate and set out in the course of his speech the "broad areas of policy" which seemed likely to present the greatest difficulty.

Firstly, there was agriculture, and the level of prices currently established by the Six. Some British producers would be better off, but others certainly would be worse off. Consumers would have to pay the higher prices for home-grown food necessary to yield the appropriate return to British farmers and also to bring the cost of imported food up to the higher levels required to protect the internal Community market. On the other hand, there would be a saving to the Exchequer through the abolition of deficiency payments. The balance of payments would be affected by the higher cost of imported foodstuffs, the necessary levies, and any additional costs of financing the Community's agricultural fund, and "those who would be our partners in the Community" must recognize that this presented a "very serious problem".

Secondly, Britain's traditional Commonwealth suppliers would be adversely affected—particularly New Zealand, for which there would have to be some special arrangement. Other Commonwealth problems had grown less serious, however, since it had become clear during the previous negotiations in 1961–63 that comprehensive trade agreements could be made with countries in Asia, while association would be available (building on the Yaoundé Convention experience) to countries in Africa and the Caribbean. Commonwealth partners would be consulted "at all stages of any negotiations".

Other important problems included the management of the domestic economy, including the unrestricted flow of direct and portfolio investment, and regional policies and the relocation of industry.

On the likely attitude of France, the Foreign Secretary said: "Some ask whether there is not still a French veto and, if so, how we propose to get round it. I do not regard this as the right approach. I do not pretend that we see eye to eye with the French government on all points of our European, Atlantic, or defence policies. Nobody . . . would seek to deny the indispensability of France to Europe, now or in the future. It is equally clear, however, and not only to us, that Britain is and always has been indispensable to Europe. Therefore we must not enter upon our discussions on the assumption that France would want to be an obstacle to the establishment of a wider and more influential Europe."

Turning to the view expressed by Edward Heath (the Leader of the Opposition) and others that the talks should be widened to include defence arrangements, George Brown stressed that the talks, and also any eventual negotiations, would be about membership of the EEC on the basis of the Treaty of Rome, which did not involve the establishment of any supranational authority dealing with matters of defence and foreign policy. Moreover, the government was "resolutely opposed" to any change in Britain's relationship with the United States as a result of joining the EEC, particularly in defence, and to any abandonment of the role which she played in the outside world.

Finally, it had been said that Britain's economic difficulties ruled out any satisfactory progress on the question of relations with the Community. The government regarded membership of the EEC as offering "no easy relief of our difficulties", but while, as the Prime Minister had stated on Nov. 10, Britain should enter the EEC only when she had secured a healthy economy and a strong balance of payments, it was "clearly sensible to proceed with these talks about possible membership of the Community at the same time as we are gathering the necessary economic strength".

In conclusion, George Brown said: "Western Europe is now divided. There is EFTA and there is the EEC. Both groupings are dynamic; both exist to promote their own development. But as their development gathers momentum, if they stay apart, the divisions must become deeper, and in that case Europe will become less and less able to play its full part in contributing to the development of those parts of the world where poverty, hunger, and lack of opportunity still constitute a major threat to our civilization. . . ."

In reply to a question in the House of Commons on Dec. 15, Wilson gave details of visits to be made by himself and George Brown early in the New Year, which took place on Jan. 15–17, 1967, Rome; Jan. 24–25, Paris; Jan. 31 – Feb. 1, Brussels; Feb. 15–16, Bonn; Feb. 26–27, The Hague, and March 7–8, Luxembourg.

A one-day conference was held in London on Dec. 5, 1966, at which Wilson explained to heads and representatives of EFTA governments the purpose of these visits, which were intended to determine whether the appropriate conditions existed in which it might be possible to activate the arrangements for a negotiation with the Community for British membership.

A communiqué issued after the meeting stated that the ministers of the other EFTA countries "welcomed" the British move as an "important step along the road to determining the prospects for a solution to the question of European economic integration in which they could all participate in an appropriate manner".

The communiqué continued: "All ministers reaffirmed their intention of keeping in the closest consultation with each other on the development of their policies and of their discussions with members of the EEC. They will review the position as it develops at any level which the situation at the moment may require."

An EFTA special ministerial meeting to discuss the prospects of European integration was held in London on April 28, 1967. The communiqué issued after the meeting was worded in part as follows:

"The EFTA governments, desirous of bringing about a single European market in accordance with the purpose of the Stockholm Convention (and having completed at the end of 1966, three years ahead of the original timetable, the establishment of the free trade area among EFTA members), recognized that, if the British government were to decide to seek a closer relationship with the EEC, that decision would open up new prospects for a solution to the question of European economic integration, in which they all intended to participate.

"The change from the present division of Europe to a single market should be as smooth as possible. Were the UK or any other member of EFTA to apply for participation in the EEC, the process of negotiation and of ratifying any ensuing agreement could hardly be short. In addition, it would be the purpose of EFTA governments that sufficient transitional periods should be provided for in order to give—should it be necessary—a reasonable opportunity to their partners in the Free Trade Area to conclude negotiations, with a view to avoiding disruption in European trade patterns . . ."

2.6 Differences within Labour Party over British entry into EEC, January–April 1967

A motion recalling the requirements for British entry into the EEC as laid down in earlier party statements—signed by 107 Labour MPs from all sections of the party—was tabled in the House of Commons on Feb. 21, 1967.

Inviting the House to note the "exploratory nature" of the visits to Common Market capitals by the Prime Minister and Foreign Secretary, it regretted the "activities of those who have seized this occasion to intensify their demand that the government should apply unconditionally for entry to the EEC"; deplored, "in particular, the speeches in which the Leader of the Opposition has invited HM Government to break its pledged word to the electorate and to other peoples of the Commonwealth"; and declared that "Britain, in consultation with her EFTA partners, should be ready to enter the EEC only if essential British and Commonwealth interests can be safeguarded".

Differences within the Labour Party over British entry had unexpectedly flared up at a routine weekly meeting of the Parliamentary Labour Party on Jan. 25. In the course of a discussion on George Brown's forthcoming participation in an all-party rally to be held on Feb. 22 under the auspices of the British Council of the European Movement, Manny Shinwell, then chairman of the Parliamentary Party and one of the leading Labour MPs opposing Britain's entry into the Common Market, was reported to have insisted that the Prime Minister should give a clear directive on the rights of ministers to address similar meetings, whether favourable or hostile to British membership. After George Brown had challenged this view and vigorously defended his right to state government policy, uproar was said to have broken out, in the course of which heated exchanges took place between Shinwell and both Brown and Richard Crossman, Lord President of the Council and Leader of the House.

Reported disagreements of a similar kind within the Cabinet were reflected by Douglas Jay, President of the Board of Trade, in a speech to a private meeting of the Parliamentary Party's finance and economic affairs group. Presenting the economic arguments for and against British entry as they affected his department, Jay was reported to have said that unconditional acceptance of the common agricultural policy would add about £200,000,000 a year to the UK balance of payments, thus leading to a serious economic crisis every three years, and result in an average increase in food prices of between 10 and 14 per cent. He further argued that Britain would be placed at a disadvantage in export markets through her production costs rising in direct proportion to her higher food costs, while those of the Six remained static, and that Commonwealth markets would be lost through the abolition of tariff preferences.

As a result of Douglas Jay's address, the Prime Minister was reported to have warned all ministers on pain of resignation to keep their Common Market utterances within the limits of the collective Cabinet decision announced to the House of Commons on Nov. 10, 1966.

On the proposition of the Prime Minister three meetings of the Parliamentary Labour Party were held, on April 6, 20 and 27, to debate the question of British entry.

2.7 Cabinet decision to apply for membership

After the meeting of ministers of the EFTA countries in London on April 28 [see 2.5] and a series of British Cabinet meetings, including sessions both at Downing Street and Chequers during the weekend of April 29–30, Harold Wilson announced in the House of Commons on May 2 that the government had decided to make an application under Article 237 of the Treaty of Rome for membership of the EEC and parallel applications for membership of both ECSC and Euratom.

The negotiations, he stated, which the government hoped would be "followed through quickly", would relate to a small number of "really important issues", identified as follows during his recent visits: problems associated with the operation of the common agricultural policy, particularly its potential effects on the cost of living and on the "structure and well-being" of British agriculture, the impact of its financial regulations on the UK budget and balance of payments, and the special Commonwealth questions concerning New Zealand and the sugar-producing countries at present safeguarded by the Commonwealth Sugar Agreement; capital movements; regional policies. Lesser issues, he added, could best be dealt with after entry.

The Prime Minister's statement was welcomed by Edward Heath, Leader of the Opposition, and by Jeremy Thorpe for the Liberals, but Manny Shinwell (Lab.) promised the "most relentless and ruthless opposition".

Replying to a large number of questions from both sides of the House, Wilson said that the government would follow the practice of the Conservative administration during the previous negotiations of making regular statements to the House about their progress. He attributed his change of view on British entry to his experience of the "actual practical working" of the Community as contrasted with his previous fears based on a "literal reading" of the Treaty of Rome, and told Michael Foot (one of the leading Labour opponents of British entry) that nuclear sharing and defence matters had not been raised during his European visits, and should, in the government's view, be confined to NATO.

2.8 House of Commons debate in May 1967—Formal application

Opening a three-day debate in the House of Commons on May 8, the Prime Minister moved the following motion: "That this House approves the statement in the Command Paper, *Membership of the European Communities* (Cmnd. 3269)." (This White Paper contained the text of the Prime Minister's statement of May 2, see 2.7.)

The motion was carried on May 10 by 488 votes to 62 (34 Labour members, 26 Conservatives, one Liberal and one *Plaid Cymru*), while a further 51 Labour back-benchers were understood to have abstained; the majority of Conservative and Liberal members voted with the government. A formal letter of application to join the EEC, with parallel applications to the ECSC and Euratom, was sent on May 10 and received in Brussels on May 11.

A motion similar to that tabled in the Commons was debated in the House of Lords on May 8–9 and carried without a division.

2.9 President de Gaulle's May 1967 press conference

At a press conference at the Elysée Palace on May 16, 1967, President de Gaulle, after declaring that he would confine himself to the general implications of British entry without prejudging the nature of possible negotiations, declared:

"The movement which seems at present to be leading England to link herself to Europe instead of keeping herself apart can only be satisfactory to France. This is why we note with sympathy the progress which appears to be revealed in this direction by the British government's declared aim and the step it has taken.

"For our part, there is no question of there being a veto, nor has there ever been one. It is simply a question of finding out whether a settlement is possible within the framework and under the conditions of the Common Market without bringing about destructive upheavals; or in what other situation, and in what other conditions, a settlement could be possible; or whether it would be desirable to preserve what has been built up until such time as it would appear conceivable to welcome an England which on her own part would have undergone a profound transformation.

"By comparison with the motives which brought the Six together, one can easily understand why England, which is not a continental country, which leans on the Commonwealth, which because of her island status has far-away commitments, and which is tied to the USA by all sorts of agreements, could not merge into a community of fixed dimensions and rigid rules.

"While this community was taking shape," President de Gaulle went on, "England first refused to join it and even showed a hostile attitude, as if she thought it represented an economic and political threat. Then she tried to negotiate for membership of the Community, but under conditions which would have extinguished the Community if she had joined. After this the British government stated that it did not wish to join the Community and set about strengthening its ties with the Commonwealth and with other European countries grouped around her in a free trade area. Now, here is England apparently adopting a new state of mind and declaring herself ready to subscribe to the Treaty of Rome, provided she is granted exceptional and prolonged delays, and that, as far as it affects her, essential changes are made in [the Treaty's] application. At the same time she recognizes that there are obstacles to overcome, which the British Prime Minister himself, with his deep experience and great foresight, has described as formidable.

"In truth, it does seem that such is the situation of the British, compared with that of the Six, that in the event of [the EEC] being changed, of there being agreement to envisage changing it, the change would involve one or other or three possibilities.

"(1) To admit that the entry of the British, with all the exceptions which will certainly accompany it, with the eruption of elements new in both their nature and number which it will naturally involve, with the participation of new states which would certainly be a corollary, would necessitate in fact building a totally new edifice, and in razing what has just been built. In that case, what would result if not the creation of a free trade zone in Western Europe, pending an Atlantic zone, which would take away from our continent its own personality?

"(2) To install between the Community on the one hand and the British and the Free Trade Zone countries on the other a regime of association, which is in any case provided for in the Treaty of Rome. . . .

"(3) Finally, to wait for the change to be brought about by the internal and external developments of which, it seems, England is showing signs. In other words, that this great people, so magificently gifted with ability and courage, should on their own behalf and for themselves achieve the profound economic and political transformation which would allow them to join the Six continentals.

"I truly believe that this is the desire of many people who wish to see a Europe appear which would have its natural dimensions, and who have for England a deep admiration and a sincere friendship. If Britain one day reached this stage, with what joy would France then greet this historic transformation."

Wilson visited Paris on June 18–20 for talks with de Gaulle. Reporting on his visit to the House of Commons on June 20 the Prime Minister revealed that, besides the Common Market, their discussions had covered the world situation, with particular reference to the Middle East, the Far East, and Africa.

On the question of British entry into the EEC Wilson said that he had told de Gaulle "why we do not believe that any of the problems arising out of our application are in any sense insoluble, why we do not intend to take 'no' for an answer", and that he had emphasized the "added compulsion we saw, in the light of recent events, for urgent action to strengthen and unify Europe in an industrial and technological sense, as a prior condition of greater political strength and influence".

2.10 Rome summit meeting of the Six
Meanwhile the British application for EEC membership, formally submitted on May 11, had been discussed at the "summit" meeting of the Six in Rome on May 29–30, 1967. In his opening address at the public ceremony marking the 10th anniversary of the signing of the Treaty of Rome, President Saragat of Italy said:

"New problems await us, among which are those concerning the geographical and historical dimensions of the Community with the accession of other countries—in the first place Great Britain, whose name is almost synonymous with political liberty. Let us express the wish that negotiations can open soon. The British application is an application from the whole nation and not simply one party of it. Labour, Conservatives, and Liberals are united in supporting the demand of the British government for membership of the Common Market, and the House of Commons has ratified it with something not far short of unanimity."

The Europe the Community was building, he continued, must be open to "all peoples holding common ideals, values, and principles, and conscious of the urgent need for the return of a European presence in the world". It must also be firmly aware of its common destiny with the United States. Furthermore, Saragat added, a European order founded solely on the concept of nation states was illusory, and would be "open to the antagonism of states and to anarchy, which would end by destroying the spirit of those nations and their very structure".

2.11 Meetings of Ministerial Council
A meeting of the EEC Council of Ministers in Brussels on June 5 broke up before discussing the British application because of the Middle East crisis, which

prevented the attendance of the French, West German, and Italian Foreign Ministers. A further meeting provisionally arranged to take place in Luxembourg on June 12 was cancelled for the same reason. Nevertheless, the British application was formally acknowledged on June 7 by Renaat van Elslande, Belgian Minister for European Affairs and chair of the Council at that time, in the following letter to Wilson:

"I have the honour to acknowledge receipt of the letter of May 10, 1967, in which your Excellency informed me of the request by the United Kingdom of Great Britain and Northern Ireland to join the European Economic Community in accordance with the terms of Article 237 of the Treaty setting up the European Economic Community. I transmitted your letter on the same day to members of the Council, which decided to set in motion the procedure provided for in the above Article. . . ."

At its next meeting in Brussels on June 26–27 the Council, while failing to agree on a Belgian proposal to give Britain an official hearing, decided to remit her application for study to the European Commission with instructions to report back in September, and agreed to discuss at its next meeting the implications for the Community of the admission of new members.

Pierre Harmel, Belgian Foreign Minister, opening the debate, referred both to the preambles of the European Treaties and to Article 237 of the Treaty of Rome and pointed out that there was a legal and political obligation on the EEC to accept new members, provided that they were democratic European countries and were prepared to endorse the Treaty and its institutions. In view of the fact that Britain had applied for membership in the prescribed manner, she should be permitted to set before the Council the problems requiring negotiation, and suggest ways of solving them.

The Belgian Foreign Minister was supported by Willy Brandt, the West German Foreign Minister, who suggested that the normal procedures for admitting new members could be implemented in conjunction with an internal ministerial study of the political and economic consequences of expanding the Community. In spite of similar statements by the Italian, Luxembourg, and Netherlands representatives, Couve de Murville (France) insisted that the Six must discuss among themselves the merits of Britain's application before giving her a hearing. In reply to Harmel, who announced that as an alternative solution he would advise the British government to state its case at the next meeting of the Ministerial Council of the WEU at the beginning of July, Couve de Murville said that such a step would have to be decided by the Permanent Council of the WEU.

At the first meeting of the new Council of Ministers of the European Communities in Brussels on July 9–10, Couve de Murville was reported to have said that the applications for membership of Britain and other EFTA countries would create a new situation for the EEC, the consequences of which might be very serious, and that unless the Six reached a common appreciation of the problems they would again be faced with the same situation which led to the breakdown of the previous negotiations in 1963.

The five other Foreign Ministers, in rejecting Couve de Murville's arguments, maintained that Britain's entry would positively strengthen the Community.

Meanwhile, at the Assembly of the WEU in Paris on June 14 a recommendation, moved by Maurice Edelman (UK, Labour), *rapporteur* of the general affairs committee, calling on the governments of the Six to give "full support" to the British application, had been passed by 55 votes to nil, with six abstentions (French Gaullists).

2.12 Preliminary Opinion of European Commission on applications for membership

The Preliminary Opinion of the European Commission on the applications for membership by Britain, the Irish Republic, Denmark, and Norway, which had been requested on June 26–27, 1967, was submitted to the Council of Ministers of the European Communities on Sept. 29, 1967, and officially published on Oct. 7. Its conclusions were as follows:

"Analysis of the chief problems involved in the extension of the Community reveals that the accession of new members such as Great Britain, Ireland, Denmark, and Norway, whose political and economic structures and level of development are very close to those of the present member states, could both strengthen the Community and afford it an opportunity for further progress, provided the new members accept the provisions of the Treaties and the decisions taken subsequently. This they have said they are disposed to do. Their accession, although it would bring great changes with it, would not then be likely to modify the fundamental objectives and individual features of the European Communities or the methods they use.

"The Commission wishes to re-state the conditions which would have to be fulfilled if extension is to take place in a satisfactory manner.

"First, the new members would, as a general rule, have to accept the arrangements adopted by the founder-members before extension, subject to any exceptional adjustments that may be made. In particular, they would have to accept:

"(1) The Community customs tariffs as they emerge from the recent multilateral negotiations in GATT [i.e. the Kennedy Round negotiations], and their gradual application to all non-member countries, along with all the rules necessary for the proper functioning of the customs union.

"(2) The basic principles of the common policies with the provision for their implementation, particularly in the economic, financial, social, and agricultural fields, and their gradual application.

"(3) The contractual obligations of the Communities towards non-member countries (association agreements, trade agreements, etc.).

"(4) The institutional machinery of the Communities as established by the Treaties and the decisions taken in application of the Treaties, subject only to those adjustments rendered necessary by the accession of new states; these adjustments will have to be designed so that the institutions shall continue to be sufficiently effective and that a suitable balance is maintained in the representation of the various member states.

"In addition, the new members, especially the main one, the UK, would have to agree with the founder-members on the solution of a number of problems which would be of vital importance for the harmonious development of an enlarged Community:

"(1) Restoration of lasting equilibrium in the British economy and its balance of payments, entailing concerted action between Great Britain and the member countries of the Community, and examination of ways and means of adjusting the present international role of sterling so that the pound could be fitted, together with the currencies of the other member countries, into a Community monetary system.

"(2) The principle of a common policy in the field of research and technology, including atomic energy, and the general lines such a policy should follow.

"(3) Financing of the Community's overall activities, including the agricultural policy.

"(4) The relations to be established with those European countries, notably any EFTA countries, which do not join the Community, and with the less developed countries, particularly the Commonwealth countries.

"To sum up, the new membership applications are impelling the Community to tackle at one and the same time the problems involved in its extension. Opinions differ as to the priority to be given to the one or the other of these objectives. The best way of overcoming the difficulty would be to try to attain them both simultaneously. But if this difficult operation is to be successfully concluded it is essential that extension should not hamper the pursuit of the normal activities of the Communities and should not subsequently entail a weakening of their cohesion or their dynamism, especially where the establishment of economic union, the requisite measures of harmonization, and the functioning of the institutional machinery, are concerned.

"The Commission is well aware that the cohesion and dynamism of the Communities depend to a great extent on the convergence of national policies in the essential fields. If full advantage is to be taken of the opportunities which extension opens up for the Community, it is apparent that member states should within a reasonable period be in a position to make progress along the road to political union.

"It follows from all the considerations set forth in this document that the Commission is not at present in possession of all the information needed to give in final form the opinion requested by the Council. . . . Choices of considerable importance for any appraisal of the impact which the new members would have on the Community are still to be made. . . . It is the Commission's opinion that, in order to dispel the uncertainty which still attaches in particular to certain fundamental points, negotiations should be opened in the most appropriate forms with the states which have applied for membership, in order to examine in more detail . . . the problems brought out in this document and to see whether arrangements can be made under which the indispensable cohesion and dynamism will be maintained in an enlarged Community."

2.13 Meetings of Council Ministers—De Gaulle's November press conference

The British, Danish, Irish, and Norwegian applications for membership were discussed in the context of the Commission's Opinion by the Council of Ministers of the European Communities at its meetings on Oct. 2–3, Oct. 23–24, Nov. 20, Dec. 11–12, and Dec. 18–19, 1967. The meetings were marked by strong French objections to British membership. In de Gaulle's 1977 autumn press conference at the Elysee Palace, on Nov. 27, he made the following comments about Britain's application:

"The idea of joining the British Isles to the Economic Community formed by the six continental states arouses wishes everywhere which are ideally very justified, but it is a matter of knowing whether and how this could actually be achieved without disrupting or destroying what already exists.

"Great Britain proposed the opening without delay of negotiations between itself and the Six with a view to entering the Common Market. It did this with truly extraordinary insistence and haste, some of the reasons for which may have been made clear by the recent monetary events. At the same time, it declared it would accept all the regulations governing the Community of the Six, which seemed a little contradictory with the request for negotiations, since why would one negotiate on clauses which one had fully accepted in advance?

"In fact, we were watching the fifth act of a play during which England has taken up very different and apparently inconsistent attitudes towards the Common Market.

"The first act was London's refusal to participate in the elaboration of the Treaty of Rome. On the other side of the Channel it was expected that this would lead to nothing.

"The second act demonstrated England's deep-seated hostility towards the building of Europe as soon as this began to be mapped out. I can still hear the notice which my friend Macmillan, then Prime Minister, served on me in Paris in June 1958, comparing the Common Market with the [Napoleonic] continental blockade and threatening at least to declare a tariff war on it.

"The third act was negotiations carried out in Brussels by [Reginald] Maudling for a year and a half, negotiations aimed at bending the Community to England's conditions. These were ended when France pointed out to its partners that it was not a question of doing that but precisely the opposite. [The President was, in fact, referring to Heath's negotiations on UK membership in 1961–63, not the abortive free trade area negotiations by Maudling in 1958.]

"The fourth act, at the start of Wilson's government, was marked by London's disinterest in the Common Market, the maintenance around Britain of the six other European states forming the Free Trade Area, and a great effort to strengthen the internal links of the Commonwealth.

"Now the fifth act is being performed. This time Britain has made its application and has embarked on all imaginable promises and pressures to get it adopted. This attitude is easily explained.

"The British people can no doubt see more and more clearly that the structures and customs of its activities, and even its national personality, are from now on put in jeopardy in the great movement which is sweeping the world—in face of the enormous power of the United States, the growing power of the Soviet Union, the renascent power of the continental nations, the new power of China, and the growing centrifugal movement apparent within the Commonwealth.

"After all, the serious economic, financial, monetary, and social difficulties with which Britain is grappling make her feel this day after day. From all this emerges a tendency to look for a framework, even a European one, which would help her to save and safeguard her own substance, allow her to play a leading role again, and relieve her of part of her burden.

"In principle, there is nothing in this which would not be salutary for her and, in a short time, satisfactory for Europe, on condition that the British people, like those whom it wishes to join, should want, and know how, to undergo the fundamental changes necessary for it to establish its own equilibrium. For it is a radical modification and transformation of Britain which is necessary for her to join the continentals. This is obvious from the political point of view.

"But today, to speak only of the economic sphere, the report addressed to the Six governments on Sept. 29 by the Brussels Commission demonstrates with the greatest clarity that the Common Market is incompatible with the economy, as it is, of England. The chronic deficit of the British economy's balance of payments demonstrates its permanent disequilibrium. In the realms of production, sources of supply, the practice of credit, working conditions, the economy includes fundamental factors which that country could not change without modifying its own character.

"The Common Market is also incompatible with the way the British get their food, both from their own agricultural production, subsidized to the highest degree, and from the supplies bought cheaply all over the world and particularly in the Commonwealth. This rules out London ever really accepting the levies provided for in the financial arrangements [of the Common Market], which would be crushing for it.

"The Common Market is incompatible also with the restrictions imposed by Britain on the outward movement of capital which, by contrast, circulates freely among the Six. The Common Market, finally, is incompatible with the state of sterling—as revealed again by the devaluation and by the loans which preceded and accompanied it. Moreover, in view of the pound's position as an international currency and the enormous external balances which weigh it down, the state of sterling would not allow it at present to become part of the solid, interdependent, and assured society in which the franc, the mark, the lira, the Belgian franc, and the guilder are joined.

"In these conditions, what could be the result of what is called the entry of Britain into the Common Market? And if one wished, in spite of everything to impose it, it would obviously mean the breaking up of a Community which has been built and which functions according to rules which would not bear such a monumental exception. Moreover, this Community would not bear the introduction among its principal members of a state which, precisely because of its currency, its economy, and its politics, is not at present a part of Europe as we have begun to build it.

"Since everyone knows the issues involved, if the Six allowed Britain in and started negotiations to this effect it would mean that they were giving their approval in advance to all the artifices, delays, and pretences which would conduce to covering up the destruction of an edifice built at a cost of so much effort and in the midst of so many hopes.

"It is true that while recognizing the impossibility of allowing the Britain of today into the Common Market as it exists, it is nevertheless possible to be in favour of sacrificing the Common Market for the sake of an agreement with Britain. Theoretically, in fact, the economic system which is practised by the Six is not necessarily the only one which Europe might practice. One can imagine, for example, a Free Trade Area covering the whole of the West of our Continent. One can also imagine a sort of multilateral treaty of the kind which will come out of the Kennedy Round, settling between 10, 12, or 15 European states their reciprocal and respective quotas and tariffs.

"But in either case it would first be necessary to abolish the Community and break up its institutions. And I tell you that France is certainly not asking for that. If, however, one or other of her partners proposed this, as is their right after all, France would examine it with the other signatories of the Treaty of Rome. But what France cannot do is to enter at present into any negotiations with Britain and its associate countries which would lead to the destruction of the European Community to which it belongs.

"And then again, that would not be at all the road which could lead to the construction of a Europe, by itself and for itself, in such a way that it would not be dependent on an economic, monetary, and political system which was foreign to it. For Europe to be able to balance the immense power of the United States it must in no way weaken, but on the contrary strengthen, the links and rules of the Community.

"Certainly, those who have demonstrated by their actions, as I have, the exceptional esteem, attachment, and respect which they bear for Britain, keenly desire to see her choose and accomplish one day the immense effort which would transform her. France is certainly quite prepared, in order to make things easy for her, to enter into any arrangement which, under the name of association or any other name, would favour, as of now, commercial exchanges between the continentals on one hand and the British, Scandinavians, and Irish on the other.

"We in Paris have certainly not been unaware of the psychological development which seems to be emerging among our friends across the Channel. Nor have we failed to recognize the merit of certain measures which they have already taken, and others which they are planning to take, for their internal equilibrium and external independence.

"In order that the British Isles can really make fast to the Continent, there is still a very vast and deep mutation to be effected. Thus everything depends in fact not on negotiations, which for the Six would be a step towards abandonment and would toll the knell of the Community, but rather on the will and action of the great British people, which would make them into one of the pillars of European Europe."

Earlier, at the outset of his press conference, General de Gaulle had been asked if it was true that, in private conversations about the British membership application, he had used the expression "I want England naked (*l'Angleterre, je la veux nue*)", as had been reported from numerous diplomatic and other sources in recent months. He replied amid laughter: "Nudity, for a beautiful creature, is natural enough and can be satisfying enough for those around her. But whatever attraction I feel towards England, I have never said that about her. It is one of those sayings which people attribute to me. . . ."

2.14 Reactions to President de Gaulle's statement

President de Gaulle's statement on Nov. 27 produced strong reactions from both the British government and France's partners in the Community.

British reactions. The Foreign Office issued the following statement on Nov. 27, 1967: "Under Article 237 of the Treaty of Rome any European State may apply for membership of the EEC. The reply has to be given by the existing members of the Community as a whole. We have made such an application in full accord with the terms of Article 237 and we expect a reply from the Community. The Council of Ministers of the Community are having a further meeting on Dec. 18–19." Wilson, answering questions in the House of Commons on Nov. 28, reiterated that the British government had no intention of withdrawing its application. Emphasizing that he had never received anything but courtesy from de Gaulle, Wilson continued: "Where there have been mis-statements of fact or wrong deductions based on a rather out-of-date approach to some of the problems of the modern world, these should be answered so that in the great debate which will continue in Europe some of these misconceptions can be dealt with once and for all."

Benelux countries. Dr Luns declared on Nov. 29, 1967, after a meeting of Benelux ministers at The Hague, that the three countries would make contact with the German and Italian governments. "Press conferences," he continued, "do not constitute a method of negotiating. There is a procedure for this in the Common Market and this procedure must be followed." The meeting of the Council of Ministers on Dec. 18 would be the "hour of truth" for the Community, and it remained to be seen how Couve de Murville would translate President de Gaulle's statements into action. There had been precedents for a government changing its opinion "in the light of official or unofficial reactions".

West Germany. A government spokesman on Nov. 29, 1967, after a meeting of the federal Cabinet, made the following statement: "The French standpoint on the question of British accession has not changed. It has rather become clearer. Nor has the German federal government's standpoint been changed by this event. Now, as before, we believe negotiations with the states willing to enter [the Common Market] should begin as soon as possible. Since the French government—judging by General de Gaulle's statements—has no fundamental objections to British accession, but, on its part, too, regards such accession as necessary for European development; and since, on the other hand, Great Britain is standing by its application, as are the other countries that are willing to enter, the German government considers it still too early to express a final conclusion about the results of the discussions currently under way in Brussels. . . ."

Italy. Amintore Fanfani, then Foreign Minister, said on Dec. 6, 1967, that de Gaulle's remarks were "not valid" and had failed to change Italy's belief that British membership of the Community was "desirable, useful, and necessary for a constructive evolution of our Continent". Devaluation of sterling had gone far towards meeting the requests of President de Gaulle and the European Commission, and repeated declarations by British ministers that their request for membership would not be withdrawn or changed faced the Six with the necessity of replying. Italy intended firmly to support the demand that a "positive response" should be given to the British application when the Council of Ministers met on Dec. 18.

According to press records, the Foreign Ministers of the Five countries, at a private meeting in Brussels on Dec. 14 during the winter session of the NATO Ministerial Council, agreed to press for a decision on the British application on Dec. 18–19, 1967.

The Dec. 18–19 Council meeting ended by recording its failure to agree on the next step to be taken, and by publishing the following statement:

"(1) The Council of the European Communities, meeting at Brussels on Dec. 19, 1967, noted that no member state has raised any fundamental objection to the enlargement of the Communities. . . One member state, however, expressed the opinion that this enlargement would profoundly alter the nature of the Communities and the methods of administering them.

"(2) All the member states were of the opinion that the restoration of Great Britain's economic and monetary situation is of fundamental importance to the question of its accession. Several member states, while fully in favour of re-establishing Great Britain's economic equilibrium, do not think that the British economy must necessarily be completely re-established at the moment of accession.

"(3) All the member states recognized that, particularly since Nov. 18, 1967, Great Britain had put into operation measures intended to consolidate its economic, financial, and monetary situation. All the member states noted that the process of re-establishing the British economy will take a certain time.

"(4) The Commission expressed the opinion that it would be advisable to open negotiations in the most appropriate form with the states which have presented requests for accession, in order to undertake the necessary further examination of the problems pointed out in its Opinion of Sept. 29, 1967, addressed to the Council, and to examine whether solutions exist which make it possible to satisfy the conditions necessary for ensuring the cohesion and vitality indispensable to an enlarged Community.

"(5) Five member states agreed with the Commission's point of view. They expressed their desire for the immediate opening of negotiations for the accession of Great Britain, Denmark, Ireland, and Norway, so that these negotiations might be undertaken in parallel with the re-establishment of Great Britain's economic situation.

"One member state considered that the re-establishment of the British economy must be completed before Great Britain's request can be reconsidered.

"(6) For this reason, there was no agreement in the Council at this stage on the next step to be taken. The President of the Council was instructed to inform the countries in question accordingly.

"(7) The requests for accession presented by the United Kingdom, Ireland, Denmark, and Norway, and also the letter from the Swedish government [see 6.4], remain on the Council's agenda."

The European Commission issued the following statement on Dec. 20: "The Commission deeply regrets the Council's failure to reach agreement on what steps should be taken to deal with the applications for membership of the Communities made by a number of European countries, in particular the United Kingdom. . . .

"The Commission appeals to all concerned to keep the consequences of the present disagreement within the narrowest possible limits. More than ever before efforts in the field of European integration will have to be pursued tenaciously, and opportunities must be sought of resuming the course, temporarily abandoned, of expanding the Communities. The Commission will do its utmost to help towards the attainment of these objectives."

2.15 British government's reaction to decision of Council of Ministers— George Brown's visits to Rome and Bonn

The reaction of the British government to the failure of the Council of Ministers to agree on the opening of negotiations was expressed in statements by the Foreign Office on Dec. 19 and by George Brown in the House of Commons on Dec. 20, 1967.

The Foreign Office statement was as follows:

"It is a matter of grave concern that the government of France has been unable to accept the unanimous view of its partners that negotiations for Britain's accession to the European Communities should start at once. This can only delay the inevitable progress towards a united Europe including Britain, which is in the interest of Europe as a whole.

"There is no question of withdrawing Britain's application. HM Government believe that, given the support of the Five governments and the overwhelming majority of opinion throughout Western Europe, European unity is bound to be achieved. HM Government will be consulting about the implications of the present situation with other European governments who share Britain's views on the future of Europe."

Brown, having paid tribute to the efforts of the Five governments and of the European Commission to secure the opening of negotiations, continued:

"The Prime Minister said in the House some weeks ago that if, contrary to our hopes and the hopes of most people in Europe, a veto were to be imposed, we should still regard ourselves as committed to our main purpose in Europe. I reaffirm that today. We continue to believe that the long-term interests of this country and of Europe require that we should become members of the European Communities.

"The communiqué which was issued after yesterday's meeting of the Community Council of Ministers made clear that our application, as well as those of the other countries, remain on the agenda of the Council of Ministers. We in turn confirm that our application stands. We do not intend to withdraw it.

"We now propose to enter into consultations with those Five members of the European Community who supported the Commission's view that negotiations should be started at an early stage.

"We shall of course also be in the closest touch with the members of EFTA and the Irish Republic. We are by no means the only country whose hopes of progress towards a genuine European unity have been temporarily disappointed.

"As regards the content of the consultations . . . which will begin at once, we for our part want to see the links between us forged as strongly as possible. But we cannot expose ourselves to any further vetoes on the part of President de Gaulle.

"As regards our relations with France, whilst we shall not indulge in any peevish or petty reaction to the present situation, it would be idle to pretend that what has happened is not a grave blow to our relationship. We think the attitude taken by the French government represents a false view of the future of our continent of Europe. We think it contains a deplorable number of mistaken ideas about the realities of the various questions at issue. We question its motivation.

"But I think it important to stress that this is not an Anglo-French affair. This is a European affair. We regret, of course, that Europe has been held back temporarily from achieving the unity which it now aspires to. But it is just because time and events in this technological age are running against Europe that we do not intend as a result of this temporary check to abandon all work along the road."

Pursuing the consultations foreshadowed in his statement, George Brown visited Rome on Dec. 29, 1967, for talks with Fanfani, and Bonn on Jan. 19, 1968 for talks with Brandt.

George Brown told the House of Commons on Jan. 24 that the West German federal government "wish to explore the ground further with the French to see whether an interim arrangement about our relations with the Community might still be agreed. I told my German colleagues that we were sceptical about this, but no one should infer from the exchange that there is a fundamental disagreement between us and the Germans on this. On the contrary, our aim and the German aim is full British membership of the Communities as soon as it can be brought about. Between us there is complete identity of purpose".

Having mentioned his talks with Fanfani, Brown declared that the Benelux countries had recently proposed various measures of European co-operation, and that the British government had been in close touch with its EFTA partners. "But," he continued, "we must pursue our policies in a wider field than EFTA. European unity is our aim. We must work out with all these others in Europe, who think as we do, the lines of common action we can take here and now to carry all of us further along this road. One thing I want to make quite clear. This course of action is not directed against France. Of course, the present Community of the Six must continue—we do not intend to hamper its work. After all, it is the Community which we ourselves will be joining some day. But what we can do outside it we shall, and that is our purpose now."

2.16 Renewal of UK–Euratom agreement
The 10-year agreement for co-operation in the peaceful uses of atomic energy which had been concluded in 1958 between Britain and Euratom was extended for another two years in an exchange of letters on Feb. 4, 1969, between Jean Rey (President of the European Commission) and Sir James Marjoribanks (Head of the British Mission to the European Communities).

2.17 WEU crisis
During February 1969 developments in the Western European Union, following a Ministerial Council meeting in Luxembourg at the beginning of the month, led to a French boycott of the WEU Council and a worsening of relations with Britain, which was further exacerbated by what came to be known as the "Soames Affair".

The French objected to what they regarded as British-inspired attempts to arrange within the framework of the WEU (comprising the Six plus Britain) for co-ordination of foreign policies, leading to the de facto creation of a seven-member European "foreign policy community". The crisis took the form of French non-attendance at a meeting of the WEU Permanent Council at its London headquarters on Feb. 14, and strong French reassertion thereafter of the principle of unanimity within the WEU, coupled with a French boycott of the WEU Ministerial Council.

The "Soames Affair" involved an official French protest to Britain on Feb. 24 over the way in which the British had disclosed to their WEU partners, and then to the press, the British version of proposals outlined by de Gaulle on Feb. 4 at a private luncheon with the British Ambassador in Paris, Christopher Soames. These proposals apparently envisaged (i) the eventual end of any need for NATO "as such, with its American dominance and command structure", once European countries had made themselves as independent of the USA as France had done, and (ii) French preparedness for political discussions with Britain as a first step in considering a looser form of free trade area in Europe, to take the place of the Common Market, and preferably with a small inner council of a European political association comprising France, West Germany, Italy and Britain.

The British press reports were refuted on Feb. 21 by the Agence France-Presse in a statement quoting "authorized sources" and entitled "a French denial", the full text of which was as follows:

"French official sources deny, contrary to information presented with a sensational character, that the President of the Republic has in the course of a recent talk with the UK Ambassador expressed orientations different from those he has publicly and constantly defined in recent years.

"They indicate that today, as yesterday, France, which remains attached to the good functioning of the European Economic Community, notes that any enlargement of this by new admissions, and especially that of Britain would lead to a complete change of the Community and, in practice, to its disappearance. It would then be possible to replace the Community by a different system.

"It is recalled that Europe can only take shape on the political plane if the nations composing it agree on a European policy of independence."

In a further statement later the same day dealing specifically with the British reports that President de Gaulle had proposed a "European Directorate of four", Agence France-Presse quoted the "authorized sources" as saying that the idea of such a "directorate" imposing its will on the small countries of Europe was "so manifestly contrary to everything that the French government has always expressed on the necessary independence of every people that it does not even merit a denial".

2.18 Discussions of European Communities' Council of Ministers on interim treaty arrangements with Britain, etc.

The Council of Ministers at its meetings on Jan. 27–28 and March 3–4, 1969, continued its discussion of a possible interim trading arrangement between the Community and Britain and the other three applicants for membership.

At the January meeting the Ministers considered a report on the interim arrangement from their permanent representatives, but, having failed to reach any decision, referred the matter to their next session. According to press reports, France's five partners agreed that the trading arrangement should be confined at first to the four applicants and linked to eventual membership of the Community, and must conform to the rules of GATT. The French Foreign Minister, Michel Debré, however, maintained that any tariff concessions should be extended to all interested European countries.

No progress was made at the March meeting in the absence of Debré, the Italian Foreign Minister Pietro Nenni, and Brandt.

2.19 Summary of developments (May 1967–June 1969)

Although Britain's application for membership of the Communities had been submitted in May 1967 [see 2.8], the French government had insisted that it should not be considered before the re-establishment of the British economy, particularly following the devaluation of sterling on Nov. 18, 1967. No agreement on the question was reached by the Council of Ministers on Dec. 18–19, 1967, and no real progress towards negotiations was made during 1968 or the first half of 1969.

In its annual report for 1968, published on Feb. 17, 1969, the European Commission maintained that there was nothing to be gained by retarding or blocking decisions which would eventually have to be adopted anyway, and asked whether it was good sense to hold up completely the start of work on enlarging the Community, despite the Opinion issued by the Commission, when all parties stated that they wanted this enlargement and knew that it would ultimately come about.

Jean Rey, then President of the European Commission, presenting this report to the European Parliament in Strasbourg on March 12, 1969, said that, having convinced their neighbours that the proper method of uniting Europe was in and through the Communities, it was up to the Communities to respond to the appeal which had been addressed to them. He stressed, however, that there could be no question of changing the nature of the Community or of transforming the Common Market into a free trade area, and that if other countries wanted to join the Community it must be "the Community as it stands, with its common policies, its political aims and its institutions".

2.20 Commission's Revised Opinion on enlargement of Communities

In view of the gradual change in the French attitude towards the enlargement of the Communities [see 2.21] following the election of President Pompidou to succeed de Gaulle and the formation of a new government under Jacques Chaban-Delmas in June 1969, progress was made during the summer of 1969 towards the resumption of contact between the European Communities and the four applicant countries, and the Commission was instructed by the Council of Ministers at its meeting on July 22–23, 1969, to bring up to date its Opinions of September 1967 and April 1968 (the second of which proposed a transitional arrangement involving negotiation of reciprocal tariff reductions, "consultation and rapprochement" through existing institutions such as the WEU and the Council of Association of the ECSC, and increased technological and scientific co-operation). This updated report, which was submitted to the Council of Ministers on Oct. 2 and published on the following day, recommended that negotiations should be opened as soon as possible and should concentrate on the major political, economic and social problems involved, and also that Community institutions and procedures should be strengthened. A summary of the main points of the new Opinion is given below.

Enlargement of Community. The four applications must be viewed together, since Denmark, the Irish Republic and Norway could hardly contemplate joining the Communities independently of Britain, nor could they without difficulty remain outside a Community enlarged by the accession of the UK alone.

Negotiations should be phased so as to ensure that all the applicant countries became members at the same time.

New members would have to accept not only the Treaties of Paris and Rome but also the decisions taken since these Treaties came into force. Enlargement problems should therefore generally be solved by means of transition measures rather than by amendments to existing rules.

Agriculture. Enlargement should not affect the financing principles of the common agricultural policy, but transition measures should be negotiated to overcome problems arising from the effects of the policy on production and consumption patterns, from the policy's financial consequences on new members, and from difficulties which might arise for Commonwealth sugar and New Zealand butter.

Adoption by the EEC of the Mansholt Plan for agricultural reform before the opening of negotiations would make it more likely that the applicant countries would agree to Community demands that they should accept the common agricultural policy as soon as they entered, including the principle of financial solidarity and its consequences.

Economic and financial problems. The Commission examined the implications of Britain's past balance-of-payments deficits and present recovery, the favourable effect of the Basle arrangements on sterling balances, and the international role of sterling. Any lasting and effective solution to these problems, it said, could be achieved correctly only through international monetary institutions but, as the issue was so important for an enlarged Community, guidelines should be established along which the Community would participate in any international action which might be taken.

Transition measures. Transitional arrangements would be necessary but should disappear according to a set timetable which should be the same for all candidates. Transition periods for industry and agriculture should be kept more or less in step; the entry into force of the Treaties of Paris and Rome and the timing of transition measures should not vary for different products or according to an entrant's own specific problems; and waivers or exceptions should be kept to a minimum.

Relations with other countries. The countries of southern Europe were at a stage of economic development which ruled out immediate membership, but they might establish preferential relations such as association if their institutions and regimes were comparable with those of the Communities' six founder-members.

For other more economically developed and democratic countries—other than those, such as Austria, which could not become full members because of their international circumstances—the Community had always considered that full membership best accorded with the Treaties' objectives. Association or preferential agreements, on the other hand, would mean that these countries might have to comply with decisions which they had not helped to take, while commitments on consultation and a multiplicity of special arrangements would cause excessive complications.

Strengthening of Community. Candidate countries must accept not only the progress which the Community had already made but also the principle of strengthening the Community, which was linked with enlargement. They should therefore start to pursue policies convergent with those already implemented in the Community so that it would be easier to solve membership problems and so that, if the negotiations were successful, the duration and scope of transition measures might be kept to a minimum.

Community institutions. A review should be made of all the Community's institutions. In particular, the Commission urged (i) that the European Parliament should enjoy real budgetary powers, that its members should be elected by universal suffrage, and that an enlargement of the Community should provide an opportunity for a redistribution of seats; (ii) that decisions of the Council of Ministers should normally be made by majority vote unless the Treaties explicitly required the contrary—i.e. basically there should be unanimity (with power of veto) on outline decisions, such as those laying down targets in specific fields, and majority voting on implementing decisions; (iii) that any adjustment of existing arrangements on weighting of Council members' votes and the level of the qualified majority should ensure that member states continued to be deterred from prolonging discussions indefinitely; (iv) that minority interests should be guaranteed by a ruling that no majority decision could be taken except on a proposal from the Commission; and (v) that powers of management should be gradually transferred to the Commission, which should retain responsibility for day-to-day decisions in close liaison with the Council and member states.

2.21 Change in French attitude—Decision at The Hague summit to open negotiations with applicant countries (December 1969)

The political changes in France during the summer of 1969 led to a more favourable attitude by the French government towards enlargement of the Communities. President Pompidou, in his first press conference after his election, stated on July 10, 1969, that France had no objection to the eventual entry of Britain or any other country.

Before this happened, however, the President said, the Six should agree among themselves on the conditions for such membership and the consequences which it might have on the future and on the very nature of the Community, because up to the present "one has often sheltered behind what was called 'the French veto' to conceal difficulties and realities".

The French government's acceptance of the Commission's revised Opinion [see 2.20] that negotiations on enlargement of the Communities should be started as soon as possible was announced by Maurice Schumann, the new French Foreign Minister, on Oct. 17, 1969.

This acceptance was, however, subject to the conditions (*a*) that the EEC's transitional period should be completed and that agreement should be reached on a new system of financing the Community's agriculture, and (*b*) that once the EEC had moved into its "definitive period" in 1970, the Six should agree on how the Community could be further developed and strengthened; this, said Schumann, would be partly eqivalent to drawing up a common negotiating position for the talks with the four applicant countries.

The important summit meeting of the Communities in the Hague, on Dec. 1–2, 1969, decided that negotiations should be opened with the four applicant countries. President Pompidou stressed in the course of a television broadcast on Dec. 15, 1969, that France was not imposing a veto on British membership of the Common Market, and he expressed the hope that the following year's negotiations would prove that Britain had really decided to turn towards Europe. Following consideration of the Commission's Revised Opinion [see 2.20] and in the light of decisions taken at the Hague summit meeting, the Council of Ministers instructed its permanent officials on Dec. 8, 1969, to begin drawing up a common negotiating position for the six member states including the following points:

(*a*) Adaptation to an enlarged Community of the agreements to be concluded by Dec. 31, 1969, on the financing of agriculture; (*b*) the Commonwealth countries' special arrangements with Britain; (*c*) the effect of British membership of Euratom and the ECSC; (*d*) measures to be taken during the transition period, and the length of this period; (*e*) the effect of an enlarged membership on the Community's institutions; (*f*) negotiating procedure; and (*g*) the economic and financial aspects of enlargement, including the question of Britain's balance of payments and sterling balances.

2.22 Action Committee for United States of Europe—Call for negotiations on British entry into EEC

A resolution calling for immediate action by the six member countries of the European Communities with a view to the opening of negotiations on rapid British entry into the EEC was made on July 16, 1969, by the Action Committee for the United States of Europe (chaired by Jean Monnet)—following the publication earlier in the month of reports by experts appointed by the Committee in March 1969 to examine the prospects and likely effects of such membership.

An estimate was published by the UK Institute of Directors on Dec. 8, 1969, of the likely gains and losses by various industries from a British entry into the EEC.

Industries most likely to gain from entry, the Institute stated, were particularly those with a high ratio of capital to output—e.g. electronics, drugs, aerospace, chemicals, and chemical, electrical and mechanical engineering; moderate gains would be experienced by industries where membership would have little direct effect—e.g. housebuilding and services, where greater economic growth might be offset by higher labour costs; "notable gains" would be made by sectors such as motor manufacturing, shipbuilding, textiles and retailing, but these would also face keener competition outside the Community and suffer from higher wage and material costs; and possible losers would include industries whose tariff protection from Community competitors would be withdrawn (e.g. scientific instruments), those dependent on a high proportion of raw materials whose price could rise (e.g. paper and footwear) and those which were expanding only slowly and whose total costs were likely to increase sharply (e.g. food, confectionery and brewing).

The Confederation of British Industry (CBI), in a report published on Dec. 17, 1969, entitled *Britain in Europe, a Second Industrial Appraisal* (its first having been issued in 1966), came to the conclusion that Britain's entry into the EEC would be to the advantage of British industry and of the industries of other

European countries, but that efforts to achieve it should be pursued only if negotiations did not involve too much deflation in Britain.

2.23 British government's "Economic Assessment" of effects of membership

The British government's "Economic Assessment" of the possible effects of membership of the European Communities on British agriculture, industry, trade, capital movements and invisible trade was set out in a White Paper (Cmnd. 4289) published on Feb. 10, 1970.

The White Paper expressed the view that "the total effect of the estimates of the cost of Britain's entry, in respect of agriculture, Community finance, trade and industry, capital movements and invisibles" produced an overall balance-of-payments cost ranging from about £100,000,000 to about £1,100,000,000; this, however, not only made "no allowance for the dynamic effects" but was "far too wide to afford any basis for judgment" and was "positively misleading" in that it was "inconceivable" that all the elements in the calculation would "work in the same direction". Nevertheless, the total balance-of-payments cost would at most involve "an additional claim on the annual rate of growth over a period of a few years of considerably less than 1 per cent of our gross national product", which would in turn "certainly be much greater" than the £39,000,000,000 which it was at present.

The Assessment concluded: "This White Paper demonstrates the need for negotiations to determine the conditions on which the opportunity for entry could be seized. Failure to reach agreement in these negotiations would not necessarily condemn Britain or the European Communities to political or economic sterility. But Europe would have lost another historic opportunity to develop its full economic potentialities in the interests of the welfare and security of its citizens; in that case the world would have lost a contribution to its peace and prosperity that neither Britain nor the countries of the European Communities can make separately."

Introducing the White Paper in the House of Commons on Feb. 10, 1970, the Prime Minister made a number of explanatory statements.

Wilson explained, in particular, that the White Paper did not allow for what it was hoped to achieve in the course of negotiations, "whether in terms of quantities and costs or in terms of periods for transition and adjustment". Nor did it attempt to estimate the cost to Britain of remaining outside the Communities if the final result of the negotiations was to produce unacceptable terms and conditions. Wilson added: "Should the negotiations not lead to acceptable terms for entry, Britain is and will be strong enough to stand on her own feet outside." The "final decision" on the question of entry, he said, did not arise on this White Paper but would have to be taken in the light of the negotiations due to begin in the summer of 1970.

In reply to Heath (then Leader of the Opposition) Wilson confirmed the importance of putting "the facts and figures . . . fairly . . . to the people as a whole", and in answer to Thorpe (the Liberal leader) he declared: "There are no options open at all in respect of the decision to open negotiations and to approach them in a determination that they should succeed if the price is acceptable."

Two-day debates were held in the House of Commons on Feb. 24–25, 1970, and in the House of Lords on March 17–18, at the end of which the White Paper was "noted" without a division in each case.

2.24 Community preparation for negotiations

Following the decision at the Hague summit meeting that negotiations should be opened with the four applicant countries, confidential papers were submitted to the Council of Ministers by the Commission during March 1970 dealing with the free circulation of goods, agriculture, the ECSC, economic and monetary policies, the Commonwealth and transitional arrangements; at meetings on April 20–21, May 11–12 and June 8–9 the Council of Ministers agreed on procedures to be followed and the main lines of principle.

In particular, it was agreed at the June meeting that negotiations would be conducted at all levels by the European Communities—i.e. not by the six individual member countries—and that negotiating meetings would, on the Communities' side, be presided over at all levels by the country currently presiding over the Council of Ministers—i.e. by Belgium up to June 30, 1970, then for successive six-monthly periods by West Germany, France, Italy, Luxembourg and the Netherlands. The Communities' standpoint would be set out and defended in the negotiations with the candidate countries either by the current President of the Council of Ministers or—by decision of the Council, and particularly when Community policies already agreed were concerned—by the Commission.

This procedure would also be followed where the negotiations were conducted at the level of permanent representatives or of any working parties which might be set up. The Commission was in addition invited to make proposals on any problems arising from the negotiations and might—particularly where common policies already agreed were concerned—be called upon to seek, in liaison with the candidate countries, possible solutions to specific problems which might arise and to report to the Council.

The ministers were also reported to have adopted the following positions on voting rights within the Council of Ministers and on the size of the Commission and of the European Parliament.

For questions within the enlarged Communities involving "qualified majority voting" in the Council of Ministers, Britain, France, West Germany and Italy should each have 10 votes, Belgium and the Netherlands five each, Denmark, the Irish Republic and Norway three each, and Luxembourg two—a total of 61 votes. The qualified majority would require 43 votes and a "blocking minority" 19, it being pointed out in the press that on this basis the combined 40 votes of the "Big Four" could not override the unanimous votes of the other six, but that the 20 votes of two of the "Big Four" could provide a "blocking minority". The size of the Commission should be increased from nine to 14, with two seats each for the "Big Four" and one each for the six smaller countries. In the European Parliament the number of seats should be raised from 142 to 208, with 36 each for the "Big Four", 14 each for Belgium and the Netherlands, 10 each for Denmark, the Irish Republic and Norway, and six for Luxembourg.

2.25 June 1970 general election in UK—Return of Conservative government
In the British June 1970 general election, which resulted in the return to power of a Conservative government with Heath as Prime Minister, the three main parties' policies were all set out in their respective manifestos.

The Labour Party said that negotiations would be "pressed with determination with the purpose of joining an enlarged Community provided that British and essential Commonwealth interests can be safeguarded"; in contrast with the 1961–63 negotiations, however, Britain would now be negotiating from a position of strength, and if satisfactory terms could not be secured she would "be able to stand on her own feet outside the Community".

The Conservative Party similarly stated that if the right terms could be negotiated "it would be in the long-term interest of the British people for Britain to join the EEC" but that "obviously there is a price we would not be prepared to pay" and that the party's sole commitment was to negotiate. A Conservative government would not be prepared to recommend to Parliament a settlement which was unequal or unfair.

The Liberal Party saw the Common Market as "an exciting experiment in the pooling of national sovereignty in the economic sphere" and as a possible forerunner of "a similar unity in foreign policy and defence", and the Liberals continued to believe that satisfactory terms could be obtained for British entry.

Back-bench opinion concerned at the possible adverse effects of British membership on conditions likely to be negotiated, on the other hand, was expressed after the re-assembly of Parliament in motions tabled by Labour members on July 21 and by Conservatives on July 23 in broadly similar terms, urging the government to insist on satisfactory safeguards for British sovereignty, food prices and the cost of living, the balance of payments, and Commonwealth and EFTA trade.

Opinion critical of membership without "far more stringent and effective safeguards" had earlier been manifested—just prior to the publication of the White Paper—in the formation on Feb. 4, 1970, of a Common Market Safeguards Campaign; this had as its executive chairman Douglas Jay (President of the Board of Trade in Wilson's government 1964–67).

2.26 Opening of negotiations—The Luxembourg meeting (June 30, 1970)

The negotiating positions of the Council and Commission of the European Communities and of the British, Danish, Irish and Norwegian governments were set out in statements at a special meeting in Luxembourg on June 30, 1970, which represented the first formal stage of negotiations.

Pierre Harmel, Foreign Minister of Belgium and at that time President of the Council of Ministers of the Communities, described the context of the negotiations as that of "a three-fold movement decided upon at the summit meeting at The Hague — the transition to the final period of the Common Market, the internal development of the Communities, and their enlargement"—which represented "three complementary aspects of the second decisive stage in the construction of Europe".

Jean Rey, the outgoing President of the Commission, emphasized that the negotiations on enlargement should not arrest or slow down the task of completing the construction of the Communities' economic and monetary union or work on agricultural structures, industrial and technological policy, common energy policy, regional policy, harmonization of taxation systems, social policy or European companies.

Anthony Barber, then Chancellor of the Duchy of Lancaster and leader of the British delegation, opened by recalling Britain's previous unsuccessful negotiations in 1961–63 and the renewed application in 1967. After stressing his government's desire to see a united and prosperous Europe and the inseparable nature of Europe's political and economic interests, Barber made it clear that the British government accepted "the treaties establishing the three European Communities and the decisions which have flowed from them". He expressed the hope that negotiations could be kept short and confined to essentials, and concluded: "I am told that the problems which you have been discussing for the last six months in preparation for these negotiations are very much the same as ours. So these are common problems for us and for you—how to enable an enlarged Community to function most effectively for the advantage of all. Our wish is to look together in the spirit of the Community for solutions which, in the words of the Commission's Opinion of 1969, will ensure the cohesion and dynamism which will be indispensable in an enlarged Community.

"After many years we now have the opportunity to realize together a Europe which has a coherent character of its own. We have the same defence interest; our political interests are growing every day progressively closer. As we develop new policies together we shall, as I have said, find it natural to develop the institutional machinery which we shall need to execute those policies. . . ."

After the formal opening session, specific proposals were put forward by Barber in Brussels on July 21 for fact-finding work in the following fields, on all except the last of which it was agreed that work should be put in hand: on agriculture and agricultural finance; dairy products, including New Zealand's "vital interest in this sector"; Commonwealth sugar; the common external tariff; the "complex task of agreeing authoritative translations of Community legislation, and certain related matters"; the European Coal and Steel Community; and Euratom.

Barber emphasized that the need for discussion of certain problems and for adaptations which the Six or Britain might think desirable "in no sense reflects any refusal on our part to adopt the common agricultural policy" which Britain would be "perfectly willing to accept . . . as member of an enlarged Community".

2.27 Negotiations (September 1970–February 1971)—EFTA position—House of Commons debate

From September 1970 detailed discussions were held at the level of deputies (i.e. permanent representatives of the Six and Sir Con O'Neill for Britain), while ministerial meetings between the Communities' Council of Ministers and Geoffrey Rippon, who took over from Barber on July 28 as Chancellor of the Duchy of Lancaster with responsibility for negotiations with the Communities, took place on Oct. 27, Dec. 8, and Feb. 2, 1971.

The principal aspects of the negotiations dealt with at these sessions were agricultural policy, arrangements for Commonwealth countries (including protection for the New Zealand dairy industry and for sugar producers in the developing countries), various trade and industrial matters, transitional arrangements, and Community finance. Although general agreement was reached on most of these subjects, the question of finance raised serious problems as regards both Britain's overall share and the contribution which she should make during the transitional period.

The EFTA Ministerial Council, meeting in Geneva on Nov. 5–6, 1970, welcomed the fact that Harmel, in his statement of June 30 [see 2.26], had said that the Community considered it desirable that agreements with the various EFTA countries should come into force at the same time.

This, the ministers said, corresponded with their own conviction expressed at the end of their previous meeting in Geneva on May 14–15, and the November communiqué reaffirmed the member countries' "strong interest in safeguarding, as an important part of an enlarged European Community, the free trade already established between EFTA countries". The ministers further noted that, with the starting of negotiations and discussions between all EFTA countries and the Communities, the procedure already agreed for a continuous exchange of information and for consultation would come fully into effect.

A two-day debate on the negotiations with the European Communities was held in the House of Commons on Jan. 20–21, 1971. During the debate Rippon described progress achieved so far and stressed that what was at stake was "the political future of Western Europe". Harold Lever, for the Labour Party, said that it would only be when the Minister came with a package agreement—if he was able to get one—that the Opposition would judge whether the package as a whole was in the interests of the country.

Opinion remained divided within both the Conservative and Labour Parties on the economic and political desirability of membership, and although there was no vote at the end of the debate a motion was tabled on Jan. 20, signed by about 100 Labour back-bench MPs, expressing the belief that "entry into the EEC on the terms so far envisaged would be against the interests of this country".

2.28 Conclusion of main phase of negotiations in June 1971
Meetings with the Communities' Council of Ministers, attended by Geoffrey Rippon, as leader of Britain's delegation, took place on March 16, from May 11 to early in the morning of May 13, on June 7 and June 21–23, 1971, when the main phase of negotiations was concluded (a White Paper, "The United Kingdom and the European Communities", being published on July 7 setting out the terms of the agreement—see 2.29).

During these later negotiations, the principal matters dealt with were sugar, New Zealand and Australian produce, capital movements and the role of sterling, fisheries, Britain's financial contribution, and agricultural transition. Sugar and New Zealand and Australian exports were in particular also the subject of discussions between Britain and the Commonwealth countries involved.

Statements on the progress of the negotiations were made by Rippon in the House of Commons on March 18, May 17, June 9, June 24 and July 14. Edward Heath said in the House of Commons on June 17 that there were six stages to be completed, viz.: (i) resolution of the major issues outstanding in the negotiations; (ii) a decision of principle by Parliament on whether the arrangements so negotiated were satisfactory and whether Britain should proceed to join the Communities; (iii) resolution of the remaining issues in the negotiations; (iv) preparation and signature of a treaty of accession; (v) drafting, Parliamentary consideration and enactment of legislation to give effect to that treaty; and (vi) deposition of instruments of ratification of the treaty by Britain and the other parties.

The conclusion of agreement on nearly all outstanding points of negotiation followed a general change of attitude by the French government during the late spring, culminating in a meeting between Heath and President Pompidou on May 20–21. Nevertheless, a warning against abandoning the Communities' "fundamental principles"—even in disguised form—was given by Jacques Chaban-Delmas, the French Prime Minister, in a speech to the French National Assembly on April 20.

2.29 Outcome of negotiations on major issues—The terms of the agreement
The July 7 White Paper (Cmnd. 4715) reviewed the course of negotiations and expressed the conviction "that our country will be more secure, our ability to maintain peace and promote development in the world greater, our economy stronger, and our industries and people more prosperous, if we join the European Communities than if we remain outside them. . . . [and] that British membership of the Communities will enhance the security and prosperity of Western Europe".

Setting out the political case for membership, it emphasized the advantages of **influence on decision-making**, as part of the Communities, with regard to global economic affairs, and, within the Communities, to influence developments on external policies, and economic and monetary union, which would otherwise move forward without any British say in the matter. On **maintenance of sovereignty** it stated that "the practical working of the Community reflects the reality that sovereign governments are represented round the table. On a question where a government considers that vital national interests are involved, it is established that the decision should be unanimous. Like any other treaty, the Treaty of Rome commits its signatories to support agreed aims; but the commitment represents the voluntary undertaking of a sovereign state to observe policies which it has helped to form. There is no question of any erosion of essential national sovereignty; what is proposed is a sharing and an enlargement of individual national sovereignties in the general interest".

Moreover, the Treaties "contain no provision expressly permitting or prohibiting withdrawal". It stressed the common European heritage and **common interests** of the UK and the Community member countries, and referred to **rejection of a North Atlantic grouping** as an alternative, since any such free trade area encompassing the United States would be dominated by the USA, and since successive US administrations "have made it clear that they would prefer to see us as members of a stronger and more united Europe than as a satellite of the United States. Similarly, the Six have firmly and repeatedly made it clear that they reject the concept that European unity should be limited to the formation of a free trade area". On the **position of the Commonwealth**, it stated: "Nor does the Commonwealth by itself offer us, or indeed wish to offer us, alternative and comparable opportunities to membership of the European Community. The member countries of the Commonwealth are widely scattered in different regions of the world and differ widely in their political ideas and economic development. With the attainment of independence, their political and economic relations with the UK in particular have greatly changed and are still changing. They have developed and are still developing with other countries trade and investment arrangements which accord with the requirements of their basic geographical and economic circumstances." It referred to the **aid given to poorer nations** by the Community countries, to the possibilities for developing Commonwealth countries of association with a wider European Community, and to the fact that the UK's share of the trade to the Commonwealth had declined sharply over the last decade.

On the economic case for membership, it referred to the **budgeting effect** of contributions to the common budget as a net cost of some £100 million in the first year, 1973, which if the structure of the budget remained unchanged could double by the fifth year, as the required proportion of UK payments to the budget rose from 8.64 per cent to 18.92 per cent under transitional arrangements. (These arrangements established a percentage of the budget which the UK would nominally be expected to pay in a ten-member enlarged Community, and then provided that actual contributions would rise gradually from 45 to 92 per cent of this nominal amount during 1973–77. They also set a ceiling on any increase in the UK contribution for the two subsequent years, 1978–79, when the direct payment system would come into effect, but the UK would not be required to pay more than 40 per cent of the amount by which the new amount might exceed the previous year's contribution.)

The White Paper estimated that gradual adoption of the common agricultural policy (the CAP) rather than purchasing food on world markets would entail an annual 2.5 per cent **increase in average retail food prices** during the transitional period (1973–77) and in 1978. It asserted that the **effect on industry** from the creation of an enlarged market should be "positive and substantial", albeit unquantifiable in advance, and, in conclusion, that the costs of joining would be more than outweighed by the advantages.

The White Paper also set out the arrangements for participation in the institutions of the Communities, in which it had been agreed that the UK should have from the start a position equal to that of France, West Germany and Italy. [See appendix 1 for details of institutional implications of enlargement.] It covered transitional arrangements on industrial tariffs and agriculture; arrangements for some degree of continuing access for sensitive

Commonwealth products; monetary issues; and accession to the ECSC and Euratom.

Transitional arrangements for industry. The government had sought "to identify as quickly as possible the advantages for British industry of integration within a single European market, while providing an adequate period of adjustment for our Commonwealth and other trading partners". Tariffs on trade between the UK and the Six were to be eliminated in five equal stages, on April 1, 1973 (assuming accession on Jan. 1 of that year), at the beginning of each of the three subsequent years, and on July 1, 1977. The common external tariff was to be adopted in four stages, 40 per cent on Jan. 1, 1974, a further 20 per cent at the beginning of each of the two subsequent years, and the final 20 per cent on July 1, 1977. Special arrangements were anticipated, however, for EFTA member countries [see chapter 6], for Commonwealth countries in Africa, the Caribbean and the Pacific and for UK dependent territories [see below], and for countries with which the existing Community had special arrangements.

Transitional arrangements for agriculture. The Community system of price supports for cereals, dairy products, beef and veal, pigmeat and sugar would be adopted in the first year of membership, but with lower threshold and intervention prices, which would move up to full Community levels in six steps over five years. In trading with countries outside the Community, for these products and for poultry and eggs, the Community system of import levies and export refunds would be phased in similarly. Trade between the UK and other Community countries in these products would be free, subject to levies and compensatory payments to equalize prices during the transitional period.

For farm products on which the Community applied a common external tariff instead of, or in addition to, its import levy system, the UK would move to gradual adoption of this tariff during the transitional period, under arrangements which were yet to be worked out in precise detail. For horticulture there would be a slower rate of tariff adjustment. For apples and pears the existing UK system of import quotas would be replaced by import levies, offsetting the difference between UK and Community prices, and these levies would then be phased out over the course of the five-year transitional period.

Commonwealth access. Special arrangements for New Zealand butter and cheese, announced on June 24 and accepted by the New Zealand government, provided for continuing access to the enlarged Community market for set quota amounts at guaranteed prices. For lamb there was no Community common market regime in place, except for a common external tariff, which stood at 20 per cent, and the UK government undertook to introduce this tariff over the transitional period, taking the view that this would not be a barrier to continuing access of an acceptable volume of New Zealand lamb to the UK market.

For sugar the UK would respect its contractual obligation to buy agreed quantities under the Commonwealth Sugar Agreement until the end of 1974, after which the developing country sugar producers within the Commonwealth would have access under association or trading arrangements with the enlarged Community; this solution had been the subject of consultations with the countries concerned on June 2–3 in London.

African, Caribbean and Pacific countries within the Commonwealth would maintain their present trading arrangements with the UK until Jan. 31, 1975, when the Communities' Yaoundé Convention would expire (the Yaoundé Convention being replaced thereafter by the enlarged Lomé Convention between the Communities and the ACP countries). UK dependent territories would be offered association with the enlarged Communities under Part IV of the Treaty of Rome, except for the European territory of Gibraltar (which at its own request would not be included within the customs area of the enlarged Communities) and Hong Kong which would be included within the generalized preferences scheme.

The Communities after enlargement would examine trade problems with India, Pakistan, Ceylon, Malaysia and Singapore. Malta already had an association agreement and Cyprus was in the process of negotiating a similar agreement.

In relations with Australia and Canada, there would not be special arrangements as for New Zealand and the developing countries of the Commonwealth, and the common external tariff and agricultural levies and tariffs would be applied by the UK gradually during the transitional period; a number of products from these two countries, however, would benefit under the various special duty arrangements which had been agreed during the UK's negotiations with the Communities.

For the Channel Islands and the Isle of Man, the UK government was seeking arrangements for a form of association short of full Community membership, allowing for the preservation of their own fiscal systems and special customs arrangements.

Financial and monetary issues. Community membership would enhance the prospect of working out arrangements in due course for the rundown of official sterling balances. The EC was currently considering UK proposals for adjusting exchange control policies to remove restrictions on capital movement within the enlarged Communities over five years, commencing with direct investment, then personal capital other than portfolio investment, and lastly portfolio investment. The introduction of value added tax from 1973 had been announced in the UK 1971 budget, and there would thus be no need for special transitional arrangements for the adoption of that system.

Coal and steel and Euratom. Tariffs for steel products would be adjusted at the same rate as for industrial products generally. Coal imports from Community countries, and exports to them, would be brought under a free trade regime. The UK would invest £24,000,000 in the ECSC reserve funds (currently amounting to some £90,000,000) in three equal annual instalments starting from the date of accession, and would gain access immediately to these reserve funds (for industrial development, workers' housing loans, new employment schemes and retraining for redundant employees, and grants for research).

The Euratom treaty, and the Euratom control system for civilian nuclear installations, would be accepted without a transitional period, except that the necessary tariff changes would take place one year after accession.

2.30 Conservative and Liberal support for entry terms—Labour and TUC opposition to entry on White Paper terms

Edward Heath, in a television broadcast on July 8, strongly supported British entry into the Common Market on the terms set forth in the White Paper. Harold Wilson's broadcast on July 9 strongly criticized the terms, however, saying that they did not satisfy the requirements on four crucial issues. Entry should not threaten "our hard-won solvency", he said, whereas the White Paper gave no figure for the balance of trade and payments impact; on Commonwealth sugar access, there were no long-term guarantees; on New Zealand food product access to Britain, nothing was stipulated after a five-year rundown period; and on capital movements, British rules would be removed but there was no agreement on what Community safeguards would apply.

At a special meeting of the central council of the Conservative Party in London on July 14, Heath explained the reasons why the government were in favour of Britain's entry into the EC on the terms negotiated and set out in the White Paper. In the course of his speech, which largely recapitulated the arguments contained in the White Paper and in his broadcast, the Prime Minister made it clear that the government did not contemplate holding a referendum on the Common Market issue.

Heath said that "it is for Members of Parliament to perform the duty for which they were elected and to take a decision on behalf of the country", and went on: "This is our traditional way of reaching great national decisions. I am absolutely sure that it is the right one for us to follow. To do otherwise, to start talking in terms of a referendum, would mean proposing a major change in our system of representative parliamentary democracy. I do not think that many of us would want to change a system which has served our country so well for so long."

The Conservative and Unionist Party, on Oct. 13, 1971, at its annual conference, approved by a majority of nearly eight to one a resolution pledging full support for Britain's entry into the European Communities on the terms negotiated by the government and set out in the White Paper. The Liberal Party, on Sept. 17, at its annual conference, also carried by a substantial majority a resolution approving Britain's entry into the EC on the terms negotiated.

The Labour Party, on the other hand, after holding a special one-day conference on the Common Market issue on July 17, carried by a large majority on Oct. 4 at its annual conference a resolution opposing British entry into the EC on the terms negotiated by Heath's government. The Trades Union Congress, at its annual conference, had passed a similar resolution on Sept. 8.

2.31 Parliamentary approval of decision to join the Communities

The longest Parliamentary debate since the war took place in the House of Commons between Oct. 21 and Oct. 28, 1971, on a government motion: "That this House approves Her Majesty's Government's decision of principle to join the European Communities on the basis of the arrangements which have been negotiated."

The six-day debate in the House of Commons—held on Oct. 21, 22, 25, 26, 27 and 28, and popularly described as the "Great Debate"—resulted in the motion being adopted by 356 votes to 244, a government majority of 112. In the House of Lords, which held a three-day debate on Oct. 26–28, an identical motion was approved by 451 votes to 58, a majority of 393. Conservative MPs were allowed a free vote in the Commons debate, whereas a three-line whip was imposed for Labour members. 39 Conservative MPs voted against the motion, while 69 Labour MPs voted for the motion despite the party whip. Five Liberals supported the motion and one voted against.

Harold Wilson said on the last day of the debate that a future Labour government would immediately give notice that it could not accept the terms which had been negotiated, "in particular the unacceptable burdens arising out of the CAP, the blows to the Commonwealth, and any threats to our essential regional policies". The EC might refuse to renegotiate, or the renegotiation might fail; the British government would explain that its posture "would be rigidly directed towards the pursuit of British interests. . . . they might accept this, or they might decide that we should agree to part".

2.32 Resolution of remaining issues in the negotiations (July 1971–January 1972)

The common fisheries policy of the existing Community, which came into force on Feb. 1, 1971, aroused considerable concern in Norway, the Republic of Ireland and Denmark as well as in Britain. It was reported that there was strong feeling among the applicant countries' negotiators that they should have been consulted over the formulation of the common policy since it did not come into force until after membership negotiations had commenced.

The European Commission forwarded its own proposals for amendments to the six member governments on June 17, 1971.

Part of the original policy stipulated that fishermen from the entire Community must have equal access to the territorial waters of other member states, with exceptions only for certain kinds of fish in specified areas which would be protected within a three-mile limit to assist communities largely dependent on these particular areas for their livelihood. The Commission's new proposals allowed for similar protection up to a limit of six miles in designated restricted areas to which access would be limited to boats based in the local ports concerned. As with the original exemptions, the additional concession was planned to extend for an initial period of five years only and was then, according to the amendment, to be reviewed with the possibility of extending the exemptions in special cases.

No agreement was reached on the basis of these proposals during the remainder of the summer, and during October and early November the Common Market countries drew up further proposals under which national governments could designate their own six-mile limits during a period of five years, although it was considered that these should not apply to the whole coastline, and that in a second five-year period these restrictions would be subject to Community approval.

It was also reported that the Community would accept further restrictions within a 12-mile limit for special cases, such as the northern coast of Norway as far south as Trondheim, the Orkneys and Shetlands, and Greenland and the Faroes. At the end of the 10 years the Commission would report on the situation as a whole and would consider if further exemptions to the standard form of the common fishing policy could be made for certain areas.

The British delegation argued in favour of more liberal treatment of the principles outlined in the Community proposals at a meeting of ministers on Nov. 9. At a ministerial meeting on Nov. 29 further progress was made, however, and Geoffrey Rippon told the House of Commons on Dec. 1 that "in addition to the Orkneys and Shetlands, it [the Communities] offered to consider the possibility of some other special areas for the United Kingdom". Rippon explained, however, that the proposals "did not go far enough to safeguard the legitimate interests of the fishing industry".

The inclusion of a review clause referring to the period beyond the 10 years of protected fishing guaranteed to the fishermen of the applicant countries was the additional concession by the Community governments at a ministerial negotiating session in Brussels which enabled an agreement to be reached on Dec. 12, although Norway remained dissatisfied with the terms offered. The review clause provided for a report before the end of the 10-year period on the coastal areas and the state of fish stocks, on the basis of which, together with the objectives of the Community's common fisheries policy, the Council of Ministers would consider subsequent arrangements.

Apart from fisheries—the major outstanding issue following the general conclusion of the negotiations on June 23, 1971—the United Kingdom delegation continued discussion of a number of minor items during the second half of 1971 and in early 1972.

Channel Islands and Isle of Man. At a ministerial meeting on Nov. 9 the UK delegation expressed satisfaction with a Community proposal designed to accommodate the Channel Islands and the Isle of Man within the framework of Article 227 (4) of the Treaty of Rome. The Communities agreed to offer these islands free trade in industrial goods within the common external tariff, and free trade in agricultural products; certain other provisions of the Treaties would not apply, and the Communities' proposals would in no way affect the islands' constitutional relationship with the United Kingdom.

At a meeting in Brussels on Dec. 17 it was stated that the islands' authorities had agreed to the proposals. It was pointed out in the British press that in particular Community tax provisions would not apply to the islands, while Community rules on the free movement of labour would not cover indigenous islanders.

Animal health. Community agreement on the maintenance of British national animal health arrangements was given at the ministerial meeting of Dec. 11–12 in Brussels. It was agreed that pending the establishment of a common veterinary policy Britain would be permitted to maintain existing arangements for protection against foot-and-mouth disease, brucellosis and tuberculosis. Imports of meat would be subject to animal and public health controls in accordance with the Community provisions. The measures would apply for five years, during which period the Community would review the situation and make appropriate proposals.

Common agricultural policy. In addition, Britain accepted the date of Feb. 1, 1973, for the commencement of the application of the common agricultural policy. It was agreed by deputies on Jan. 7, 1972, that Britain's request for export restitutions on grain-based spirits, particularly whisky, from the Community Agricultural Fund would be accounted for in a separate protocol, while differences over Community and British varieties of hops for beer manufacture would be settled during an interim period.

Industrial policy. Among the issues deferred until after membership was effected was the definition of areas in Britain where aids to industry would be limited. In the progress towards regional development policy in the Communities, the six existing members had limited development aids to 20 per cent of any investment in the more industrially developed "central area" of the Communities.

Nationality and movement of labour. On Jan. 14 agreement was reached on a definition of British nationality, following Dutch concern over the possibility of a large-scale influx into the Netherlands of sections of the British immigrant population after membership had been completed. It was decided that Britain's definition of a British subject as a person who was not subject to immigration control and who enjoyed full rights of entry into the United Kingdom should be attached to the Treaty of Accession. A safeguard clause was also included permitting any Community country concerned about excesses of movement of immigrant labour from one country to another to request action from the Commission or, should the Commission refuse, from the Council of Ministers.

2.33 Arrangements for consultation

To enable applicant countries to participate in the formulation of policies which developed after signature of the Treaty of Accession on Jan. 22, a consultation procedure was included in the Treaty allowing the candidates to make their interests known. Their views would be expressed through an interim committee consisting of permanent representatives (of the Six) and Commission represen- tatives, and consultation would take place after the Council of Ministers had reached preliminary outline agreement on a topic. In the event of serious difficulties the applicant country concerned would be able to request further discussion at ministerial level.

2.34 Signature of Treaty of Accession (Jan. 22, 1972)

The Treaty of Accession to the European Communities, consisting of a number of separate documents, was signed in the Egmont Palace in Brussels on Jan. 22, 1972, by the Prime Ministers of the United Kingdom, Ireland, Denmark and Norway.

The signing ceremony was delayed for nearly an hour by an incident involving
Heath. As the British Prime Minister was entering the Egmont Palace a young woman
rushed forward and threw a plastic bottle of black ink at him, the ink hitting him in the
face and drenching the lapels and shoulders of his suit. As a result the ceremony was
delayed for 55 minutes while Heath, who was otherwise unharmed, changed into
another suit.

Many leading figures of the post-war movement for European unification were
present at the Brussels ceremony, among them Jean Monnet (then aged 84), popularly
known as the "father of Europe"; Walter Hallstein, first President of the European
Commission; Harold Macmillan, the former Prime Minister who made Britain's
original application for EEC membership which was vetoed by General de Gaulle;
Lord George-Brown, who (as George Brown) was Foreign Secretary when the British
Labour government made a second application for EEC membership, also vetoed by
France; and Sir Christopher Soames, British Ambassador in Paris, who with Heath
played a leading role in the European negotiations in the early 1960s. Macmillan, Lord
George-Brown, Sir Christopher Soames and Duncan Sandys were all present in
Brussels at the personal invitation of Heath, as was also Jeremy Thorpe, leader of the
Liberal Party. An invitation to Harold Wilson was declined after the Shadow Cabinet
had decided unanimously on Jan. 17 to reject the Prime Minister's invitation to the
Labour Party to be represented at the Brussels ceremony; Lord George-Brown,
however, one of the Labour Party's leading pro-marketeers, accepted Heath's in-
vitation in a private capacity.

Prior to the signing of the Treaty of Accession by the four new members,
and also by the original Six, speeches stressing the historic nature of the
occasion were made by Gaston Thorn, Foreign Minister of Luxembourg and
President of the Council of Ministers of the European Communities; by
Gaston Eyskens, Prime Minister of Belgium, on behalf of the host country;
and by Franco Maria Malfatti, President of the European Commission. The
British signatories, in addition to Heath, were Sir Alec Douglas-Home,
Foreign and Commonwealth Secretary, and Geoffrey Rippon, the government's chief negotiator in the negotiations with the EC. The four new
members—the United Kingdom, Ireland, Denmark and Norway—signed the
Treaty of Accession in that order, which was the order in which application
for membership of the Communities had been made by the four countries.

The British, Irish, Danish and Norwegian Prime Ministers all made
speeches after signing the Treaty of Accession. Heath spoke as follows:

"We market today, with this ceremony, the conclusion of arduous negotiations over
more than 10 years which have resulted in another great step forward towards the
removal of divisions in Western Europe. This uniting of friendly states within the
framework of a single Community has been brought about by the sustained and
dedicated work of many people. Their efforts were essential to the success which we
are celebrating.

"My tribute here is to all who have laboured in this great enterprise—not only to
those who have negotiated, ministers and officials, together with the members of the
Commission who have contributed so much, but to all who, in their many different
ways, have supported and advanced the idea of a united Europe. Just as the
achievement we celebrate today was not preordained, so there will be nothing inevitable about the next stages in the construction of Europe. They will require clear
thinking and a strong effort of the imagination.

"Clear thinking will be needed to recognize that each of us within the Community
will remain proudly attached to our national identity and to the achievements of our
national history and tradition. But at the same time, as the enlargement of the

Community makes clear beyond doubt, we have all come to recognize our common European heritage, our mutual interests and our European destiny. Imagination will be required to develop institutions which respect the traditions and the individuality of the member states, but at the same time have the strength to guide the future course of the enlarged Community.

"The founders of the Community displayed great originality in devising the institutions of the Six. They have been proved in the remarkable achievements of the Community over the years. It is too early to say how far they will meet the needs of the enlarged Community. For we are faced with an essentially new situation, though one which was always inherent in the foundation of the Community of the Six, which was visualized in the Preamble to the Treaty of Rome and which has been created by its success. Let us not be afraid to contemplate new measures to deal with the new situation.

"There is another cause for satisfaction. 'Europe' is more than Western Europe alone. There lies also to the east another part of our continent; countries whose history has been closely linked with our own. Beyond these countries is the Soviet Union, a European as well as an Asian Power. We in Britain have every reason to wish for better relations with the states of Eastern Europe. And we do sincerely want them. Our new partners on the Continent have shown that their feelings are the same. Henceforth our efforts can be united.

"The European Communities, far from creating barriers, have served to extend East-West trade and other exchanges. Britain has much to contribute to this process, and as members of the Community we shall be better able to do so. Britain, with her Commonwealth links, has also much to contribute to the universal nature of Europe's responsibilities.

"The collective history of the countries represented here encompasses a large part of the history of the world itself over the centuries. I am not thinking today of the age of imperialism, now past; but of the lasting and creative effects of the spread of language and of culture, of commerce and of administration, by people from Europe across land and sea to the other continents of the world.

"These are the essential ties which today bind Europe in friendship with the rest of mankind. What design should we seek for the new Europe? It must be a Europe which is strong and confident within itself. A Europe in which we shall be working for the progressive relaxation and elimination of East-West tensions. A Europe conscious of the interests of its friends and partners. A Europe alive to its great responsibilties in the common struggle of humanity for a better life.

"Thus this ceremony marks an end and a beginning. An end to divisions which have stricken Europe for centuries. A beginning of another stage in the construction of a new and greater united Europe. This is the task for our generation in Europe."

2.35 The Treaty of Accession
The three principal documents making up the Treaty of Accession to the European Communities—popularly referred to in the press as the Treaty of Brussels—were:

(a) The "Treaty concerning the accession of the Kingdom of Denmark, Ireland, the Kingdom of Norway and the United Kingdom of Great Britain and Northern Ireland to the European Economic Community and the European Atomic Energy Community".

(b) The "Decision of the Council of the European Communities of Jan. 22, 1972, concerning the accession of the Kingdom of Denmark, Ireland, the Kingdom of Norway and the United Kingdom of Great Britain and Northern Ireland to the European Coal and Steel Community".

(c) The "Act concerning the conditions of accession and the adjustments to the treaties", covering under a number of heads the negotiations between Britain, Ireland, Denmark and Norway with the Six over the previous 18 months. Unlike (*a*) and (*b*), which were relatively short documents, (*c*) was an Act of great complexity and detail, embodying 161 Articles and with numerous annexes.

As regards (*a*) and (*b*), a separate procedure was required for accession to the European Economic Community and Euratom on the one hand, and to the European Coal and Steel Community on the other, because of legal differences between the original treaties—the Treaties of Rome and the Treaty of Paris respectively—under which these organizations were created.

The textual provisions of (*a*) and (*b*) are given below.

Treaty on Accession of Britain, Ireland, Denmark and Norway to EEC and Euratom. Consisting of a Preamble and three Articles, this Treaty was worded as follows:

Preamble. "His Majesty the King of the Belgians, Her Majesty the Queen of Denmark, the President of the Federal Republic of Germany, the President of the French Republic, the President of Ireland, the President of the Italian Republic, His Royal Highness the Grand Duke of Luxembourg, Her Majesty the Queen of the Netherlands, His Majesty the King of Norway, Her Majesty the Queen of the United Kingdom of Great Britain and Northern Ireland;

"united in their desire to pursue the attainment of the objectives of the Treaty establishing the European Economic Community and the Treaty establishing the European Atomic Energy Community;

"determined in the spirit of those Treaties to construct an ever closer union among the peoples of Europe on the foundations already laid;

"considering that Article 237 of the Treaty establishing the European Economic Community and Article 205 of the Treaty establishing the European Atomic Energy Community afford European states the opportunity of becoming members of these Communities;

"considering that the Kingdom of Denmark, Ireland, the Kingdom of Norway and the United Kingdom of Great Britain and Northern Ireland have applied to become members of these Communities;

"considering that the Council of the European Communities, after having obtained the Opinion of the Commission, has declared itself in favour of the admission of these states;

"have decided to establish by common agreement the conditions of admission and the adjustments to be made to the Treaties establishing the European Economic Community and the European Atomic Energy Community, and to this end have designated as their plenipotentiaries . . .

[*Here follow the signatures of the various plenipotentiaries.*]

"who . . . have agreed as follows:

Article 1. "(1) The Kingdom of Denmark, Ireland, the Kingdom of Norway and the United Kingdom of Great Britain and Northern Ireland hereby become members of the European Economic Community and of the European Atomic Energy Community and Parties to the Treaties establishing these Communities as amended or supplemented.

"(2) The conditions of admission and the adjustments to the Treaties establishing the European Economic Community and the European Atomic Energy Community necessitated thereby are set out in the Act annexed to this Treaty. The provisions of that Act concerning the European Economic Community and the European Atomic Energy Community shall form an integral part of this Treaty.

"(3) The provisions concerning the rights and obligations of the member states and the powers and jurisdiction of the institutions of the Communitites as set out in the Treaties referred to in paragraph 1 shall apply in respect of this Treaty.

Article 2. "This Treaty will be ratified by the High Contracting Parties in accordance with their respective constitutional requirements. The instruments of ratification will be deposited with the government of the Italian Republic by Dec. 31, 1972, at the latest.

"This Treaty will enter into force on Jan. 1, 1973, provided that all the instruments of ratification have been deposited before that date and that all the instruments of accession to the European Coal and Steel Community are deposited on that date.

"If, however, the states referred to in Article 1(1) have not all deposited their instruments of ratification and accession in due time, the Treaty shall enter into force for those states which have deposited their instruments . . .

Article 3. "This Treaty, drawn up in a single original in the Danish, Dutch, English, French, German, Irish, Italian and Norwegian languages, all eight texts being equally authentic, will be deposited in the archives of the government of the Italian Republic, which will transmit a certified copy to each of the governments of the other signatory states."

Decision of Council of European Communities on British, Irish, Danish and Norwegian Membership of European Coal and Steel Community. This document likewise consisted of a Preamble and three Articles and was worded as follows:

Preamble. "The Council of the European Communities;

"having regard to Article 98 of the Treaty establishing the European Coal and Steel Community;

"whereas the Kingdom of Denmark, Ireland, the Kingdom of Norway and the United Kingdom of Great Britain and Northern Ireland have applied to accede to the European Coal and Steel Community;

"having regard to the Opinion of the Commission;

"whereas the conditions of accession to be determined by the Council have been negotiated with the aforementioned states;

"has decided as follows:

Article 1. "(1) The Kingdom of Denmark, Ireland, the Kingdom of Norway and the United Kingdom of Great Britain and Northern Ireland may become members of the European Coal and Steel Community by acceding, under the conditions laid down in this Decision, to the Treaty establishing that Community, as amended or supplemented.

"(2) The conditions of accession and the adjustments to the Treaty establishing the European Coal and Steel Community necessitated thereby are set out in the Act annexed to this Decision. The provisions of that Act concerning the European Coal and Steel Community shall form an integral part of this Decision.

"(3) The provisions concerning the rights and obligations of the member states and the powers and jurisdiction of the institutions of the Community as set out in the Treaty referred to in paragraph 1 shall apply in respect of this Decision.

Article 2. "The instruments of accession of the Kingdom of Denmark, Ireland, the Kingdom of Norway and the United Kingdom of Great Britain and Northern Ireland to the European Coal and Steel Community will be deposited with the government of the French Republic on Jan. 1, 1973.

"Accession will take effect on Jan. 1, 1973, provided that all the instruments of accession have been deposited on that date and that all the instruments of ratification of the Treaty concerning Accession to the European Economic Community and the European Atomic Energy Community have been deposited before that date.

"If, however, the states referred to in the first paragraph of this Article have not all deposited their instruments of accession and ratification in due time, accession shall take effect for the other acceding states. . . .

"The government of the French Republic will transmit a certified copy of the instrument of accession of each acceding state to the governments of the member states and of the other acceding states.

Article 3. "This Decision, drawn up in the Danish, Dutch, English, French,

German, Irish, Italian and Norwegian languages, all eight texts being equally authentic, shall be communicated to the member states of the European Coal and Steel Community, the Kingdom of Denmark, Ireland, the Kingdom of Norway and the United Kingdom of Great Britain and Northern Ireland."

2.36 French referendum on enlargement

In a referendum held on April 23, 1972, the French people gave their approval to the enlargement of the European Communities to include the United Kingdom, Denmark, the Irish Republic and Norway. The French government's Bill authorizing ratification of the Treaty of Accession to the European Economic Community and Euratom, signed by the prospective members, was supported by 68.31 per cent of those who cast valid votes and opposed by 31.68 per cent. However, the government's success was tempered by a large number of abstentions, amounting to 39.75 per cent of the total electorate, while a further 6.99 per cent returned blank or spoiled papers.

President Pompidou had announced the referendum at a press conference on March 16, although the official political campaign did not open until April 12.

The Gaullist UDR, their governing partners the Independent Republicans, and the centre parties and Radical Party, took up position in support of a "Yes" vote, whereas the Communist Party recommended a "No" vote and the Socialist Party and Unified Socialist Party proposed a "justified abstention".

Of the six original members of the Communities, France was the only one to have decided on a referendum as the means of ratifying the Treaty of Accession, the other five relying on normal parliamentary procedure. Of the four applicant countries, Denmark, Ireland and Norway had all decided to hold referendums, planned for Oct. 2, May 10 and Sept. 24–25 respectively, although the Norwegian vote would be consultative only.

2.37 Appointment of Britain's two members of the European Commission

Sir Christopher Soames (52), British Ambassador in Paris, and George Thomson (51), who held many ministerial posts in the 1964–70 Labour government, were appointed by Heath on Oct. 8, 1972, as Britain's two members of the Commission of the European Communities with effect from Jan. 1, 1973.

2.38 Passage of European Communities Bill in UK Parliament (February–October 1972)

The European Communities Bill, providing for the United Kingdom's entry into the European Communities from Jan. 1, 1973, was presented to Parliament on Jan. 26, 1972, and given its second reading in the Commons on Feb. 17. After a prolonged committee stage on the floor of the Commons, it received its third reading on July 13, and eventually became law on Oct. 17. Although debated exhaustively and at great length by the House of Commons, where there were nearly 100 divisions on the legislation, and subsequently by the House of Lords, the Bill emerged from its parliamentary passage without any amendments, its provisions remaining exactly as they had been when originally published.

The second reading in the Commons on Feb. 17 came at the end of a three-day debate, largely recapitulating on the October 1971 "Great Debate" [see 2.31]; the vote was 309 in favour (Conservatives and five Liberals) and 301 against (279 Labour, 15 Conservatives, one Liberal—Emlyn Hooson—and six others). Harold Wilson said on Feb. 18 that the vote "made it clear that the Prime Minister has no shred of authority for pursuing his European policy" and that he should seek a fresh mandate at a general election.

The committee stage was to have begun on Feb. 29, but was temporarily held up to enable the House to debate an Opposition motion of censure on Sir Robert Grant-Ferris, Chairman of Ways and Means (Deputy Speaker), in protest at his ruling that numerous amendments which had been put down to Clause 1 of the Bill were out of order. The censure motion was debated on March 1 and rejected by 309 votes to 274—a government majority of 35. The committee stage proper begain in the House later the same evening (March 1). On March 6 Peter Shore (Labour) moved an Opposition motion condemning the government for framing the European Communities Bill "with the intention of removing the possibility of substantial amendment" and saying that this was "a gross breach of faith in the light of undertakings previously given that the Bill and the Treaties could be freely discussed". This motion was debated the same day and rejected by 317 votes to 270, and on March 7 the House went on to the second day of the committee stage, which was not completed until the first week of July.

On April 18, when Clause 1 of the Bill (defining "the Treaties") was still under discussion, divisions took place on two important amendments moved by Labour and Conservative opponents of Britain's entry into the Communities. The first, in the name of three members of the Opposition front bench (Michael Foot, Peter Shore and Fred Peart), asked that the Bill, if enacted, should not come into force "until a general election has first been held and the express consent of the British people (to entry into the EC) thereby obtained"; it was defeated by 301 votes to 272. The second amendment, sponsored by six Conservative back-bench anti-marketeers, concurred with the view expressed in the Opposition amendment and also asked that the Bill should not come into force "until a consultative advisory referendum. . . . has first been held, thereby enabling the government to assess the extent to which the Treaty of Accession has the full-hearted support of the British people". This amendment was defeated by 284 votes to 235.

The Prime Minister, Edward Heath, in reply to questions earlier the same day, had ruled out the possibility of a referendum, declaring that in the United Kingdom "we have a fully effective and representative parliamentary system for debating and deciding issues such as entry into the European Communities", and adding that the "consent of the people has already been given, through the parliamentary machine, by a majority of 112" (i.e. in the "Great Debate" of October 1971).

On April 27, by which time the Commons had spent 88 hours (10 days) on the committee stage and were still only on Clause 2, Robert Carr (who had succeeded William Whitelaw as Leader of the House) announced the government's intention to introduce a timetable—the "guillotine" procedure—for the rest of the committee stage; specifically, a total of 12 more days in committee, bringing the total time for the committee stage to 170 hours (or 22 days) on the assumption that the House rose at 11 pm every night. The motion for the "guillotine" was approved on May 2 by 304 votes to 293, a government majority of 11.

Clause 2 was finally passed on June 14 by 296 votes to 288—a government majority of eight. This clause, the heart of the Bill, gave the force of law in the UK to present and future Community law, without further enactment in the UK. It provided for payments to and receipts from the Communities, and for Orders in Council or regulations to be made to implement obligations or exercise rights under the Treaties. This clause was described by Peter Shore (Labour) as the most serious attack on the power of Parliament, on British democracy and on the freedom of action of any British government, involving a transfer of sovereignty to the non-elected institutions of the Communities.

After 21 days in committee and 92 divisions, with government majorities varying between four and 54, the Commons on July 4 completed its consideration of the Bill's 12 clauses, the last of which was adopted on that date by 217 votes to 206—a government majority of 11. Subsequent to the adoption of Clause 2, the government's majority had fallen to five votes on June 22 on Clause 6 (imposing the common agricultural policy) and to eight votes on June 27 on Clause 7 (making arrangements for the financing of the Sugar Board when Britain entered the Communities).

The committee stage was finally completed on July 5, after 96 divisions (the last on a new clause, moved by the Opposition, on the form of procedure to be adopted in passing Orders in Council and statutory instruments). As the Bill had gone through without any amendment, no report stage was necessary and it proceeded directly to its third reading in the Commons. This was given on July 13 by 301 votes to 284—a government majority of 17.

In the House of Lords—where, as in the Commons, the Bill went through all its stages without amendment—the Bill was given a second reading on July 26, after a two-day debate, by 189 votes to 19, a goverment majority of 170; the official Opposition did not vote against the Bill because it had already been passed by the Commons. The committee stage in the Lords was completed on Aug. 10, having occupied four days during which there were 17 divisions, with government majorities ranging from 66 to 126 votes. Two days, Sept. 12–13, were allotted for the report stage in the Lords (unlike the Commons, a report stage is possible in the Upper House even if no amendments have been made during the committee stage), and on Sept. 20 Parliamentary action on the Bill was completed when the House of Lords gave it a third reading by 161 votes to 21—a government majority of 140.

2.39 Ratification of Treaty of Accession by other signatories

Among the existing members, ratification of the treaty was approved in Belgium by the Senate on June 30, 1972, and by the Chamber of Deputies on Dec. 8; in West Germany by the *Bundestag* on June 21 and by the *Bundesrat* on July 7; in Italy by the Chamber of Deputies on Dec. 5 and by the Senate on Dec. 19; in Luxembourg by the Parliament on Dec. 20; and in the Netherlands by the Second Chamber of the States-General on Sept. 14 and by the First Chamber on Nov. 14. In France, President Pompidou was authorized to ratify the treaty in a law of May 3, which followed the referendum held on April 23.

In Denmark, Royal Assent to the ratification was given by Queen Margrethe on Oct. 11, following the referendum approving Danish membership, while in Ireland the Third Amendment to the Constitution Bill was approved in a referendum on May 10 and subsequently signed by President de Valera on June 8.

2.40 First summit conference of the Six and the heads of state or government of the three acceding countries

The future policies of the enlarged Communities were discussed in Paris on Oct. 19–20, 1972, at a summit conference of the Nine (the Norwegian government having decided, following the negative vote in the consultative referendum on Sept. 24–25, not to ratify the Treaty of Accession—see 5.10). The conference discussed in particular the questions of monetary union and regional and social policy: coverage of the institutional implications of the enlargement of the Communities is given in appendix 1.

2.41 Enlargement of the Communities to nine members as from Jan. 1, 1973—Adoption of agricultural policy from Feb. 1

The United Kingdom, the Republic of Ireland and Denmark became members of the European Communities on Jan. 1, 1973, in accordance with the provisions of the Treaty of Accession.

The UK (and Denmark and Ireland) formally adopted the common agricultural policy on Feb. 1, 1973, on the basis of an agreement reached in Brussels on Jan. 24. The five-year transitional period for the implementation of the CAP thus began on Feb. 1.

3: IRELAND: APPLICATION AND ACCESSION

3.1 Chronology of events

July 31, 1961	Initial request for membership of EEC
Nov. 29, 1961	UK White Paper on special UK relations with Ireland
Oct. 23, 1962	EEC Council of Ministers approves proposal for negotiations put forward by Ireland
Jan. 7, 1963	Initial application for membership of ECSC and of Euratom
Jan. 29, 1963	Breakdown of Community negotiations with Britain following de Gaulle's press conference on Jan. 14 and before opening of formal negotiations with Ireland
Jan. 13, 1964	Couve de Murville–Lemass talks in Dublin, joint statement on Franco-Irish relations
Dec. 14, 1965	UK–Irish Free Trade Agreement signed
Jan. 7, 1966	*Dáil* approves UK–Irish Free Trade Agreement
Jan. 24, 1966	Lemass statement that UK–Irish Free Trade Agreement would not affect Irish application to EEC
May 11, 1967	Presentation of formal reapplication for membership of EEC, ECSC and of Euratom
Sept. 29, 1967	EC Commission Opinion on enlargement
Nov. 2–4, 1967	Lynch–de Gaulle talks in Paris support Irish membership
Dec. 19, 1967	Renewed French emphasis on obstacles to British entry to EC
Dec. 1–2, 1969	Hague summit urging restart of negotiations
June 30, 1970	Negotiations open
Jan. 22, 1972	Signature of Treaty of Accession
May 10, 1972	Referendum decision in favour of accession
June 8, 1972	Presidential ratification of Accession Treaty
Jan. 1, 1973	Irish accession to European Communities

3.2 Initial application (1961–63)

The Irish application and eventual accession to the European Communities was particularly closely related to that of the United Kingdom. Defence was also a key issue, since Ireland was the only country which was not a member of NATO to join the EC and the possibility of Community co-operation on defence questions was seen as a potential threat to the country's neutrality.

During the 1950s, Ireland did not participate in European multilateral trading agreements, relying instead on special agreements with Britain. Nevertheless, Sean Lemass, the *Taoiseach* (Prime Minister), announced in the *Dáil Éireann* (lower house of parliament) on Aug. 1, 1961, that his government had formally served notice the previous day that the Irish Republic was applying for full membership of the EEC, the text of the application being published on Aug. 3. (A first application for membership of the ECSC and Euratom was not made until Jan. 7, 1963.) A statement to the EEC Council of Ministers outlining the Irish government's reasons for applying and describing the state of the Irish economy was made by Lemass on Jan. 18, 1962.

Earlier, after a meeting between Edward Heath, representing the UK government, and representatives of the EEC governments, held on Oct. 10, 1961, a communiqué was released as a UK government White Paper on Nov. 29 [see also 1.7]. It included the following statement: "There is one other European country I should like to mention, namely, the Irish Republic. We have special trading arrangements with the Irish, deriving from the days when they were part of the United Kingdom. I do not think it necessary to describe these in detail. I will limit myself to saying that we in the UK were pleased to see that the Republic had applied for membership of the Community. If their application succeeds—as we hope it will—our trading arrangement with them will be subsumed in the wider arrangements of the enlarged Community, and no special problems need arise."

Discussions continued throughout 1962 and the EEC Council of Ministers on Oct. 23, 1962, gave its assent to the proposal for negotiations made by the Irish Republic.

3.3 Irish–French discussions (1964)

Although the Irish application to the EEC (together with those of Denmark and Norway) lapsed with the breakdown of Britain's negotiations in January 1963, Ireland retained good relations with the EEC governments and, in particular, with France.

The French Foreign Minister, Maurice Couve de Murville, paid an official visit to the Irish Republic on June 11–12, 1964, during which he was received by President Eamon de Valera and had talks with Lemass and the Foreign Minister, Frank Aiken. A joint communiqué (June 13) said that:

(1) The two Foreign Ministers had noted "with satisfaction that no difficulties exist in Franco-Irish relations, which are characterized by a friendship deeply rooted in history and by a mutual and profound sympathy between the two peoples";

(2) "Close cultural relations . . . founded on a community of civilization" traditionally existed between the two countries, and it was desirable to "develop cultural exchanges", to "increase the number of [exchange] scholarship holders and students, which had already been growing for several years", and to develop the teaching of French in Irish schools. The ministers had agreed to begin preparing a cultural agreement;

(3) Economic relations between the two countries had been "closely reviewed", the ministers having "noted with satisfaction that trade had more than doubled since 1961 and that this growth was taking place in both directions". They hoped for a further increase in trade "balanced in so far as may be possible in the mutual interest of both countries", and trade talks would open in Dublin on July 6 [see below]. They had also noted increasing French participation in Irish industrial progress and recognized the value of French investment in the Irish economy.

It was understood that relations between the Irish Republic and the EEC had also been among the topics discussed. Couve de Murville referred to this aspect of the talks when reporting on his visit to the French Cabinet on June 17, 1964.

According to the communiqué issued after this Cabinet meeting, Couve de Murville said that he had "noted that the Irish government wished to find a formula for rapprochement with the EEC"; that he had "verified the Irish government's interest in developing its ties with Europe in whatever form might be possible"; and that he had "given an assurance that France was favourable to such a rapprochement and to the development and forging of links between Ireland and the Common Market".

As foreshadowed in the joint communiqué, Franco-Irish trade talks were held in Dublin on July 6–9. An official statement recorded agreement to continue the existing trade agreement, "with provision for increased import facilities in respect of certain products", and said that increased French investment in Irish industry and possible arrangements to stimulate tourist traffic between the two countries had also been discussed.

3.4 Irish–UK Free Trade Area Agreement (Dec. 14, 1965)

As regards Irish–UK relations, a Free Trade Area Agreement was signed in London on Dec. 14, 1965, by Harold Wilson and Lemass (the British and Irish Prime Ministers), providing principally for the abolition on July 1, 1966, of all the remaining British import duties on Irish goods and for the elimination in 10 equal annual stages from July 1, 1966, of Irish duties on most British exports. The Free Trade Area Agreement was approved by the *Dáil* on Jan. 7, 1966, after a four-day debate.

Lemass, moving approval of the agreement, exchanges of letters, and understandings, said that the agreement provided the Irish Republic with "a fair balance of advantages" and was intended to regulate trading arrangements with Britain until it became "absorbed in an agreement for our membership of a wider international trading group, whether EFTA or the EEC or a combination of both".

Explaining the negotiations leading to the signature of the agreement, Lemass mentioned the unsuccessful negotiations between 1956 and 1959 for the creation of a European free trade area; Ireland's decision not to participate in EFTA "because of our expectations at that time that pressures to open up the EEC to include Britain and other West European countries were likely to build up"; largely unsuccessful discussions with Britain in 1960 following the establishment of EFTA; the applications by both Britain and the Irish Republic for membership of the EEC and the breakdown of these negotiations; a meeting between Lemass and Harold Macmillan (then British Prime Minister) in 1963; and the meetings between Lemass and Wilson.

The idea of negotiating a free trade area with Britain while awaiting developments in the EEC, he went on, had first been put to the British government by Ireland; it was "not an arrangement which anybody asked or urged us to accept but one which we ourselves desired and which we proposed because we considered that it was necessary in this country's interests".

Following the breakdown of the Brussels negotiations in January 1963, the Irish government had decided to continue with the process of reducing industrial protection which they had initiated in 1962 "in anticipation of, and as part of our preparations for, our membership of the EEC". This decision had been based on three main considerations: (i) that the policy of protection had ceased to be effective in promoting industrial expansion and had been replaced by a policy of capital grants, technical assistance, and tax inducements; (ii) that protection was in some instances supporting inefficiency and high costs; and (iii) that the Irish Republic had to be made ready in all aspects of its economic organization to meet the situation with which it would be faced when membership of the EEC became possible—which it was assumed would be before 1970. It had therefore been decided to embark on this course of tariff reduction regardless of any reciprocal advantages which other countries might be willing to give to the Irish Republic.

The new agreement had to be considered against the background of the European situation as it was developing. Within 12 months (i.e. the end of 1966) all the principal countries of Western Europe would have completely removed the tariffs and other trade restrictions against one another within either EFTA or the EEC. Moreover, the Irish government assumed that within some period of time EFTA and EEC member states would come together in an enlarged free trade area or common market and had decided to make industrial reorganization plans accordingly.

The negotiation of a new trade agreement with the UK was necessarily the first step in the general reorganization of Ireland's external trading arrangements; this agreement settled the conditions under which her agricultural trade could be carried on and had to be concluded before the question of EFTA membership could even be considered.

The government intended that Ireland should join the EEC as soon as possible, and Irish industrialists had to face up to the possibility that on acquiring membership of the EEC Ireland might have to accept a more rapid rate of tariff reduction or might not be able to retain all the safeguards and escape clauses negotiated in the British agreement. It would be "fatal" to "go on without making any changes either in respect of our own protective tariffs or in our trade arrangements with Britain until membership of the EEC became possible for us or until some now unforeseeable development took place in the European trade situation". Moreover, there were "no trading conditions negotiable with the EEC which would at the same time permit the preservation of our preferential access to the British market".

In conclusion, Lemass stressed that this was "a trade agreement and nothing more". It had been entered into on Ireland's own initiative and in her own interests. There were no non-trade conditions or political implications in it, except to the extent that the Irish government saw it "facilitating our subsequent membership of the EEC on the basis of full equality of status and opportunity with other members".

Liam Cosgrave (Leader of the Opposition) moved a *Fine Gael* amendment expressing the *Dáil's* concern with the inevitable effect of the freeing of trade on employment and emigration, and deploring the fact that the agreement was "unbalanced" and that the concessions obtained were "small in the immediate future and limited and insecure thereafter".

"The *Taoiseach*, he said, had argued that the agreement was more balanced than an agreement with the EEC would have been and that it offered a longer transitional period, but the fact was that the agreement with Britain had no provisions for a stabilization fund or social fund to cater for redundant workers such as was provided in the EEC.

As regards relations with the EEC itself, Cosgrave suggested that in the same way that Austria "appeared to have succeeded in reaching some conclusion" on getting some form of association with the EEC there was "surely . . . some in-between arrangement that would have been possible for this country".

Lemass referred to the Anglo-Irish agreement and also to the Irish government's attitude towards Irish membership of the EEC in an address to the Consultative Assembly of the Council of Europe on Jan. 24, 1966.

In its Second Programme for Economic Expansion announced in the autumn of 1963 and designed to cover the seven-year period to 1970, he said, the Irish government had based its timetable of unilateral tariff reductions on the assumption that Ireland would be a member of the EEC before 1970, and two across-the-board reductions of 10 per cent each had already been made.

Ireland could not have developed links with the EEC without serious damage to her special trading relationship with Britain, and it was therefore natural that the Irish government should concentrate its efforts on improving trading relations with the UK "in a way that would be consistent with the eventual participation of both countries in an enlarged European Community". The conclusion of the Anglo-Irish agreement had been facilitated by the high degree of free trade already existing between the two countries and by "the energetic measures we have been taking to prepare the Irish economy for the kind of trading conditions that will be encountered when the opportunity comes to join in an enlarged European Community".

Apart from the immediate trading benefits which it conferred, the agreement was important for Ireland in that it marked a step closer to Europe and so helped to "dispel much of the uncertainty which in recent years has handicapped us in the taking of fundamental decisions affecting the future course of our economy". Ireland was prepared to consider other possibilities, such as seeking membership of EFTA, to enable her to participate in a wider European grouping as a further interim step towards her ultimate objective of forming part of an economically integrated Europe. Whether that objective was to be reached directly by entry into an enlarged European Community or via EFTA, "we should hope that the terms of transition would correspond to those of our free-trade arrangements with Britain". These terms were designed to "afford us a reasonable opportunity of effecting, without undue disturbance to our economy, the change-over to free-trading conditions" and thus to "prepare ourselves for participation in a single European market".

At a press conference before his address on Jan. 24, Lemass said that as EFTA did not deal with agriculture it had not so far been considered to Ireland's advantage to become a member. The advantages had been enhanced, however, and the disadvantages diminished, now that the position of Irish agriculture had been established in the agreement with Britain. If the EEC resolved its difficulties and if the EEC and EFTA appeared likely to draw together, membership of EFTA would become important to Ireland, while if the position in Europe did not change then the Irish government would have to consider taking some action in regard to EFTA in the course of the next year or two.

3.5 Reapplication (1967)
The Irish Republic's formal requests for the reactivation of its applications for membership of the EEC, the ECSC, and Euratom, were presented in Brussels on May 11, 1967, the same day as the handing over of Britain's applications, by the Irish Ambassador to the EEC, Sean Morrisey.

Prime Minister Jack Lynch told the *Dáil* on May 11 that the request to the EEC asked the Council of Ministers to fix an early date for the opening of negotiations on the original Irish application for membership of Aug. 3, 1961, consideration of which had been suspended after the breakdown of the previous British negotiations in January 1963, in accordance with the Council's decision of Oct. 23, 1962, to do so on a date to be mutually agreed. The government, Lynch continued, had informed the chairman of the Council of Ministers that it wished negotiations on its application to be conducted, as far as possible, concurrently with those of Britain, and that arrangements should be made for the views of both countries to be fully considered on all matters concerning Anglo-Irish trade.

Prior to the steps taken in Brussels, Lynch had visited London on May 1 for talks on British and Irish entry with Wilson and the then Commonwealth Secretary, Herbert Bowden, which were described in a communiqué as a continuation of those held in London in December 1966. (The latter talks, which took place on Dec. 19, 1966, between Lynch and Wilson and the Foreign Secretary, George Brown, had been concerned both with Britain's possible entry into the Community and the fall in Irish exports of cattle to the UK.)

Lynch, accompanied by Charles Haughey (Minister for Finance), made a tour of EC capitals during June and July, 1967, and in talks with the relevant governments and also with the European Commission in Brussels they were given full support for the Irish application. The two ministers' visits took them to the following capitals: The Hague (June 21), Bonn (June 27), Rome (July 21), Brussels (July 26–27) and Luxembourg (July 28).

After a debate in the *Dáil* on July 25–26, 1967, a government motion, moved by Lynch, approving the decision to reapply for membership of the EC was carried without a division. An amendment by Brendan Corish, leader of the Labour Party, seeking to delay a decision until the government had disclosed the full implications of membership on national sovereignty, trade, employment, industry, and agriculture, and the political terms of the agreement to be negotiated, was defeated by 68 votes to 18, with *Fine Gael* abstaining. A *Fine Gael* amendment, moved by Cosgrave (Leader of the Opposition), "deploring" the failure of the government to take more realistic preparatory steps towards membership, was defeated by 68 votes to 40.

3.6 Franco-Irish talks (November 1967)

Due to the close relations between Ireland and Britain, and in line with the Opinion on enlargement of the EC Commission of Sept. 29, 1967 [see 2.12], discussions about the Irish application for membership of the EC followed closely those of the British application. However, the main problem for the Irish application was the French attitude to British membership [see 2.13].

Prime Minister Lynch, accompanied by Haughey, visited Paris on Nov. 2–4, 1967, for talks with de Gaulle about Ireland's application for membership of the European Communities, and to sign a cultural agreement between Ireland and France which had been negotiated earlier in the year. During his visit, which was the last of a series to EC capitals, Lynch also had discussions with Georges Pompidou, the French Prime Minister.

At a luncheon in the Elysée Palace in honour of Lynch on Nov. 3 President de Gaulle declared: "We are now faced with an essential task, the construction of Europe. In order for this Europe to be European, it must require the existence of the Community of six continental states, and it is of capital importance that this Community should reinforce and develop itself. It must also involve association with the Community of other West European states. Finally, it must admit of détente, entente, and co-operation with the states of the centre and the east of our continent. Everything indicates that Ireland can and must be associated with the accomplishment of this great task."

After his talks with the President, Lynch told a press conference on Nov. 3 that he was convinced that the French government had no objection in principle to British membership of the European Communities. The difficulties concerning British entry, particularly those affecting the position of sterling and the balance of payments, had been discussed in a broad context, and, although the President had not mentioned a specific date for the opening of negotiations, he had indicated that the French government expected them to begin at some stage. Lynch added that there had been no suggestion during the talks that Ireland should consider negotiating for membership without Britain.

Reporting to the *Dáil* on his visit on Nov. 7, Lynch said that President de Gaulle and his ministers had assured him that there was no objection in principle to Ireland's membership of the European Communities, and that they looked forward to the day when it would be possible. In mentioning the difficulties presented by the British application for membership, the President had referred to the suggestion he had previously made in public on more than one occasion that Britain might accept some form of association with the EC. He inquired, added Lynch, whether Ireland had given any thought to a similar approach in its case.

"I explained," Lynch continued, "why Ireland's application was for membership and the importance for Ireland of simultaneous accession with Britain. The President stated that, in the event of progress not being possible for a considerable time on the British application for membership, it might be helpful for us to have an interim arrangement with the Communities pending full membership. I expressed appreciation of his offer of support and good will in this connexion, but emphasized that our application, which is at present before the Council of Ministers, is for full membership and that we hope for an early favourable response to this."

Lynch added that his discussions with the governments of the Six and with the European Commission in Brussels had resulted in a greater understanding of Ireland's position and had advanced her candidature for membership of the Communities. It was now clear that all six governments and the Commission had no objection in principle to Ireland's application, which presented them with no major problems. Furthermore, they all accepted the importance for Ireland of simultaneous membership with Britain.

Despite the traditional positive aspects of Franco-Irish relations, the Irish application to the EC was held up by the French opposition to British membership during 1968, and was only revived after the election of President Pompidou in June 1969.

3.7 Reopening of negotiations (June 30, 1970)
Negotiations on the Irish application for full membership of the European Communities were opened on June 30, 1970, in Luxembourg along with those for the other three applicant countries. These developments followed the Communities' agreement at the summit meeting of their members' heads of state and government in The Hague on Dec. 1–2, 1969, on the principle of enlargement to include other countries [see 2.21].

The Irish government's assessment of the political and economic case for membership of the Communities, and of the likely effects of such membership, was set out in a White Paper published in Dublin on April 20, 1970.

At present, the White Paper said, the Communities were still at an early stage in their political evolution, and members were bound only by the terms of the Treaty of Rome which imposed no specific obligations in the political field. Membership would afford Ireland an opportunity of participating fully in the movement towards European unity and would give her a voice in the shaping of the political development of the Communities, as in other aspects of their activities. The scope of the Treaties of Rome and Paris (the latter establishing the ECSC) was wider than other treaties and agreements such as those creating the United Nations and the General Agreement on Tariffs and Trade to which Ireland was a party, and they involved a range of limitations on the freedom of action of member states of the European Communities. Accession would accordingly necessitate an amendment of the Constitution. It was,

furthermore, recognized that as the Communities evolved towards their political
objectives those participating must be prepared to assist, if necessary, in the defence of
Europe.

On the economic effects, the White Paper admitted that there would inevitably be
problems in the short term, but estimated that in the long run they would be
significantly outweighed by gains from membership. Moreover, access to the enlarged
Communities would greatly enhance the attractions of Ireland as a base for new
foreign industrial investment. Ireland's system of grants for encouraging industrial
development would, it was considered, be consistent with the objectives of the Treaty
of Rome, although they would come under review in the Communities. In general,
membership would provide conditions more favourable to the development of the
Irish economy than would be obtainable outside.

As regards agriculture, membership would provide improved outlets at re-
munerative prices for most of Ireland's production. Areas most likely to benefit were
cattle and beef, milk and dairy products, and sheep and lambs; producers of pigs,
poultry and eggs would have to meet higher feed costs, but these effects could be offset
by more efficient production; cereals might show a swing from wheat to coarse grains,
with perhaps no significant overall change in acreage; production of sugar beet and
potatoes might show little alteration; but horticulture would be likely to encounter
difficulties due to increased competition from the Communities. Overall, the volume
of gross agricultural output by the later part of the 1970s could be of the order of 30–40
per cent above the present level.

Other aspects where membership might have direct effects included the adoption of
a value added tax system; the co-ordination of Irish economic and monetary policies
with those of other member states; and the implementation of equal pay for women.
In connexion with the last-named factor, the cost in the private sector could not be
readily estimated; in the public sector, however, the abolition of sex-differentiation
would cost £1,250,000 a year, while the abolition of marriage-differentiated scales and
the adjustment of scales for grades employing only women could bring the total cost to
over £9,000,000 a year. The requirement of free movement of workers was not likely
to have any significant effect on the Irish labour market.

In overall terms, the higher prices for agricultural products could result in a rise of
11–16 per cent in food prices which, after adjustments of consumption patterns, might
mean an increase of 3–4½ per cent in the consumer price index spread over the whole
of the transitional period. On the question of costs, the White Paper estimated that
Ireland's contribution to the running of the Communities could be of the order of
£19,000,000 a year as from the end of the transitional period but might well be less. At
the same time, membership would give rise to a saving of at least £36,000,000 a year in
Exchequer support to agriculture.

The position of the Irish government and its particular concerns regarding
the negotiations were explained by Dr Patrick Hillery, the Minister for
External Affairs, at the formal opening of negotiations in Luxembourg on
June 30, 1970.

The Minister reaffirmed that his government accepted the aims of the Communities
as set out in the Treaties of Rome and Paris and the decisions taken to implement
them, and recalled the position taken both in 1961 when Ireland first applied for
membership of the EEC and again in 1967, when she formally requested the
reactivation of her application. The government accepted that the political objectives
gave the Communities their "meaning and purport", and was closely following the
deliberations of the member states on political unification. Furthermore, it also
expressed its willingness to participate in the development of economic and monetary
union and to accept the Treaties' economic obligations.

Turning to the problems of agriculture, Dr Hillery said that Ireland accepted the objectives of the common agricultural policy and considered that participation should afford a secure basis for the balanced development of her agriculture and should not present any major difficulty. Certain aspects would need to be discussed, however, including the EEC's regulations relating to animal and plant health and future arrangements for fisheries.

As regards industry, the Minister pointed out that in the period from 1960 to 1969 the volume of industrial production had increased by about 100 per cent, equivalent to 7 per cent per annum, while over the same period the volume of industrial exports had increased threefold and in 1969 represented over half of total merchandise exports. In view of the increasing capacity of Irish industry as a whole to meet the competitive challenges involved, it was felt that in the longer term the structure and efficiency of Irish industry generally would be strengthened. Particular points which would have to be considered included certain sensitive industries, financial and fiscal incentives for the expansion of industry, and the problem of "dumping".

One of the most important elements in negotiations over transitional arrangements was Ireland's trading relationship with the United Kingdom, which was the market for over 70 per cent of total Irish exports and was the supplier of over 50 per cent of her imports. The 1965 Anglo-Irish Free Trade Area Agreement [see 3.4] included provision for the progressive application of free-trade treatment by Ireland to British industrial goods over a nine-year period to mid-1975, and because of its importance to the Irish economy it was "essential that agricultural and industrial trade between Ireland and the UK during the transitional period should continue with the least possible disturbance".

In respect finally of procedural arrangements, Hillery emphasized his government's concern not only that procedures should be settled before substantive negotiations took place but also that all four applicant countries should be parties to any discussions undertaken for this purpose. The procedures should provide for a reasonable degree of parallelism in the negotiations with each applicant country, and simultaneous accession to the Communities by the applicants was "of course essential".

Furthermore, the procedures should permit the participation of each applicant country in negotiations on all matters affecting its interests, so that decisions were not taken without reference at all stages to the other applicant countries directly involved —e.g. in respect of negotiations with the UK on certain matters in the agricultural sector which were of vital interest to Ireland. (This question of following closely the course of discussions with both the UK and other applicants in matters of concern to Ireland, and of having Irish views taken into account before decisions were reached, had also been stressed by Lynch, the Prime Minister, in the application presented to the EEC on May 11, 1967.)

3.8 Negotiations (1970–71)

Negotiations on the Irish application proceeded roughly in parallel with those with the UK. Unlike Britain, however, Ireland and the other two applicant countries were generally prepared from the start to accept equal transitional periods for agriculture and industry, but were concerned that the EC's new fisheries policy—which came into force on Feb. 1, 1971, and would open members' territorial waters to the fleets of other members after five years — should not be applied to the detriment of their own fishing industries. The Communities, for their part, proposed to all the four applicants the same timetable for the alignment of industrial tariffs over a period of four and a half years from the beginning of the transition period and for the introduction of the common external tariff.

A further common concern of the three smaller applicant countries was that they should be brought into consultations over matters which affected more than one applicant at an early stage of negotiations, and that in any case there should be a full exchange of information; this concern reflected largely the fear that terms of membership might be settled bilaterally between the Communities and the United Kingdom, and that there might then be little possibility of the other countries' interests being taken into account.

In all, ten ministerial–level negotiating sessions were held between Ireland and the European Communities. Initial sessions after that which took place on June 30, 1970, were held on Sept. 21–22, Dec. 15 and March 2, 1971, while subsequent key sessions took place on June 7 and Dec. 12, 1971.

Prior to the settlement of several of the major items in the negotiations for membership, Dr Hillery stated in a speech in County Kerry on May 22, 1971, that "theoretical talk about so-called alternatives to membership must now be regarded as *passé*". Referring to those who said that they had fears concerning entry into the Communities, Dr Hillery said: "I think this country has had its fill of fear and pessimism. It is high time that we eliminated the last vestiges of that national inferiority complex which history has imposed on us. We are an adult nation capable of taking care of ourselves in the world outside".

Dr Hillery added that the negotiations were now set on a steady course to successful conclusion and that this had been more than confirmed by the recent meeting between President Pompidou and Edward Heath [see 2.28]. "I would strongly urge everyone in this country," he declared, "those in industry and farming, employers, management and labour, and the public generally, to come firmly to grips with the reality that, in 18 months' time, Ireland will be a member of the European Communities."

Details are given below of the main topics discussed during the negotiating sessions, in elaboration of the general items outlined in the April 1970 White Paper and by Dr Hillery on June 30, 1970 [see 3.7].

Transition period. Although ideally the Irish government would have preferred a longer transition period for industry than for agriculture—the opposite of the UK standpoint—it proposed to the Communities that the period of transition should be the same in both sectors, and in November it announced acceptance in principle of a five-year period. At the December 1970 meeting Dr Hillery also stated that the five-year period should apply to such matters as the free movement of capital and labour and equal pay.

The timetable suggested by the Irish Republic at a meeting of deputies on Jan. 19, 1971, was, as regards Ireland's tariffs on EC industrial goods, a progressive elimination over the period from April 1, 1973, to Jan. 1, 1978, with the common external tariff being implemented at the same rate except that the first two stages would be combined into a single reduction on Jan. 1, 1974. The Communities' proposals, on the other hand, were in each case the same as those put to the UK. In the agricultural sector, the Irish government proposed a progressive five-stage elimination of the differences between Irish and EC prices, with a final alignment in 1977. For goods covered by the Anglo-Irish Free Trade Area Agreement the abolition of tariffs between the two countries should take place as planned on July 1, 1975.

Ireland made no request similar to that of the UK that the five-year transitional period for tariff alignment should be followed by a further period of three years during which the Communities' financial arrangements should be finally applied in stages.

Industrial and agricultural transition provisions. At a meeting in Brussels on April 27, 1971, the Irish delegation accepted the proposals of the six existing members with regard to the transitional arrangements, which would extend through five stages over 4½ years for agricultural products and over five years for industrial products. At the same time Ireland accepted Community proposals for adjustment of Irish tariffs to the common external tariff of the EC in five stages spread over five years.

This acceptance was confirmed at the full ministerial negotiating meeting on June 7, 1971.

Special treatment. Ireland was reported initially to have requested that the jute and motor assembly industries should receive special tariff treatment after the five-year transitional period, but later to have withdrawn the request in respect of jute. The Republic also asked to be allowed to retain tariff quotas for an unspecified number of years for plywood, wood pulp, newsprint, raw aluminium and wattle tanning extracts.

Fisheries. Special concern was expressed by Ireland at the possible effect on her inshore fishing industry of the new Community fisheries policy which, the government feared, might lead to over-exploitation of Ireland's fish resources. It was pointed out that Ireland herself possessed no deep-sea fishing fleet.

In the final fisheries agreement reached on Dec. 12, 1971, Irish coastal waters within a 12-mile limit for the stretch of the west and south coasts from Lough Foyle in the north to Cork in the south were exempted from immediate free access by other Community member countries during the transition period. In addition, the Irish east coast from Carlingford Lough to Carnsore Point was protected for crustaceans and molluscs only.

Agricultural finance. At the meeting on June 7, 1971, the Irish delegation also received satisfactory assurances on immediate access to Community funds for agricultural finance, calculated to represent a saving of £30,000,000 in export subsidies which would be recovered from the EEC's Agricultural Fund.

Anti-dumping measures. It was also agreed on June 7 that the new member states would be able to take measures at national level during the transitional period against the dumping of imports from third countries, while Community negotiators further declared themselves willing to include in the Accession Treaty a clause enabling Ireland to protect itself against dumping by member states. It was decided that Ireland would be empowered to take protective measures at national level during the transitional period in cases of great urgency, although these measures would have to be submitted to the Commission for subsequent review.

Community finance. Agreement on Irish contributions to the Community budget was reached at a ministerial meeting in Brussels on June 29, 1971, which foresaw an eventual Irish contribution of 0.6 per cent of the total budget, corresponding to the Irish share of the gross national product of the Community of 10 nations. It was calculated that Ireland would pay approximately £4,000,000 in the first year of membership—a figure equal to 45 per cent of the maximum Irish contribution, while by 1978 she would pay her full 100 per cent share, representing a figure of approximately £9,000,000.

Industrial development. Following a meeting in Brussels on July 12, 1971, when the Irish delegation was granted an extension for protection in respect of imported motor cars up to 1985, further progress was made in Luxembourg on Oct. 18 with agreement on an industrial development protocol to be appended to the treaty.

This protocol noted that Ireland was in need of a policy of industrialization and economic development and would benefit from all Community procedures and resources to this end, as well as recognizing that any schemes offered by Ireland would receive sympathetic consideration. The effect of this concession was to allow firms benefiting from export tax relief procedures to continue to do so for the life of the agreements concerned. The relief scheme would be reviewed after membership had been achieved, but it was indicated that new schemes would be considered favourably. Dr Hillery was reported to have stated after the meeting that the agreement would permit Ireland to maintain an advantage over other areas of the enlarged Communities until after 1990.

Sugar beet. The negotiations were completed at a meeting in Brussels on Jan. 13, 1972, when final agreement was reached on the size of the sugar beet quota, for which a figure of 150,000 tonnes was decided.

3.9 Conclusion of negotiations (December 1971)—Signature of Accession Treaty (Jan. 22, 1972)

For each of the applicant countries except Norway [see 5.6] negotiations were concluded in all essentials at a ministerial session held on Dec. 12, 1971. The Accession Treaty (which comprised three documents—see 2.35) was signed by all four countries and by the existing Community member countries on Jan. 22, 1972, in Brussels.

Shortly before that date a White Paper was published in Dublin on Jan. 15, 1972, on the political and economic effects of accession.

Political implications. In a passage assessing the political implications of membership, the White Paper pointed out that while the treaties involved no political obligations it was clear that the founders of the Communities had gone beyond the purely economic, commercial and social spheres and that wider political initiatives would occur, particularly with regard to developing countries. The paper also discussed the causes and effects of the limitation on national powers inherent in the treaties, stating in this connexion: "The Treaties establishing the three European Communities are wider in scope than has been usual in international agreements. Moreover, they prescribe for the institutions of the Communities greater powers of decision than has been normal in international organizations. There are, as a consequence, corresponding limitations on the freedom of action of the member states of the Communities. It is important to bear in mind that these limitations relate only to those economic, commercial and social matters which are covered by the Treaties."

The White Paper said that membership could be regarded as a pooling or sharing of sovereignty by the member states in a Community context rather than as a "loss" of sovereignty by the individual member state. "One of the major problems facing small countries such as Ireland is how to exercise their national sovereignty as fully as possible in today's highly complex and interdependent world. For these countries, indeed for most countries other than the major powers, the real freedom, as distinct from the national right, to take national action and pursue policies in the economic and trading sectors is circumscribed to a very great extent by the complex nature of international economic and trading relationships."

Special arrangements. The White Paper noted certain special arrangements made during the negotiations which would have a special significance for industry. These were: (i) the transitional periods for the gradual dismantling of Irish tariffs and of quantitative restrictions in relation to trade in industrial products with the other member states of the enlarged Communities and for the gradual alignment of duties with the common external tariff applicable to non-member countries; (ii) the special anti-dumping regime which would be annexed to the Treaty of Accession; (iii) the arrangements applicable to industrial incentives and the corresponding Protocol which would be annexed to the Treaty of Accession.

Effects of free trade. It was pointed out that the majority of Irish industry would feel the impact of free trade some time before the home market was opened to European competition, through the Anglo-Irish Free Trade Area Agreement [see 3.4] which would reach maturity in 1975.

The White Paper made an assessment of the general economic prospects and of the prospects for various sectors. Employment in manufacturing industry was expected to rise by about 50,000 net during the period from 1970 to 1978 due to the influx of new industry. During the same period the output of manufacturing industry was expected to achieve an annual growth of 8½ per cent, compared to 6½ per cent during the 1960s.

Agriculture. With reference to agriculture it was stated that beef and dairy product prices would be subject to particularly substantial increases during the transitional period. The two sectors together accounted for about 60 per cent of total agricultural output and, with the stimulus of the increasing prices, it was expected that they would account for the major part of the expansion in Irish agriculture following accession to the Communities. Some expansion of sheep and pig output was also anticipated, while the acreage under tillage was expected to remain in balance due to an increase in barley growing and some fall in wheat production.

The White Paper stated: "On the basis of prices and costs obtaining in the Communities in 1970–71, it has been projected that the volume of gross agricultural output will increase by about one-third by 1978 and, allowing for the higher EC price levels, the increase in the value of output will be over 75 per cent." The Paper predicted that the decline in agricultural employment, which had averaged about 10,000 annually during the 1960s, would fall to 7,000 annually between 1970 and 1978, when employment on the sector might be of the order of 225,000. In parallel with the reduction in the numbers leaving agriculture, it was forecast that incomes would rise. "Some farming costs will also increase but, provided that vigorous and sustained efforts are made at all levels to promote greater efficiency and productivity, it is estimated that, at 1970–71 EC prices, family farm incomes will by 1978 be twice as high as in 1970; increases in EC prices between now and 1978 mean that actual farm incomes will be considerably higher."

Economic growth. In the economy as a whole it was estimated that the annual national growth rate would average nearly 5 per cent over the eight-year period, although the rate of expansion was likely to be uneven in the early years of the transitional period when the tariff reductions under the Anglo-Irish Free Trade Area Agreement were still incomplete and when the increases in agricultural incomes had not made their full impact on the economy. Total net employment was expected to increase by 50,000 by 1978, representing an annual increase of over 6,000 compared to a little over 1,000 in the 1960s. As stated above, employment in industry would rise by 50,000 and that in services by about 60,000, but at the same time agricultural employment was expected to fall by about 60,000 over this period.

Finance. Contributions and benefits involved in participation in the European Investment Bank and in the European Coal and Steel Community were expected to result in an annual net saving to the Exchequer of the order of £25,000,000 to £30,000,000 over the period up to 1980.

Prices. The White Paper stated that it was impossible to make an estimate of the effect of membership on industrial prices, but that as agricultural prices would be controlled it was anticipated that there would be an increase of between 0.7 and 1.0 per cent in the consumer price index. As regards food prices, these would rise by between 2 and 3 per cent each year for five years.

Conclusion. In a summary of its assessment of the implications of membership the White Paper stated: "The government consider that the terms of accession which have been negotiated for Ireland are satisfactory; they will greatly facilitate the adjustment of the economy to the obligations of membership while at the same time enabling us to take effective advantage of the opportunities which membership will provide."

At the signing ceremony held on Jan. 22, 1972, Jack Lynch, the *Taoiseach*, made a speech which he began in Irish and continued in English as follows:

"We mark by our gathering here today and by the signing of the Acts of Accession of the four applicant countries to the European Communities the culmination of many months of intensive and arduous negotiations. The successful outcome of the negotiations is a gratifying measure of the political will which has clearly existed on the part of the Community and each of the applicant countries to find mutually acceptable solutions to the problems which presented themselves. The manifestation of this political will and this mutual understanding points towards a future of beneficial and constructive co-operation by our 10 countries in the enlarged Communities.

"Today is also a beginning—the beginning of a new phase in the creation of a wider and stronger Europe. The heads of state or government of the present member states at their historic meeting in The Hague in December 1969 charted the future course of the movement towards the construction of Europe. They inspired the idea of the 'triptych'—the three-fold movement for the completion of the Communities, for their internal development and strengthening, and for their enlargement. Under this inspiration major progress has been made, and the third element in this three-fold movement—the enlargement of the Communities—is now being taken a decisive step forward.

"We have set ourselves the entry date of Jan. 1, 1973. As far as we in Ireland are concerned, we now have to fulfil the necessary constitutional requirements. My government are convinced that the Irish Parliament and people share the government's conviction that the political and economic future of Ireland lies in co-operation with the other member states in the enlarged Communities and that they will decisively approve the entry of Ireland to the Communities.

"Ireland is the youngest of the states represented here today. However, we are one of the oldest nations of Europe. Geography has placed us on the periphery of the continent. But we are an integral part of Europe, bound to it by many centuries of shared civilization, traditions and ideals.

"Ireland, because of historical circumstances, did not participate in the past in all the great moments of European experience, but the Irish people have in many periods of our history been deeply involved in the life and culture of the European mainland. Since statehood, my country, conscious of its European past, has sought to forge new and stronger links with the continent. In this we were renewing and revitalizing historic bonds.

"A distinguished Irishman has written: 'My only counsel to Ireland is that to become deeply Irish she must first become European.' He also wrote over 60 years ago: 'If this generation has, for its first task, the recovery of the old Ireland, it has for its second the discovery of the new Europe.'

"Since these words were written Europe has been devastated by two world wars, and it has been the task of a later generation of Europeans to begin the construction of a new Europe based on unity and co-operation amongst its peoples. We in Ireland seek to share in this noble endeavour. We have responded to the call made by the founding fathers of the Communities to other countries of Europe who shared their ideals to join in their efforts to establish the foundations of an ever closer union among the European peoples. My government see in the European Communities the best hope and the true basis for the creation of that united and peaceful Europe.

"We recognize that the enlargement of the Communities will pose its own problems. For the present member states it will be a matter of adjusting to the workings of a Community of Ten. For the new member states there will be the challenges of integrating into a Community already established and developed.

"These will be no easy tasks but, from the record of the Community of Six since its establishment and from our successful experience together in the negotiations, we draw confidence that the difficulties of accession and transition will be overcome and that the effective and constructive working of the enlarged Community will be assured. There is, however, much to be done; the coming year will be a vital period of preparation. The consultation procedure which was agreed in the negotiations will enable the process of integration for the applicant countries to commence and to proceed.

"In this period before the Community is enlarged our countries will also look beyond the immediate problems of accession and transition. We should engage in examining together what the Community's future course should be after enlargement. For the Community of Ten cannot of its very nature, no more than the Community of Six, remain static; it will be a continuous creation; it must evolve and progress in the direction of the unity in Europe which the architects of the original Community envisaged.

"Another of the tasks which, I suggest, our 10 governments must face in the context of the enlargement of the Communities, is to examine carefully how the institutions may best be equipped for their respective roles after enlargement. I have in mind here particularly the role of the European Parliament. All recognize a government's obligation to involve the people of the nation as closely as possible in the processes of government.

"There will equally be an obligation on us jointly to bring the peoples of the enlarged Communities into closer contact and involvement with the decisions, policies and workings of the Communities. It is in this surely that there is a major role for the European Parliament. The Irish government consider it of the highest importance that the part to be played by the Parliament in the enlarged Communities should be the subject of the closest study by our governments acting together.

"The enlarged Communities, as they evolve towards that greater unification in Europe which their founders envisaged, can be a vital force for peace in the world and can make an ever-increasing contribution to the economic and social progress of the developing nations. We attach the utmost importance to the emphasis placed by the member states at the summit meeting in The Hague on the promotion of rapprochement among the peoples of the 'entire European continent'.

"Great thoughts, Mazzini said, make great peoples. Robert Schuman saw that a united Europe would be achieved not in one step but by many concrete measures. The creation of the European Communities was the first practical expression of the vision of Schuman and the other founding fathers. Their development and achievements have brought significantly nearer the realization of the goal of unity in Europe. The Communities' enlargement will bring this realization even closer.

"At our signing here today of the Act of Accession, which marks a decisive step towards the future co-operation of our 10 countries, it is surely appropriate that we should draw hope and inspiration from the achievements of the past 20 years and the vision which made them possible."

3.10 Referendum (May 10, 1972)
A referendum on constitutional changes enabling the Irish Republic to become a member of the European Communities was held on May 10, 1972, and resulted in approval of membership by a ratio of almost five votes to one in a poll in which 71 per cent of the electorate participated. The referendum was held several months after the Irish signature of the Treaty of Accession to the Communities in January and after Parliamentary approval for the constitutional changes.

Membership of the European Communities necessitated a constitutional amendment which, according to Article 46 of the Irish Constitution, "shall, upon having been passed or deemed to have been passed by both Houses of the *Oireachtas* (parliament), be submitted by referendum to the decision of the people in accordance with the law for the time being in force relating to the referendum". The Third Amendment of the Constitution Bill, 1971, was passed by the *Dáil* on Jan. 26, 1972, and by the *Seanad* (Senate, upper house of parliament) on March 8.

The wording of the amendment was as follows: "The state may become a member of the European Coal and Steel Community (established by Treaty signed at Paris on the 18th day of April, 1951), the European Economic Community (established by Treaty signed at Rome on the 25th day of March, 1957), and the European Atomic Energy Community (established by Treaty signed at Rome on the 25th day of March, 1957). No provision of this Constitution invalidates laws enacted, acts done or measures adopted by the state consequent on membership of the Communities, or prevents laws enacted, acts done or measures adopted by the Communities, or institutions thereof, from having the force of law in the state."

The political parties took up their positions on the question of membership in a debate in the *Dáil* on June 2, 1971, when the two largest parties, *Fianna Fáil* and *Fine Gael*, were in favour of entry, while the Labour Party—with 17 of the total of 144 seats—confirmed its opposition. By January 1972 the opposition to entry into Europe consisted principally of the Labour Party, a number of leading trade unions, the New Republican Unity Party, and both sections of *Sinn Féin*, the political wing of the Irish Republican Army, all of which were grouped in the Common Market Defence Campaign—launched on Jan. 22, 1972, with a rally coinciding with the signature of the Treaty of Accession in Brussels.

During a *Dáil* debate on the terms of entry on March 23, 1972, an amendment in the name of Justin Keating (Labour), deploring the inadequacy of the negotiations for membership and rejecting the terms set out in the White Paper of the preceding January, was defeated by 56 votes to 16, the *Fine Gael* deputies abstaining. A government motion that the House take note of the White Paper was then passed by 89 votes to 16, the *Fine Gael* members voting on this occasion with the government.

Brendan Corish, the leader of the Labour Party, had said during the debate that his party objected in principle to the whole concept of the EC and was not in agreement with the philosophy of free trade expressed in the Treaty of Rome. He also stated that political union as the objective of European integration involved very serious implications for Ireland which had not been explained by any member of the government. With reference to agriculture Corish said that farmers with small and medium-sized holdings, representing 70 per cent of the Irish farming community, would be encouraged to abandon farming but would have no guarantees of subsequent employment. On April 17 Corish further warned that membership of the EC would mean an overall 23 per cent rise in food prices.

At the conclusion of the debate Dr Hillery, the Minister of Foreign Affairs, announced that a referendum would be held on May 10, 1972.

In an information leaflet assessing the implications of membership of the European Communities, the Department of Foreign Affairs calculated that British and Irish membership would result in progressive integration of the economies of the two parts of Ireland, although this would not automatically lead to political reunification. On the other hand *Sinn Féin* argued that membership of the Communities could entail an acknowledgment of existing political boundaries.

Prime Minister Lynch, opening *Fianna Fáil's* referendum campaign at a meeting in Dublin on April 17, described EC entry as an opportunity to advance substantially the economic and social well-being of the people of Ireland.

Lynch told an audience of party members that the case against entry concentrated on the two issues of loss of jobs and a rise in the cost of living. He went on: "We have never denied that free trade would cause problems for some firms. For over 10 years we have used money, time and energy in making Irish firms more efficient so that they could compete with imports. . . . If we stay out we would still have to make some form of trade arrangement with Britain and the other EC members. That agreement would require industrial free trade, so that firms threatened by free trade would be no better off while the rest of us would be worse off because we would lose the benefits of membership."

Referring to the cost of living, Lynch said that the Opposition was presenting a "wildly exaggerated picture" of the effect of membership on food prices in an attempt to "frighten people into blind opposition to the EC". In each year of the five-year transitional period, Lynch said, higher prices for farmers would mean an increase of "2p to 3p for each pound we spend on food"; he commented that since other prices would not be affected "the change in the overall cost of living during the transitional period will be much smaller than a penny in the pound each year".

The Prime Minister told the meeting that opposition to EC membership, which claimed to be based on economic grounds, was really of a political nature "concerned chiefly with sovereignty and the political future of the Communities". He discounted claims that membership would perpetuate divisions in Ireland, arguing on the contrary that to stay outside the EC would confer on the border "the status of a frontier, both economic and political, between ourselves and the rest of Europe".

The Irish Congress of Trade Unions forecast on April 20 that there would be an "economic catastrophe" if the country voted in favour of membership on May 10, and claimed that the direct result would be the loss of up to 35,000 jobs. However, the 350,000 members of the Congress were reported to be divided on the EC issue.

In a statement to the *Dáil* on April 18, Dr Hillery gave a further account of the reasons for the application to join the Communities, describing it as "one of our most important single foreign policy decisions, certainly since the last war, and perhaps since the founding of the state".

Dr Hillery emphasized that the choice did not lie between joining or retaining the status quo. "Our choice", he said, "must be between joining or putting in jeopardy the special trading relationship we have with Britain—the market for some 70 per cent of our exports". The Republic, he went on, was joining Europe not only for her own interests but also because of a concern for "Community interest—that common interest which is really a form of enlightened national interest". He believed measures at Community level could bring economic and social progress ensuring a "constant improvement in the living and working conditions of our peoples".

Dr Hillery declared that those concerned with the building of the European Communities had not been wholly concerned with their own interests, and added: "The Community is a curious mixture of bargaining and negotiation about prices and quotas, on the one hand, and efforts to build common institutions and to lay the groundwork for a closer unity in Europe on the other. Underlying all these activities, however, is a strong current of a more idealistic kind—a determination to promote certain common values; a strong will to ensure that Western Europe, which has so much in common and so much of worth in its culture, will never tear itself apart again in internal hostilities. A strong motive of its founders was to promote these more idealistic concerns by knitting the member states of the Community together in a multitude of ways affecting their direct as well as their common interests. It would be a mistake to concentrate so much on each of these individual 'stitches' that we do not see the larger pattern which they are slowly forming."

Shortly before the referendum the government announced a revised regional development policy designed to derive maximum benefit from the aid available for such development within the Communities. The Industrial Development Authority proposed the creation of 55,000 new jobs in the period from 1973 to 1977, which, taking into account redundancies, would result in a net increase of 38,000 jobs.

The ballot paper for the referendum asked the question: "Do you approve of the proposal to amend the Constitution contained in the undermentioned Bill?" and cited the Third Amendment to the Constitution Bill, 1971. Under Article 47 of the Constitution the proposal for the amendment would be regarded as approved if a simple majority of the people voted in favour of its enactment into law. Enactment would then require the signature of the Bill by the President of the Republic.

Polling took place on May 10, and the results announced the following day showed that 1,041,880 voters had voted in favour of membership compared with 211,888 against, a total of votes representing 71 per cent of the electorate. Of the total poll the "Yes" votes accounted for 83 per cent and the "No" votes for 17 per cent, while spoiled votes accounted for less than 1 per cent of the total. In terms of the entire electorate the "Yes" votes accounted for more than 58 per cent and the "No" votes for 12 per cent.

There was a clear "Yes" majority of over 70 per cent in each of the 42 constituencies, reaching as much as 92 per cent in Donegal North-East and 90 per cent in Galway North-East, and the lowest being 73 per cent in Dublin South-West. However, Inishbofin and Owey Island, both off the Donegal coast, voted "No". The lowest poll was recorded in Galway West, at 62 per cent, and the highest in Mid-Cork, at 77 per cent. The total poll was almost 6 per cent lower than in the 1969 general election but was 5 per cent higher than in the previous referendum in 1968 and almost 13 per cent higher than in the 1959 referendum, which had coincided with a presidential election.

Lynch welcomed the result, stating: "This is a great victory for the Irish nation. Such a massively favourable vote is a great tribute to our people's innately sound judgment." He added: "This emphatic vote of the Irish people emphasizes their firm desire to take their place in a united Europe and to contribute to its economic, social and cultural progress."

The then President of the Commission of the European Communities, Dr Sicco Mansholt, said that the result of the Irish referendum would make a great impression on the other applicant countries still facing referendums.

3.11 Final ratification (June 8, 1972) and accession (Jan. 1, 1973)
Following the favourable result of the referendum, the Third Amendment to the Constitution Bill, 1971, was signed by President de Valera on June 8, 1972, and on Jan. 1, 1973, Ireland acceded to the European Communities along with the United Kingdom and Denmark.

The appointment of Dr Hillery, who had been Minister for Foreign Affairs since 1969, as the Irish member of the Commission had been announced on Sept. 26, 1972.

4: DENMARK: APPLICATION AND ACCESSION

4.1 Chronology of events

Jan. 4, 1960	EFTA Treaty of Stockholm signed
July 31, 1961	British and Danish announcement of intention to apply to EEC
Aug. 10, 1961	Formal application for EEC membership
Oct. 26, 1961	Negotiations begin
March 16, 1962	Formal application for ECSC and Euratom membership
Jan. 29, 1963	Breakdown of negotiations following de Gaulle's press conference on Jan. 14
Sept. 27, 1966	Government statement on possible Nordic approach to EEC
Oct. 21, 1966	Dahlgaard statement opposing Danish membership of EEC at that time
May 11, 1967	Formal reapplication for EEC, ECSC and Euratom membership
Sept. 29, 1967	Commission Opinion on enlargement
Dec. 19, 1967	Renewed French emphasis on obstacles to British entry to EC
Jan. 23, 1968	Danish elections result in formation of centre-right coalition government
Feb. 4, 1968	Draft treaty for Nordek customs union
Nov. 22, 1968	EFTA Vienna compromise agreeing separate entry of EFTA members to EC
Dec. 1–2, 1969	Hague summit urging reopening of negotiations
June 30, 1970	Negotiations reopen
Nov. 6, 1970	EFTA statement on agreements with EFTA members not applying to EC
Sept. 21, 1971	Danish elections bring Social Democrats back to power
Oct. 9, 1971	New government states intention of continuing application
Dec. 16, 1971	Danish parliament approves continuation of application
Jan. 22, 1972	Treaty of Accession signed
Oct. 2, 1972	Referendum decision in favour of membership
Oct. 11, 1972	Royal assent given to instrument of ratification
Dec. 31, 1972	Denmark leaves EFTA

Jan. 1, 1973   Danish accession to European Communities

Feb. 27, 1986   Danish referendum in favour of approving package of EC
                 reforms [see 12.14]

4.2 Background—Initial application (1960–63)
Danish foreign policy in the decades preceding accession to the European
Communities reflected the country's economic and cultural links with Britain,
Scandinavia and West Germany.

Like Britain and Ireland, Denmark first applied for membership in the
early 1960s, reapplied in 1967 and acceded on Jan. 1, 1973, becoming the only
Scandinavian member of the Communities, given that Norway, which had
also applied, decided not to proceed with accession following a referendum
showing a clear majority opposing membership of the EC.

Denmark did not take part in the formation of the EEC at the time the
Treaty of Rome was drawn up in 1957, but participated instead in the
formation of the European Free Trade Association (EFTA) and signed the
Treaty of Stockholm on Jan. 4, 1960. Nevertheless, the statement made by
Harold Macmillan, the UK Prime Minister, in April 1961 in favour of Community membership [see 1.4] was welcomed by the Danish government. At a
meeting of the NATO Council on May 9 of that year Jens Otto Krag, then
Danish Foreign Minister, expressed his government's approval of the prospective British negotiations, adding that if these were to take place Denmark
"would also want to initiate such negotiations with the EEC".

Swedish criticism of the apparent about-turn in Danish policy, away from Nordic
co-operation and the free trade area concept towards the full customs union of the
EEC, led to an understanding reached at a meeting in London in June 1961 whereby
those countries about to apply to enter the EEC agreed not to do so until terms could
be found that were acceptable to all the EFTA member countries and not just those
applying for membership.

After the Bonn Declaration of July 18, 1961 [see 1.3], in which the six EEC
governments stated that they wished to see an expansion of the role of the
Communities in developing European unity, both the Danish and UK governments announced on July 31 that they were applying for membership.

On the same day a communiqué, known as the "Geneva Declaration", was issued
by the EFTA Council following an EFTA ministerial meeting held in Geneva on July
28. This described the two applications as providing "an opportunity to find an
appropriate solution for all EFTA countries and thus to promote the solidarity and
cohesion of Europe". It also said that the EFTA member countries would "examine
with the EEC the ways and means by which all members of EFTA could take part
together in a single market embracing some 300,000,000 people".

The Danish government formally applied for full membership of the EEC
on Aug. 10, 1961, on the same day as the British government, although the
formal application for membership of the ECSC and Euratom was not made
until March 16, 1962. On Oct. 26, Krag made a statement explaining his
government's application, following which formal negotiations started on
Nov. 30, 1961.

Krag's statement was in many ways similar to that made on Oct. 10, 1961, by
Edward Heath, then UK Lord Privy Seal [see 1.7], UK accession being widely

regarded as a prerequisite for Danish accession, in particular because of the heavy, though decreasing, dependence of Denmark's chief export (agricultural products) on the UK market. Two other essential conditions were seen by Krag to be the accommodation of the other EFTA countries not applying for Community membership in any accession agreement, and the maintenance of Denmark's special relations with other Nordic countries.

During 1962 negotiations were conducted in parallel with British negotiations and six sessions were held at ministerial level. However, negotiations were broken off following meetings in December 1962 between Harold Macmillan (the UK Prime Minister) and President de Gaulle of France and President Kennedy of the United States, leading to de Gaulle's statement of January 1963 imposing an effective veto on the UK application.

The collapse of the UK negotiations was crucial to the Danish position, especially because of the agricultural question. While Krag (who had taken office as Prime Minister in September 1962) was visiting de Gaulle on Jan. 26–29, 1963, the French President reportedly offered him the possibility of Denmark alone becoming a member or an associate member of the EEC; however, after consultations with the UK government, such a solution to the issue was turned down by the Danish government.

4.3 Second application (1966–67)

The first official moves towards a renewed Danish application were made in 1966, in the context of Denmark's relations with her Scandinavian neighbours. The possibility of Denmark alone or of the three Nordic full members of EFTA (Denmark, Norway, and Sweden) together approaching the EEC with a view to joining the Community was mentioned again by Krag, in an address to the Consultative Assembly of the Council of Europe in Strasbourg on Sept. 27, 1966.

"There is," said Krag, "an intensive debate in Denmark about the question how we can help to get European co-operation on the move again. In that respect the Nordic countries might, perhaps, be able to play a part. . . . I do not think that an isolated Danish entry into the Common Market would solve Denmark's problems. Nor would it be desirable from an overall European point of view. But we must keep our minds open to any opportunity that could lead to a solution to Europe's market problems. We intend in the near future to discuss our views with Sweden during the visit by the Swedish Prime Minister [Tage Erlander] to Denmark at the beginning of October. I think that the matter should be taken up among all the Nordic countries at the coming session of the Nordic Council next February. A Nordic initiative—if it should prove possible—may have an importance of its own, also as an appeal to the United Kingdom and France to re-establish the contacts that were broken off in January 1963 and to resume the negotiations in which, among others, Denmark took part simultaneously. . . ."

The Assembly approved on Sept. 28 a resolution which, inter alia, expressed the wish for a resumption of association negotiations between the EEC and the United Kingdom and other EFTA member countries. Krag's proposals, however, were not favourably received in Norway and Sweden.

A Norwegian Foreign Ministry spokesman stated on Sept. 27, 1966, that Norway's existing application for membership of the EEC was based on a decision of parliament affirming that her membership was conditional upon Britain also joining; Gunnar Lange, the Swedish Minister of Commerce, stated in a broadcast on the same day that any new joint approach by Denmark, Norway and Sweden was "excluded at present without Great Britain"; and Erlander said in Copenhagen on Oct. 4 at the beginning of his visit to Denmark that he doubted whether the Nordic countries alone should undertake any initiative, and suggested that they should rather discuss what could be done within the framework of EFTA. Kaare Willoch, then Norwegian Minister of Commerce and Shipping, said in a speech in the *Storting* (Norwegian parliament) on Oct. 20 that the Danish initiative had come as a surprise to the Norwegian government, and that while it was natural for the Scandinavian countries to co-operate in bringing an end to the division of Western Europe into the EEC and EFTA blocs they should be careful not to weaken the links between the EFTA countries.

Tyge Dahlgaard, who had been appointed Danish Minister for Trade, Shipping, and European Market Relations on Sept. 20, 1966, stated in a radio interview on Oct. 21 that "Denmark may consider joining the Common Market alone in about a year's time if neither Britain nor Norway and Sweden are approaching the Six, but for the time being it is out of the question for Denmark to join the EEC".

The formal renewal of the Danish application for membership of the EEC was presented in Brussels on May 11, 1967, by Kaj Larsen, chargé d'affaires of the Danish mission to the European Communities. Earlier the same day, the *Folketing* (Danish parliament) had approved the government's decision (announced on May 10 by Dahlgaard) to re-apply for entry, by 150 votes to 20 (Socialist People's Party), with one abstention (Faroe Islands member). In his statement Dahlgaard had said that, apart from measures needed to protect fisheries in the Faroe Islands and Greenland, his government would not ask for any special arrangements in the negotiations.

A Danish explanatory memorandum was handed to Jean Rey, then President of the European Commission, on July 17, 1967. This stressed Denmark's willingness to assume all obligations arising from the Treaty of Rome and the ECSC Treaty and the regulations issued under them; stated that Denmark wished to participate in the further economic and political developments of the Communities; and expressed the hope that other EFTA countries would be given the opportunity to negotiate on their membership or other appropriate links with the Communities, with special emphasis on "positive solutions" for the other Nordic members.

The memorandum proposed that the duty-free customs arrangements within EFTA be maintained during the period required for the negotiations of the EFTA countries with the Communities, and expressed the wish for a short transitional period for the removal of customs duties for industrial goods. It was pointed out that Denmark's agricultural policy would be adjusted to the requirements of the Common Market before Denmark's formal adherence to the EEC so that no transitional period would be necessary for Danish agriculture, but it was suggested that Denmark should participate in the relevant negotiations between the EEC and Britain, since the incorporation of British agriculture in the Common Market would affect vital Danish interests.

The memorandum also mentioned that it would be necessary to carry on consultations on special questions such as social security provisions for foreign workers, and the sale of farmland and farms to foreign nationals. As far as Greenland and the Faroes were concerned, it was suggested that a statute might be worked out for them similar to that for the French Overseas Departments and that special attention should be paid to their fishery interests. Finally, the memorandum expressed the wish that the negotiations should be conducted and concluded simultaneously with those between Britain and the European Communities.

At a meeting held on June 26–27, 1967, the Community Council of Ministers requested the European Commission to prepare an opinion on the enlargement of the Community. The preliminary Opinion of the Commission on the application for membership of Britain, Ireland, Denmark and Norway was submitted to the Council of Ministers on Sept. 29, 1967, and published on Oct. 7, 1967.

This supported the applications, arguing that all four should be considered together and that negotiations should aim for the simultaneous entry of all the applicants. The Opinion also recognized that the three smaller countries would have fewer adjustment problems than Britain [see 2.12 for further details].

During the last four months of 1967, there was intense diplomatic activity between the four applicant countries and the six EC countries. However, during the course of five meetings of the EC Council of Ministers held in the last three months of 1967, the French established a block to the entry of Britain which continued throughout 1968.

4.4 Nordek negotiations (February 1968–April 1970)
Following the breakdown of negotiations with the European Communities in December 1967, interest in a Nordic customs union (over and above the economic co-operation already afforded through the Nordic Council and EFTA) was revived in early 1968. (In Denmark after a general election held on Jan. 23, 1968, a centre-right coalition government of Conservatives, Radical Liberals and *Venstre* Liberals led by Hilmar Baunsgaard had in February taken over from the minority Social Democratic government led by Krag.)

In 1954, soon after the creation of the Nordic Council the previous year, discussions had taken place on the possibility of forming a customs union between Denmark, Norway and Sweden (Finland at that time not yet being a member of the Council). Following further consultations, a draft treaty for the creation of a customs union covering about 80 per cent of trade between the four Scandinavian countries, including Finland, had been presented to the governments concerned in July 1957 and published on Oct. 20, 1957. By this time, however, negotiations had begun on the establishment of a European free trade area, and after the EEC and Euratom treaties had entered into force in 1958 it was agreed in 1959 to set up the European Free Trade Association between Austria, Denmark, Norway, Portugal, Sweden, Switzerland and the United Kingdom. In view of these developments the idea of a Scandinavian customs union had lapsed, although a convention on Nordic co-operation was signed in March 1962 between Denmark, Finland (associated with EFTA since June 1961), Iceland, Norway and Sweden.

In accordance with a Danish proposal agreed in February 1968 during the 16th Nordic Council meeting in Oslo, a special conference was held in Copenhagen on April 22–23 of the Prime Ministers of Denmark, Finland (Dr Mauno Koivisto), Norway (Per Borten) and Sweden (Erlander), together with their Foreign and Trade Ministers, Iceland being represented by its Minister of Commerce. A preliminary report on the economic problems of establishing Nordek was published on Jan. 14, 1969, and on Feb. 4, 1970, in Stockholm, a draft treaty on the establishment of a customs union and other measures of economic co-operation between Denmark, Finland, Norway and Sweden (Nordek) was signed by officials of these countries. The scheme was approved by the Nordic Council at its 18th full assembly meeting held in

Reykjavik on Feb. 7–12, and it was proposed that the necessary institutional framework should be set up with effect from Jan. 1, 1971.

However, developments during 1969 following the resignation of de Gaulle on April 28 and culminating in the Hague summit of the Six in December served to cast doubt on the future of the Nordek idea. Furthermore after a general election held in Finland on March 15–16, 1970, President Urho Kekkonen announced on April 6 at the opening of parliament that Finland was interested in establishing trade arrangements with the EC provided this could be done without compromising Finland's policy of neutrality. Further meetings on the Nordek project were cancelled.

Per Haekkerup (Danish Foreign Minister 1962–66) in 1969 summed up his country's approach to the idea of a Nordic customs union as follows: "It is the stated policy of Denmark that Nordic economic integration is in no way an alternative to our European objective. It is a prerequisite for Denmark that a Nordic treaty be worked out in such a way that it positively improves the possibilities of the Nordic countries to participate in an enlarged European Community."

[For the February 1969 crisis within the WEU which followed proposals for co-operation between the Six and Britain put forward at a WEU ministerial council meeting in October 1968 by Pierre Harmel, the Belgian Foreign Minister, see 2.17.]

4.5 Resumption of negotiations (1969–70)

Following the election of President Pompidou and the formation of a new French government under Jacques Chaban-Delmas in June 1969, progress was made during the summer of 1969 towards the resumption of negotiations between the EC and the four applicant countries. At a meeting held on June 22–23, 1969, the EC Council of Ministers asked the Commission to revise its Opinion on enlargement of September 1967 [see 2.12], and the Commission submitted a revised Opinion to the Council on Oct. 2, 1969 [see 2.20].

This Opinion urged that negotiations be started as soon as possible, stating that all four applicants should be treated together, that new members should be expected to accept the EC as it existed in 1969 and that enlargement problems should be solved by means of transition measures, rather than by amendments to existing values.

The opening of negotiations between the European Communities and Denmark was preceded by the publication in March 1970 of the report of a government commission which estimated that membership would raise the export of agricultural products to the EC countries by 2,300,000,000 kroner (£125,000,000) p.a., or by about 50 per cent of the 1968–69 level. Under existing arrangements, the Commission said, Denmark would have to pay about 800,000,000 kroner a year into the European Agricultural Guidance and Guarantee Fund, but this would be more than offset to the extent of 1,000,000,000 kroner through the abolition of agricultural subsidies. It was estimated that membership would involve a rise of about 1.2 per cent in the price of foodstuffs.

Negotiations were opened on June 30, 1970, and at this first meeting Prof. Nyboe Andersen, the Danish Minister of Economic Affairs and European Integration, made a statement to the Communities stressing in particular his government's wish for as short a transitional period as possible. After re-calling the decision of the Danish parliament in May 1967 to authorize the government to resume negotiations for Danish membership of the European Communities, together with the UK and in the expectation that other Scandinavian countries would also find solutions for their relations with the

Communities, Prof. Andersen affirmed his government's readiness to accept the European Treaties and subsequent decisions, the Communities' plans for further development, and the political aims of the Communities.

In the light of co-operation already attained between the five Nordic countries (Denmark, Finland, Iceland, Norway and Sweden)—particularly in the fields of labour, social security, legal harmonization, education and culture—and of progress over the past 10 years within EFTA, Prof. Andersen expressed his government's hope that the creation of a new and stronger European Community would be accompanied by the preservation of the significant results achieved in these other groupings.

All factors considered, the Danish government wished for no period of transition and was ready to accept the full obligations of membership immediately the treaties enlarging the Communities had been ratified, since for more than 10 years Denmark had "borne what we find to be a disproportionate share of the burden caused by the economic division of Europe, in particular through damage to our traditional agricultural exports". The government recognized, on the other hand, that the other applicant countries did want some transitional period and that the Communities were disposed to accept this, but asked that efforts should be made to avoid "unreasonable repercussions on a country which has no desire, no interest, and certainly no responsibility for a period of transition which may have to apply to all applicant countries".

The Danish government was firmly resolved to confine the problems of negotiation to a minimum, of which the following were the most important:

Customs union. The initial step towards a common external tariff, and the initial internal tariff reduction, should each be "substantial", and the gradual adoption of the common external tariff should be effected at a tempo which did not exceed that of the removal of the internal tariff barriers. In connexion with the transitional period, Denmark must also reserve the right to use the provisions of the Treaty of Rome relating to tariff quotas for certain products.

Transitional arrangements for agriculture. If a transitional period for agriculture should prove necessary, it should be as short as possible. It should begin as soon as the treaty of accession entered into force, with a substantial step towards Community price levels in line with the first approximation of tariffs; the new member countries should benefit from a Community preference immediately their entry took effect; there should be parallelism between the growing advantages obtained during the transitional period and the contributions paid to the Agricultural Guidance and Guarantee Fund during the various stages of the transitional period; the obligations in the field of establishment in agriculture should at the earliest enter into force at the end of the transitional period; and the removal of Denmark's existing benefits on the British market under Danish-British agreements should be viewed in the light of the other provisions for transitional arrangements and should be the subject of discussions between the UK, the Communities and Denmark.

Economic and monetary co-operation. Because of its balance-of-payments situation, Denmark might have to request that a transitional period in the agricultural sector should be accompanied by transitional arrangements also with regard to the liberalization of capital movements.

Faroe Islands and Greenland. The possibilities of special arrangements would have to be discussed for these territories in the same way as had been agreed for overseas territories of the present member states; the government did not visualize association but rather a solution within the framework of Denmark's own membership. A solution of this problem was of vital importance for the populations of both Greenland and the Faroes, which numbered only some 40,000 each.

Institutions. Denmark considered it important that the European Parliament should be given an increasingly significant role.

Finally, Prof. Andersen urged that problems of common interest should not be considered solved until they had been discussed in substance with all interested countries; for certain defined areas it should be agreed not to finalize negotiations with any single country without giving other interested countries a fair chance to have their interests taken suitably into account. These topics included, for Denmark, the transitional period for agriculture, financial arrangements, institutions, fisheries policy, and such new areas of co-operation as monetary and economic union. In addition, each applicant country should be given the chance to advance in its negotiations to the same extent as other countries, so that it should become possible for all the negotiations to reach approximately the same level of completion at the same time.

All four applicant countries were concerned that their entry into the EC would not disadvantage non-applicant members of EFTA. The EFTA Ministerial Council, meeting in Geneva on Nov. 5–6, 1970, welcomed the intention expressed by the EC that Community agreements with EFTA countries should come into force at the same time as the four applicants joined the EC [for full details of which see chapter 6].

4.6 Progress of negotiations (late 1970–1971)
Following the opening of negotiations on June 30, 1970, eight ministerial-level sessions and 16 deputy-level meetings were held during which discussions centred on Denmark's request for a short transitional period, the position of Greenland and the Faroe Islands, beer production, tariff quotas and fisheries.

Products on which Denmark was reported to have asked for tariff quotas were palm and linseed oil, cocoa beans, raw tobacco, unworked lead and sea salt. On the question of fisheries, discussions covered such aspects as freedom of access to territorial waters, market organization especially for frozen fish, pricing policy, and imports from third countries. (Denmark's fishing limit had been extended from three to 12 nautical miles from July 1, 1967, this limit having earlier been similarly applied to both Greenland and the Faroe Islands.)

However, accession negotiations with Denmark proved in general less problematic than those with the UK in particular, and also, for instance, than those with Norway, where the fisheries question was of greater importance to the economy [see 5.4, 5.6]. There were fewer political problems over Denmark's acceptance of the treaties and existing Community legislation, not least because the Danish economy had over the preceding decade undergone a restructuring process aimed at establishing a stronger and more competitive industrial sector and at the progressive harmonization of Danish economic regulations with those of the EC.

Negotiations were largely completed by July 12, 1971, when Prof. Andersen announced at a ministerial meeting that the main difficulties had been resolved. Matters concluded by then are detailed below.

Industrial tariffs. At a meeting of deputies on May 24, 1971, the Danish delegation agreed to the terms for the industrial transition period, allowing for five reductions of 20 per cent each in the Danish tariff on industrial imports from EC countries, this agreement being confirmed at a ministerial meeting on June 7. Denmark also agreed to the terms accepted by the British delegation relating to the adoption of the common external tariff.

Agriculture—financial transactions. On June 7 the Danish delegation further confirmed that it had accepted the principles arising out of Community negotiations with Britain on the common agricultural policy and the transitional provisions applicable to financial transactions. However, with reference to the transitional provisions in the agricultural sector, the Danish delegation stated that Denmark would encounter difficulties with a certain number of horticultural products which were protected against imports by quantitative restrictions due to be abolished in accordance with the Communities' proposals. There were similar reservations on beef and livestock.

Community finance. Further progress was made at a meeting of deputies on June 29 when the Danish delegates agreed to the financing of Community policies and the system of own resources, thus endorsing an earlier British agreement of June 21–23.

Nordic trade. At the next ministerial meeting on July 12 Prof. Andersen repeated a request that a satisfactory solution should be found to the safeguarding of the free trade already established between the Nordic countries.

4.7 General elections (Sept. 21, 1971)

In general elections to the *Folketing* (parliament) held on Sept. 21, 1971, key issues were Denmark's application to join the EC and also the Danish economic situation. On the former the Social Democrats were internally divided, although officially the party supported full Danish membership of the EC, provided that certain conditions could be fulfilled, such as British entry to the EC and satisfactory solutions for Norway and Sweden. The Socialist People's Party was alone in opposing entry outright.

The elections resulted in the resignation of the Conservative, Radical Liberal and *Venstre* Liberal coalition government of Baunsgaard, which had held power since the previous election in 1968, and the reappointment on Oct. 11 of Krag as Prime Minister of a minority Social Democrat government (his previous term of office having lasted from 1962 until 1968).

The poll on Sept. 21 resulted in a hung parliament, for although the Radical Liberals, to which Baunsgaard belonged, were able to maintain their position unchanged, the *Venstre* Liberals and the Conservatives sustained losses of four and six seats respectively. The Social Democrats and Socialist People's Party, on the other hand, gained eight and six seats respectively.

Voting later held in the Faroes on Oct. 5 resulted in the election of another Social Democrat and one representative who declined to take part in internal Danish politics. With the informal support of the Socialist People's Party and one deputy each from Greenland and the Faroes, Krag's new government commanded a majority of one in the *Folketing*.

Speaking at a press conference on Oct. 9, 1971, after announcing his Cabinet, Krag said that his government intended to continue the EC negotiations and that he hoped that an agreement with the six member countries could be signed before the end of the year.

4.8 Conclusion of negotiations

The remaining outstanding details on the terms of membership were settled at a meeting of deputies in Brussels on Dec. 21, 1971, when it was agreed that there would be a five-year period during which the Danish monopoly on liquid milk supplies to some Danish dairies could continue and that there would be a similar period during which legislation on pharmaceutical products could be adapted to Community regulations. On the same day the Danish delegation received assurances from the Communities that they were in agreement with the principle of continuation of the Nordic free labour market after Denmark and Norway had joined the Communities.

A final meeting on Jan. 14, 1972, concluded the negotiations, including the outstanding details relating to the fishing industry, Denmark being granted protection for a stretch of the coast of west Jutland from Thyboroen to Blaavandshuk and for the Faroes and Greenland.

In a report on the outcome of the negotiations, prepared in December 1971 during the drafting of the Treaty of Accession, the Danish government made comments on various aspects of the negotiations and of Community policies.

Economic and monetary policy. On economic and monetary policy the report noted that at a ministerial meeting on Nov. 9 a statement was made in which Ivar Norgaard, the new Danish Minister of Foreign Economic Affairs, declared: "The Danish government attaches importance to the Communities' objective of achieving closer co-operation in the field of economic policy, including monetary harmonization. . . . The attitude of the Danish government towards future plans for co-ordination of economic policy will be governed by the extent to which these decisions harmonize with our national aims. The Council of Ministers has adopted a resolution on economic and monetary union with which my government can concur. . . . Our participation in future co-ordination must in no way preclude the Danish *Folketing* from implementing an economic policy—including primarily a taxation and social policy—that will secure greater equality between the individual groups in our society."

Institutions. In its comments on the European institutions, the report referred to the views of certain member states in support of nominating members to the European Parliament by direct election in the individual countries. It added: "It has been the Danish contention during negotiations with the Communities that it is important that the European Parliament should be delegated an increasingly powerful role."

Agriculture. Describing the terms negotiated for agriculture, the report stated: "The transitional arrangements agreed by negotiation represent a vast improvement in the earning capabilities of the Danish farming industry. The sales value of the main agricultural commodities will rise by an average of about 25 per cent by the end of the transitional period." On full adoption of Community prices it was estimated that increased earnings on the home market would be the equivalent of £19,400,000 (350,000,000 kroner) and that increased earnings from exports would be £105,500,000. The higher prices on the home market were estimated to total 7 per cent, resulting in a "modest rise" in the cost of living. It was calculated that the food price increases would be reflected in a rise of 1½ per cent in the cost-of-living index, corresponding to 0.2–0.3 per cent per year for each of the five transitional years. This annual figure was described as "substantially lower" than the annual rise in home market prices over the previous five years. In fact it was noted that the price of eggs, poultry and certain grades of pigmeat would drop at the start of the transitional period, as the current level of Danish prices in these sectors was higher than Community prices.

Community budget. The report calculated that Denmark's share of the total Community budget would rise from 1.07 per cent in 1973 to 2.03 per cent in 1977, a contribution lower than Denmark's share of the gross national product of the enlarged Communities which was at that time 2.4 per cent. In cash terms these figures would represent payments of £13,900,000 in 1973 rising to £38,900,000 in 1977.

Customs union. With reference to the terms applicable to Denmark in the operation of the customs union, the report noted that the Communities had agreed to duty-free quotas for lead bullion and to duty-free imports of palm oil and cocoa beans from those African countries already associated with the Communities and from those Commonwealth countries which would receive similar terms from 1975, but rejected Danish requests for duty-free quotas in respect of linseed oil and tobacco.

It was stated that the effects for Danish industry of keener competition as a result of the customs union were difficult to assess, but that the restructuring of Danish industry with the attendant closures of unproductive enterprises would continue. The trend towards greater specialization would continue and an increasingly large share of Denmark's industrial output would be exported, in parallel with a growing requirement for imports of industrial goods.

Adoption of the common external tariff in respect of third countries was calculated to bring higher costs for raw materials and semi-finished goods at present entering duty-free, which would increase the overall import value by 2–3 per cent or £16,700,000, assuming that imports from the Communities were raised in price by a similar amount to take advantage of the new situation.

Scandinavian relations. In connexion with the maintenance of existing trade relations with the other Scandinavian countries, the government stated: "The continued existence of co-operation at a Scandinavian level in a situation in which the Scandinavian countries will have different forms of association with the European Communities is a matter of the greatest importance to Denmark. Although the issue was not the subject of negotiations it was ascertained during the course of technical discussions with the Communities that none of the Scandinavian agreements will conflict with Community rules."

4.9 Position of the Faroe Islands and Greenland

Final agreement on the position of Greenland and the Faroes was reached at a last negotiating session on Jan. 14, 1972. As a dependency of Denmark, Greenland was to become an integral part of the Communities, although in the October 1972 referendum on membership [see 4.13] a majority of 70 per cent of the Greenland electorate opposed accession. (The island's subsequent acquisition of internal autonomy in May 1979 and its ultimate withdrawal from the Communities in February 1985 are covered in chapter 9.)

The Faroe Islands, on the other hand, already enjoyed internal autonomy under Danish sovereignty, and were consequently to be given special external associate status under the Accession Treaty, whereby the islands participated only in the Communities' free trade arrangements with a similar status to the remaining EFTA countries and were not covered by other common Community policies, including fisheries. No referendum was therefore held in the Faroes, although the islands' *Lagting* (parliament) was given the opportunity to present by the end of 1975 a proposal for EC membership should it so wish. Subsequent *Lagting* votes however, confirmed the islands' approval of existing arrangements.

4.10 Parliamentary approval of signature of Accession Treaty—Initial decision to hold referendum

Following visits by Prime Minister Krag to Bonn, Paris and London during November 1971, the Danish *Folketing* approved on Dec. 16 the Danish signature of the Treaty of Accession to the Communities by 141 votes to 32 (all 17 members of the Socialist People's Party, 11 Social Democrats and four Radical Liberals). This vote fell just short of the five-sixths majority of *Folketing* representatives required by the 1953 Constitution for the delegation of "powers vested in the authorities of the realm . . . to international authorities"; therefore, under the Constitution, a referendum was necessary for such legislation to be implemented.

In fact, however, as in Norway, pressure for a referendum to be held on the issue of membership had built up while negotiations with the EC were still in progress. Accordingly, the *Folketing* had already decided on May 18, 1971, to hold a referendum (although in contrast to the Norwegian procedure, the Danish vote was to be taken after the issue had been debated and voted upon in the *Folketing* and would be binding).

The May 18 vote to put the final decision on membership to a popular vote was supported by 132 votes to 12 with two abstentions. It was brought by the Social Democrats, who were in opposition at the time, but commanded 62 seats in the *Folketing* or 34.6 per cent of the vote, which was above the one third of parliamentary members required by the Constitution before legislation could be submitted to the electorate.

Consequently, even if five-sixths of the members of the *Folketing* voted in favour as required by the Constitution the decision would still be reversed by a referendum if more than 50 per cent of the votes cast, constituting at least 30 per cent of the entire electorate, were against entry. Conversely, a Danish vote in the referendum in favour of entry to the Communities would not be the sole means of ratification of the Treaty of Accession if the government could obtain a majority of at least five-sixths in a vote in the *Folketing* (although the Dec. 16 vote fell short of this requirement).

4.11 Signature of Accession Treaty (Jan. 22, 1972)

At the ceremony for the signing of the Accession Treaty held in Brussels on Jan. 22, 1972, Jens Otto Krag made the following speech after he had signed the Treaty.

"More than ten years have passed since I, in October 1961, as Foreign Minister on behalf of the Danish government, presented Denmark's application for membership of the European Communities. We saw then the applications of Ireland, Norway, the United Kingdom and Denmark as a natural and logical consequence of the co-operation which the countries of Western Europe had established in so many fields after the war. We still hold that view. We had, admittedly, not expected that it would take so long to reach the end of the road. But we have not been waiting in silence. Hardly any question has been discussed so much, not only in Denmark but also in the other countries of Western Europe. At every opening of the Danish parliament, in all major parliamentary debates in Denmark, in all ministerial meetings of EFTA since its start, in the Nordic Council, in the Council of Europe, at visits to the European capitals, one of the principal subjects has been how the economic split-up of Western Europe could be overcome.

"I am referring to these past events because they explain the satisfaction we feel in the present situation where, at long last, we are about to sign the Treaty of Accession.

"I find it appropriate, therefore, to take this opportunity to thank all those who have helped bring about this situation. I think, above all, of those who, by mutual concessions and flexibility, brought about the political conditions for the opening of negotiations and for their successful completion. But I think also of those who, especially in the last few months, have been working round the clock to bring before us the texts of the agreements we are signing today.

"Not so very many years ago it would have sounded like something out of a fairy-tale or wishful thinking if we had been told that European countries, which had been warring [with] each other for centuries, would be able to sign a treaty like the one before us.

"Let me end by making three wishes for the future of the European Communities.

"My first wish is that the new member countries will add a positive element to the development of the Communities and thereby strengthen their vitality, efficiency and dynamism. I am well aware that this implies that we too must learn to understand and respect the interests of other member countries and in a proper democratic way to solve the future problems in a manner satisfactory to all parties concerned and so also to the Communities.

"The second wish is that the Communities will pursue their internal policies in a progressive spirit of social consciousness. We have learned how to achieve economic growth. But we still have to learn how to administer it in a way that will not only bring more material wealth to us all but also correct social imbalances for the benefit of the least privileged. At the same time the problems of preservation and improvement of the human environment as a whole in the industrial society become ever more acute. We can solve these problems by common action. Each country itself will hardly be able to.

"In conclusion, the third wish . . . is that the external policies of the Communities will be open and outward-looking. I am thinking first of the other EFTA countries, including not least the other Nordic countries, Sweden, Iceland and Finland. These countries have taken part in European co-operation since the last war. Without arrangements with them our co-operation would not be complete.

"I am thinking also of growing trade and understanding with the countries of Eastern Europe in the spirit of negotiation and détente.

"Nor should we forget the importance of close co-operation with the United States and Canada. Both in the fields of trade, monetary affairs and security is the destiny of Western Europe closely bound up with that of North America. It will not be our interest to loosen these ties.

"Last, but not least, I think of the developing countries, the poor world outside Europe and North America. An enlarged European Community will acquire an economic and commercial strength which imposes on the Communities a special responsibility for the solution of the problems of the Third World. It will be one of the most urgent tasks of the Communities to live up to this responsibility.

"It is with the confidence that the European Communities will fulfil these wishes that I sign my name to the Treaty of Accession and will recommend it for approval by the Danish parliament and the Danish people. It is the hope of the Danish government and of the majority of the Danish parliament that this historic decision will contribute to secure the peace of Europe, further our economic development and thereby create the foundation for new social progress, also for the poorest countries of Europe. In this context and in full freedom European culture and scientific progress will have their best possibilities."

4.12 Folketing approval of ratification of Treaty—Second parliamentary vote in favour of referendum (Sept. 8, 1972)—Referendum campaign

On Sept. 8, 1972, the *Folketing* approved the Enabling Act ratifying the Treaty of Accession to the European Communities by 141 votes in favour to 34 against, with two abstentions—i.e. again slightly under a five-sixths majority.

Those voting in favour included 58 of the 70 Social Democratic members, all 31 Conservatives, all 30 *Venstre* Liberals and 22 of the 27 Radical Liberals. Those voting against comprised 12 Social Democrats, four Radical Liberals, all 17 members of the Socialist People's Party and one of the two members representing Greenland. The two Faroese members abstained, while the two remaining members of the *Folketing*, one Greenland member and one Radical Liberal, were absent during the vote due to illness.

Although, as stated above, the holding of a referendum had already been approved in May 1971, the *Folketing* voted once again on the same issue in accordance with the Constitution which in Article 43 specifies that a referendum should be held on an issue involving the delegation of national sovereignty when the *Folketing* had failed to achieve a five-sixths majority. A unanimous vote in favour of a referendum was accordingly taken immediately after the Sept. 8 decision in favour of membership.

During the spring of 1972 the parties which had formed the government at the time of the decision to hold a referendum—the Conservatives, the Radical Liberals and the *Venstre* Liberals—had pressed the new Social Democratic government led by Krag to arrange for the vote to be held before the

Norwegian referendum. However, at a party conference the previous summer, the Social Democrats had agreed on a resolution declaring that in the event of a Norwegian refusal to join the Communities "a new situation would be created". Consequently, after the Norwegian government had announced the date of its own referendum on March 3, 1972, Krag announced on March 7 that the Danish referendum on membership of the European Communities, for which the date had already been postponed on Jan. 24 from June until September, would be held on Oct. 2, 1972, one week after the Norwegian referendum on Sept. 24–25.

Although the largest trade union, the General and Semi-skilled Workers' Union, voted to oppose Danish membership of the Communities in April 1972, the Trade Union Confederation decided in favour of entry on May 18 by 524 votes against 406 with 38 abstentions. During the summer the principal opposition outside parliament was expressed by a "National Front against the Common Market", which continued its campaign on the basis of an assertion that membership was unconstitutional.

At a special meeting held on Sept. 10, 1972, after a party conference, the Social Democrats, who had been divided on the EC issue, voted in favour of joining the Communities by 272 votes to 95, with one blank vote.

Krag, speaking both as Prime Minister and as leader of the party, emphasized that membership would reduce the risk of unemployment and at the same time would contribute towards Scandinavian co-operation, as even if Norway decided to remain outside the Communities the Scandinavian countries would have at least one spokesman in Brussels to watch over their interests.

The campaign in favour of membership concentrated mainly on the economic advantages, particularly with regard to prospects for Danish agriculture and the balance of payments.

Although of diminishing importance in total economic production and trade, agricultural products still accounted for about one quarter of total exports in 1970 and were expected to benefit from access to the six countries of the existing Communities and from continued trade with the UK, a traditional market for Danish bacon and dairy products. The Danish agricultural industry had also achieved a high rate of productivity during the 1960s due to a reduction in the number of farms and in the number of farm workers (by almost 50 per cent), while output had increased. Thus the Danish industry was in a favourable position to take advantage of the high price support system of the EC's common agricultural policy, which was designed to assist less efficient farmers.

Danish exports to the six existing countries of the Communities and to the United Kingdom accounted for 41.6 per cent of total exports in 1970, while the corresponding figure for imports amounted to 47.1 per cent. Exports to these trading partners had been growing at an annual rate of about 5 per cent during the previous eight years, but imports had been growing faster, thus aggravating the current balance-of-payments deficit which had amounted to 4,050,000,000 kroner (then £225,000,000) in 1970. However, trade between the Scandinavian countries had also developed quickly so that by 1970 Norway and Sweden had together replaced the United Kingdom as the largest export market with a combined share of 24 per cent of Danish exports compared with 14 per cent in 1960.

Krag gave a further warning on the importance of the economic issues when he announced on Sept. 21 that a devaluation of the Danish krone would be inevitable if the referendum resulted in a majority of "No" votes.

During the following days speculative pressure on the krone in the financial markets increased, and when the result of the Norwegian referendum became known on Sept. 26 it was announced in Copenhagen that foreign currency dealings would be suspended until Oct. 3.

4.13 Vote in favour of EC membership—Political reactions

In contrast to the negative vote in Norway [see 5.10], the Danish referendum resulted in a substantial majority in favour of membership. 1,958,115 votes were recorded for entry (representing 63.3 per cent of the total 3,093,806 "Yes" and "No" votes) and 1,135,691 against (36.7 per cent), with 11,907 blank votes and a further 7,409 spoiled or invalid papers. These figures represented an overall participation of 90.1 per cent of the total electorate of 3,453,763 registered voters, of whom 56.7 per cent voted in favour of membership and 32.9 per cent against. [For February 1986 referendum in favour of approving package of EC reforms see 12.14.]

While the final votes were being counted Krag told a press conference in Copenhagen: "The decision which the people of Denmark have taken is historic, and the government can only record its pleasure and gratification. We have accepted an offer from Europe not just for economic advantage. We wish to participate in the construction of Europe and to contribute what we have to offer to that Europe." Expressing his regret that Norway had not taken the same decision, Krag affirmed: "It will be our special duty and responsibility to try and unite European and Nordic co-operation. We will not forget Nordic co-operation nor give it second priority."

The Danish decision was warmly welcomed in several European countries, the British Prime Minister, Edward Heath, describing it as "a great day for Europe", while the West German government stated that it was convinced that "the entry of Denmark is in the political as well as the economic interests of all parties concerned". The Italian Prime Minister, Giulio Andreotti, said that his government was "deeply satisfied", and in The Hague the Dutch Prime Minister, Barend Biesheuvel, commented that the Danish economy was so closely tied to that of the United Kingdom that a decision not to join would have resulted in "technical problems". At a meeting of Community Ministers of Agriculture in Luxembourg on Oct. 3, Jacques Chirac, the French Minister, described the decision as "good for Danish agriculture and good for French agriculture", while the chairman of the meeting, Pierre Lardinois, the Dutch Minister, affirmed that the Community "definitely needs Denmark among us if we are to regulate the markets of Western Europe".

In Norway, Trygve Bratteli asserted that the Danish decision would in no way inhibit Nordic co-operation, but the President of the Commission of the European Communities, Dr Sicco Mansholt, warned that Denmark could not act as a bridge between the Communities and the Nordic countries. Dr Mansholt also criticized the use of referendums as a means of taking European policy decisions, claiming that such a vote "can be influenced too easily by questions and problems not directly concerned". He added that he hoped that Norway, Sweden, Switzerland and Spain would eventually join the Communities although he noted that Spain would first have to adopt "democratic structures".

4.14 Resignation of Krag—Appointment of Joergensen as Prime Minister

Despite the convincing victory of his government's policy in the referendum, Krag announced his resignation both as Prime Minister and as leader of his party to the *Folketing* on Oct. 3, only a few hours after the final result was known. He explained that he had wanted to resign for some time and pointed

out that he had spent 25 years in politics "and this seemed a good time to go".
Krag nominated his Foreign Minister, Knud Borge Anderson, as caretaker
Prime Minister, but later in the day the Parliamentary Social Democratic
Party announced that Anker Joergensen, chairman of the General and
Semi-skilled Workers Union, had been nominated to succeed Krag as Prime
Minister and leader of the party.

The nomination was approved by the party's executive committee on the
following day, and on Oct. 5 Joergensen was formally appointed Prime
Minister by Queen Margrethe. On leaving the Amalienborg Palace
Joergensen said that he hoped for "political stability which will allow the
government to complete its full term", which was due to end in 1975. He
added that there would be no Cabinet changes and that he fully accepted a
policy statement made by Krag immediately before his resignation.

Joergensen (50) had been a member of the *Folketing* since 1964 but had never held
Cabinet office before, having devoted much of his time to trade union activities, which
had led to his appointment as chairman of the General and Semi-skilled Workers
Union in 1968. His views in favour of membership of the European Communities had
resulted in his voting against the majority of his union, which had rejected the
government's European policy at a congress earlier in the year [see 4.12].

4.15 Final ratification and accession (Oct. 11, 1972, Jan. 1, 1973)— Appointment of Danish Commissioner

Following the favourable referendum result, the final step in the procedure
establishing Danish membership of the Communities was taken on Oct. 11,
1972, when Queen Margrethe of Denmark gave the Royal Assent to the
instrument of ratification, and on Jan. 1, 1973, Denmark acceded to the
European Communities. [For details of the dates of ratifications by existing
EC member countries of the Treaty of Accession for all the applicant
countries see 2.39.]

Finn Olav Gundelach (47), was sworn in as the Danish member of the
Commission on Jan. 9, 1973, and was allocated responsibility for the internal
market and customs union. Gundelach, a career diplomat, had served in the
Danish delegation to the United Nations in Geneva from 1955 and later took
part in negotiations within the GATT until his appointment as Danish
ambassador to the EC in 1967.

5: NORWAY: APPLICATION AND REJECTION

5.1 Chronology of events

April 30, 1962	Initial application to EEC
May 2, 1962	Application for ECSC and Euratom membership
July 4, 1962	Negotiations open
Jan. 14, 1963	De Gaulle's press conference opposing UK membership of EEC
Oct. 12, 1965	Appointment of Borten as Prime Minister of non-Socialist coalition
Sept. 27, 1966	Negative Norwegian reaction to Danish proposal for Nordic approach to EEC
July 24, 1967	Formal reapplication
Sept. 29, 1967	Commission Opinion on enlargement
Dec. 19, 1967	Renewed French emphasis on obstacles to British entry to EC
Feb. 4, 1968	Draft treaty for Nordek customs union
June 15, 1969	Pompidou elected President of France
Dec. 1–2, 1969	Hague summit urging reopening of negotiations
June 5, 1970	Government statement on negotiating position regarding Norwegian agriculture and fisheries
June 30, 1970	Negotiations reopen
Feb. 1, 1971	New EC fisheries policy into effect
March 2–13, 1971	Replacement of Borten coalition by Bratteli Labour government
March 30, 1971	Confirmation of government decision to hold referendum
Jan. 22, 1972	Signature of Accession Treaty
Sept. 24–25, 1972	Referendum decision against membership
Oct. 12–18, 1972	Resignation of Bratteli and appointment of Korvald minority coalition government
Oct. 25, 1972	Request for negotiations on trade agreement
May 14, 1973	Signature of Special Relations Agreement

5.2 Initial application (May 1962–January 1963)

Norway had initially sought economic integration with other European
countries through EFTA, so that when the United Kingdom, the country's
largest single market, Ireland and Denmark, part of its important Nordic
market, all applied to join the EEC in mid-1961, it was widely thought that
Norway would also do so soon, to maintain its access to key markets. Political
considerations, however, stalled this application until April 30, 1962, when
the Labour government of Einar Gerhardsen wrote to the Council requesting
that formal negotiations be opened.

Essential to any such move was an amendment to the Constitution (such as had
already existed since 1953 in Denmark—see 4.10) to permit the transfer of sovereign
powers from the Norwegian authorities to international bodies if approved by an
appropriate majority of *Storting* (parliament) members. Several attempts to introduce
such a change had been made over the preceding decade and the amendment was
eventually passed on March 8, 1962, by 115 votes to 35. The vote was regarded in part
as a preliminary test of attitudes towards the possible political impact of an application
for EEC membership, which was under consideration by the government at the time.
The only party to vote en bloc in favour was the opposition Conservative Party, while
the Centre Party, representing agricultural interests, and the Socialist People's Party
voted against, and all the other parties were split in their voting patterns.

A three day *Storting* debate on various possible forms of membership or association
with the EEC resulted in a vote on April 28, 1962, by 113 votes to 37 in favour of an
application for full membership. The voting pattern was similar with only the Conservative Party voting unanimously in favour of membership.

In a letter sent to the Commission in Brussels two days after the debate
Halvard Lange, the Foreign Minister, wrote that his government "would be
thankful if negotiations about conditions for accession could be begun in the
near future", and, referring to the "special problems" raised by accession
"because of the country's geographical location and economic structure",
added that his government hoped it would be "possible, through mutual
understanding, to reach satisfactory solutions to these problems during the
negotiations". In an initial session with the Council of Ministers on July 4,
1962, particular reference was made by Lange to the need for the protection
of Norwegian fisheries and agriculture.

Formal negotiations began with a ministerial level meeting on Nov. 12, but
the French veto of UK membership in January 1963 meant that substantial
negotiations were never actually opened.

5.3 Reapplication (July 24, 1967)

The four-party coalition government of Per Borten, which in October 1965
had been the first non-Socialist government to come to power since 1935
(except for one month in 1963), reacted against Danish proposals made on
Sept. 27, 1966 concerning an independent role for the Nordic countries in
Europe [see also 4.3], and stated that the Norwegian application for
membership of the Community was conditional upon Britain also joining.
Accordingly, once the British reapplied on May 11, 1967, the formal
Norwegian reapplication followed on July 24, 1967.

This application for membership of the EC was made in the form of a letter
from John Lyng, the Foreign Minister, to the President of the Communities'
Council of Ministers, and was presented in Brussels on July 24 by Jan

Halvorsen, Norwegian Ambassador to the European Communities. In his letter Lyng, after referring to Norway's original application received on May 2, 1962, asked for negotiations aimed at an eventual agreement on Norwegian membership of the EEC. He also expressed his government's endorsement of the ECSC and Euratom Treaties.

The government's proposal for full membership, contained in a White Paper presented to the *Storting* on June 16, included a promise, on the completion of negotiations and without prejudice to the government's final decision, to arrange a referendum on the question of entry. The White Paper also stated that special agreements would be sought on agricultural and fishery problems, and that in the event of failure to secure satisfactory terms the government would have to consider associate membership or some other alternative solution.

Having considered the White Paper, the foreign relations committee of the *Storting* early in July endorsed the government's proposal, although the majority of its members, representing the Conservative and Labour parties, also expressed the view that the *Storting* would have to consider the situation again if the application failed, and recommended postponement of any final decision about the proposed referendum until the *Storting* had studied the results of the negotiations. Representatives of the Centre, Christian People's, and Liberal Parties, on the other hand, supported the government's view that associate status should be considered in the event of full membership proving unattainable, and proposed the organization of a referendum as soon as the outcome of the negotiations was known.

After a three-day debate the *Storting* approved the government's policy on July 13 by 136 votes to 13 (four Centre Party members, three Christian People's Party members, four Labour Party members, and the two deputies of the Socialist People's Party).

During the debate the opposition was led by Hans Borgen, a member of the Centre Party, who suggested that the government should conduct the negotiations without asking ab initio for membership, and that any application for membership should be made dependent on the prior assurance of favourable terms for Norway's agriculture and fisheries; moreover, the Norwegian negotiations should be co-ordinated with those of Sweden and Finland. Borgen's formal motion to that effect, however, was supported by only 16 votes and the request for special terms for Norwegian agriculture and fisheries was not expressly mentioned as a condition in the Norwegian application.

After the breakdown in these negotiations in December 1967 [see 2.14], Norway took part in negotiations to establish a Nordic customs union or Nordek as proposed by the Danish government [see 4.4], but these were stalled by the Finnish government after The Hague summit of December 1969 had indicated a change in EC attitudes.

5.4 Reopening of negotiations (June 1970)
Formal negotiations for membership of the European Communities were restarted on June 30, 1970, at a meeting in Luxembourg.

In a document published beforehand on June 5, 1970, the government expressed its wish to become a full member of the European Communities, but said that if certain conditions were not met—principally permanent exceptions for Norwegian agriculture and suitable arrangements for fisheries—Norway would instead have to seek associate or other appropriate status. This policy document was approved by the *Storting* on June 25 by 132 votes to 17; those voting against the government comprised seven members of the Centre Party (out of a total of 20), seven Labour members and three members of the Christian People's Party (another of the coalition parties).

At the Luxembourg meeting on June 30, Norway's position was explained by the Foreign Minister, Svenn Stray.

Trade. Total exports of goods and services amounted to about 40 per cent of Norway's gross national product; these exports were, however, centred on a limited number of important markets—four-fifths of her commodity exports going to Western Europe—and were concentrated on a few categories of products. The government attached decisive importance to the preservation of the free market created within EFTA, and also stressed that during the negotiations solutions must be found which would secure the continuation of the free trade and other forms of co-operation already achieved between the Nordic countries.

Regional policy. This must constitute an essential element of the future European industrial policy. Moreover, Norway's population would represent only 1.5 per cent of that of a 10-member Community; in such a "far-flung and sparsely-populated country" the maintenance of settlement in the various regions would always be a problem of primary importance, and this presupposed that satisfactory conditions existed for agriculture and fisheries.

Agriculture. In order to secure a settlement in all parts of the country, the pre-servation of an agricultural industry of about the current extent and character was necessary, while for the purpose of maintaining a "state of preparedness" it was of decisive importance to have an agricultural industry which offered possibilities for providing the population with a minimum supply of foodstuffs.

The area of arable land amounted to only three per cent of Norway's total area, and her agricultural production amounted to only 0.5 per cent of that of an enlarged Community. On a European scale this production was marginal, and "special arrangements of a lasting character in favour of Norwegian agriculture should accordingly not have any perceptible effect on European agriculture". The most important agricultural products were those derived from domestic animals (which accounted for about 80 per cent of agricultural income) and fruit and vegetables in certain regions; on the other hand, Norway imported practically all her requirements of sugar and cereals for human consumption, half her needs of fodder grain, and large quantities of fruit and vegetables. Norway was a considerable net importer of foodstuffs, and membership in an enlarged Community would entail substantially increased foreign exchange expenditure.

Norway's policy aimed at securing for the agricultural population the same level of income as that enjoyed by people engaged in other industries. This meant a relatively high price level, and if Norwegian agriculture had to adapt itself to current prices within the EC there would result a loss of income of between 40 and 50 per cent. Satisfactory arrangements would therefore have to be found which would secure for farmers the necessary economic basis for continuing their profession; since the com-petitive handicaps under which Norwegian agriculture operated were of a permanent character, such arrangements must also be made on a permanent basis.

Fisheries. In the coastal districts fisheries were to a large extent the basis of settlement, and in many districts there were few or no employment alternatives. Norwegian fisheries were largely coastal, and questions connected with the fishery limit were therefore of "vital importance". Norway assumed that since negotiations for an enlargement of the Communities had now been opened, the applicant countries would be given the opportunity to express their views on the common fisheries policy.

Capital movements and establishment. Rules governing these would raise certain problems. Norway was traditionally a capital-importing country, but the form and size of capital imports for further development gave rise to special problems owing to the structure of Norwegian industry, with small enterprises disposing of little capital of their own. Moreover, Norwegian legislation embodied a concession system which made it possible to control the exploitation of natural resources with due regard to economic and social considerations, and the government would like to discuss problems associated with this.

ECSC and Euratom. In relation to the Treaty of Paris certain questions would arise, inter alia, in connexion with coal production in Spitzbergen, while Euratom posed few problems apart from that connected with security control, which must, however, find its solution in a larger context.

Political co-operation. After touching on technological and scientific matters, pollution and the protection of the environment, and economic and monetary matters. Stray stated that his government favoured a constructive European co-operation designed to strengthen the peoples of Europe both economically and politically, so as to enable them to play an ever-increasing part in the efforts to safeguard international peace and security. It was understood that discussions on future political co-operation would take place in other contexts, and such co-operation should also offer possibilities for even greater efforts in favour of the large group of developing countries.

Referendum. Before the *Storting* took a final stand on the result reached in negotiations, a referendum would be held of a consultative character.

Co-ordination of negotiations. The negotiating timetable should be the same for all four applicant countries, and negotiations should be terminated at the same time in respect of all the participating countries. In principle, the negotiations should proceed at the same pace, and it was necessary to establish an effective consultation procedure for the negotiations with the various countries. On the Norwegian side, for example, the government would wish to take part in all negotiations which touched upon questions relating to fisheries policy.

Norwegian negotiations for membership were complicated both by difficulties over the protection of the Norwegian fishing industry and also over maintaining adequate subsidies for Norwegian agriculture. The procedures were further delayed by disagreement on European policies which led to the formation of a new Norwegian government in March 1971 under the leadership of Trygve Bratteli.

5.5 Resignation of Borten as Prime Minister—Formation of Labour government under Bratteli (March 2–13, 1971)

The resignation on March 2 of Borten and his coalition government resulted from a leakage to unauthorized persons of a confidential state paper on the report of a conversation between the Norwegian Ambassador in Brussels, Jan Halvorsen, and Jean-François Deniau, a member of the European Commission, which was believed to deal with matters relating to Norway's projected membership of the EC and was published by the Norwegian newspaper *Dagbladet*. On Feb. 24 Borten stated that neither he nor his staff were responsible for the leak to *Dagbladet*, but on Feb. 26 he admitted that he had shown the document on Feb. 15 to an unauthorized person (Arne Haugestad, a lawyer who was leader of the movement against Norway's joining the EC— see also 5.8) during an air journey, and expressed regret at this "indiscretion". (Haugestad categorically stated that he was not the source for the *Dagbladet* report.)

In a statement on March 2 to the *Storting*, Borten accepted responsibility for having disclosed details from classified state papers to unauthorized persons, expressed regret for having done so, and said that the only "natural solution" was that the government should tender its resignation. Borten stated that the ministers of his own party—the Centre Party—did not consider the question of the leak to be of sufficient importance to justify the resignation of the government, but the ministers of the other coalition parties—the Conservative, Liberal and Christian People's parties—took a contrary view. Later in the day Borten accordingly tendered his resignation to King Olav.

After an unsuccessful attempt to revive the coalition, a new government drawn entirely from the Labour Party was formed on March 13 by Trygve Bratteli, the Labour leader.

5.6 Negotiations (September 1970–January 1972)

Negotiations at ministerial level took place on Sept. 22 and Dec. 15, 1970, and, after a postponement due to the formation of the new government, on March 30, 1971. Discussion at these meetings and at meetings at the level of deputies covered the following main subjects:

Finance. Norway was reported to have pointed out that her share of EC finance in 1978 after the end of the transitional period might be about 2.2 per cent of the total budget, even though her gross national product would then be only 1.77 per cent of that of the enlarged Communities. This share of the budget was estimated to amount to $97,000,000 in 1978, of which $36,000,000 would come from customs duties, $30,000,000 from agricultural levies, and $31,000,000 from the proceeds of a value added tax.

Tariff quotas. These were requested for cocoa beans, raw tobacco, raw lead, sea salt, and palm and linseed oil.

Fisheries. Norway pointed out that the existing six EC countries had a total catch of 1,700,000 tons in 1969, whereas the catch of the four applicant countries was 4,800,000 tons. Moreover, the six EC members currently imported about 500,000 tons net a year while the four applicants together exported about 750,000 tons; there would, therefore, in the enlarged 10-member Communities, be a net surplus available for export of 250,000 tons instead of a deficit, and the whole fisheries position would be very different from what it was at present in the six countries. Attention should be paid, Norway maintained, both to this export problem and also to the market position for frozen, salt and dried fish as well as fresh fish. Finally, Norway was reported to have expressed particular disappointment that the EC should have proceeded to draw up its fisheries policy while the four applicant countries had only just begun negotiating and without consulting with the applicants, and to have stressed her concern that her 12-mile fishing limit (introduced in 1961) should be preserved beyond the proposed five-year period in the northern coastal waters.

At the third ministerial meeting between the Norwegian delegation and the representatives of the six member countries on March 30, 1971, Norway's new Foreign Minister, Andreas Cappelen, reaffirmed Norwegian interest in pursuing the negotiations, repeated his country's concern over fishing and agricultural problems, and also announced that Norway would hold a referendum on membership of the Communities.

After a meeting on June 8 in Oslo, when senior government ministers from the five Nordic countries reaffirmed their support for continuance of the free trade arrangements developed through the Nordek agreement, the Norwegian parliament voted on June 17 by 113 votes to 37 to continue negotiations for entry into the European Communities; those voting against comprised all 20 Agrarians, eight members of the Labour Party, five Liberals and four members of the Christian People's Party. Under the Norwegian Constitution membership would be rejected if, on completion of the negotiations, the terms should be opposed by 38 or more votes of parliament's 150 members (i.e. 25 per cent or more). At the same time a motion was passed calling on the government to prepare alternative arrangements for an association agreement with the EC.

Substantive negotiations did not in effect take place until after early June 1971, when key issues regarding UK accession had been settled in principle. Details of the main negotiating subjects considered from June 1971 onwards are summarized below.

Agriculture. At a ministerial meeting on June 21 Cappelen made a further request for special consideration for Norway's agricultural industry. It was explained that as Norwegian agriculture constituted only 0.5 per cent of the enlarged Communities' total production and consisted of only a small range of products, it was felt that the Communities could tolerate exceptions to its policy, and Cappelen specified that the exceptions should take the form of lasting arrangements for subsidies both in support of particular regions and products and of general income in some cases.

Following visits to Norway in October by Deniau, EC Commissioner responsible for negotiations for enlargement, and by Michel Cointat, French Minister of Agriculture, it was announced at a ministerial meeting in Luxembourg on Oct. 19 that the Communities recognized the special problems of Norwegian agriculture and that solutions would be proposed based on a transitional period during which Norwegian price support systems would be allowed to continue until replaced by a system of direct subsidies to producers.

These measures were put to the Norwegian delegation at a meeting in Brussels on Nov. 3, when the Community representatives insisted that Norway must accept the common agricultural policy after the interim period and that the subsidies must fit within the framework of the Treaty of Rome.

A special protocol to be appended to the Treaty of Accession was completed at a negotiating session on Dec. 21, when the Norwegian delegation accepted a proposal under which Norwegian agriculture would continue to be supported by the existing system for a three-year period and horticulture for five years, after which the problems would be resolved within the terms of the common agricultural policy.

Community budget. On June 30 the Norwegian delegation accepted the Communities' proposals concerning its contributions to the budget of the enlarged Communities. The Norwegian payment would rise from £9,600,000 in 1973 to about £29,000,000 in 1977, a contribution relative to Norway's share—assessed at 1.66 per cent—in the total gross national product of the 10 countries.

Institutions. At the same meeting (June 30) the Norwegian delegation also accepted proposals regarding Norwegian participation in the Community institutions.

Shipping. At a further meeting of deputies on July 20 the Community representatives agreed to allow continuing Norwegian control over foreign investment in the shipping industry, which provided 9 per cent of the country's gross national product, including £350,000,000 in freight charges. The controls would be allowed to continue until common policies on the rights of establishment had been worked out on a Community basis.

Relations with other EFTA countries. Shortly after the first contacts between senior governmental representatives of the six EC member countries and those of the EFTA countries not making application for membership, Cappelen stated in Brussels on July 27 at a ministerial meeting that it was essential that a comprehensive agreement be worked out with Sweden and with the other countries involved.

Norway's insistence on special treatment for its fishing industry was given support by the Italian Prime Minister, Emilio Colombo, when he met his Norwegian counterpart, Bratteli, in Rome on Jan. 5, 1972. Following a series of talks with governmental leaders in the other member countries, Bratelli's government presented a proposal to the Communities on Jan. 10 for a special protocol maintaining a 12-mile limit for the whole of the stretch of coastline from Landesnes to the most northerly point at the junction with the Soviet border. This limit would have included 97 per cent of the value of the

Norwegian catch and would have included a 500-mile section of coast south of Trondheim which the Communities had previously refused to envisage as eligible for a 12-mile limit.

No agreement was reached on these proposals, and the Norwegian delegation continued to reject Community insistence on the principle of the transitional nature of the exemptions from the common fisheries policy. However, following a Cabinet meeting in Oslo on Jan. 13 Sören Sommerfelt, the leader of the Norwegian negotiating delegation, was given a new mandate to continue the talks, and agreement was finally reached on Jan. 14. Under this, the Communities agreed to grant protection within a 12-mile limit as far south as Egersund (only about 50 miles north-west of Landesnes) and also accepted a form of words which would allow protection to continue beyond 1982 under conditions to be arranged at the time.

On Jan. 21, Knut Hoem, the Norwegian Minister of Fisheries, resigned having explained in a letter to Bratteli that he was opposed to the terms negotiated for Norwegian entry into the European Communities and thus could not support signature of the Treaty of Accession.

It was reported that Hoem was satisfied with the arrangements for the 10-year transitional period, which granted Norwegian fishermen protection within a 12-mile limit along most of the Norwegian coast, but was not prepared to accept as sufficient guarantee the political assurances given by the Community negotiators in respect of continued safeguards beyond 1982.

The results of the Norwegian negotiations were explained in a White Paper published in Oslo on March 10, 1972, in which the government recommended membership of the Communities and examined the consequences of adhesion.

In particular, it was submitted that membership was a necessity for the country's shipping industry, which earned 40 per cent of Norway's foreign exchange and for which the enlarged Communities represented 60 per cent of its market. In general terms, the White Paper rejected the possibility of a commercial agreement with the EC as an alternative to full membership, as this would reduce the economic growth of the country and would also prohibit the Norwegian government from participating in European decisions affecting Norway.

5.7 Signature of Treaty of Accession (Jan. 22, 1972)

Bratteli attended the ceremony for the signature of the Accession Treaty in Brussels on Jan. 22, 1972 and spoke as follows:

"It is an honour and a pleasure for me to represent the Norwegian government at the signing of the Treaty of Accession to the European Communities. Our application for membership does not date from yesterday. It has been actively upheld ever since 1962 by the successive governments and *Stortings*, since it stands for our natural interest, which is closer and more committed co-operation, in the political, economic and cultural fields, with our traditional partners in Europe.

"The recently concluded negotiations have defined for Norway, as they have for the three other applicant countries, the terms of this accession. The Norwegian government considers that the outcome of these negotiations constitutes a satisfactory basis for Norway's accession to the European Communities. It is now for the Norwegian people and the *Storting* to take the final decision in this important matter, in keeping with our democratic and parliamentary traditions. We need the support of the people to reinforce our links with Europe and proceed further along the path followed by the European Communities in order to ensure for the peoples of Europe peace and security, well-being and happiness, to assume the responsibility we have towards the underprivileged countries of the world. The enlargement of the Communities will provide greater scope and new opportunities to attain those common aims which are so important for our own peoples and for the rest of the world. These can be attained if our political action, our progressive and pragmatic co-operation are founded on confidence and frank solidarity between partners. It is the Norwegian government's firm resolve to give concrete expression to this confidence and solidarity.

"In the Communities, the ideal must not be too far removed from reality, nor the periphery too far from the centre. It would be rather pointless to find, in Brussels, solutions to our common problems if we were unable to convince our peoples that the common objectives are also their own and that solutions which have been reached are reasonable and fair.

"We are working, in our countries, to still extend democracy to fresh sectors of society. We see in the Community the possibility of also introducing democratic forms of decision-taking into international co-operation.

"A Community which extends from Sicily to Finmark must find various and flexible means of action to solve the different problems which are raised by the evolutionary trends of society in the different regions. In this context we attach importance to the aim of the Treaty of Rome, which is to ensure a harmonious and balanced development of all the regions in the Community.

"We consider it as a primordial task for the Communities to foster social policy and to raise it to ever higher levels. It is equally important to develop regional policy so as to strengthen, with the aid of pooled resources, the basis of economic activity in the peripheral regions. The economic integration of which the enlarged Community is the basis will place us in a better position to solve the problems of effecting changes in economic activity and ensuring employment. By means of a common industrial policy we will be better able to master the problems introduced by large multi-national corporations into our economies and into the world economy. It is only by common action that we will be able effectively to protect the environment.

"These, then, are the essential tasks for our societies. But the enlargement of the Communities must also be seen in a broader political context. Efforts to bring about greater unity in Europe have now reached a major crossroads. In this part of the world we have travelled a long way towards reconciliation, peace and stability. This is a further step towards a solution of the problems facing less favoured peoples in other parts of the world. Thanks to the enlargement of the Communities, the peoples of Europe will be able to look to the future with greater confidence."

5.8 Decision to hold referendum (March 1971)

The decision to hold a consultative referendum was confirmed by Cappelen, the Minister of Foreign Affairs, on March 30, 1971, shortly after the formation of the Bratteli government. No provision for a referendum is included in the Norwegian Constitution, and the final decision on the membership of an international organization such as the European Communities was subject, under Article 93 of the Constitution, to a three-quarters majority being achieved in the *Storting* (i.e. 113 of the full membership of 150 being in favour). However, the government had the support of only a minority in the *Storting*, and it was considered that the referendum would in effect be decisive, Bratteli having announced on Aug. 23, 1972, that he would resign if the vote went against membership.

Of the four parties in the outgoing coalition, the Conservatives, Liberals and Christian People's Party were in general favourable to Norway's entry into the EC; the

Centre Party—which represented mainly agrarian interests—had, however, many reservations on whether Norway should join the European Common Market, and had expressed concern at the possible position of Norwegian farmers in such an eventuality. The Labour Party was in favour of Norway's entry into the EC if the terms were right, although some elements in the party—notably on the left wing—were opposed to entry into the Common Market.

5.9 Referendum campaign

During the negotiations on terms applicable to Norwegian membership there had been particular difficulty in reaching agreement on safeguards for the fishing and agricultural communities in Norway, which were expected to be subjected to fierce competition from parallel industries in the rest of the Communities unless continued protection was arranged. Although provisions were eventually made to allow for a degree of protection in the final terms negotiated, many Norwegians continued to express anxiety and opposition to membership.

The opposition campaign was led by the People's Movement against Norwegian Membership of the Common Market (*Folkebevegelsen Mot Norsk Medlemskap i Fellesmarkedet*) which was founded in August 1970 and launched its campaign in the autumn of that year. Based initially on the farmers' organizations which had opposed membership since 1962, it quickly came to draw support from individuals and groups cutting across party lines within the *Storting* and also from outside the normal parliamentary channels.

On April 19, 1972, shortly after the publication on March 10 of the government's final White Paper on membership [see 5.6] the People's Movement issued its own "White Paper" laying down detailed arguments against accession.

Opposition was expressed towards specific issues such as the fisheries question, where the existing Six had agreed on a Community fisheries policy disregarding Norway's position on the same day negotiations had reopened in June 1970 and where the guarantees given in the protocol as to what would happen after the 10-year transition period were deemed inadequate. In general the anti-EC campaign tapped "Norwegian popular fears of loss of sovereignty" which Toivo Miljan in his book "The Reluctant Europeans" (Hurst and Co., London, 1977) saw as contributing directly to the subsequent Norwegian referendum result. Community reports published in 1969–70, such as the Davignon Report on political co-operation and the Werner Report on economic and monetary union [see also 6.2] were held up as evidence that the future development of the European Communities could infringe upon national sovereignty to a greater extent than would originally have been approved at the time of Norway's scheduled accession and beyond what a small country such as Norway might be able to influence.

Despite the vigorous and efficient anti-Common Market campaign Erik Ribu, chairman of the Norwegian government's common market committee and Under-Secretary of State for Trade and Shipping, on June 21, 1972, predicted that 60 per cent of the electorate would vote in favour and that even a narrower result would be sufficient to enable the three-quarters majority to be obtained in a final vote in the *Storting*.

Ribu estimated that, of the 150 members, only 40 were opposed to entry and that three of these at least were likely to be persuaded to vote in favour following a referendum which approved membership. The governing Labour Party held 74 seats in the *Storting*, although 11 of these were held by opponents of Norwegian entry into the Communities, and was supported in its European policy by the 29 Conservative Party members and by factions of the Christian People's Party (14 seats) and of the Liberal Party (13 seats). The Centre (Agrarian) Party, holding 20 seats, was unanimously opposed to Norwegian membership.

Announcing his decision to resign in the event of rejection of membership in the referendum, Bratteli told a Labour Party rally on Aug. 23 that he wanted the "people's support" for his government's EC policy and warned that defeat on the issue would "create a very serious situation for the country", making it impossible for the government to continue in power. The statement was described by Hans Borgen, chairman of a group opposing membership [see also 5.3], as constituting "intolerable pressure" on voters, while Per Borten commented that he was surprised that Bratteli had asked for support rather than for advice from the consultative vote.

In response to suggestions that, in the event of a negative vote, the Labour Party might form a new government under a different Prime Minister, Bratteli declared on Aug. 26 that "a negative result at the referendum will destroy the basis for the present government, not only in relation to the EC but in a number of other fields". Bratteli added that "no new Labour government can negotiate with the EC about anything other than full membership", thus rejecting the often advocated suggestion that Norway should abandon plans for full membership in favour of a trade agreement.

On Aug. 28 the 11 Labour Party MPs opposing Norwegian membership called on the people to "vote according to their convictions" despite Bratteli's threat to resign.

Kaare Willoch, leader of the Conservative Party, added his support to Bratteli when on Aug. 28 he affirmed that his party would refuse to be part of a government whose main task was to negotiate a trade agreement with the Communities, but he indicated that a temporary coalition formed solely to negotiate such a limited agreement could expect passive co-operation from the rest of the *Storting* despite its "narrow and motley parliamentary basis", provided it "followed a moderate course on other issues". He suggested that a more permanent government could be formed after the next parliamentary elections (which could not be held until September 1973—the end of the four-year period of the existing *Storting*).

In the closing stages of the campaign, which had been vigorously contested for several months both within and outside the formal political framework, Willy Brandt, the West German Chancellor, joined Bratteli in addressing a public meeting in Oslo on Sept. 14 organized by the "Yes to the Common Market" group. (Brandt's support was regarded by the government as an important feature since he had lived in Norway during the earlier part of the Nazi regime in Germany, acquired Norwegian citizenship when deprived of his German nationality, and during the German occupation of Norway had stayed in Sweden.)

On this occasion Brandt described the Communities' policy as one which involved "a constructive attitude with regard to neighbouring countries which have not joined the Communities, co-operation with the countries of Eastern Europe and also well defined relations with regard to the United States and other large industrial nations".

Although a large majority in parliament and most newspapers had been consistently in favour of Norwegian membership of the European Communities, it was considered in the foreign press and by a number of independent surveys that public opinion had generally remained against the principle of entry.

In an interview with *The Guardian* on Sept. 23, Bratteli commented: "Since early this year I have felt the whole time that there was a fair chance to get through. But it is a very strange picture. The Labour Party is no problem at all because there is a considerable majority in the organization and among the voters. But in some other groups there have been developments, changes, especially in the later months." Bratteli explained much of the opposition as a reflection of the general mood of protest in the world. "No to the Common Market," he said, "has been a rallying point for all protesting groups—Maoists, Stalinists, Leninists, conservatives and religious groups. I think the temper of the discussions we have had has been bound to this special situation. It's protest against this modern world, against the modern industrial society, the education system and so on. If there is a 'No' [vote], many of these people will be surprised to find all the evils are still there."

5.10 Vote against membership of European Communities (Sept. 24–25, 1972)—Subsequent amendments to the Treaty of Accession

Polling was held over two days, and the 2,647,000 eligible voters were asked to reply "Yes" or "No" to the question: "Do you think Norway should join the European Communities?" The northern and rural communities were reported to have voted heavily against membership, and the final figures recorded a majority of "No" votes, which amounted to 1,099,389 or 53.5 per cent of the total poll, while the "Yes" votes amounted to 956,043 or 46.5 per cent. The voting figures represented a poll of 77.6 per cent of the electorate.

Bratteli commented immediately after the last votes had been cast: "In my opinion European integration is a long-term trend, which will not be stopped by this decision in Norway. But how Norway will handle this problem in the future is impossible to say."

On Sept. 26 the Norwegian government informed the representatives of the Community countries in Brussels that Norwegian participation in the consultative negotiating committees was to be withdrawn and that Norway would not take part in the summit meeting planned to open on Oct. 19 in Paris involving the countries of the enlarged Communities. Halvorsen, Norwegian Ambassador to the Communities, announced on the same day that the Norwegian government had decided not to submit a proposal for membership to the *Storting*.

Some of the foreign reactions are described below.

United Kingdom. The British government announced on Sept. 26 that the Norwegian decision would have no effect on British plans to join the Communities on Jan. 1, 1973, but Labour Party spokesmen suggested that the pressure for a referendum on membership would be intensified. However, the legislation for British entry had already passed through all the necessary parliamentary stages and required only the granting of the Royal Assent and the depositing of the instrument of ratification of the Treaty of Accession before becoming final.

Soviet Union. The newspaper *Pravda* declared on Sept. 27 that the principal argument against the Communities had been the "political aspect of the problem" and that the Norwegians had "justly" been alarmed at the movement towards "political and even military integration" which was implied in the plans of the "supranational bodies" of the Communities.

Finland. Kalevi Sorsa, the Finnish Prime Minister, referred in a speech on Sept. 26 to the possibilities of reinforcing Nordic co-operation which were raised by the Norwegian decision, and commented that the "interdependence and mutual influence" among the peoples of Denmark, Finland and Sweden had for long been a "strong characteristic" of Northern Europe.

Sweden. A communiqué published on Sept. 26 noted that the Swedish government "will do what it can to support the Norwegian government in its efforts to obtain a satisfactory solution with regard to the Communities", and added that Nordic co-operation "will be able to develop and deepen whatever form of co-operation with the Communities is chosen by each of the Nordic countries".

France. President Pompidou stated on Sept. 26 that he "regretted" the result of the referendum and hoped that it would not influence the Danish voters who faced a similar decision the following week.

European Communities. Sicco Mansholt, President of the European Commission, declared in a radio programme on Sept. 26 that the decision was "a step back for Europe", and commented: "Europe is in a phase where economic and monetary problems play too great a part. We have not yet created a social and democratic Europe."

The Norwegian failure to ratify the Treaty of Accession did not prevent its application to the other three applicant countries—Denmark, the Republic of Ireland and the United Kingdom—as provision had been made in the Treaty to meet such an eventuality. Article 2 stated that if the instruments of ratification had not been deposited "in due time" (i.e. before Jan. 1, 1973) by all the candidate countries the Treaty would enter into force for those which had done so.

However, the Treaty documents required a number of modifications in the event of a failure to ratify by one or more applicants. The articles mainly affected included those covering (i) official languages of the enlarged Communities, which would have included Norwegian; (ii) national representation on various committees; (iii) the composition of the Commission; (iv) the composition of the Court of Justice, which was to have included one Norwegian judge out of a total of 11; (v) voting rights in the Council of Ministers, where Norway was to have had three votes in cases where a qualified majority was required; (vi) national contributions to the Community budget, to which Norway would have contributed 1.66 per cent in the first year.

In addition to these requirements, the Treaty of Accession and its attendant documents provided that the Council of Ministers could declare those parts of the Treaty which referred expressly to a non-ratifying country to have lapsed, or could otherwise adjust them. Thus, Norway's special protocols referring to fishing, agriculture and the status of Spitzbergen could be deleted from the text.

5.11 Resignation of Bratteli—Formation of Korvald coalition government (March 1972)

In accordance with his earlier statements, Bratteli confirmed on Sept. 27 that he and his government would resign, but announced that the resignation would be delayed to enable the government to fulfil a number of functions connected with the opening of a new session of the *Storting*. (The delay allowed the government to present the budget for the coming year and also enabled discussions to take place between the political parties on the formation of a new government.)

Bratteli tendered his resignation to King Olav on the morning of Oct. 7, and on the same day the King entrusted the formation of a new Cabinet to Lars Korvald, a prominent advocate of a trade agreement with the Communities as an alternative to full membership and leader of the small Christian People's Party, which held only 14 seats in the *Storting*. In the meantime, Bratteli was requested to remain in office at the head of a caretaker government.

Korvald's task of forming a government was complicated by the limited number of political allies to whom he could turn in the *Storting*. The referendum had reflected the views of only a minority of parliamentary opinion, and Korvald was thus forced to open discussions with the Centre Party, the Liberals and the dissidents from the Labour Party who had voted against EC membership, since the Conservative Party and the bulk of the Labour Party had been in favour.

He was nevertheless able to announce on Oct. 12 that he had succeeded in forming a minority coalition government comprising his own party, the Centre Party, and a faction of the Liberal Party opposed to full membership of the Communities.

Korvald presented his Cabinet list to King Olav on Oct. 16 and, having been sworn in on the following day, the new government took office on Oct. 18. The Cabinet comprised six ministers from the Centre Party, five from the Liberal Party and four from the Christian People's Party. It was represented in the *Storting* by only 39 of the 150 members, including 20 Centre Party members, 14 CPP members and five Liberals, the remaining eight Liberals being supporters of EC membership who had refused to participate in a government which would negotiate only a trade agreement as an alternative.

Korvald made a policy statement in the *Storting* on Oct. 24 which concentrated primarily on the need to reach a trade agreement which would "satisfactorily secure trade between the European Economic Community and Norway and form a basis for co-operation in other fields".

In addition, the statement confirmed Norway's policy of continuing membership of EFTA and NATO, stressing that the basis of such participation was "the principle of equal co-operation between free and independent nations". With regard to international economic co-operation, Korvald stated that the government would "influence capital transactions with other countries and establishments across the borders with the intention of securing vital national interests", and similarly intended to "establish political control of the economic tendencies towards concentration and in this context [to] deal especially with problems of foreign participation in Norwegian industry".

The policy statement also drew attention to Norwegian concern over protection of the fishing industry; declared that the government would work for a "strengthening of the sovereignty of the coastal states over fishing in adjoining sea areas" within the context of a UN Conference on the Law of the Sea planned for 1973; and added: "The question of an extension to the fishery limit will be considered." As regards the shipping industry, Korvald affirmed that it was "important for Norway to counteract tendencies towards protectionism in international shipping", and that the government would "take care of these interests in international negotiations and agreements".

It was reported on Oct. 24 that the Norwegian ship owners' association had requested the Minister for Commerce and Shipping, Hallvard Eika, to provide for mutual co-operation and consultation with the Communities on shipping questions in any trade agreement which Norway might conclude.

5.12 Request for opening of trade negotiations with EC (Oct. 25, 1972)
Korvald announced on Oct. 12 that his new government would negotiate a free trade agreement with the Communities as an alternative to the full membership which had been rejected in the referendum, and on Oct. 16 he told a press conference that negotiations could be completed by April 1. However, Gunnar Rogstad, managing director of the Norwegian export council, had warned on Sept. 26 that, if such an agreement were to follow the same pattern as those negotiated with other non-applicant members of the European Free Trade Association [see chapter 6], there would be difficulties over terms for the principal Norwegian exports.

Rogstad emphasized that the model of the Swedish free trade agreement with the Communities could not simply be transferred to Norway, as among Norwegian exports there was a larger proportion of products considered by the EC as "sensitive" or as a threat to Community industry. It was thus estimated that more than 40 per cent of Norwegian exports would be subject to special conditions delaying the removal of tariff barriers in the event of a trade agreement being negotiated. The products concerned would include paper and board, aluminium, ferro-alloys and non-ferrous metals, all of which had been the object of protracted disagreements during the negotiations with the non-applicant countries. Furthermore, Norway was also faced with the task of re-negotiating terms for trade in fish, of which almost half was directed to the countries of the enlarged Community of nine members and which had been the most difficult obstacle to the successful conclusion of negotiations on terms for full membership.

(Norwegian exports to the six existing countries of the Communities and to the United Kingdom and Denmark amounted to 54.8 per cent of total exports in 1970, while the corresponding figure for imports amounted to 53.4 per cent. The continuing importance of the EC as an export market was indicated by an increase in the proportion of Norwegian exports to the six original members, which rose to a share of 29.7 per cent in 1970 compared with 25.7 per cent in 1960, despite EC customs tariffs and the parallel development of free trade within EFTA.)

The free trade agreements negotiated by the non-applicant EFTA countries with the Communities had allowed for free trade to be maintained between Denmark, Norway and the United Kingdom on the one hand and the six non-applicants on the other, but no specific provisions had been made in the event of one or other of the acceding countries withdrawing its application. Thus the Norwegian position with regard to trade with both Denmark and the United Kingdom was unclear. However, on Oct. 5 the Norwegian Ambassador in London, Paul Koht, sent a note to the Foreign Office requesting Britain to help prevent the reimposition of tariff barriers on Norwegian exports after Jan. 1, when Britain ceased to be a member of EFTA. On Oct. 6 Denmark and Norway agreed that free trading arrangements for industrial products applicable during 1972 should be extended throughout 1973, after which a "solution must be found by means of an arrangement between Norway and the enlarged EC".

Dagfinn Vaarvik, the Foreign Minister, subsequently announced that the new government had made a formal request to the Communities on Oct. 25 for the opening of negotiations on a trade agreement. It was reported in Brussels that the Norwegian letter to the Communities recalled the commitment made at the summit conference in Paris on Oct. 19–20 to seek a "speedy solution" to the problems of Norwegian relations with the EC.

During a two-day debate in the *Storting* on the government's policy statement, Korvald declared on Oct. 30: "Our aim is to conclude these negotiations before April 1 next year, and we hope to get a development clause in the agreement like the one which Sweden has obtained in her agreement with the Market." Willoch, chairman and parliamentary leader of the Conservative Party, stated on the same day that the possibility of full membership must be kept open and that in the meantime a trade agreement should contain "a clear and purposeful development clause", which would emphasize that Norway wished to establish closer co-operation in such fields as shipping and monetary policies and environmental protection. However, Borten, leader of the Centre Party, criticized the "unwillingness to accept the result of the referendum" and maintained that the government had no mandate to negotiate any arrangement which would open the way to gradual entry into the Communities.

5.13 Norwegian trade relations with the UK

During October certain concessions in the British exchange control regulations in respect of Norway were withdrawn following the Norwegian decision not to proceed with membership of the Communities. The Bank of England stated in a series of notices that permission announced in the 1972–73 budget for official exchange (as opposed to investment currency) to be used by UK residents for direct investment in Norway was to be withdrawn, while at the same time Norwegian sterling loan facilities in the UK were to be limited.

Jon Norbom, the Norwegian Finance Minister, announced on Nov. 2, however, that Britain had agreed to a preliminary arrangement allowing most Norwegian industrial goods tariff-free access to the British market during 1973, although an expiring agreement concerning exports of Norwegian frozen fish fillets to Britain was still subject to renegotiation.

The British government considered that such an agreement with Norway was compatible with its commitments to the European Communities, since no change in the UK tariff with respect to third countries was required until Jan. 1, 1974, and the existing zero tariff arrangements between the two countries—concluded under the terms of the EFTA agreements—could thus be maintained throughout 1973. However, (i) the UK would apply levies on imports of certain Norwegian products subject to the EEC common agricultural policy, and (ii) qualification for free entry of the broad range of industrial products would be subject to EFTA rules of origin only until March 31, 1973, after which date the UK would make its first tariff adjustments with the Communities and would thus have to comply with the Community rules of origin.

The British and Norwegian governments accordingly exchanged notes on Nov. 7 establishing the legal basis for the continuance of free trade relations between the two countries pending the conclusion of an agreement between Norway and the EC.

5.14 Negotiations on trade agreement with the Communities

Exploratory talks between Norway and the European Commission had started in Brussels on Nov. 9, 1972, following the Norwegian government's submission of a formal request for negotiations on a trade agreement on Oct. 25. Full-scale negotiations began in February 1973 and an agreement was initialled on April 16. The bargaining which took place in this period, and which extended the negotiations beyond the April 1 deadline originally envisaged, centred on three main problems:

(1) The Norwegian government objected to the proposed transitional arrangements for the abolition of tariffs by the EC on "sensitive" industrial products, particularly unwrought aluminium. On aluminium they wanted a shorter transitional period than the 10 years proposed by the Commission and also a higher initial annual "ceiling" than the duty-free 190,000 tons put forward by the Commission, in order that Norway might continue her traditionally duty-free exports of aluminium to Britain and Denmark. On some other "sensitive" industrial products the Norwegians also wanted shorter transitional periods and higher ceilings.

(2) Norway sought the concession of a low tariff not only on her substantial exports of fish fillets (the normal EC rate being 15 per cent), but also on other fish products such as tinned fish, frozen prawns, hardened fish fats and fatty acids (which were likewise subject to a high external tariff). The Commission, while prepared from the outset to concede a lower tariff on fish fillets, had reservations about the other items, which it regarded as agricultural products. An important factor in the bargaining on fish was the Norwegian government's policy statement of Oct. 24, 1972, that the question of an extension to the present fisheries limit of 12 miles would be considered.

(3) The third principal element in the negotiations was the reduction in Norwegian tariffs on certain EC exports, notably wine and some horticultural products, which either the Commission sought from Norway or which Norway offered as concessions for its demands on fish and aluminium.

5.15 Signature of Special Relations Agreement (May 14, 1973)

A Special Relations Agreement providing for free trade in industrial products was signed in Brussels on May 14 between the European Economic Community and the European Coal and Steel Community on the one hand and Norway on the other. The agreement, which was ratified by the Norwegian parliament at the end of a debate held on May 24–25, was to come into operation on July 1, providing for the progressive abolition of customs duties on most industrial goods between Norway and the EC countries in five stages between July 1, 1973, and July 1, 1977. Special provisions were also contained relating to fish and certain sensitive industrial products.

The agreement had the effect of establishing for Norway a similar "special relationship" with the EC to that already negotiated with the other "non-joining" members of EFTA, namely Austria, Finland, Iceland, Portugal, Sweden and Switzerland [see chapter 6]—although no decision had been taken in Helsinki by April 1 on whether to sign the Finnish agreement, while that part of Iceland's agreement dealing with fish exports remained inoperative pending a satisfactory settlement of the "cod war". The agreement signed with Norway also ensured that the enlargement of the EC from six to nine members would not result in any significant reimposition of tariffs between Norway and her former EFTA partners (Britain and Denmark).

The main provision of the agreement was a commitment by both sides to abolish all tariffs on industrial goods in five successive cuts, as follows:

July 1, 1973	20 per cent
Jan. 1, 1974	20 per cent
Jan. 1, 1975	20 per cent
Jan. 1, 1976	20 per cent
July. 1, 1977	20 per cent

As with the other EFTA "non-joiners", the timetable was therefore to be basically the same as that governing the removal of tariffs between the original Six and the three acceding countries; however, in the case of the other EFTA countries (except Finland and, partially, Iceland) and the new members the first tariff cut came into effect on April 1, 1973.

The agreement also incorporated a number of compromises on the points mentioned above:

Fish products. Fish fillets and frozen prawns were to be subject to tariffs of 3 per cent and 7.5 per cent respectively (compared with the normal common external EC tariff of 15 per cent and 20 per cent respectively). These reductions were to be applied in stages over a four-year period beginning on Jan. 1, 1974. In the same period Britain and Denmark, whose free trade with their former EFTA partner had earlier been extended to the end of 1973, were to build up their tariffs on Norwegian fish fillets to the 3 per cent level. It was also understood in this context that these concessions would be suspended if Norway were at any time to make a unilateral extension of her fishing limits, a condition which closely resembled the one made in 1972 in the case of Iceland. On the other fish products under discussion, the only concession granted was a reduction in the tariffs on some kinds of tinned fish.

Sensitive products. On unwrought aluminium Norway secured the concession of a reduction in the transitional period from 10 to nine years. No increase was achieved in the initial 190,000 tons ceiling proposed by the Commission, but a formula put forward by Denmark was adopted, according to which the ceiling on unwrought aluminium was to be increased if the system for the temporary admission of imports for processing in the EC and then for re-exporting was not working satisfactorily. For other sensitive products such as magnesium, silicon carbide, ferro-alloys, zinc, artificial textile fibres, paper and cardboard, the agreement specified various tariff-free quotas as well as transitional periods varying from seven to 11 years. In general these represented only slight concessions to Norway beyond the original negotiating position of the Commission.

Agriculture and wine. The agreement specified that for semi-manufactured agricultural products tariffs would be removed in respect of that proportion of the product considered to be industrial. Norway also undertook to remove tariffs on wine from EC countries and also on some fruit and vegetables.

Coal and steel. A separate agreement signed at the same time on matters relating to the European and Steel Community provided for the achievement of free trade in Treaty of Paris products by July 1, 1977, on the same schedule of tariff cuts as for other industrial goods.

The main agreement also contained clauses relating to its supervision and possible extension, including the establishment of a joint Norway-EC supervisory committee, which would meet normally twice a year to settle customs arrangements and rules of origin, and an evolutionary clause providing for an extension of the scope of the agreement by negotiation at the request of either partner.

5.16 Parliamentary ratification of agreement—The "Crotale" controversy (May–June 1973)

Although it was reported that there was some disappointment in Norway at the outcome of the negotiations, particularly in industrial circles with regard to the provisions on aluminium, the trade agreement was ratified by the *Storting* after a debate on May 24–25. However, controversy was provoked during this debate when the chairman of the *Storting's* foreign affairs committee, Helge Seip (Liberal), raised the question of the "Crotale affair", with the result that the Foreign Affairs Committee was instructed to hold an official enquiry into the matter.

The "Crotale" controversy broke out in Norway on March 28, when it was alleged in the foreign affairs committee that the Norwegian government had attempted to secure better terms in the negotiations for the trade agreement by offering to buy the French Crotale rocket system, and had used the possibility that the Crotale system would be bought in order to exert pressure on the French government, which had consistently opposed the granting of better terms for Norwegian exports of aluminium to the EC. For the government, Eika replied to the committee that the question of buying the French system had indeed been touched upon in the course of talks with French officials in Paris. However, it was later made known that the idea of linking the rocket purchase with easier terms for aluminium was first put forward by the French themselves when the former Labour government under Trygve Bratteli had been in power, although the government had at the time refused to link the two questions.

At the end of the two-day debate the agreement was approved by a unanimous vote on May 25, and on June 8 the Norwegian government survived, by 77 votes to 73, a motion of no-confidence on the Crotale affair brought against it in the *Storting* by the Labour Party. Korvald, the Norwegian Prime Minister, expressed his regrets at the conduct of the government in the affair and admitted that it had been envisaged that the purchase of the rockets could be linked with the securing of better terms for aluminium exports to the EC.

6: EUROPEAN FREE TRADE ASSOCIATION: EC RELATIONS WITH REMAINING EFTA COUNTRIES

6.1 Chronology of events

Dec. 12, 1961	Austrian and Swedish requests for special arrangements with EEC
Dec. 15, 1961	Swiss application for economic association with EEC
June 4, 1962	Portuguese approach to EEC
Nov. 10 and 24, 1970	Opening of discussions between EC and non-applicant EFTA countries (including Finland and Iceland for the first time)
June 16, 1971	Commission Opinion on possible agreements with non-applicant EFTA countries
Nov. 9, 1971	Council approval of negotiating mandate
Dec. 3, 1971	Opening of negotiations at ambassador level
July 21, 1972	Resignation of Paasio government in Finland
July 22, 1972	Signature of Special Relations Agreements
Oct. 25, 1972	Austrian *Nationalrat* approves Agreement
Nov. 29, 1972	Approval by Liechtenstein *Landtag* of application of Swiss Agreement to Liechtenstein
Dec. 3, 1972	Approval of Agreement in Swiss referendum
Dec. 12, 1972	Swedish *Riksdag* approves Agreement
Dec. 13, 1972	Portuguese National Assembly approves Agreement
Jan. 1, 1973	Entry into force of Agreements
Feb. 28, 1973	Icelandic *Althing* ratifies Agreement
Oct. 5, 1973	Finnish signature of Agreement
Nov. 16, 1973	Finnish *Eduskunta* approves Agreement
Nov. 19–20, 1975	Conclusion of agreement on West German fishing rights in Icelandic waters
June 1, 1976	Signature of interim agreement ending fisheries dispute between Iceland and UK
July 1, 1977	Abolition of bulk of tariff duties between EFTA and EC countries at end of transitional period
Jan. 1, 1985	Establishment of free trade in industrial goods between EC and EFTA countries

6.2 Negotiations with non-applicant EFTA countries

The Communities opened discussions in November 1970 with those members of the European Free Trade Association (EFTA) which, unlike the UK, Denmark and Norway, had not applied for full membership of the Communities—i.e. Austria, Iceland, Portugal, Sweden and Switzerland—and with Finland, which at that time was an associate rather than a full member of EFTA. The positions of Austria, Sweden and Switzerland—the three neutral countries among the full EFTA members—were put to the EC Council of Ministers on Nov. 10, and those of Finland, Iceland and Portugal on Nov. 24.

This widening of the talks followed a meeting of the Council of Ministers on Oct. 26–27 which agreed that full membership could be granted only to countries accepting all the Communities' rights and obligations and all their aims, including both economic and monetary union and also political union. For other European countries which could not make this commitment, it would be possible to conclude trade agreements involving no share in decision-taking.

The question of economic and monetary union had been dealt with by a committee under the chairmanship of Pierre Werner, the Prime Minister of Luxembourg, which had presented an interim report to the Council of Ministers at its meeting on June 8–9, 1970, and a final report on Oct. 26. Political unification had been examined by a committee chaired by Vicomte Etienne Davignon, political director of the Belgian Foreign Ministry; this committee's report had been approved in principle by the Council of Ministers on July 20, 1970, and finally adopted on Oct. 27.

Sections dealing with the background to each country's position [except Portugal, for which see 11.4] are given below. [For Norway's May 1973 Special Relations Agreement, concluded on the model of those concluded by other EFTA countries after Norway's decision against Community membership, see 5.15 above.]

6.3 Austria

Austria had originally requested a special arrangement with the EEC on Dec. 12, 1961, when Sweden also made a similar application. At a first hearing on July 28, 1962, Dr Bruno Kreisky, then Austrian Foreign Minister, made a statement on his country's position and after the breakdown of negotiations for British membership in 1963, the Austrian request was never formally withdrawn. Preliminary discussions were renewed with the EEC Commission in mid-1963, exploratory talks opening on July 4 and continuing on Nov. 4–7, 1963.

Speaking in Vienna on Nov. 14, 1963, Dr Fritz Bock, the Austrian Trade Minister, said: "The results of the exploratory talks in Brussels have proved that association between Austria and the Common Market does not pose any insuperable difficulties. Austria's arrangement with the Common Market must, in view of the country's special position, take the form of an exceptional treaty, which would not serve as a model for others." A full report of these talks was sent by the Commission to the Council of Ministers.

The EEC Foreign Ministers discussed on Oct. 13, 1964, the opening of formal negotiations on the renewed Austrian request for association. All member countries again confirmed their desire for a solution to the problems which faced Austria, but remained divided over the terms under which the Commission should be authorized to start talks. Whereas France, West

Germany, and Luxembourg unreservedly backed the Commission's view that the EEC should grant Austria an arrangement involving full economic union, with only those deviations rendered necessary by her neutrality, Belgium, Italy, and the Netherlands expressed reservations and proposed that plans for an association agreement should be studied.

After the committee of permanent representatives (Coreper) had further examined the issues involved, the Council at its session on March 1–2, 1965, unanimously decided that the Commission should be given a mandate for a first round of negotiations with the Austrian government, covering the removal of trade barriers between the EEC and Austria, customs duties between Austria and non-member countries, the harmonization of Community and Austrian policies, and the setting up of the necessary machinery. The negotiations, which opened on March 18 and ended on June 25, led, according to a joint communiqué, to a wide rapprochement of views on certain matters.

Press reports made it clear, however, that the Austrian suggestion of a double membership for herself of EFTA and the EEC had not been accepted by the EEC, which feared that any tariff-free access for Austria to both economic groupings would risk wide economic distortion. The EEC proposal was said to have been that after a year, which would allow Austria to renounce her EFTA membership and to start adjusting her tariff rates to those of the EEC, she should introduce substantial tariff reductions vis-à-vis the Six and that, as she gradually enjoyed more of the benefits of reduced tariffs from the Six, she should make a compensating move in raising tariffs vis-à-vis EFTA.

A further three rounds of negotiations were held from Sept. 28 to Oct. 1, 1965, from Dec. 6 to 10, 1965, and from Jan. 31 to Feb. 3, 1966.

These negotiations covered principally the mutual dismantling of barriers to trade, the harmonization of tariffs, agricultural preferences, harmonization of economic policies and the avoidance of distortions of competition, the problem of Austria's trade with East European countries, institutional questions, and problems connected with the neutrality obligations contained in the 1955 Austrian State Treaty and constitutional law.

After a report on the negotiations had been submitted to the EEC Commission at the end of March by Jean Rey, Commission member responsible for external affairs, a group of experts from EEC member states held its first meeting on April 25 to examine the progress of the negotiations.

At a meeting of the EFTA Council on May 12–13, 1966, in Bergen, Norway, Dr Bock, the Austrian Vice-Chancellor and Minister for Trade and Reconstruction, denied reports that Austria did not wish to make the final 20 per cent EFTA tariff reduction at the end of 1966; he stated, however, that no decision could be taken before the autumn, when it would be clearer what stage Austria's negotiations with the EEC had reached. Later, at a meeting of the Austrian cabinet on July 11 it was agreed that a speedy resumption of negotiations with the EEC and an early conclusion of a treaty were becoming increasingly urgent; only in this way, it was stated in a communiqué issued after the meeting, could the sound development of the Austrian economy and a high level of employment be ensured.

Negotiations on special arrangements between Austria and the EEC were resumed on Dec. 13, 1966, after a lapse of 10 months.

At an EEC Ministerial Council meeting on Oct. 26–27, 1966, it was agreed that the permanent representatives should prepare a new second partial "mandate" dealing principally with customs tariffs, agriculture, and trade with East European countries. Although this report was to have been adopted at a Ministerial Council meeting on

Nov. 24–25, consideration was postponed at the request of France—the reason given being that various Foreign Ministers (including Maurice Couve de Murville, the French Foreign Minister) would be unable to attend—and it was not until the following Council meeting on Dec. 6–7 that the permanent representatives' report was discussed.

In the meantime, President Nikolai Podgorny of the USSR had paid an official visit to Austria on Nov. 14–21, 1966. At a meeting with members of the Austrian government on Nov. 15 President Podgorny reaffirmed the Soviet Union's opposition to any Austrian arrangement with the EEC, which the Soviet government considered would be contrary to the provisions of the Austrian State Treaty; at the same time he denied that the Soviet Union was bringing any pressure to bear on Austria.

President Podgorny spoke further on this subject in the course of a radio and television broadcast on Nov. 20, saying: "As friends of Austria we must say in all frankness that an arrangement with the Common Market, in whatsoever form, would in our opinion result in Austria being bound not only by economic but also by certain political obligations. This in turn would lead intentionally or unintentionally to a departure from the State Treaty and from the tested course of neutrality which is so advantageous to the Austrian people. . . ."

At the EEC Council meeting on Dec. 6–7, the ministers held a short closed session without the Commission members, at the request of Couve de Murville. It was reported in the press that Couve de Murville had referred (i) to discussions on the Austrian position between President de Gaulle and Alexei Kosygin, the Soviet Prime Minister, who was that time visiting France (although no reference was made to Austria in any of Kosygin's speeches in France or in any official communiqués); and (ii) to the fact that France was the only EEC member country which was also a signatory of the Austrian State Treaty.

The "partial negotiating mandate" was approved by the Council on Dec. 7 and for internal tariffs envisaged the elimination of tariffs on goods traded between Austria and the Six EEC countries at the end of a four-year period, while the Community's common external tariff was to be introduced on most products over a three year period.

The subsequent seventh round of negotiations lasted from Dec. 13 to Dec. 16, 1966. Discussion centred mainly on the rate of industrial tariff reduction, with Austria requesting the EEC countries to lower their tariffs on Austrian goods by 25 and 35 per cent respectively in the first two stages instead of 15 and 45 per cent as proposed by the Community. Exemptions were sought by Austria for antibiotics, while the EEC proposed special arrangements for aluminium, wood, cellulose, and paper. The Community approved in principle that Austria should have a "large degree of autonomy" in developing an independent commercial policy towards Eastern Europe in order to "establish a harmonious development of trade" with East European countries, and it was proposed that this subject and the question of agricultural trade should form the main topics to be discussed at the next round starting on Jan. 31, 1967.

During 1967 further progress was delayed largely as a result of the dispute with Italy over the question of the South Tirol which was not settled until the end of 1969 (when after more than eight years of negotiations Italian government proposals for increased autonomy for the German-speaking population of Alto Adige or South Tirol, which had been ceded by Austria to Italy in 1919, were agreed on by the German-speaking minority, the Austrian government and parliament and approved by the Italian parliament).

Shortly before the settlement of this dispute, and following the general change in the French attitude towards an enlargement of the Communities, the Austrian government stated on Nov. 4, 1969—a month prior to the Communities' Hague summit meeting—that it hoped that Austria's special interests arising from her international status would be respected in any consideration of the future of the Communities and of their enlargement.

In view of the changed circumstances following the Hague summit meeting, discussions were held at official level on Dec. 17–18, 1969, while on Feb. 17–18, 1970, Otto Mitterer, then Austrian Minister of Trade and Industry, and Dr Kurt Waldheim, then Foreign Minister, held talks in Brussels with Rey and Pierre Harmel, the Belgian Foreign Minister.

At these meetings, Austrian representatives proposed that an interim preferential trade arrangement should be concluded with the Communities involving mutual tariff reductions on industrial goods of 30–40 per cent in two steps, as the first stage in the creation of a free trade zone between Austria and the Communities. This proposal was designed to conform with requirements under Article XXIV of the General Agreement on Tariffs and Trade, which permits preferential arrangements only under given circumstances and subject to certain conditions, relating particularly to most-favoured-nation treatment. Austria further urged that any arrangements should be agreed before the opening of formal negotiations on the enlargement of the full membership of the Communities. The Communities stressed that any arrangement must be a temporary one, the object of which must be the early implementation of part of a global agreement.

Although no progress was made during the spring and summer of 1970, Austria's special position was outlined to the Communities' Council of Ministers in Brussels on Nov. 10 by Dr Rudolf Kirchschläger, then Foreign Minister, following the Council's decision on Oct. 26–27 to authorize the European Commission to begin technical negotiations for a partial interim trade arrangement on the basis of directives approved by the Council.

Any arrangement with the Communities, Dr Kirchschläger said, must enable Austria to continue to respect in full her obligations arising from her permanent neutrality and from the 1955 State Treaty. This also meant that Austria should in peacetime exercise complete freedom and independence in her relations with third countries, including trade relations, and that she might not take part in any Community action against third parties other than on purely economic grounds. Furthermore, in case of war or the threat of war, Austria must have the right to suspend the application of any specific clauses of the agreement or to terminate the whole agreement itself. In view of these special factors, the object during the negotiations would be to produce arrangements which respected the common economic demands and interests of both Austria and the Communities, including the maintenance of political stability in central Europe.

In 1969, Dr Kirchschläger continued, 41 per cent of all Austria's exports had gone to the six countries of the Communities, compared with 50 per cent in 1958 before the establishment of the EC, while as regards imports the level had increased slightly over this period from 54 to 56 per cent; as a result, Austria's deficit in trade with the Communities had risen from $158,000,000 to $596,300,000. In relation to EFTA countries and Finland, the value of Austrian exports had increased five-fold since the formation of the Association in 1960, and in 1969 had represented 26 per cent of exports (12 per cent in 1959); the value of imports from EFTA had quadrupled over the same period. A 10-member Community would take an estimated 51 per cent of Austria's exports and supply about 65 per cent of her imports.

In view of these changes in trade over the past 12 years, particularly the growth in relation to EFTA, Austria maintained that an enlargement of the Communities should not be allowed to lead either to a retention of trade barriers between the Communities and EFTA members which had not applied for membership or to a rebuilding of barriers between the four new members of the Communities and the other EFTA countries. The Hague summit meeting decisions should therefore be so interpreted as to mean that enlargement should in no way affect or reduce the present level of economic integration.

Because of the provisions of Article XXIV of GATT, any agreement between Austria and the Communities should lead to the removal of all tariffs, quantitative restrictions and similar barriers to trade in respect of all trade between Austria and the Communities in the EEC and ECSC sectors. Although limited exchanges of trade privileges would give some relief, they could not create the fully dynamic situation which would result from the complete liberation of the market from all trade restrictions. At the end of the EEC's transitional period, and with the prospective accession of the four applicant countries, the Communities would be largely rounded off and consolidated, and there should be no technical or economic difficulties which might hold up solutions for countries such as Austria. Joint efforts should therefore be made to find a form of participation which, while safeguarding Austria's special status, permitted extensive economic collaboration.

After reiterating the importance of upholding progress already achieved by EFTA in the field of freedom of trade, Dr Kirchschläger referred inter alia to the mutual facilitation and intensification of trade in the agricultural sector, technical co-operation, economic and monetary collaboration, and the need to keep negotiations with the applicant and non-applicant countries running parallel.

At meetings on Nov. 25–26, on Jan. 5, 1971, and in mid-March 1971, the two sides discussed principally the size and implementation of tariff reductions, quantitative import restrictions on the part of the EC, agriculture, reservations by the EC on the treatment of special steels, and the Austrian paper industry.

6.4 Sweden

Like Austria, Sweden first made an application to the EEC on Dec. 12, 1961, for a form of economic association with the EEC falling short of full membership. A statement on the Swedish position was made on July 28, 1962, by Gunnar Lange, the Swedish Minister of Commerce. The revived Swedish application, made in July 1967 after the UK, Danish and Irish reapplications in May, was however generally regarded as not wholly excluding the possibility of full membership of the Communities, and it was not until March 1971 that full membership was finally ruled out as a possible form of association with the European Communities.

In a letter presented in Brussels on July 28, 1967, by Sten Lindh, Swedish Ambassador to the European Communities, Lange requested negotiations "with a view to enabling Sweden to participate in the extension of the EEC in a form which is compatible with a continued Swedish policy of neutrality". The letter stated: "The Swedish government is desirous to remind the Community of its strong interest in participating in the work for a uniform economic solution in Europe. . . . It is of essential importance in this connexion to preserve the progress which has been made within EFTA and thereby the duty-free Nordic market." The letter also expressed Sweden's wish to negotiate for membership of the ECSC and Euratom.

Delivering the letter, Lindh made a verbal statement declaring that the continuation of Swedish neutrality was the "determining factor" in any negotiations, and hoped that the latter would be conducted as far as possible concurrently with those of other EFTA countries. The government's decision to ask for negotiations with the EC "on the broadest possible basis" consistent with its policy of neutrality had been announced on July 7 after consultations with the advisory council on foreign affairs, and the exact form of Lange's letter was drafted after a further meeting of the Council on July 26.

Developments during 1969 culminating in the Hague summit meeting led to renewed consideration of the enlargement of the Communities, but in the case of the Scandinavian countries the question was complicated by the fact that negotiations were currently being conducted over the creation of a Nordic customs union and other measures of Nordic economic co-operation (Nordek—see 4.4) between Denmark, Finland, Iceland, Norway and Sweden.

After the opening of Community negotiations with the four applicant countries on June 30, 1970, the Swedish government on Aug. 5 accepted an invitation from the Communities to take part in discussions on Sweden's relations with the Communities. In its reply, the government stressed that as far as possible these should be conducted parallel with those being held with Denmark and Norway for full membership.

In his address to the Communities' Council of Ministers on Nov. 10, Kjell-Olof Feldt, the Swedish Minister of Trade, accepted the principle of a customs union and a common agricultural policy, but emphasized his country's determination to safeguard her position of neutrality.

Sweden, Feldt said, wished to take part in the enlargement of the Communities by means of comprehensive, close and lasting economic relationships, subject to the maintenance of her policy of neutrality. An essential element of any agreement would be the establishment of a customs union, and Sweden was also prepared in principle to accept the common external tariff. In this connexion, Feldt pointed out that in 1969 Sweden's imports from the six EC countries had amounted to about $2,000,000,000 or one-third of all her imports, and that her export deficit vis-à-vis these countries had been about $430,000,000. At the same time, the Nordic countries as a whole had together imported almost $5,000,000,000 from the EC and thus represented the Communities' second largest market after the United States.

After stating that Sweden supported measures for greater freedom of movement of workers, services and capital, and co-operation in the fields of social and economic policy, Feldt said that the aims for a common agricultural policy, as set out in the Treaty of Rome, corresponded with those of Sweden and that market organization for various agricultural products was similar in Sweden and the Communities, so that no special problems were envisaged in this respect. In both industry and agriculture Sweden envisaged the need for transitional arrangements, with appropriate synchronization between progress in the freeing of trade in industrial goods, in the achievement of the agricultural common market, and in the application of financial rules.

As already emphasized both in 1962 and again in 1967, Sweden insisted on being able to pursue policies in the future appropriate to a neutral country, and she could not therefore accept obligations which would "render illusory" the possibility of choosing neutrality in the event of war. Moreover, this policy must be supported by a strong military defence structure, and the economy must be so organized that the country could endure for a considerable time a large-scale blockade. Sweden could not embark on any co-operation in the fields of foreign, economic, monetary or other policy which would in her view jeopardize her ability to pursue this neutrality. Accordingly, Sweden could not participate within a certain grouping of countries in any binding form of co-operation in foreign affairs aimed at the establishment of common policies, and limits would be set to the extent to which she could accept a transfer of the right of decision-making to international institutions within the framework of economic and monetary union.

Finally, Feldt turned to the question of Nordic co-operation—especially in the fields of travel, free movement of labour, social benefits and free trade in industrial goods. Trade between the Nordic countries had doubled in the past seven years, and progress in all these fields must not only be maintained but also continued and increased. In this connexion, the minister stressed the common interest of the EFTA countries that the free market achieved so far should be retained as part of an enlarged European Community. Discussions with Sweden should, he said, be conducted as far as possible in parallel with those with Denmark and Norway, but the exact form of any association of Sweden with the Communities should be decided at a later stage. This procedure would have the advantage that further information could be obtained for an evaluation of the situation from the point of view of neutrality.

Exploratory talks were held with the European Commission on Dec. 17 and in the second week of March 1971. The government found it impossible, however, to reconcile Sweden's traditional policy of neutrality with the requirements of membership of the Communities—particularly in the light of the Werner and Davignon reports [see 6.2] and initial meetings on the coordination of foreign policy. Sweden's decision not to apply for full membership was accordingly announced by the Prime Minister, Olof Palme, on March 18.

In a memorandum issued at the same time, it was stated that Sweden would instead seek some special form of agreement involving a customs union for both industrial and agricultural products, with each party's rights and obligations clearly set out. Sweden would not be represented on the Communities' Council of Ministers, and special institutional arrangements would have to be worked out.

6.5 Switzerland

The Swiss application for economic association with the EEC was made on Dec. 15, 1961, shortly after the initial Austrian and Swedish applications, and a first hearing was held on Sept. 24, 1962.

The Swiss government's case for the reopening of exploratory talks was presented to the Council of Ministers on Nov. 10, 1970, by Ernst Brugger, head of the Federal Economy Department, who emphasized the importance of Switzerland's "permanent armed neutrality" and asked that arrangements should be worked out to respect and uphold this status.

Switzerland's neutrality, Brugger said, represented an element of stability in world politics, and any limitation would produce a new factor of uncertainty. The maintenance of the credibility of Switzerland's policy therefore set certain limits to the curtailment of national sovereignty.

Both sides should seek as comprehensive solutions as possible, particularly since increased European integration would make existing bilateral agreements with members of the Communities invalid or meaningless. At the same time, the particular characteristics of Swiss direct democracy must be upheld. Switzerland was accordingly seeking exploratory talks which would make clearer each party's needs, and Brugger emphasized that his government had no preconceived attitudes and was not at the present stage putting forward detailed proposals.

After pointing out that an enlarged Community would provide about 75 per cent of Switzerland's imports and purchase nearly 60 per cent of her exports, and that Switzerland imported $1,500,000,000 more a year from the Communities than she exported to member countries, the minister said that it was essential that trade relationships should be made as liberal as possible; arrangements should therefore be made consistent with Article XXIV of GATT—i.e. a comprehensive removal of barriers to trade. In the context of global arrangements Switzerland would suggest a rapid dismantling of barriers and substantial steps in the reduction of restrictions.

Switzerland's agricultural policy had generally the same aims as that of the EC but, due partly to natural conditions, the price level in Swiss agricultural production was considerably higher than in the Communities. In addition, there was basic parity between agricultural and other industrial incomes, whereas the adoption of the present EC agricultural arrangements would result in a fall of about 50 per cent in the net income of Swiss farmers.

Other topics which would need to be discussed included services, freedom of movement, technical barriers, drug regulations, insurance, patent law, and transport policies. Brugger laid particular stress on the high proportion of foreign workers in Switzerland. Other matters referred to by the minister included recent work carried out by the Communities in the fields of industrial policies, research, energy, regional policies, and above all economic and monetary union.

The talks which Switzerland sought should define each side's interest in close co-operation in specific fields, and the government hoped that talks would be opened immediately. Any tariff reductions between the Communities and the four applicants for full membership should be made parallel with reductions vis-à-vis non-applicant EFTA countries.

Discussions were subsequently opened at official level on Dec. 16, 1970, and the fact-finding stage was concluded on March 5, 1971.

6.6 Soviet reaction to discussions with neutral countries

Soviet opposition to any form of membership of the Communities by Austria, Sweden or Switzerland was expressed by Andrei Kuznetsov, political commentator of the Soviet Communist Party newspaper *Pravda*, on Jan. 6, 1971. Entry into the Communities by these three neutral countries, he said, would have an adverse effect on the political climate in Europe through the establishment of close political ties. The Community negotiators were showing "no intention of accepting the conditions advanced by the neutral countries" by separating the economic aspects from the political, and Kuznetsov maintained that European integration was assuming an "ever more clearly defined political nature".

Detailed discussions began between the European Commission and Finland on Jan. 6, 1971, and were continued on March 22–26, the position of Finland (and of Iceland and Portugal) having been discussed initially with the Communities at ministerial level on Nov. 24, 1970.

6.7 Finland

The country's particular position as regards the Soviet Union meant that at that time Finland was an associate rather than a full member of EFTA (although it eventually acquired full membership in January 1986), and did not in the early 1960s open discussions along with other Scandinavian countries on closer association with the European Communities. As the prospects of Denmark, Norway and Sweden acceding to the Communities became increasingly likely, President Urho Kekkonen of Finland sought to avoid his country's exclusion from key economic markets "in view of Finland's vital interests in maintaining her trading position in all markets", as he stated in a speech on July 23, 1970.

At the November 1970 meeting Olavi Mattila, Minister for Foreign Trade, pointed out that exports of goods and services accounted for 25 per cent of Finland's gross national product. Over the past 10 years the share of Finland's foreign trade held by EFTA countries had risen from 32 to 41 per cent while that of EC countries had dropped from about 32 to 26 per cent; the Nordic countries alone now accounted for over 20 per cent and the Soviet Union for 15 per cent. Within these totals, the share of goods other than the traditional wood-based products had increased over the past decade from 23 to about 50 per cent in EFTA trade and from 12 to 23 per cent in EC trade. Mattila also explained that trade with the Soviet Union was based on five-year agreements under a tariff agreement signed in 1961, (while four days before the meeting, i.e. on Nov. 20, 1970, the 1948 Finnish–Soviet Treaty of Friendship and Co-operation had also been renewed five years before its expiry).

Any solution leading to full membership of the Communities was precluded by virtue of Finland's special position, but foreign trade was of great importance to the development of the Finnish economy, and the government requested that talks with the Communities should cover principally (i) the dismantling of barriers to trade, especially through tariff arrangements for industrial goods which would permit the continuation of Finland's present duty-free trade; (ii) the avoidance of such undes-irable side-effects as deflection of trade and unfair competition; (iii) arrangements compatible with Article XXIV of GATT; (iv) solutions in the agricultural sector — agricultural exports to EC countries amounting to only 4.6 per cent of total Finnish exports and being "insignificant" in the context of Community trade; and (v) the institutional framework, in which Finland did not envisage participation.

Finland must retain the integrity of decision-making under all circumstances in both trade and other matters, since any compromise of this principle could undermine the credibility of her neutrality. She recognized, at the same time, that the Communities had political goals as well as arrangements which affected the sovereign decision-making power of member countries, and it was for these reasons that she could not ask for membership.

6.8 Iceland

The country had become a member of EFTA on March 1, 1970, after a formal application to EFTA made on Jan. 23, 1969, and although a member of the Nordic council, had not participated in the abortive Nordek negotiations [see 4.4]. Detailed discussions opened on Jan. 8, 1971, following ministerial-level talks with the Communities on Iceland's position on Nov. 24, 1970.

At the Nov. 24 meeting Gylfi Gislason, the Minister of Trade, emphasized the disadvantages which would result for Iceland if Britain, Denmark and Norway became members of the Communities without any other action being taken, since she would lost her duty-free access to those markets for industrial goods under EFTA. Trade with the present six EC member countries currently represented about 27 per cent of Iceland's imports and 16 per cent of her exports; that with the six EC members plus the four applicants for membership accounted for about 55 and 40 per cent respectively; and that with the combined EC countries and the other EFTA members to 68 and 52 per cent respectively.

Membership of EFTA had been designed not only to ensure a more favourable position for Iceland's traditional fisheries exports but also to create conditions and a climate conducive to greater diversification. New tariffs on industrial goods could undermine Iceland's newly initiated programme of industrial development, while the admittance to the EC of the largest fish-producing nations in Europe could also restrict the markets for Icelandic fish products in the enlarged Community to such a degree as to cause grave difficulties for Iceland. All parties in parliament agreed, nevertheless, that a solution was not to be found in membership of the EC, and that some other form of agreement must be found.

Any such agreement should, however, (i) give Iceland the same privileges with regard to unrestricted duty-free exports to EC countries as she currently enjoyed in EFTA countries; (ii) enable Iceland to export her fish products free of duty to the enlarged Community, provided such exports did not disrupt normal market condi-tions: (iii) give EC members the same privileges in Iceland as EFTA countries, and allow them to acquire the same tariff privileges as those countries in the future in accordance with the terms and conditions of Iceland's accession to EFTA; (iv) permit Iceland to continue to have the same right as she had at present within EFTA to control imports for a limited number of commodities, including petroleum products.

At a press conference in Brussels Gislason explained that one principal factor excluding EC membership was that Iceland would be obliged under the terms of the Communities' fisheries policy to grant the fleets of other member countries unrestricted access to her territorial waters.

6.9 Commission guidelines for negotiations (June 16, 1971)

The Commission had recognized the impending problem of the non-candidate EFTA countries (and Finland as an associate member of EFTA) as early as October 1969, when it had raised the question in its "Opinion" on the enlargement of the existing Community [see 2.20]. Furthermore, during negotiations for membership of the EC the three EFTA applicant countries had emphasized the need for special arrangements to maintain the free trade positions with the rest of EFTA; in the absence of any other arrangement the UK, Denmark and Norway would have to re-establish tariff barriers against their former EFTA partners, who would in turn be obliged to reinstate their own tariff barriers against the three applicants.

During the course of EFTA ministerial meetings in 1970 and early 1971 the necessity of maintaining free trade among all existing EFTA members was stressed on several occasions, and it was noted that the Communities had also indicated that agreements with the non-candidates should come into force in parallel with the agreements for full membership. After an EFTA ministerial meeting at Reykjavik, Iceland, on May 13–14, 1971, a communiqué was published stating that "the exploratory talks of recent months between the EFTA countries not seeking membership and the Communities should provide a suitable basis for the forthcoming negotiations".

The European Commission summarized the results and conclusions of its preliminary discussions with the EFTA non-candidates in an "Opinion" published on June 16, 1971, which outlined the principal features of possible agreements.

Basic principles. The Commission explained that under the Community treaties elimination of trade barriers should be linked with measures designed to prevent both deflection of trade and distortion of competition, and that certain concessions regarding free movement of workers, liberalization of services, and wider trade in agricultural produce could only be envisaged if the measures were sufficiently wide-ranging to ensure an adequate balance between benefits and obligations on both sides. It was also pointed out that, while some of the countries concerned might be able to achieve the material requirements for free trade, "insuperable difficulties" would be encountered in institutional management, a problem which would lead to countries having to conform to decisions in whose formulation they had had no part.

It was considered either that there should be no removal of trade barriers at all between the enlarged Communities and the remaining EFTA countries or, alternatively, that the EFTA trading system would be applied to the whole of the enlarged Communities. However, as a further alternative it was suggested that the choice could be postponed for two years—1973 and 1974—during which time all EFTA countries, including the new members of the EC, would continue to trade freely among themselves while maintaining tariff barriers with the original six members.

It was stressed that one of the difficulties was that the only point of common interest among the six countries was the wish to establish a free trade system with the Communities. Beyond that, each country had its own requirements for an agreement, Sweden, for example, being prepared to go further than a straightforward tariff agreement and to accept the common agricultural policy, competition rules and the free movement of labour concept due to the country's strong links with Norway and Denmark. Switzerland would also accept some Community rules, the Commission noted, but would insist on freedom of action in external relations and would not wish to participate in the Communities' decision-taking machinery. Austria wanted broad co-operation with no institutional links at all, while Finland was interested only in free trade for industry. Portugal and Iceland similarly presented particular difficulties because of their relatively undeveloped economies, which were heavily dependent on non-industrial economic sectors such as agriculture and fishing.

It was recommended that the basis to be adopted for the tariff reductions would be the tariffs applying on Jan. 1, 1972 (the date of the fifth and final Kennedy Round tariff cut under the General Agreement on Tariffs and Trade), and that the timetable to be adopted should be a five-year transitional period as agreed for the candidate countries.

Rules of origin. The Commission considered that a system to eliminate deflections of trade brought about by tariff differences as applied to third countries could be based on rules of origin, whereby free trade was restricted to goods wholly or partly produced in the free trade area concerned. (Rules of origin had not been drawn up for the Communities, since trade operated within a customs union having a common external tariff; the EFTA agreement, on the other hand, included only elimination of tariffs between its members with no common position with regard to third countries.)

It was pointed out that such a system would be acceptable as the volume of imports into the EFTA countries from outside the Community of Ten was relatively small. However, the Commission stated that it would not be possible to consider a system of "cumulative origin", as proposed by several of the non-candidate countries, since this would involve products originating from outside the free trade area being considered as eligible for tariff-free trade if they had been subject to further processing in an EFTA non-candidate country.

Quotas. Quantitative import restrictions on a limited basis could, the Commission considered, be eliminated without difficulty in the Communities, in Sweden and in Switzerland, although Finland and Austria had stated that certain restrictions would have to be maintained for political reasons.

Competition. In the field of competition, restrictive practice rules would have to be provided in cases which were not covered by Community treaty rules and which would be incompatible with the operation of the trade agreements. There would also have to be an escape-clause mechanism in the event of a dispute which might involve withdrawal of tariff concessions or the introduction of quantitative restrictions.

Taxes and controls. No harmonization of tax systems was envisaged, but the Commission stated that distortion resulting from tax adjustment at frontiers would have to be prevented, for example by prohibition of any fiscal measure or practice discriminating against imports. Provision would also have to be made guaranteeing freedom of payments and transfers relating to trade in goods covered by the agreements, and exchange controls and similar restrictions would have to be removed. Anti-dumping and other protective measures on the part of the Community countries would be the responsibility of the Community institutions alone.

Legal framework. A more general problem, later raised by the United States as the primary basis for objections to Community agreements with the non-candidate EFTA countries, was that the accords would have to comply with the General Agreement on Tariffs and Trade, Article XXIV of which states inter alia that "a free trade area shall be understood to mean a group of two or more customs territories in which duties and other restrictive regulations of commerce are eliminated on substantially all the trade between the constituent territories in products originating from such territories".

The Commission considered that to comply with GATT the agreements might be based on a system involving the removal of obstacles to trade only for industrial products. Special measures would have to be taken for products subject to the Treaty of Paris (i.e. European Coal and Steel Community products), arrangements could be made for agricultural and fishery products from Portugal and Iceland, and separate agreements could be worked out for certain countries in respect of fair treatment of Community workers and of co-operation in transport matters.

The agreements would be reviewed at the end of the transitional period, i.e. in 1978, and it would be possible to withdraw subject to one year's notice.

Agriculture. Although Portugal and Iceland were considered as special cases, the Commission recommended that for the other four countries there should be no agreement on free trade for agricultural products, as exports of these goods over the three preceding years had represented only 6.7 per cent of their trade with the Communities. It specified that for Portugal tomato, fish preserve and cork products would be eligible for concessions, and that for Iceland fisheries products (representing 80 per cent of exports) would be covered.

Special cases. The Commission made several suggestions concerning products of particular concern to one or more of the non-candidate countries.

It was considered that "immediate and full application" of measures to remove tariff barriers in the paper industry, of great importance for Finland, Sweden and Austria, would create "serious problems" for the Community industry. It was suggested that solutions could be found to ensure that the Community paper industry was provided with pulp on the best possible terms and that the firms concerned would be protected from excessive competition from "more favourably placed procedures".

The Swiss watch and clock industry had already been the subject of some difficulty during the Kennedy Round negotiations, and the Commission recommended that the industry would have to adapt itself to the rules of the agreement made at the time.

Detailed changes in existing practice in the iron and steel industries, transport, and movement of workers were also mentioned by the Commission as being necessary in certain cases.

Shortly before the negotiating mandate was discussed in detail by the EC ministers [see 6.10], the EFTA Council and the Joint Council of EFTA and Finland met at ministerial level in Geneva on Nov. 4–5, 1971, after which a communiqué stated that the ministers considered that negotiations should "start soon and be pressed forward as rapidly as possible".

The communiqué added: "Ministers asked the Council at official level to examine the legal and other implications which will arise in the event of some members acceding to the European Communities and others establishing special relations with the Communities. They were informed of the intention of the United Kingdom to give notice on Dec. 31, 1971, of its withdrawal from EFTA to come into effect on Dec. 31, 1972."

6.10 Amendments to negotiating mandate

After discussion by the EC Ministers in July 1971, when the alternative solution of maintaining a two-year tariff standstill was rejected, the broad outlines of the negotiating mandate as suggested by the Commission were finally approved on Nov. 9. In addition, further concessions were made to Portugal and Iceland permitting the tariff reductions to be spread over seven years instead of five, as laid down for the other four countries. There would be no obligation for the non-candidates to harmonize their legislation, but any movement in this direction would be welcomed by the Communities. It was agreed, mainly at French insistence, that the industrial products list on which tariffs would be removed would include exceptions in certain sensitive sectors.

Proposed basis for agreements. The agreements would be based on Article XXIV of GATT and on Article 113 of the Treaty of Rome, which states that in the event of the conclusion of tariff or trade agreements the common commercial policy should be based on uniform principles and that third country agreements should be negotiated by the Commission on authority from the Council of Ministers.

No definite decision was taken on the Commission's recommendation to exclude agricultural products from the negotiations with the four more industrialized countries, but the Council agreed that the Commission should examine individual concessions as recommended by the six EC member governments' permanent representatives.

Rules of origin. The Council made a decision that the rules of origin should be the same as those applied between the Community and the associated African states, while the application of a system based on cumulative origin should be treated more flexibly along the lines of preferential systems negotiated with African and Mediterranean countries. (Under the Yaoundé Agreements with the associated African states, a product originating from a third country qualified for duty-free access to the EC if it underwent sufficient transformation in the associated country to transfer its classification from one heading to another under the Brussels Tariff Nomenclature. In other EC association agreements a more straightforward system stipulated that only goods wholly produced within the associated country qualified for duty-free access.)

Safeguard measures. The Commission's decision on central EC control of anti-dumping measures was turned down by the Council, which decided that each Community country would be free to apply safeguard measures in the event of regional, structural or employment difficulties. As a concession to the Commission it was agreed that this safeguard mechanism should be reviewed after a year with a view to transferring the right of decision to the Community institutions.

Paper products. The ministers expanded the Commission's suggestion on paper products to specify a 12-year period during which the duties could be abolished, although their application might be further postponed by automatic application of the safeguard clause in the event of difficulties for EC member countries.

"Sensitive" products. The mandate also included a list of "sensitive products" for which the Council of Ministers required a transitional period of eight years (instead of five as for most industrial products), with in addition no tariff cuts during the first three years. The list of items included aluminium, lead, zinc, silicons, magnesium, ferro-alloys (except ferro-nickel and ferro-manganese), tungsten, molybdenum, tantalum, antimony and other special metals, wool and cotton fabrics, grindstones, mechanical pulp, asphalt and stone slabs, bricks and other building materials, including fireproof slates; tariff protection was also requested on synthetic fibres against Sweden, Austria and Finland, and against Sweden alone for stainless steel pipes, ball-bearing tubes and road tractors for goods trailers.

Immediately before the ministerial meeting approving the negotiating mandate, the United States protested against the impending negotiations in a verbal message delivered to the Commission and to the six member governments on Nov. 5, 1971. Ralf Dahrendorf, Commissioner for External Trade, was reported to have replied to the message on Nov. 8 stating that the protest would have no effect on the Communities' negotiations and that the action constituted a direct interference in the autonomous policies of the Communities. The then President of the Commission, Franco Maria Malfatti, was reported to have said at the Council meeting the same day that the arrangements envisaged with the EFTA countries conformed with the rules of GATT and would not discriminate against third countries.

6.11 Opening of negotiations (December 1971)

Following the agreement on final instructions for the negotiations on Nov. 29, 1971, the Commission opened bilateral negotiations on Dec. 3 at ambassadorial level, but the talks were hampered by disagreement among the Community countries and with the non-candidates over the contents of the list of sensitive products and by other technical matters. Some of these points of dispute were resolved at a meeting of EC Ministers on Jan. 31–Feb. 1, 1972.

It was decided at this meeting to base the definition of rules of origin on existing Community provisions in preferential relations with third countries, although each country's case would be examined individually. It was also agreed that EC members would study changes to be made to the list of processes which could be applied to goods and which affected the origin of the product.

The Community ministers agreed to make concessions on trade in a number of processed agricultural products provided satisfactory reciprocity was given. The offers would be made to particular countries, including for example a reduction to 10 per cent in the tariff on beer for Sweden, Finland, Portugal and Iceland only. In addition three categories of "sensitive" products were established, including a system of flexible surveillance for products such as stone, asphalt, bricks and tiles, tractors, semi-finished copper materials and possibly plywood products; a system of strict surveillance involving import quotas valid after 1977 on products such as silicons and ball-bearings; and thirdly a tariff freeze for three years to be followed by a system of strict surveillance applying to carbon and alloy steels, tubing for ball-bearings, stainless steel tubing, most ferro-alloys, aluminium, lead, tungsten, molybdenum, and other special metals.

Discussion during the subsequent negotiations centred mainly on these sensitive products, the proposed 3-year tariff freeze, and the question of agricultural products. After the first two rounds of plenary negotiations the Commission, in March, completed a report on the progress made and recommended the Council of Ministers to agree on a more flexible mandate in the light of the difficulties encountered.

In particular, the Commission suggested that the Communities should abandon their proposal for a tariff freeze on the sensitive products during the first three years of the eight-year transitional period. In addition it suggested that the Communities should also withdraw requests for unilateral concessions on agricultural products, considered by France, Italy and the Netherlands as fair compensation for permitting the non-candidate countries tariff-free access for most industrial products. (The four more industrialized non-applicant countries had insisted during the negotiations that any tariff cuts in the agricultural sectors should be reciprocal.) Furthermore, the Commission recommended further Community tariff concessions on agricultural product imports from Portugal and on fish from Iceland, and also suggested that concessions on processed agricultural products should be uniform and not subject to individual arrangements with each country as originally proposed.

The tariff freeze on sensitive products would have meant that in 1975 the four neutral countries (Austria, Sweden, Switzerland and Finland) would have cut their tariffs to 40 per cent of their original levels, while the Six would have made no cuts at all on 73 per cent of their total industrial imports from Finland (of which 63 per cent comprised paper products and 10 per cent other sensitive products, including non-ferrous metals). Similarly, no cuts would have been made on 33 per cent of industrial imports from Sweden and 10 per cent of imports from Austria.

The EC Ministers, meeting in Luxembourg on April 24–25, 1972, agreed to abandon the proposed tariff freeze and decided that in its place there should be a gradual reduction in tariffs from the beginning of the agreements in January

1973, amounting to a reduction of one-fifth of the tariff levels during the first three years with the remaining reductions spread over the five-year period to the end of 1980.

Paper. In the case of paper, the ministers proposed that the Commission should offer the non-candidate countries a tariff reduction of 2 per cent spread over the first four years on the existing total tariff of 12 per cent, with larger reductions over the subsequent eight years, so that the tariff would be completely eliminated by the beginning of 1985. In addition, the ministers proposed that the three EFTA countries which intended to become full members of the Communities (the UK, Denmark and Norway) and which would continue their tariff-free trade in most industrial products, should initially introduce a tariff on their imports of paper from their former EFTA partners amounting to 4 per cent, applied in three annual stages. There would be a standstill period from 1976 to 1981, after which the tariff would be progressively reduced to zero in parallel with cuts to be made by the six original Community members. The three countries would, however, be permitted to maintain a limited duty-free import quota of paper products until 1980.

Agriculture. The debate over the inclusion of agricultural products in the agreements was not resolved, although Germany, France, Belgium and Luxembourg all agreed that the Community should follow the Commission's advice to exclude them except in the cases of Portugal and Iceland. However, both the Netherlands and Italy remained in favour of an agricultural agreement, insisting that a formula should be found to permit exports to EFTA countries. Italy in particular opposed Community concessions to Portugal on wine and tomato concentrate (recommended by the Commission) without obtaining the right to export its own agricultural products, of which tomato concentrate and wine formed an important part.

The EFTA ministers met in Geneva on May 4–5, 1972, to consider the amended Community position on the negotiating terms.

A communiqué issued after the meeting stated: "All ministers expressed their satisfaction that the first stage of the negotiations . . . had now been completed and that agreement had been reached on a number of important constituent parts of the prospective special relations agreements. On the other hand, ministers noted with concern that a number of problems of crucial importance to the individual non-candidate countries remained unsolved. They stressed the importance of reaching balanced solutions which would be mutually satisfactory and safeguard free trade already established between EFTA countries." The communqiué also noted that, as the agreements were planned to come into force at the same time as the Treaty of Accession, negotiations should be concluded before the summer recess.

It was agreed at the Geneva talks that the last ministerial meeting of the eight EFTA member countries and Finland would be held on Nov. 16–17, 1972, during which amendments to the 1960 Stockholm Convention, which established the original organization, would be discussed with a view to forming a "mini-EFTA" including the five non-candidate EFTA countries and Finland.

6.12 Differing positions of non-applicant EFTA countries

As predicted by the Commission in its initial guideline report on the negotiating mandate in June 1971, the positions of the non-candidates differed considerably both among themselves and in relation to those of the Communities (which had been formulated in consultation with the four applicant countries). The various attitudes of the five EFTA members and Finland are summarized below.

Sweden. Shortly after the EC terms had been decided in November 1971, Palme, the Swedish Prime Minister, was reported to have predicted great difficulties for relations between the Communities and Sweden, and it was suggested that the Swedish government did not expect a final form of agreement to be reached before February or March 1973. Hans von Delwig, director of Sweden's Iron and Steel Board, was reported to have said that the Community offer on treatment of sensitive products was "clearly unsatisfactory" and "visibly less favourable than expected", and that it would affect Swedish suppliers of special steels, who employed 45,000 workers (three-quarters of the country's total steel industry work force), and perhaps cause employment difficulties. Similar reactions were reported from the Swedish paper industry.

These views were confirmed in the series of working party meetings which followed the start of negotiations in December. There was particular concern in the Swedish delegation regarding the limitations on future evolution of the trade agreement towards what the Swedes hoped would eventually constitute a broader field of co-operation. However, the Commission stated that it had no authority to negotiate on these matters.

The Swedish government had earlier clarified its position on the nature of the agreement in a policy statement published on Sept. 6, 1971, which argued that, while free trade in industrial products formed a good starting point for negotiations, the mutual advantages of co-operation should be maximized by (i) creating favourable conditions for planning by governments and enterprises, (ii) covering other important fields besides customs duties and trade regulations and (iii) permitting further development so that co-operation could be widened and deepened.

In particular the Swedish government suggested that free trade in industrial goods would function at its best if all signatory countries adopted the same duties in relation to third countries, thus requiring Sweden to harmonize its tariffs with the common external tariff of the Communities. Sweden would also adopt other trade regulations as necessary, including tariff legislation, elimination of non-tariff barriers and co-operation on a common commercial policy with regard to third countries.

Beyond trade affairs the Swedish government also proposed that application of Community rules on competition should extend to Commission jurisdiction over Swedish firms and the application in Sweden of the case law of the Community Court of Justice. In return Sweden should be represented on the Consultative Committee on Cartels and Monopolies.

Other fields in which Sweden suggested that there should be co-operation and mutual consultation included medium- and short-term economic planning, monetary questions, industry, technological research, energy and human environment.

Austria. Austrian relations with the Communities were at a more advanced stage than those of the other non-candidate countries, as negotiations on a partial interim trade agreement had been sanctioned by the EC Council of Ministers in October 1970 and continued during 1971 [see 6.3]. Progress in these negotiations was taken into account at a further ministerial meeting in November 1971, when additional measures for the negotiating directives stipulated that the interim agreement must conform with the mandate agreed for the opening of negotiations to solve the problems raised for EFTA in general by the enlargement of the Communities. Negotiations on the interim agreement were completed at a meeting on Dec. 15–16, although additional changes in detail would be necessary when the discussions on the final accord were themselves concluded. However, despite this progress disagreement over procedural matters prevented an early application of the interim measures, which would have involved a 30 per cent cut in tariffs both at Austrian and at Community borders until the full agreement was established.

Commenting on June 17, 1971, on the Commission's guideline report on the trade agreements (i.e. the "Opinion" published on the previous day—see 6.9), Dr Josef Staribacher, the Austrian Minister of Commerce, expressed the hope that the Council of Ministers would "approve this report which corresponds to our requests". Dr Staribacher had discussed the agreement during the previous week with Kosygin, the

Soviet Prime Minister, during a visit to Moscow. In an interview with *Le Monde* on June 17 Dr Staribacher said: "We did not go to Moscow to obtain a change in the Soviet position on the Common Market problem, but I believe that my explanations have largely contributed to reduce Moscow's distrust of our position; I do not expect any difficulty from this quarter."

The Austrian Chancellor, Dr Kreisky, visited government leaders of the Communities and the UK during late February and early March 1972 to discuss Austria's proposed relationship with the enlarged Communities. At a press conference in Brussels Dr Kreisky was reported to have stated that agriculture would be "a very, very important element" in the agreement. In common with representatives of all the other non-candidate countries Dr Kreisky expressed concern over the list of sensitive products on which tariff reductions would be delayed, and suggested that the Austrian paper industry, employing 20,000 workers, would be especially vulnerable.

During the negotiations Austria indicated that the special relations agreement should have some agricultural content, including the maintenance of existing agricultural accords with the Communities. In particular there was concern over Austrian beef and dairy exports to the Communities. The agricultural issue was considered to be particularly important because the governing Socialist Party needed the assistance of the People's Party, which drew its support partly from the farming community, to achieve the two-thirds parliamentary majority required to ratify any treaty with the European Community countries.

Finland. The Community proposals on paper products were of most concern to Finland, and in an article published in March the Central Association of Finnish Forest Industries claimed that Finland exported only 2,000,000 tons of paper to the Communities and applicant countries in 1970, compared with total consumption in the ten countries of 27,400,000 tons, of which 22,100,000 tons were produced within the area of the ten states. It was stated that Finland thus only supplied 7.3 per cent of the paper and board consumed in the area and that Sweden and Finland together supplied less than 15 per cent. Similarly, out of a total consumption by the Ten of 21,700,000 tons of wood fibre for the paper and board industry, only 1,300,000 tons, or about 6 per cent, was imported from Finland.

At the opening of talks on Dec. 13, 1971, Finland's chief negotiator, Pentti Uusivirta, accepted an industrial free trade area as the basis for future relationships with the enlarged Communities. However, on Feb. 2, 1972, President Kekkonen told the Finnish *Eduskunta* (parliament): "The preliminary proposals which were submitted yesterday [Feb. 1] by the Commission are such that they amount to economic sanctions for our wood-based manufacturing industry. Although these proposals are not definitive, it can be said without doubt that the exceptional manner in which our principal export product is being treated is unacceptable."

Switzerland. In approving the European Commission's guideline report on the agreements to be negotiated with the non-candidate countries, Brugger, head of the Federal Department of Public Economy, commented on June 21, 1971, that it served as a "useful basis for the settlement of relations between Switzerland and the EC" and that the proposed solution raised no "institutional difficulties", conformed with GATT rules, and did not affect "Switzerland's indispensable autonomy in preserving its neutrality".

In the subsequent negotiations during the winter of 1971–72, the Swiss delegation to the negotiations, led by Paul Jolles, head of the trade division of the Federal Department of Public Economy, was concerned over the inclusion of aluminium, metal alloys, paper and chocolate on the list of sensitive products, but few major difficulties were reported during the discussions.

The issue said to be of principal concern to the Swiss people was the possibility of broader agreements after the free trade accord had been signed. In this context Pierre Graber, head of the Swiss Political (Foreign Affairs) Department, stated on May 13 that the agreement with the EC would be an end in itself "without any evolutionary character", but at the same time he added that he was "sure" that the agreement would be the subject of a national referendum, to be held probably in December 1972.

Iceland. Iceland's negotiations were severely handicapped by the unilateral Icelandic decision announced in August 1971 to extend its fishing limits from 12 to an average of 50 nautical miles from the coast from Sept. 1, 1972, and by the Communities' subsequent refusal to conclude an agreement until the proposed extension was abandoned. Einar Ágústsson, the Icelandic Minister of Foreign Affairs, explained his government's reasons for the new limit in discussions on April 20 with Dr Sicco Mansholt, the Commission's President, and with Jean-François Deniau, another Commissioner.

At a meeting in Luxembourg on April 25 to discuss a revised mandate the EC Ministers decided that the Communities' offer to Iceland (cuts of about 50 per cent in the common external tariff) was conditional on an agreement between Iceland and the UK and West Germany, the two countries mainly affected by the fishing limit extension. However, Thorhaller Ásgeirsson, the chief Icelandic negotiator, stated that the EC condition was "entirely unacceptable".

6.13 Conclusion of negotiations—Signature of Special Relations Agreements (July 1972)

During the final three rounds of negotiations on June 7–21, July 5–6 and July 13–20, 1972, particular attention was paid to exceptions involving longer transitional periods for a number of "sensitive" products against which the Community countries wanted continued protection. As in the earlier discussions from December to April there was also considerable debate on the issue of inclusion of unprocessed agricultural products in the terms of the agreements, mainly at the insistence of Italy and the Netherlands, but it was eventually agreed that trade in agricultural products could be discussed outside the context of the Special Relations Agreements (except in the cases of Portugal and Iceland).

The agreements were concluded in Brussels on July 22, 1972, between the European Economic Community and the European Coal and Steel Community and Austria, Finland, Iceland, Portugal, Sweden and Switzerland (together with Liechtenstein), completing the establishment of a free trade area of 16 countries embracing both the enlarged Communities and EFTA.

At a ceremony in the Palais d'Egmont in Brussels the agreements were signed by representatives of all countries concerned with the exception of Finland, whose representatives only initialled the agreements since the Finnish government had resigned on July 19 [see 6.20]. The agreements were to be effective from Jan. 1, 1973, when the UK, the Republic of Ireland, Norway and Denmark were due to become full members of the Communities, and were to be ratified by the governments of the countries concerned.

The agreements provided for the gradual achievement of free trade in industrial goods between the six original members of the Communities and the Republic of Ireland on the one hand and each of the EFTA countries which had not applied for full EC membership on the other, while at the same time preserving the existing free trade among all countries which were members of EFTA at the time of the signature of the agreements, including the UK, Norway and Denmark. Tariffs on the great majority of industrial goods were to be eliminated over a transitional period of 4½ years (see table), when cuts would also be made on a number of processed agricultural goods. Special arrangements were made for several of the EFTA non-applicant countries, particularly for Iceland and Portugal, and for certain groups of products, notably paper. (The final establishment of free trade in industrial goods between the EC and the EFTA countries did not actually take place until Jan. 1, 1985, when the last tariffs remaining in Finland were eventually removed.)

The table below shows in the centre column the schedule of tariff cuts to be applied by the six existing Community countries and Ireland on the one hand and the non-applicant EFTA countries on the other to the bulk of trade in industrial goods. The right-hand column shows the cuts to be made on sensitive products by the Community countries and Ireland.

Date	Percentage of original tariff	
1.4.73	80	95
1.1.74	60	90
1.1.75	40	85
1.1.76	20	75
1.7.77	0	60
1.1.78	—	40*
1.1.79	—	20
1.1.80	—	0

*with a minimum level of 3 per cent in most products.

The total value of imports in the area covered by the 16 countries, including trade between each state, amounted to $141,166,000,000 in 1970, calculated in terms of the parity of the dollar at that time. The corresponding figure for exports was $133,380,000,000. This trade accounted for almost 40 per cent of the world's total imports and exports in 1970.

The Special Relations Agreements differed fundamentally from the terms reached for full membership with the other three EFTA countries and Ireland in that (i) the six countries would have no power of decision in Community affairs, and (ii) they would not take part in any institutions except in a joint executive committee which would normally meet twice a year to manage the free trade arrangements, particularly those related to customs matters and to rules of origin. There were also basic differences with other trade agreements negotiated by the Communities (association agreements, e.g. with Turkey, the Yaoundé and Arusha preferential agreements with developing countries, and general tariff preference agreements), which involved only a small degree of reciprocity in trade concessions.

There was little discussion on the general character of the agreements during the seven months of negotiations despite the variety of views among the EFTA countries concerned. However, clauses in the preambles of all the agreements, with the exception of that with Finland, left open the possibility of further evolution in relations with the Communities beyond strictly commercial fields.

6.14 Delayed tariff reductions and quantitative restrictions
Although the agreements included no permanent exceptions to the free trade arrangements for industrial products, there were a number of special provisions affording extended tariff protection for individual countries and groups of countries for up to 11 years, compared with 4½ years for the majority of trade.

Imports of Communities and Ireland. On certain products regarded by the Communities as particularly sensitive the existing members of the Communities and Ireland would eliminate tariffs against some of the EFTA countries at a slower rate incorporating cuts in the original tariff of 5 per cent each on April 1, 1973, Jan. 1, 1974, and Jan. 1, 1975, of 10 per cent on Jan. 1, 1976, of 15 per cent on July 1, 1977, and of 20 per cent each on Jan. 1, 1978, 1979 and 1980 [see table above].

Sensitive products. The following products would be subject to the sensitive products tariff schedule applied to imports from all the EFTA non-candidate countries, with the exception of Portugal for which a separate system was agreed: ferro-alloys, excluding ferro-nickel and products covered by European Coal and Steel Community agreements [see 6.19]; unwrought aluminium, aluminium waste and scrap; unwrought lead; unwrought zinc, zinc waste and scrap; wrought or unwrought tungsten, molybdenum, tantalum, cadmium, chromium, germanium, hafnium, manganese, niobium, antimony, titanium, vanadium, uranium, zirconium, rhenium, gallium, indium and thallium.

For imports from Austria, Finland and Sweden the sensitive products list also included continuous and discontinuous filament textile fibres for the manufacture of artificial and synthetic textiles; for Austria and Sweden certain alloy and high carbon steels were listed; while for Sweden alone a range of stainless and normal steel pipes were specified.

Quotas. In addition to the tariff regimes applied to these products a system of "indicative ceilings" or quotas was included in the agreements with the aim of preventing excessively rapid growth of Community imports which might lead to disruption of markets. Imports of a number of other less sensitive products would also be closely monitored so that similar arrangements could be made if necessary.

Imports exceeding the ceilings could be made liable for the remainder of the year to the full rather than the reducing rate of the common external tariff at the request of the Commission or any member country. Ireland, being neither a member of EFTA nor of the existing Communities, would in these circumstances apply the appropriate "most-favoured-nation" tariff, while the UK, Norway and Denmark would apply a gradually increasing proportion of the common external tariff until July 1, 1977, when the tariffs applied by these three new members of the Communities and the six existing members would be equal.

Not all the sensitive products were to be subject to the ceilings at the start of the agreement on Jan. 1, 1973, but Community member countries would be permitted to impose them in later years on request. The initial level of ceilings to be imposed in 1973 would be based on average imports into the Communities in the years 1968–71 plus an additional factor of 5–15 per cent, varying according to the product. In subsequent years the ceiling could be increased by 5 per cent annually (3 per cent in respect of cork products), although the Communities could maintain the levels of earlier years subject to consultation.

Imports of EFTA non-applicant countries. Community restrictions on sensitive products were balanced to some degree by parallel measures applied by some of the EFTA countries concerned to imports from the Communities.

Switzerland, for example, decided that paper product imports from the existing members of the Communities and from Ireland would be subject to the same schedule of tariff reductions as that applied by the Communities, while *Sweden* decided to apply the Communities' sensitive product schedule of cuts to some steel product imports. *Austria's* restrictions covered almost all products on the Communities' list of sensitive products, whereas *Finland* was permitted to defer tariff reductions on a very much larger range of products imported from the Communities and Ireland, although restrictions would be only small on imports from the UK, Norway and Denmark. The products affected by the Finnish restrictions included agricultural and electrical machinery, textiles, shoes and lorries.

6.15 Provisions for paper trade

Agreement on special terms for paper product imports to the Communities and to its prospective members proved one of the most difficult problems to be resolved during the negotiations. The issue had been further complicated on July 11, when Geoffrey Rippon, Chancellor of the Duchy Lancaster and the chief British negotiator, called upon the Communities to modify their proposal for a 4 per cent British duty on paper imports to an 8 per cent duty to be applied by 1977, when it would equal that to be then applied by the Communities in the course of their own series of tariff cuts. The Community tariff was currently set at 12 per cent, while the UK imported all paper products from its EFTA partners at zero duty.

Despite opposition from Denmark and Norway, which supported Sweden and Finland in their opposition to the British proposal, a ministerial meeting in London on July 20 agreed on a compromise formula which would impose duties on a small part of British paper product imports. The countries principally affected were Finland (for which paper accounted for 42 per cent of total exports), Sweden and Austria.

Tariff arrangements. It was agreed that, while almost all trade in industrial products between EFTA countries would continue to operate without tariff restrictions, paper product imports to Britain, Denmark and Norway would be subject to a tariff increasing to a maximum of 8 per cent in 1977 and thereafter declining to zero in parallel with the tariff reductions agreed with the Communities and Ireland. The table below illustrates the agreed tariff schedule for the main products concerned.

Date	Community tariff per cent	Acceding countries' tariff per cent
1.4.73	11.5	0
1.1.74	11.0	3.0
1.1.75	10.5	4.5
1.1.76	10.0	6.0
1.7.77	8.0	8.0
1.1.78	8.0	8.0
1.1.79	6.0	6.0
1.1.80	6.0	6.0
1.1.81	4.0	4.0
1.1.82	4.0	4.0
1.1.83	2.0	2.0
1.1.84	0	0

Duty-free quotas. During this period duty-free quotas would, however, be applied in respect of imports from Austria, Finland, Sweden and Switzerland to the acceding countries. The precise levels and coverage of these quotas would not be settled until 1973, but it was agreed that in the case of the UK they would cover the bulk of trade in a reference period related to the average of imports in 1968–71. It was reported in the press that about 80 per cent of the trade in paper products between the UK and the producing countries would be covered by the quotas and that a supplementary clause in the agreement provided for a review of the quantities concerned in 1975.

Rippon explained in his statement to the Commons that the solution "took full account of the difficulty in which the British paper industry finds itself at present, and was also acceptable to our partners in the Communities and EFTA". In answer to questions he added that, taking into account the duty-free quotas on paper, the arrangements made with respect to Sweden and Finland "provide for 90 per cent of the present trade to this country to come in duty-free".

6.16 Processed agricultural products
The agreements included trade concessions on a number of processed agricultural products (most of which were covered by an existing Community regulation)

involving a schedule of tariff cuts over a 4½-year period to cover the industrial content of the products, and also a sliding-scale element to compensate for the difference between world and Community prices for agricultural raw materials.

The protection offered to the Community producers of agricultural raw materials would not be eliminated, since the EFTA non-applicant countries would not participate in the Community common agricultural policy which guaranteed higher prices than on the world market as a result of annual contributions by member countries to a joint fund.

The Community terms were matched broadly by reciprocal offers from each of the EFTA countries concerned, although there were a number of exceptions and additions—for example the trade in whisky was to be the subject of further negotiations, including discussion of arrangements for the UK during the transitional period.

6.17 Rules of origin
New rules of origin would apply from April 1, 1973, the date of the first tariff cuts, and would be based on those applied in the Communities' existing association and preferential trade agreements such as those with the Mediterranean countries and with the Yaoundé and Arusha countries. They would also incorporate process rules for specific products similar in principle to those applied by the UK in respect of the generalized system of preferences for developing countries negotiated in the context of the UN Conference on Trade and Development (UNCTAD). This system broadly involved a requirement that a product should have been transformed sufficiently to justify its inclusion under a different heading in the Brussels Nomenclature, although a list of exceptions and variations was also included in several important product sectors.

In addition, trade between the non-candidate EFTA countries and the three acceding EFTA countries would continue to operate under EFTA rules during the transitional period, although there would be a further system of concessions and controls for goods produced in the UK, Norway and Denmark which incorporated products originating in the six existing members of the Communities or in Ireland.

The combination of various methods of assessing origin was the result of considerable discussion at all stages of the negotiations, when countries with particular interest in one or other product attempted to win concessions to assist their domestic industries. Some of the principal products affected by the modifications eventually agreed upon included manufactured foodstuffs (including concessions on imported sugar content of confectionery, of importance to Switzerland), chemicals, leather, footwear and textiles.

To take account of the particular needs of European industrial production, provisions were made to allow a certain degree of "cumulation" whereby, subject to certain conditions, goods which had already qualified under the rules of origin in one country in the free trade area would maintain their "originating" status when further processed in any other country covered by the agreements.

6.18 Rules of competition
Although the non-candidate EFTA countries were not obliged to harmonize their competition policy rules with those of the Communities, a number of specific practices were forbidden in as much as they would adversely affect trade under the terms of the agreements.

These included (i) agreements between undertakings, decisions by associations of undertakings and concerted practices between undertakings which had as their object or effect the prevention, restriction or distortion of competition in regard to production or trade; (ii) any abuse by one or more undertakings of a dominant position within the territories of the parties to the agreements; (iii) government aids which distorted or threatened to distort competition by favouring certain undertakings or the production of certain goods.

In the event of any claims of distortion of competition as a result of one of the above situations, the appropriate committee set up to administer each agreement would attempt to resolve the problem; failing a solution, the country concerned was permitted to take steps such as the withdrawal of the relevant tariff concessions. In the case of export aids remedial action was permitted before consultation in the committee.

Additional safeguards. Other escape and safeguard clauses were included to cover balance-of-payments difficulties, anomalies arising as a result of differences between levels of most-favoured-nation tariffs on raw materials or intermediate products, dumping, and sectoral and regional difficulties. Except in the case of balance-of-payments difficulties, all these matters were to be discussed in the committee concerned before action was taken, although unilateral action was not completely excluded.

6.19 Coal and steel agreements

Separate agreements on matters concerned with the ECSC provided for the achievement of free trade in Treaty of Paris products by July 1, 1977, on the same schedule of tariff cuts as for other industrial goods, and included the elimination of quotas and other trade restrictions. In addition, the six EFTA countries agreed to observe the pricing and competition rules of the ECSC and, with the exceptions of Switzerland and Iceland, to undertake the administration of the rules themselves.

As in the general industrial trade agreements, the Community specified that certain alloy and high carbon steels should be regarded as sensitive products and were subject to the extended transitional period arrangements, and in the case of Austria and Sweden were also subject to indicative ceilings. Both Portugal and Finland were permitted to make special provisions.

6.20 Positions of EFTA non-applicant countries

Some special provisions for individual countries and the attitudes of those countries to the agreements are outlined below.

Austria. In addition to the main agreement, Dr Kreisky, the Chancellor, and Dr Staribacher, Minister of Trade, signed an interim agreement at the Brussels ceremony on July 22 enabling a 30 per cent tariff cut on all industrial products to be made on Oct. 1, 1972, and including a 5 per cent cut on sensitive products such as paper and aluminium, the former otherwise conforming to the agreement reached in London on July 20. Negotiations on the interim agreement had started earlier than those held in parallel with the other EFTA countries, and were the consequence of long-standing Austrian efforts to reach a settlement with the Communities since 1961.

In the light of the earlier failures and of the recent success Dr Kreisky told the Austrian parliament on July 25 that differences between the UK and France had obstructed the establishment of a large free trade area. He stated: "The Brussels agreements proved that the way towards a general solution to the problems of European integration could only be cleared on the day when France and Great Britain reached agreement. The era of large continental and sub-continental markets has begun."

Dr Kirchschläger, the Foreign Minister, reaffirmed that the agreements with the

Communities in no way changed the external policy of neutral Austria, although on Aug. 18 the Soviet government expressed anxiety over the future of Austrian neutrality in a memorandum referring to the Soviet position with regard to the formation of economic and political blocs.

Karl Schleinzer, leader of the People's Party, accused the goverment of weakness during the negotiations and in particular deplored the omissions in the agreement with respect to the agricultural sector. He also proposed several complementary economic measures on which would depend the ratification by his party of the agreements, but nevertheless greeted the Brussels accords as a "historic success". The interim settlement was to be ratified on Sept. 14 and the full Special Relations Agreement on Oct. 25.

Finland. The minority Social Democrat government of Rafael Paasio (which had been formed in February following general elections in October 1971) resigned on July 19, three days before the planned signature of the agreement in Brussels. Announcing the resignation, Mauno Koivisto, the Finance Minister, declared that "only a majority government can take the responsibility of signing the trade agreement with the European Common Market". He stressed however, that no specific foreign policy issue had occasioned the government's resignation, which he said had resulted from a combination of internal and foreign policy problems. The day after the government's resignation, the Communist Party renewed earlier attacks claiming that it had failed to clarify its position on the agreement with the Communities.

Interparty negotiations eventually resulted in the formation of a centre-left coalition government, which was led by Kalevi Sorsa, the Social Democratic leader and out-going Foreign Minister, and was sworn in on Sept. 4. Nevertheless the Special Relations Agreement was not signed by the Finnish government until over a year later in October 1973 [see 6.23].

Finland was most directly concerned with the dispute over the restriction on trade in paper products and as a result imposed her own restrictions on imports from the Communities to cover about 30 per cent of trade in industrial products. Otherwise the Finnish agreement was similar to those applicable to the other EFTA countries, except that (i) it contained no "evolutionary clause" by which the parties might at a future date extend their co-operation into other fields, and (ii) whereas the other EFTA countries were obliged to give 12 months' notice of withdrawal, a period of three months was specified in the case of Finland.

Iceland. As in the case of Portugal, it was considered during the negotiations that Iceland's dependence on exports of fish and fish products justified special arrangements to favour this industry, and also to assist the development of other industrial sectors. On this basis the Communities and Ireland undertook to eliminate tariffs on industrial goods over the standard period of 4½ years, while Iceland's own tariff barriers would be removed over a period extending in most cases to the be-ginning of 1980. The three acceding EFTA countries had already eliminated their barriers against Icelandic products since Iceland had become a member of EFTA, and Iceland agreed to continue its own schedule of tariff cuts with these countries (initial cuts having already been made) in parallel with reductions on goods from the Com-munities and Iceland starting in 1974.

Iceland was also granted duty-free trade with the Communities and Ireland for frozen fish fillets, subject to certain minimum price requirements, while canned herrings would benefit from a 50 per cent tariff reduction. The concessions on fish and fish products, which constituted 80 per cent of Iceland's total exports, were dependent on a settlement of the fishing limits dispute satisfactory to all members of the enlarged Communities.

In addition Iceland was granted a tariff quota of 30,000 tons annually of aluminium out of its total production of 77,000 tons, with provision for a 5 per cent increase each year.

Sweden. Although Sweden had earlier been in favour of extensive co-operation with the Communities beyond the limits of a trade agreement, the Brussels settlement was welcomed by Feldt (Minister of Commerce) as the most comprehensive economic agreement in the field of trade policy to which Sweden had been a party. Feldt pointed out that free trade in Western Europe had long been a central objective of Swedish trade policy and that the agreement gave stability and durability to Sweden's relations with West European countries.

Referring to Sweden's longer-term objectives, Feldt said further co-operation in the economic field was covered by the reference in the agreement to a framework for additional negotiations. The constructive spirit in which the agreements had been concluded was considered by Feldt as a promising starting point for the future extension of co-operation.

Switzerland. The Swiss agreement with the Communities was complemented by a separate accord on watches and clocks extending the scope of an arrangement concluded in June 1967 in the context of the Kennedy Round tariff negotiations. The last 10 per cent reduction in tariffs incorporated in the 1967 settlement should be applied on Jan. 1, 1973, and all other remaining duties would be removed in equal parts of 20 per cent over five years, thus avoiding the continuation of some trade barriers as originally proposed by the Communities.

In exchange the Swiss agreed to more liberal conditions permitting French, Italian and West German producers of partly finished watches and components to continue supplies to the manufacturers of complete watches, which would retain their trade description as originating in Switzerland.

Another agreement appended to the main body of the document signed in Brussels referred to a protocol drawn up in Rome in June 1972 on the subject of foreign workers in Switzerland, a matter which had been of particular concern to Italy and which had caused considerable difficulties in Switzerland, where there was an unusually high proportion of foreign residents.

The agreement with Switzerland applied also to Liechtenstein, which forms a customs union with Switzerland and whose representative participated in the negotiations.

6.21 Approval of Special Relations Agreements in Switzerland, Austria, Portugal and Sweden (October–December 1972)

The agreements were approved in Austria by the *Nationalrat* (lower house of parliament) on Oct. 25 (the interim agreement having been approved on Sept. 14), in Sweden by the *Riksdag* on Dec. 12 and in Portugal by the National Assembly on Dec. 13.

The Special Relations Agreement between Switzerland and the European Communities was approved in a national referendum on Dec. 3, 1972, by 1,345,057 votes to 509,350 in a 51.2 per cent poll. The Liechtenstein *Landtag* (parliament) on Nov. 29 had approved the application of this agreement to Liechtenstein.

Under the terms of Article 89 of the Swiss Constitution a referendum is only obligatory in the case of approval of an international agreement when the treaty is concluded for an indefinite period. However, although the Special Relations Agreement provided for withdrawal in any year, the Swiss government (*Bundesrat*—Federal Council) announced in a message to the Federal Parliament on Aug. 25 that the importance and possible duration of the agreement justified the holding of a referendum.

The *Nationalrat* (lower house) approved the terms of the agreement on Sept. 21 by 151 votes to 7, and on Sept. 25 also approved by 122 votes to 32 the Federal Council's proposal to submit the agreement to a referendum. However, on Sept. 27 the *Ständerat* (upper house) rejected the proposal to hold a referendum by 19 votes to 18, although unanimously approving the terms of the agreement itself. It was considered by some Swiss legal authorities that the referendum issue should be settled within a strictly constitutional context, but after a further vote in the *Nationalrat* on Oct. 3

approving the holding of the referendum by 108 votes to 38, the *Ständerat* also voted in favour on the same day by 21 votes to 14.

6.22 Entry into force of Agreements (Jan. 1, 1973)

On Jan. 1, 1973, Special Relations Agreements entered into force between four of the seven remaining members or associates of EFTA on the one hand and the EC on the other, thus inaugurating a programme of tariff reductions and other measures which would lead to a free trade area embracing the 13 countries concerned.

It was intended that the free trade area should be further extended when (i) the Finnish government had signed the terms of a Special Relations Agreement which had been initialled in July but not formally signed by the end of 1972; (ii) a similar agreement had been negotiated by the Norwegian government with the Communities following the Norwegian decision not to become a full member [see 5.10]; (iii) the Icelandic parliament had approved the agreement signed in July with the Communities.

6.23 Finnish signature and ratification of Agreement (Oct. 5 and Nov. 16, 1973)

Finland's Special Relations Agreement with the European Economic Community and the European Coal and Steel Community was signed in Brussels on Oct. 5, 1973. The delay of over 14 months between the initialling of the agreement and its signature was caused partly by internal Finnish political difficulties and partly by uncertainty over the attitude of the Soviet Union.

Within Finland, the agreement had been criticized by a section of the Social Democratic Party, which constituted the leading element in the country's coalition government, and was strongly condemned by the Communist Party as being in contravention of Finnish neutrality. However, the council of the Social Democratic Party on Sept. 19 had decided to accept the agreement in the light of the passage through parliament of certain legislation giving the government extensive new powers over the economy, particularly prices. Opposition to these laws by the Communists (on the grounds that they were preparing the way for the EC agreement) meant that they had not been approved earlier although proposals had first been put forward in December 1972.

As regards the uncertainty over the Soviet attitude, the signing by Finland of a co-operation agreement with Comecon in May was considered by the Finnish government as providing a balance to the EC agreement, and following an unofficial visit to the Soviet Union on Sept. 2–3 by President Kekkonen, the latter, at an extraordinary meeting of the Finnish cabinet on Oct. 3, gave the government authority to proceed with the signature in Brussels.

At the same time, President Kekkonen published a commentary on the subject in which he said that the agreement with the EC was "purely commercial", having as its aim the guaranteeing of Finnish competitiveness. He stressed that the agreement was compatible with all Finland's international treaties, and added: "We have built our foreign policy on relations of good neighbourliness and on the determined observation of the agreements which we have concluded. In this respect nothing has changed, nothing will change."

However, on Oct. 12 the Soviet Communist Party newspaper *Pravda* prominently published the text of a statement by the Finnish Communist Party urging the Finnish parliament not to ratify the agreement—a development which was interpreted by many observers as indicating continued opposition to the agreement on the part of the Soviet government. Under the terms of the text signed in Brussels, the agreement had to be ratified by Finland before the end of November for it to come into force on Jan. 1, 1974.

On Nov. 16 the *Eduskunta* (parliament) duly ratified the agreement by 141 votes to 36, only the Communists voting against. The agreement therefore came into effect on Jan. 1, 1974, with a 40 per cent cut in tariffs on industrial goods, to bring the timetable of tariff reductions for Finland into line with the one already in operation between the European Communities and the other EFTA countries.

6.24 Icelandic ratification of Agreement (Feb. 28, 1973)—Conclusion of fisheries dispute (June 1976)

Despite the failure of attempts to resolve the fisheries dispute between Iceland and the UK and West Germany, which followed the former's declaration of a 50-mile fishing limit as from September 1972 [see 6.12], Iceland ratified the Special Relations Agreement on Feb. 28, 1973. On the same day the EC issued a formal reminder to Iceland that a settlement had to be reached by March 31 if Iceland was to draw the full benefits from the agreement when the latter came into force on April 1.

Subsequently it was reported from Brussels on March 20 that the European Commission had asked member governments of the Nine to agree to a postponement of that part of the agreement covering Icelandic fish exports, pending a satisfactory solution to the "cod war". The Commission's proposal was ratified by the Council of Ministers at its meeting in Brussels on March 22, and a Council meeting held on June 25–26 in Luxembourg postponed the first tariff cuts on fish exports from Iceland which had been due to take place on July 1, 1973. The issue was not resolved until three years later after both West Germany and the UK had concluded agreements with Iceland and tariff cuts were eventually made from July 1, 1976.

When West Germany and the UK on April 14 and June 5, 1972, respectively instituted proceedings against Iceland at the United Nations' International Court of Justice the Icelandic government refused to recognize the court's jurisdiction on the dispute. A ruling, given on July 25, 1974, and also rejected by the Icelandic government, found that the Icelandic regulations extending exclusive fishing rights to 50 miles were not opposable (applicable) to either the United Kingdom or West Germany; that Iceland was not entitled unilaterally to exclude UK and West German fishing vessels from the disputed area; and that the parties were under a mutual obligation to undertake negotiations in good faith for the equitable solution of their differences.

The ruling was followed by a further extension as from Oct. 15, 1975, of Iceland's fisheries limit from 50 to 200 nautical miles and on July 16 the Commission informed the Icelandic government that its decision was "likely to prejudice the interests of several [EC] member states and thus of the Community as a whole". The Commission added that plans for new arrangements to enable Iceland to benefit from tariff reductions on her fish exports to the Communities (then liable to 15 per cent duty) would be suspended. Another "cod war" between the UK and Iceland ensued and led to the severance of diplomatic relations between the two countries from February 1976 until June 2, the day after an interim agreement was signed in Oslo. Under this agreement the number of British trawlers fishing within Iceland's 200-mile limit (which was not formally recognized by the UK) was limited to an average of 24 a day. An agreement on West German fishing rights in Icelandic waters had also been concluded at a meeting on Nov. 19–20, 1975 in Bonn, on condition that the Icelandic–UK dispute was also settled.

In the light of the settlement of the fisheries dispute with the UK, it was announced by the European Commission in Brussels on June 15, 1976, that the government of Iceland had been informed that tariffs on Icelandic fish and fish product imports to the EC member countries would be reduced as from July 1, 1976 (generally by 80 per cent and for some items abolished altogether), as if the reduction had taken effect in mid-1973 as originally planned.

7: RENEGOTIATION OF UK MEMBERSHIP TERMS

7.1 Chronology of events

Feb. 28, 1974	General election and return of minority Labour government pledged to renegotiate membership terms
April 1, 1974	Delivery to EC Council of Ministers of British demand for renegotiation
June 4 and 18, 1974	Detailed exposition of British requirements
Oct. 10, 1974	General election and return of Labour government with renewed commitment to renegotiation and to submitting new terms to electorate for decision on continuing membership
Dec. 9–10, 1974	Paris summit of the Nine as first "European Council" and proposals for budgetary correction mechanism
Jan. 23, 1975	Announcement by British government of intention to hold referendum by June
March 10–11, 1975	Dublin summit of Nine as European Council and agreement on budgetary correction mechanism
March 12, 1975	Wilson's statement of completion of renegotiations
March 18, 1975	British government recommendation of "yes" vote in referendum on continuing UK membership
April 9, 1975	House of Commons vote approving government recommendation
June 5, 1975	Referendum and two-to-one vote favouring continuing membership of Communities

7.2 Election of Labour government in 1974—April 1 statement on renegotiation of terms of British membership of Communities

The Feb. 28, 1974, general election resulted in the fall of the Heath government and the formation on March 4 of a minority Labour government under Harold Wilson. Labour's election manifesto had included a pledge to seek renegotiation of the 1971 accession agreement, as foreshadowed by Wilson when parliament had debated the terms of accession at the time [see 2.31]. The new government's demand for a major renegotiation was delivered on April 1, 1974, by James Callaghan (as Foreign and Commonwealth Secretary) to the EC Council of Ministers meeting in Luxembourg.

His statement (also published as a UK government White Paper) amplified the passages on the Communities from his March 19 foreign policy statement to the Commons, while on March 21–22 he had paid an official visit to West Germany and discussed the renegotiation issue with Chancellor Willy Brandt.

Callaghan told the Council of Ministers on April 1 that "we shall negotiate in good faith, and if we are successful in achieving the right terms we shall put them to our people for approval", but that "if we fail, we shall submit to the British people the reason why we find the terms unacceptable and consult them on the advisability of negotiating the withdrawal of the UK from the Community". The Labour government intended to "stop further processes of integration, particularly as they affect food taxes", while the re-negotiations were in progress.

He continued: "In view of the great importance of the issue of membership of the Community, my government is now engaged in a root and branch review of the effect of Community policies and will place before you in due course in detail the proposals which we would wish to see the Community adopt in order to remedy the situation.

"In particular, we are examining with great care the working of the common agricultural policy; the estimates for future contributions to and receipts from the Community budget; the Community's trade and aid policies towards the Commonwealth and developing countries; and how far in practice the existing rules, as they are interpreted, interfere with the powers over the British economy which we need to pursue effective regional, industrial and fiscal policies."

He referred to positions adopted by the October 1972 Paris summit of the Nine which, he said, "seemed to lay down a rigid programme under which **economic and monetary union**, including permanently fixed parities, would be achieved by 1980", an objective which he assessed as "dangerously over-ambitious: over-ambitious because the chances of achieving by 1980 the requisite degree of convergence of the rates of growth of pro-ductivity and wages rates, of investment and savings seemed to us to be very small; dangerous because of the impossibility for any country, particularly a country with a relatively low growth rate, to manage its own economy efficiently and provide for full employment if it accepted permanently fixed parities without such convergence having been achieved". However, he conceded that "proposals now being considered do not provide for automatic movement towards permanently fixed parities", and that "you will find our objections very much lessened if we can all agree that there can be no question of trying to force the pace, of compelling member countries to accept permanently fixed parities if this means accepting massive unemployment, or before their economies are ready".

On the Paris summit's expressed intention of moving to **European union** by 1980, he said that such a transformation "seems to us to imply a change which is quite unrealistic and not desired by our peoples, certainly not by the British people", and he went on: "I understand that work on clarifying this issue is about to begin within the Community. I shall watch carefully to see if this clarification will help to relieve our anxieties."

On the **common agricultural policy**, where as an importer of much of its food Britain would suffer a heavy balance-of-payments burden from high prices (although many Community prices were at present lower than world prices), there were also problems of surpluses, notably of butter, and of the high cost of operating the CAP, which accounted for 80 per cent of the Community budget. Concerning **Commonwealth and developing countries**, improvements would be sought for overseas suppliers (notably of sugar and New Zealand butter) and Britain hoped to see serious improvement in the Communities' generalized system of preferences (GSP) for agricultural and industrial trade. Britain would also seek generous terms for the access to Community markets for African, Caribbean and Pacific (ACP) countries, in the negotiations currently under way for what was to become the Lomé Convention, and in the field of aid "the Community should look wider than those countries eligible for association". On the question of "whether existing rules interfere with the **powers over the British economy** which we need to pursue effective regional, industrial, fiscal and counter-inflationary policies", the Labour government would "want to be sure that, in cases where jobs are in danger or where there is a need to sustain and develop valuable industrial capacity, we can give aid quickly and effectively . . . [and that] we can continue to give our own assisted areas the help which they need".

Community budget. "Finally, I come to the Community budget. Here fundamental changes are required. Britain's income per head and her rate of growth are lower than in many of your countries. I take it you would agree that the out-turn of the Community budget should not in all justice result in massive subsidies across the exchanges from my country to yours. This is not acceptable.

"We are not asking for charity. We seek a fair deal. In 1973, only paying 8½ per cent of the Community budget in accordance with the transitional key, we were already the second largest net contributors. At the end of our normal transitional period we shall be paying over 19 per cent, well over the 16½ per cent which is our likely share of [gross national product] at that time.

"If the full 'own resources' system were to be applied to us with no changes in 1980, we should find ourselves paying still more, perhaps several percentage points more, of the Community budget—in even sharper contrast with the relatively low share of GNP we can then expect to have.

Procedure of renegotiation. " . . . We do not wish to disrupt the work of the Community more than is necessary during the period of renegotiation. I shall come back to the Council at an early date with detailed proposals on the common agricultural policy, the treatment of the Commonwealth and of developing countries, the Community budget and other areas of difficulty in the economic field. I hope you will agree then to have a general discussion, and to agree how certain of our requests for changes in the Community arrangements should be handled. . . . We shall have to reserve the right to propose changes in the Treaties if it should turn out that essential interests cannot be met without them.

External relations. " . . . The image of the Community in the United Kingdom is not good. My country wishes to remain a member of an effective Atlantic alliance and there is therefore concern about the degree of disagreement between the Community and the United States. . . . We shall not always be able to agree with the United States, but the Community, in devising its procedures and its common positions, must always try to work with America whenever it can.

"Conversely, America must try and work with us. Only if the Nine work harmoniously with the US, both on economic issues in the framework of the Community and on political issues in the framework of political co-operation, shall we surmount the difficulties to which President Nixon and Dr Kissinger have recently drawn attention.

"We should also like to work with you to produce a stable, healthy and co-operative relationship with all those countries or groups of countries with whom Europe's life is intimately connected, for example with Japan, Canada and other industrialized countries; with the Commonwealth and the Community's associates; with the Arab countries; and with the Soviet Union and Eastern Europe.

"We are ready to intensify political consultation and co-operation. But before we can do so we need to agree on our broad aims. I should certainly like to see if we can do this together. . . .

Conclusion. "So to conclude, we shall work for an early and successful result to what we in Britain have come to call renegotiation. Meanwhile, we shall participate in the work of the Community and act in accordance with Community procedures, subject only to not proceeding with further processes of integration if these seem likely to prejudge the outcome of the negotiations.

"Our aim will be to get an agreement which can be regarded as providing a fair balance of advantage for each of our countries. If this can be achieved successfully, renegotiation will not damage the Community but will strengthen it."

Reactions from the other Foreign Ministers to Callaghan's statement were reported to have been generally reserved—some showing varying degrees of understanding for the British government's position, but all indicating opposition to any course of action which would undermine the basis of the Community. The French Foreign Minister in particular, Michel Jobert, was understood to have left open the possibility of Britain securing some changes but to have ruled out firmly any revision of the basic Community Treaties.

Following this general statement in Luxembourg on April 1, Callaghan presented a more detailed exposition of British requirements at a meeting of the Council of Ministers held in Luxembourg on June 4.

At a meeting of the Agriculture Ministers of the Nine held in Luxembourg on June 18, the UK Minister of Agriculture, Fisheries and Food, Fred Peart, gave further clarification of the British government's "ideas and proposals for the improvement of the common agricultural policy and certain related matters".

7.3 Measures to improve parliamentary supervision of Community developments

Opening a House of Commons debate on the European Communities on June 11, 1974, Callaghan announced four measures intended to ensure that the British parliament was kept informed of developments related to the European Communities: (i) more frequent debates, both on the renegotiation and on the general progress of the Communities; (ii) the allocation of a part of question time exclusively to Community affairs; (iii) the monthly announcement to parliament of the following month's Community business; and (iv) the publication of a report every six months on affairs inside the Communities and on the government's attitude to them.

The establishment of Select Committees on European Community Secondary Legislation, for both the House of Commons and the House of Lords, had been announced on May 2.

7.4 Reaffirmation at second 1974 election of Labour commitment to renegotiation and pledge to hold referendum or further general election on results of the renegotiation—Paris summit meeting of the Nine in December 1974

Having secured an overall parliamentary majority (of three seats) at a general election on Oct. 10, the Wilson government pursued its policy of renegotiation in the latter part of 1974, aiming to give the electorate the opportunity to express a judgment on the desirability of Community membership once the new terms had been established.

Labour's October election manifesto committed the government to submitting the results of renegotiation to the verdict of the British people, expressed through the ballot box, within 12 months. (The Conservative manifesto on the other hand stated that "the terms secured by the last Conservative government were supported by those members of the previous Labour government most qualified to judge them", and that withdrawal "would confront us with the choice of almost total dependence on others or retreat into weak isolation". The Liberals for their part expressed "continued faith in our membership".)

Prior to a summit meeting of the Nine held in Paris on Dec. 9–10, 1974, Wilson had talks with West German Chancellor Helmut Schmidt (Brandt's successor) at Chequers on Nov. 30–Dec. 1, and with President Valéry Giscard d'Estaing in Paris on Dec. 3. Wilson on Dec. 7 (i.e. two days before the Paris summit) publicly stated that if the British renegotiations were successful he would commend the revised terms to the British people.

Considerable resistance was put up by the French delegation at the Paris summit to the British demand for a revised method of calculating contributions to the Community budget—this being one of the basic British renegotiation requirements. However, late in the evening of Dec. 10, after Wilson had reportedly warned that he could see "no hope whatsoever for successful renegotiations" if the British demand on the Community's budget were not met, a compromise agreement was finally reached under which the Community institutions were to work out an appropriate "correcting mechanism".

In the communiqué of the Paris summit the heads of government recalled "the statement made during the accession negotiations by the Community to the effect that, 'if unacceptable situations were to arise, the very life of the Community would make it imperative for the institutions to find equitable solutions'" and they confirmed that "the system of 'own resources' represents one of the fundamental elements of the economic integration of the Community". However, they invited "the institutions of the Community (the Council and the Commission) to set up as soon as possible a correcting mechanism of a general application which, in the framework of the system of 'own resources' and in harmony with its normal functioning, based on objective criteria and taking into consideration in particular the suggestions made to this effect by the British government, could prevent, during the period of convergence of the economies of the member states, the possible development of situations unacceptable for a member state and incompatible with the smooth working of the Community".

At a press conference given at the end of the meeting on Dec. 10, President Giscard referred to it as "the last European summit" and "the first European Council". Whereas previous summits had been attended by "a large number of experts", the present conference had been "a meeting solely of heads of government and Foreign Ministers, held throughout exclusively in their presence", in the manner of a national council of ministers. The more regular future meetings of the heads of government provided for in the communiqué would, he added, take the form of a European Council of this new type.

7.5 Announcement of British referendum

In a statement to the House of Commons on Jan. 23, 1975, outlining "the means by which the British people will decide the issue of our membership of the European Community", Wilson announced that, provided the renegotiations had been completed in time, a referendum would be held "not later than the end of June". The text of his statement was as follows:

"It is the declared policy of the government that, once the outcome of our renegotiation of the terms of membership is known, the British people should have the right to decide, through the ballot box, by means either of a general election or of a referendum, whether Britain should continue in membership of the European Community or should withdraw. The government have decided that this should be done by means of a referendum.

"Prolonged uncertainty and delay on the decision of the British people are in the interests neither of Britain nor of other members of the Community. After 15 years of discussion and negotiation it is an issue which all of us in this House and in the country want to see settled; and uncertainty about the future of British membership is inhibiting the work of the Community.

"The government are committed to putting the issue to the people before Oct. 10 this year. Provided that the outcome of renegotiation is known in time, we intend to hold the referendum before the summer holidays, which means in practice not later than the end of June. . . .

"When the outcome of renegotiation is known, the government will decide upon their own recommendation to the country, whether for continued membership of the

Community on the basis of the renegotiated terms, or for withdrawal, and will announce their decision to the House in due course. That announcement will provide an opportunity for the House to debate the question of substance. . . .

"The circumstances of this referendum are unique, and the issue to be decided is one on which strong views have long been held which cross party lines. The Cabinet has, therefore, decided that if, when the time comes, there are members of the government (including members of the Cabinet) who do not feel able to accept and support the government's recommendation, whatever it may be, they will, once the recommendation has been announced, be free to support and speak in favour of a different conclusion in the referendum campaign. . . .

"The government propose within a very few weeks to publish a White Paper on the rules and arrangements for conducting the referendum. The White Paper will set out the various possible courses on each issue and the government's proposals on such matters as the information policy of the government during the referendum campaign, broadcasting arrangements during the campaign, the question of expenditure by campaigning groups, the form in which the question is to be put to the British people, and arrangements for conducting the poll, the counting of the votes and the announcement of the result. . . . The debate on the referendum White Paper will enable the government to take full account of the views expressed by [MPs], and by public opinion generally, in drafting the necessary legislation for the referendum. . . ."

7.6 Commission's proposals on correcting mechanism for budget contributions—Agreement on budgetary correcting mechanism at March 1965 Dublin meeting of European Council

The Commission's proposals on budget contributions published on Jan. 30, 1975, bore the title "The Unacceptable Situation and the Correcting Mechanism". The proposals provided for a compensatory refund mechanism to be triggered under certain budgetary and economic conditions, their detailed contents being as follows:

Unacceptable situation. An "unacceptable situation" would be regarded as existing if a member country, in addition to being a disproportionate contributor to the Community budget [see below], was also in economic difficulties, the latter being defined as the concurrent existence of (i) a per capita gross national product (GNP) below 85 per cent of the Community average, (ii) a rate of growth of per capita GNP below 120 per cent of the Community average, and (iii) a balance-of-payments deficit on current account.

Disproportionate contributions. A member state would in principle be regarded as making disproportionate contributions to the Community budget if its actual payments under the system of "own resources" expressed as a percentage of the total budget exceeded its percentage share of the Communities' GNP, subject to recognition of the different character of the three classes of own resources designated under the Treaty of Luxembourg of April 1970, namely, agricultural levies, customs duties and value added tax—VAT. Whereas payments from VAT (or based on relative GNP pending agreement on VAT—see below) were to be regarded (principally at the insistence of France) as obligations of the member states concerned, agricultural levies and customs duties, which derived from Community-level trade, were regarded as Community resources. Thus certain thresholds and ceilings were to be applicable to the operation of the refund mechanism [see below].

Correcting mechanism. A disproportionate payment as defined above would entitle a member state to a refund calculated on the basis of a rising percentage scale applicable to particular bands (tranches) of the actual payment expressed as a percentage of payments that would have been made under a GNP-based scheme, as follows:

Overpayment Tranches per cent	Refund per cent
100–105	No refund
105–110	50
110–115	60
115–120	70
120–125	80
125–130	90
130 and above	100

It was further specified that the correcting mechanism would be applied only where percentage contributions were more than 110 per cent of the country's share of Community GNP. Moreover, the amount of actual refund could not exceed (i) two-thirds of the total excess payment, (ii) the net foreign exchange costs to a member state arising from the Community budget transactions, or (iii) its contribution to own resources deriving from VAT, whichever of these three ceilings was the lowest. (The first two ceilings were understood to have been entered at the insistence of the West German government.)

Activation of mechanism. A member state would apply for the correcting mechanism to be put into operation, and the Commission would assess the reality of the situation by reference to the pre-established criteria. If appropriate, the necessary refund would be entered in the next draft budget for approval by the Council of Ministers. The Commission's proposals envisaged that in practice a member state would have to enter a claim at the end of the first half-year of apparent over-payment and specified that the criteria as to "economic difficulties" would be considered in the light of the figures for the last three years expressed as a moving three-year average, and the criteria as to "disproportionate contributions" to the Community budget in the light of the forecasts for the current year. Any amount required for a refund would be entered as "expenditure necessarily resulting" in the budget for the following year; it might if necessary be adjusted on the basis of the correcting mechanism according to the actual outturn of the forecasts of the contribution to Community financing.

Trial period. The Commission suggested that the proposed arrangements could be operated for a trial period of seven years, at the end of which the Community authorities "would consider the conditions of application of the mechanism and take steps accordingly".

At a meeting of the Council of Ministers on Feb. 10 in Brussels, the Commission's proposals for a correcting mechanism were broadly welcomed, and in the House of Commons on Feb. 27 Callaghan described them as a "remarkable advance". A meeting of the Council of Ministers in Brussels decided on March 3 to refer the proposals for final decision at a meeting of the heads of government of the nine member countries of the Communities in Dublin on March 10–11, 1975. At this meeting, (one of the more frequent sessions of the heads of government as a "European Council" envisaged by the Paris summit conference in December 1974) it was decided that the budgetary correcting mechanism as laid down in the paper prepared by the European Commission should be applied with the following modifications:

"(1) The criteria concerning the balance-of-payments deficit and the two-thirds ceiling are dropped.

"(2) The following provisions will be incorporated into the agreed mechanism: (i) the amount of the correcting mechanism shall be up to a ceiling of 250,000,000 European units of account (EUA); however, as soon as the amount of the Community budget exceeds 8,000 million EUA, the ceiling shall be fixed at an amount representing 3 per cent of total budget expenditure; (ii) when a moving average drawn up over three years indicates that the balance of payments on current account of the country in question is in surplus, the correction shall only affect any difference between the amount of its VAT payments and the figure which would result from its relative share in the Community GNP."

In a statement to the House of Commons on March 12, Wilson stated that the Dublin meeting had rejected certain suggested changes in the Commission's proposals for a correcting mechanism which would have been unfavourable for Britain, and maintained that the modifications adopted were to Britain's advantage.

He went on: "The two main changes were on the operation of the balance-of-payments criterion and on the proposed limits on refunds. . . . Under the balance-of-payments criterion proposed by the Commission, a member state would have ceased to be eligible for a budget refund if it had run a balance-of-payments surplus on average for three years. This criterion was modified so that, even if a country has a balance-of-payments surplus on average over three years, it can continue to qualify for a refund related to its VAT contribution, provided that it meets the other criteria.

"On the limits on refund, the Council agreed to drop the Commission's proposal that refunds should be limited to two-thirds of the amount by which a country's share of the budgetary contribution exceeded its share of the Community's GNP. We got rid of the two-thirds limitation. Instead, the Council agreed upon a ceiling of 250,000,000 EUA on the amount of a refund to any qualifying country in any single year. This would give a refund at current exchange rates of up to about £125,000,000 in any year to a member state that qualifies. It was also agreed that, if and when the total Community budget came to exceed 8,000 million EUA, the ceiling from then on should be 3 per cent of the budget total.

"The arrangements which the Community has now agreed would, if Britain remains a member of the EEC, give us an assurance of a repayment of hard cash if we found ourselves in the future paying an unfair share of the Community budget."

7.7 Access for New Zealand dairy produce

Among the renegotiation demands presented to the Council of Ministers on June 18, 1974, by Fred Peart, was a requirement that the Communities should discuss arrangements for continued access for New Zealand dairy produce beyond the five years to 1977 provided for under Protocol 18 of the British Act of Accession. The New Zealand government's desire that a firm commitment should be made in respect of the British demand constituted the main purpose of visits by the New Zealand Prime Minister, Bill Rowling, to London on Feb. 9–17, 1975, and subsequently to Brussels (on Feb. 17–18), Bonn (Feb. 18–19) and Paris (Feb. 20–23).

Another aspect of Peart's requirements—that the pricing arrangements under Protocol 18 should be reviewed annually—had been met on Nov. 19, 1974, when the Council of Ministers agreed that the Community levy on (British) imports of New Zealand butter and cheese should be reduced to provide for an effective 18 per cent increase in the price received by New Zealand producers, which had hitherto been based on the average UK market price in 1969–72. (In 1974 New Zealand dairy exports to the UK market were subject to maximum quotas of about 160,000 tons of butter and 60,000 tons of cheese, which had not been completely filled due to drought conditions in New Zealand, actual shipments having reached 130,000 tons of butter and 20,000 tons of cheese. Under Protocol 18 these would fall to about 140,000 tons and 15,000 tons respectively by 1977.)

Following Rowling's visit to London, the British government informed its Community partners of its wish that Article 5 of Protocol 18 providing for a review of the New Zealand arrangements in 1975 should be activated and that the Dublin meeting should express a commitment in this respect.

Rowling was understood to have obtained a further commitment that the British government would raise with the Community the effects of Britain's gradual upward alignment to the 20 per cent external Community tariff on lamb and mutton, which he claimed was eroding the profit margins of New Zealand producers on the fixed UK price; he was also reported to have discussed the implications for New Zealand of the possible introduction of a common agricultural policy regime for sheepmeat.

At the Dublin meeting of the European Council on March 10–11, 1975, the heads of government adopted a statement of intent to reach agreement on continued access for New Zealand dairy produce after 1977.

"They invite the Commission to present a report in order to prepare the review provided for in Article 5 [of Protocol 18 of the British Act of Accession] and to submit as soon as practicable a proposal for the maintenance after Dec. 31, 1977, of special import arrangements as referred to in that article. They observed that the institutions of the Community have already carried out certain price adjustments in the framework of the protocol [see above]. In the same spirit, the Community, which remains attached to a fair implementation of the protocol, is ready to review periodically and, as necessary, to adjust the prices having regard to the supply and demand developments in the major producing and consuming countries of the world, and also to the level and evolution of prices in the Community—including intervention prices—and in New Zealand, taking, moreover, into account cost developments in New Zealand and trends in freight charges.

"As regards the annual quantities to be established by the Community institutions in the framework of the special arrangements after 1977, these should not deprive New Zealand of outlets which are essential for it. Thus, for the period up to 1980, these annual quantities, depending upon future market developments, could remain close to effective deliveries under Protocol 18 in 1974 and the quantities currently envisaged by New Zealand for 1975.

"They note that Protocol 18 provides that the exceptional arrangements for the import of cheese cannot be maintained after Dec. 31, 1977, and that this situation and the problems which may arise from it will be given due attention with appropriate urgency, taking into account also the considerations in the following paragraph.

"The heads of government note, moreover, that New Zealand and the Community together provide the major part of world exports of dairy products. They therefore express the wish that, in the same spirit with which the Community approaches the application of Protocol 18, an ever closer co-operation be developed between the institutions of the Community and the New Zealand authorities with the objective of promoting in their mutual interest an orderly operation of world markets. Such a co-operation, apart from its intrinsic value, should provide a basis from which to achieve, in a wider framework, the conclusion of an effective world agreement such as is envisaged in Protocol 18."

Wilson told the UK House of Commons in his March 12 statement that the guidelines adopted by the Dublin meeting represented "a substantial improvement" on the existing provisions of Protocol 18.

"First, it was agreed that annual imports of butter for the first three years after 1977 (from 1978 to 1980) may remain close to deliveries in 1974 and 1975. The heads of government accepted what had been strongly urged on us by the New Zealand government—the need for periodic review of the prices received by New Zealand — and provided for these to be adjusted as necessary to take account, among other things, of future developments in the levels of Community intervention prices.

"In the existing protocol signed in 1972 the special arrangements for cheese expire altogether after 1977, but it is now accepted that this creates problems which, in the words of our agreement yesterday, will be examined by the Community with due urgency. In other words, we have now kept open the option for some continuing imports of New Zealand cheese after 1977, when they were due to cease under the 1971 terms. The Commission has been invited to bring forward its report for the review of the protocol together with the necessary proposals. I would expect this to be done during the summer."

7.8 Presentation of March 1975 report and White Paper on results of renegotiation—Recommendation of "yes" vote in forthcoming referendum on membership

Harold Wilson said at the end of his March 12 statement in the Commons on the Dublin meeting that he had "made it clear to the other members of the Council that, with these agreements on the budget and on New Zealand, we had now taken our discussions within the Community on renegotiation as far as they could go".

Before the Dublin meeting, Callaghan had on March 3 indicated to the Council of Ministers that Britain wanted a complete review of the operation of the European Coal and Steel Community, particularly with a view to re-establishing national control over investment, pricing policy and mergers in the steel industry. However, he had made it clear that this new request did not constitute a renegotiation demand and could be dealt with after the UK referendum on Community membership.

Wilson announced in the House of Commons on March 18 that the Cabinet had decided to recommend that in the forthcoming referendum (subsequently fixed for June 5) the British people should vote for continued British membership. He gave his assessment of the renegotiation as follows:

Common agricultural policy. "Objective One. 'Major changes in the common agricultural policy [CAP] so that it ceases to be a threat to world trade in food products, and so that low-cost producers outside Europe can continue to have access to the British food market.' The Minister of Agriculture [Fred Peart] . . . in his statement to the Council of Ministers on June 18, 1974, . . . asked for: (i) the establishment of firm criteria or pricing policy, taking account of the needs of efficient producers and the demand/supply situation; (ii) greater flexibility, taking account of the need for appropriate measures to deal with special circumstances in different parts of the Community; (iii) measures to discourage surpluses and to give priority to Community consumers in the disposal of any surpluses which arise; (iv) improvement in the marketing regimes for some major commodities, particularly beef, with a view to avoiding surpluses; (v) the improvement of financial control; and (vi) better access for certain commodities from outside the Community, with particular regard for the interests of Commonwealth producers and of the consumer.

"Now as to the outcome. On the 'supply of food at fair prices', in the three CAP price settlements since the government took office, the Minister of Agriculture has succeeded in keeping price increases below cost increases, and thus in real terms reinforcing the downward trend in CAP prices. This would benefit consumers and taxpayers and also is designed to reduce the risk of surpluses. Increasingly, price proposals are being related to the costs of efficient producers and the supply/demand situation, and this approach is reaffirmed in the Commission's report on the CAP stock-taking.

"On the 'greater flexibility for special circumstances and improved systems of market regulation, especially beef', the Minister has secured changes for beef under which member states are no longer obliged to maintain high prices for producers by buying beef into store and denying it to consumers. Instead, they can let it go to consumers at reasonable prices and make up returns to producers by deficiency payments partly financed by the Community. In addition, special encouragement has been given for sugar production in the UK. More generally, the monetary arrangements have been used to differentiate the percentage price increase between member states. There has been more flexibility in the use of national aids.

"On the 'requirements of measures to discourage surpluses and to pay more regard to consumers', the downward pressure on CAP prices is itself a safeguard against surplus production—together with our proposals, now being pursued, for the reduction of support buying prices for milk products and cereals when surpluses start to arise. Then there is the recent practice that any surpluses which do develop are run down by cheap supplies to Community consumers rather than being unloaded on world markets. We have had this in the beef subsidy for pensioners and in the increased butter subsidy. British consumers again benefit from the monetary import subsidies paid to countries which have devalued, and from special measures to keep Community prices below world prices, particularly the sugar import subsidy which is financed by the Community.

"On the objective of 'improved financial control', some progress has been made — better estimates of costs and budgetary implications of new proposals, tighter monitoring of expenditure and the introduction of precautions against fraud.

"On 'access for third-country foodstuffs', in 1971 we condemned the failure to provide security for Commonwealth Sugar Agreement producers. . . . But we have now got assured access for up to 1,400,000 tons of sugar from developing countries, for which we pressed from 1971 onwards, so this objective has been achieved. (Moreover, during the recent world market sugar shortage, British refiners and manufacturers had purchased 170,000 tons of sugar to maintain continuity of supplies with the aid of Community subsidies of £36,000,000.)

"On 'access for New Zealand dairy produce', in the autumn of 1974 we secured an increase of 18 per cent in the prices paid to New Zealand to ensure continued supplies, and at Dublin we got agreement on the broad lines of the continuing arrangements for access of New Zealand dairy produce after 1977. No commitments had been made in 1971, but so far as butter is concerned, the Commission have been instructed to prepare in the next three or four months a draft based on the maintenance of butter imports from New Zealand to Britain at around the level of 1974–75 deliveries, together with price proposals to which the New Zealand government attach the greatest importance. On cheese, the protocol to the treaty of entry ruled out any more access for New Zealand cheese of the kind provided for in 1973–77. But last week's statement has left the matter open, and we have given notice that we shall pursue it in the Protocol 18 review. We shall press this very hard.

"Improved access for other foodstuffs has been secured as a result of GATT negotiations, the trade sections of the Lomé Convention, the Mediterranean agreement and the Community's 1975 generalized scheme of preferences which has now been agreed. Improved access, too, for tropical oils, Canadian cheddar, soluble coffee and lard, though no achievement yet on access for certain other foods such as canned fruit and hard wheat. We have requested levy-free quotas for hard wheat and flour, and put on record that we shall at an early date seek elimination or reduction of the tariff on New Zealand lamb.

Community budget. "Objective Two. On the Community budget the manifesto commitment was: 'New and fairer methods of financing the Community budget. Neither the taxes that form the so-called own resources of the Communities, nor the purposes, mainly agricultural support, on which the funds are mainly to be spent, are acceptable to us. We would be ready to contribute to Community finances only such sums as were fair in relation to what is paid and what is received by other member countries.' It rapidly became clear that we could best secure our objectives not by seeking to overturn the system of financing the budget from 'own resources' but by correcting its unfair impact by a mechanism which would provide a refund to us. I reported to the House a week ago and set out the corrective mechanism proposals . . . which satisfactorily met what we then proposed, involving a refund of up to £125,000,000 a year.

Economic and monetary union. "Objective Three. Economic and Monetary Union [EMU]. The manifesto commitment is as follows: 'We would reject any kind of international agreement which compelled us to accept increased unemployment for the sake of maintaining a fixed parity. . . . We believe that the monetary problems of the European countries can be resolved only in a world-wide framework.' Since that commitment was made there has been a major change in the attitude of other European governments to the practicability of achieving EMU by 1980. As a long-term objective it was restated in the Paris communiqué, but for all practical purposes it has been tacitly abandoned. For example, the second stage due to start on Jan. 1, 1974—15 months ago—has never been adopted, and practical work has been virtually at a standstill for a long time. There is no prospect of our coming under pressure to agree to an arrangement, whether in relation to parity commitments or otherwise, threatening the level of employment in Britain. . . .

Regional, industrial and fiscal policies. "Objective Four. Our election manifesto of February 1974 stated our objective as: 'The retention by parliament of those powers over the British economy needed to pursue effective regional, industrial and fiscal policies.' On regional policy, since the turn of the year, and in the context of our renegotiations, the Commission have had an intensive discussion with us and other member governments and have now formulated the principles under which they propose to implement their role in the co-ordination of regional aids. Their hierarchy of assisted areas conforms to ours. No forms of national aids are ruled out in principle, and there is no interference with our existing regional aids. There is a particular problem relating to assistance given by the Highlands and Islands Development Board, for which a derogation is being obtained. In discussing the way in which regional aids might be changed to meet new circumstances, the Commission have furthermore acknowledged that national governments are the best judges of what is required in their own country, and that the Commission will be prepared to consider changes in national aid systems compatible with the Common Market, when they are justified by problems of employment, unemployment, migration and by other valid requirements of regional development policy which constitute essential national problems. The Commission have further accepted that urgent action by governments may be necessary and that treaty procedures will not hold this up.

"We have not met with any serious difficulties from the EEC in the conduct of industrial policy during the past year. . . . Article 222 of the Treaty of Rome specifically permits nationalization; and government participation in the equity of a firm does not in itself raise problems under the treaty. The Commission have accepted that in urgent cases we will provide aid without first giving them an opportunity to comment. . . . The Commission have not yet commented on the Industry Bill. The proposals for the National Enterprise Board and for planning agreements have much in common with arrangements in other member states; they are in no way incompatible with the treaty, provided that the government's powers are not exercised so as to damage the competitive position of undertakings in other member states—a principle which we accept, as we have in the case of regional policy. . . .

"Steel is more difficult. . . . I am satisfied that potential problems over prices can be resolved by close contact between the government and the Steel Board, and possible difficulties about mergers are also capable of a solution. There is nothing in the Treaties of Rome or Paris, or in practices or policies under the treaties, which precludes us from extending nationalization of the present private sector, even total nationalization. On the control of private investment . . . the Foreign and Commonwealth Secretary [Callaghan] gave notice at the Council of Ministers on March 3 that it might be necessary to ask for treaty revision, if there is no other way of solving the problem. If, as part of the control of the economy, the government, any government, have to hold back the level of new investment in the public steel sector, it is unacceptable that the private sector should be free to expand where it wants, and by as much as it wants, thus adding to the inflationary pressure on resources. . . . Since it is well known that other member countries have met with those and similar problems, and have found administrative means of dealing with it, I told the other heads of government in Dublin that we would study the methods they have used, whether by environmental controls, planning controls, industrial development certificates, or other means.

"Were this to fail, we could still have recourse to extending public ownership, or to proposing treaty revision. The reference in the manifesto objective to fiscal policies has not proved difficult. There are proposals for certain measures to harmonize the structure of some indirect taxes, but any which were objectionable to us would require our agreement. I will come to this again on VAT.

Capital movements. "Objective Five. Capital movements. The manifesto commitment says: 'Equally we need an agreement on capital movements which protects our balance of payments and full employment policies.' We have made use of the relevant articles of the Treaty of Rome to revert to broadly the same exchange control regime as applied before entry. We can continue to take action under those articles to protect our balance of payments.

Commonwealth and developing countries. "Objective Six. The Commonwealth and developing countries. The manifesto said: 'The economic interests of the Commonwealth and the developing countries must be safeguarded. This involves securing continued access to the British market and, more generally, the adoption by an enlarged Community of trade and aid policies designed to benefit not just associated overseas territories in Africa but developing countries throughout the world.' I have referred to Commonwealth sugar and New Zealand dairy products. Another major achievement was the Lomé Convention (signed on Feb. 28, 1975, in the Togolese capital). What was achieved—and a great tribute is due here to the work of [Judith] Hart, the Minister of Overseas Development—is the transformation of a paternalistic arrangement with a restricted range of mainly ex-French and Belgian colonies or territories, in which they had to offer the Community reciprocal trade benefits, into a relationship based on co-operation with 46 countries in Africa, the Caribbean and Pacific (22 from the Commonwealth). The new convention governs access, without requiring reciprocity, a completely new scheme for stabilization for commodity earnings, and much increased aid. It has rightly been described as historic. For this and other reasons, almost all Commonwealth countries, advanced and developing, have expressed their hope that Britain will stay in the Community.

"As to Asian countries, such as India, Sri Lanka, Bangladesh and Pakistan, a good deal has been done for them already. They have benefited from EC emergency aid to those countries most seriously affected by the oil price rises. India has an agreement with the EC, and the other three are negotiating them. The generalized scheme of preferences has been much improved, and earlier this month the Council of Ministers agreed to work for continuing improvements to the scheme, with particular emphasis on the interests of the poorest developing countries, including those of the Indian sub-continent. But it cannot at this stage be claimed that all the problems so far as Asian countries are concerned have as yet been solved. In principle, yes, but there is so far no commitment about financial provision.

Value added tax. "Objective Seven. Value added tax (VAT). The manifesto commitment is: 'No harmonization of value added tax which would require us to tax necessities.' The proposals now being discussed in the Community are concerned with agreeing a uniform assessment base for VAT. They provide for our system of zero rating. We will be able to resist any proposals which are unacceptable to us. That was not the position four years ago. Contrary to the situation four years ago, this is no longer a real threat. So far from harmonizing, a number of countries are insisting on increasing the number of VAT rates within their own tax systems, and it seems there is no danger to our freedom here at all.

Conclusion. "To sum up, therefore, I believe that our renegotiation objectives have been substantially, though not completely, achieved. . . . What now falls to be decided is whether, on these terms—the renegotiated package as a whole—the best interests of Britain will be best served by staying in or coming out. . . .

"So, I do not believe that in taking this decision we are entering into a narrow regional grouping to the detriment of our world-wide relationships. . . . We have to face the fact that practically the whole Commonwealth, deciding on the basis of their own interests, want Britain to stay in the Community. . . . Relations with the United States are closer and better than they have been at any time, certainly in this generation, and in some contrast to what they have been in very recent times. Nothing in today's decision will in any way weaken that relationship.

"A fundamental change, not in the treaty but in the practice, has been brought about by the new system of heads of government summits of a regular routine character, started with that convened by President Giscard in Paris last September, and continued by the December meeting, and now the Dublin meeting. This system has already de facto reasserted a degree of political power at top level, not only over the month-by-month decisions, but over the general method of operation of the Market. This does not mean it has become a Europe *des patries* [the phrase attributed to President de Gaulle of France in 1961–62 to describe his concept of the European Community]. It is a Community. But, as compared with even a year ago, vital interests of individual nations are now getting much more of a fair hearing, and the political power in asserting those interests has certainly increased more than appeared possible in the battles of 1971, 1972 and 1973: more, in my view, than even a year ago, when the result of the February election made the manifesto objectives for the first time no longer a domestic, political argument, but a governmental mandate for renegotiation. . . ."

7.9 Dissent within Cabinet over government's "Yes" recommendation

Seven members of the Cabinet "availed themselves of the licence to differ" on the government's recommendation: Michael Foot (Secretary of State for Employment); Eric Varley (Secretary of State for Energy); Barbara Castle (Secretary of State for Social Services); Tony Benn (Secretary of State for Industry); Peter Shore (Secretary of State for Trade); William Ross (Secretary of State for Scotland) and John Silkin (Minister for Planning and Local Government).

Foot, Castle, Benn, Shore and Silkin, together with Hart (Minister of Overseas Development), who was not a member of the Cabinet, on March 23 issued a statement giving their reasons for dissenting from the recommendation, on the grounds that the results of renegotiation "have fallen far short of our minimum aims".

The material balance-sheet of membership was markedly unfavourable, they said, but "the gravest disadvantages are political. The rights of our own people and the power of parliament remain at the end of the negotiations subordinate to the non-elected Commission and Council of Ministers in Brussels. . . . To Western Europe we offer continued co-operation and alliance, as we do to our friends in other continents. What we deny is both the benefit and the reality of a special and exclusive relationship with the Common Market; and what we reject is the underlying purpose to create a new single state in Western Europe. . . . As democrats and socialists we believe that Britain, freed from the restraints of the Common Market, can better serve the world community of which we are part and the aims of our own people for a better and fuller life."

7.10 Parliamentary votes approving government's "Yes" recommendation
The House of Commons on April 9 at the end of a three-day debate approved by 396 votes to 170 on a free vote the following government motion: "That this House approves the recommendation of HM Government to continue Britain's membership of the Community as set out in the White Paper on the membership of the European Community" [published on March 27].

The 396 votes for the government's motion were made up of 249 Conservatives, 135 Labour and 12 Liberals. The 170 votes against the motion comprised 144 Labour, 7 Conservatives, 11 Scottish Nationalists, 6 Ulster Unionists and 2 *Plaid Cymru*. A total of 60 members did not vote (including 34 Labour and 18 Conservatives).

The House of Lords approved a similar motion on April 22 by 261 votes to 20.

7.11 The referendum (June 5, 1975)
The Referendum Bill, which was given its second reading in the Commons on April 10 (by 312 to 248) and received the Royal Assent on May 8, established that the question should be "Do you think that the UK should stay in the European Community (Common Market)" and that the result should rest on a simple majority. The government would deliver to each household a less technical version of the White Paper on the new terms, its own recommendation for a Yes vote entitled "Britain's new deal in Europe", and documents containing statements by the two opposing campaign organizations, Britain in Europe (the umbrella campaign for a Yes vote) and the National Referendum Campaign (for a No vote), both of which would receive £125,000 from public funds.

A special Labour Party conference on April 26 approved by 3,724,000 votes to 1,986,000 a recommendation from the party's national executive committee (NEC) that Britain should leave the EC. The main speakers in support of the NEC statement were Bryan Stanley, general secretary of the Post Office Engineering Union, and Michael Foot. Both Wilson and Callaghan spoke in favour of the government's recommendation for continued membership of the EC. The general council of the Trades Union Congress (TUC) on April 23 formally approved a document opposing Britain's continued membership of the European Community, but at the same time stressed that individual unions would be free to express a contrary view.

In the referendum on June 5, the electorate voted in favour of continued membership of the European Communities by a two-to-one majority. England, Wales, Scotland and Northern Ireland all registered "yes" majorities; of the 68 counties and regions on which counting was based, only two Scottish island areas—Shetland and the Western Isles—returned majority votes against Community membership.

There were 17,378,581 Yes votes (67.2 per cent of valid votes) and 8,470,073 No votes, and 54,540 spoilt papers, in a turnout of about 64 per cent (compared with 78.8 per cent and 72.8 per cent at the two general elections in 1974).

The TUC general secretary Len Murray said on June 6 that the TUC accepted the result of the referendum, and he indicated that it would lift its boycott of Community institutions (principally the Economic and Social Committee).

Harold Wilson said in a Commons statement on June 9 that "the debate is now over . . . the historic decision has been made", that "I now say to our partners in the Community that we look forward to continuing to work with them in promoting the Community's wider interests and in fostering a greater sense of purpose among the member states", and that "it also follows from the decision to remain in the Community that this country should be fully represented in all the Community's institutions". He went on:

"I have said that if renegotiation succeeded and if our recommendation was endorsed by the country we should feel it right that this House should be fully represented in the European Assembly [i.e. the European Parliament, which had been boycotted by the Labour Party since Britain's accession to the Community]. A recommendation to this end will now be made to the Parliamentary Labour Party."

8: GREECE: APPLICATION AND ACCESSION, GREEK MEMORANDUM POSITION OF TURKEY

8.1 Chronology of events

July 25, 1959	EEC acceptance in principle of Greek request for association
July 9, 1961	Signature of Association Agreement
Nov. 1, 1962	Entry into effect of Association Agreement
April 21, 1967	Military coup in Greece
July 1974	Restoration of civil regime
Nov. 26, 1974	Greek government's aide-mémoire to Community expressing wish for full Community membership
Dec. 2, 1974	First meeting of EEC–Greece Association Council since restoration of Greek democracy
June 12, 1975	Submission of formal Greek application for negotiations on accession
January–February 1976	Delivery of Commission's Opinion recommending pre-accession period, and rejection of Opinion by Community Council of Ministers
April 28, 1976	Signature of additional protocol extending Greek association—from Six to Nine
July 27, 1976	Ministerial conference marking formal opening of accession negotiations
Feb. 28, 1977	Signature of second financial protocol under Association Agreement
Feb. 7, 1978	Resolution of Council of (Foreign) Ministers on completion of accession negotiation by end of year
Dec. 21, 1978	Compromise agreement on length of transitional period to follow Greek accession
April 3, 1979	Successful conclusion of accession negotiations
May 28, 1979	Signature of Treaty of Accession in Athens
June 25–28, 1979	Greek parliamentary debate and ratification of Treaty
Dec. 16, 1980	Finalization of arrangements for Greek participation in European Regional Development Fund
Jan. 1, 1981	Greek accession as tenth state of European Communities

Jan. 12, 1981	Entry into European Parliament of 24 Greek members nominated by national parliament
Oct. 18, 1981	Greek general election resulting in victory for Pasok party critical of Community membership
Oct. 18, 1981	Concurrent direct election of Greek members of European Parliament
Nov. 26, 1981	Outlining by Andreas Papandreou at European Council of new Greek government's policy with regard to EC
March 1982	Submission of Greek memorandum
June 17–19, 1983	European Council recognition of "special problems" of Greece
July 1, 1983	First assumption by Greece of rotating presidency of Community Council of Ministers
March 29–30, 1985	Launching at European Council meeting in Brussels of Integrated Mediterranean Programmes
June 2, 1985	Pasok general election victory following campaign emphasizing benefits obtained from Communities by outgoing Pasok government
Sept. 2, 1986	Signature in Heraklion, Crete, of first programme involving Community aid for Greece under Integrated Mediterranean Programmes

8.2 1962 Association Agreement
The six member countries of the EEC on July 25, 1959, accepted in principle a Greek request for association with the EEC in a customs union, with provision for a move to full membership when Greece's economic progress permitted. After two years of negotiations covering the detailed provisions of the association, the EEC Council of Ministers gave its final approval on June 12, 1961, to an Agreement which was then signed on July 9, 1961, and entered into effect on Nov. 1, 1962.

It was pointed out in the press at this time that about 40 per cent of Greece's agricultural products were exported to the Six, while about 60 per cent of her industrial imports came from the Six.

The chief topics covered in these negotiations were as follows:

(i) The date at which tariff reductions by Greece vis-à-vis the Six should commence and the speed at which they should be effected, having regard to the state of developments of the Greek economy.

(ii) The expansion of markets for Greek agricultural products (especially tobacco and citrus fruits) in the six member countries of the EEC. Italy expressed particular concern at the possible effects which Greek exports might have on her own exports of citrus fruits, but a compromise was finally reached [see below] whereby a ceiling was fixed on the quantity of fruits which might be exported by Greece under conditions of equal treatment with exports by EEC member countries. A compromise was also eventually reached with Italy on the level of Italian imports of Greek tobacco.

(iii) Greece's trade relations with third countries, in which connexion Greece demanded the right to accord favourable treatment to products imported from third countries in order to promote the export to those countries of her own agricultural products, so long as the EEC could not guarantee that Greece's output of these products would be fully absorbed in the markets of the EEC member countries.

(iv) The nature of an "escape" clause [see below].

(v) The granting of loans to Greece by the EEC. Originally the EEC had proposed to make new loans dependent on the settlement of Greece's pre-war debt totalling the equivalent of £75,000,000 (with an additional £75,000,000 representing accumulated unpaid interest since 1941); of this sum, nearly 80 per cent was in sterling, 17 per cent in dollars, and the remainder in French francs.

Greece put forward the argument that only a very small portion of the debt was owned in EEC member countries, that Germany and Italy had been responsible for war devastation in Greece, and that post-war reparations had been insufficient to enable Greece to develop her economy to the point at which she could resume repayment of the debt. A statement issued by the Greek Ministry of Finance on Aug. 24, 1960, declared that Greece had "repeatedly expressed her eagerness for a settlement of the pre-war public debt based on the capabilities and needs of the Greek people . . . in spite of the terrible trial of her economy during the war and post-war periods and the need to concentrate all her resources and capabilities on her economic development"; discussions had, however, revealed a conflict on basic points which made agreement impossible.

Eventually, however, an accord on the unconditional granting of loans was reached and embodied in a special protocol [see below].

The main provisions of the final agreement are summarized below:

Greek association with the EEC. Under Article 238 of the Treaty of Rome Greece would not become a full member of the EEC but would associate herself with it on the basis of a customs union, with the prospect of her incorporation into the Community when the progress of her economy allowed her to assume fully the obligations deriving from the Rome treaty.

The object of the association was defined as the "continuous and balanced strengthening of trade and economic relations between the contracting parties, having particular regard to the need to secure an accelerated development of the Greek economy".

Internal tariffs between Greece and EEC member countries. A customs union would become fully effective after a transition period during which Greece would receive special consideration. In principle she would reduce her tariffs over 12 years from the date of the Agreement coming into force, at the rate of 10 per cent immediately, 10 per cent at the end of each 18-month period for the first nine years, and a further 10 per cent at the end of each of the remaining three years.

In order to assist in the development of Greek industry, however, there would be special concessions in the case of most industrial goods produced in Greece, the transition period for these lasting 22 years. Thus, during the first 10 years tariffs would be reduced by a total of 20 per cent, i.e. a 5 per cent reduction on the date of the Agreement coming into effect, and three reductions of 5 per cent each at intervals of 2½ years; from the end of the 10th year until the end of the 22nd, the remaining 80 per cent of the original tariffs would be reduced at the rate laid down for normal tariff elimination, i.e. one-tenth (or 8 per cent of the original tariff) at the end of the 10th year, one-tenth at the end of each 18-month period for the next nine years, and one-tenth at the end of each of the last three years. It was estimated that the 22-year transition period would apply to approximately one-third of Greece's imports from the Community.

Tariff reductions which had already taken place among the six member countries of the EEC, as well as any further reductions, would, upon the Agreement coming into effect, immediately and automatically apply to Greek products. Thus the tariff would immediately be reduced by 30–40 per cent for Greek industrial products and by 20–30 per cent for Greek agricultural products, all tariffs vis-à-vis Greece being completely eliminated by 1969 at the latest.

In order to protect newly established industries, Greece would be permitted during the 12-year transition period to impose new tariffs or to increase existing ones by a maximum of 25 per cent ad valorem, provided that imports from the EEC of the products affected did not exceed 10 per cent of the total imports from the member countries of the Community in 1958. These tariffs might be maintained for nine years and would then be progressively reduced, being eliminated in any case by the end of the 22-year transition period.

External tariffs. Greece accepted the tariffs of the EEC's common external tariff scale, so that at the end of the 12- or 22-year transition period (whichever applied to the articles in question) goods imported from third countries would be subject both in Greece and in the EEC member countries to a common external tariff.

In the case of tobacco, raisins, olives, colophony, and turpentine (the five products in which Greece has a "special and increased interest") the following special provisions in favour of Greece would apply during the first 12 years: (i) the ad valorem tariff of the common external tariff scale on Oct. 1, 1960, might not be modified by more than 20 per cent without the prior consent of Greece, e.g. the EEC ad valorem tariff vis-à-vis third countries of 30 per cent on tobacco might not be reduced below 24 per cent; (ii) the prior approval of Greece would also be sought before any special tariff quotas were granted by the EEC member countries for more than 22,000 tons out of the total of 130,000 tons of tobacco imported annually from third countries, and for more than 15 per cent of the annual EEC imports from third countries of raisins, olives, colophony, and turpentine.

For up to 10 per cent of her imports from third countries, Greece would be permitted to grant special tariff quotas without the prior approval of the EEC, provided the special tariffs would equal those currently applied for corresponding imports from EEC member countries.

Quantitative restrictions. These would be progressively eliminated between Greece and the EEC. In particular, the equivalent of 60 per cent of Greek private imports from EEC countries in 1958 would be permanently liberalized within one year, rising to 75 per cent at the end of the fifth year and to 80 per cent at the end of the tenth year. Global quotas for EEC member countries equal to Greece's imports from those countries in the first year after the Agreement came into effect would be increased from the third to the tenth year by 10 per cent per annum on a cumulative basis; after the tenth year the rate of increase would be raised to 20 per cent for each 18-month period, all quantitative restrictions being eliminated by the end of the 22-year period. The expansion of import quotas and import liberalization already effected or to be carried out in the future between member countries of the EEC would be extended to Greece.

Special agricultural provisions. The Agreement aimed at harmonizing the agricultural polices of the signatory countries, so that Greek agricultural products would receive equal treatment with similar products of the Six. If for any reason Greece found that such a harmonization for a particular product ran contrary to her interests, she might decline to implement it, in which case she would be entitled to enjoy at least a most-favoured-nation status as regards her relations with the Community for that particular commodity.

All Greece's key farm products (tobacco, raisins, olives, etc., and all fruit and vegetables) would immediately enjoy equal treatment with similar products of the six member countries of the Community. For Greek wines quotas had been fixed covering the normal maximum annual exports in recent years, within which they would enjoy equal treatment; these quotas would be increased whenever the quotas prevailing among the Six underwent an increase.

At the special insistence of Italy, a protocol was added providing that if the export trade of any EEC member country was adversely affected by Greek exports of citrus fruits, grapes, and peaches, the EEC Council of Ministers might decide that Greek exports of these products which were in excess of the amount stipulated in the protocol would not enjoy the status provided by the Agreement. The limits were set at 22,000 tons for citrus fruits, rising to 45,000 tons by the end of the fifth year; 15,000 tons for fresh grapes, rising to 31,000 tons; and 40,000 tons for peaches, rising to 83,000 tons. After the fifth year the limits would be agreed by both sides until Greek agricultural policy was completely harmonized with that of the Six. In the case of citrus fruits, the limits might be subject to revision if Greece experienced particular difficulties with her exports to third countries with which she was linked by bilateral clearing agreements.

A more rapid tariff reduction by the Six would be applied to Greek exports of raisins and tobacco, viz. the tariffs in force on Jan. 1, 1957, would be halved immediately the Agreement came into force, and would be completely eliminated in the case of raisins within six years and in the case of tobacco by the end of 1967.

The French *Monopole du Tabac* would stabilize its purchases of Greek tobacco at the average level of the years 1957–59, and would increase them in the same proportion as those countries which imported tobacco freely; the Italian Tobacco Monopoly would procure from Greece at least 60 per cent of its purchases of tobacco for internal consumption (i.e. excluding tobacco destined for re-export), with a guaranteed annual minimum value of $2,800,000.

The tariff and quota status for imports of other farm products by either side would become permanent at the level in force when the Agreement came into effect. In the case of meat and dairy products, however, Greece would grant limited tariff reductions amounting in general to 20 per cent within the first 10 years but to 40 per cent for ham, 35 per cent for cheeses, and 30 per cent for butter.

Other provisions. The Agreement also provided for the establishment of a common economic policy on the model of the Treaty of Rome, taking into account the needs and resources of Greece. The movement of workers, services, and capital would be liberalized; a common policy would be established for vocational training and the exchange of young workers; and tax legislation, currency policy, transport systems, and the rules of competition would be harmonized. The Council of the Association [see below] would determine the exact conditions for the implementation of these provisions.

Institutions. The application of the Agreement would be supervised by a newly created Council of the Association, composed of members of the Council of Ministers and of the Commission of the EEC and of the Greek government. Each side would have one vote and the Council would take its decisions on the basis of unanimity; if it found itself unable to solve the differences submitted to it, it might refer them to the European Court of Justice or to arbitration. In the latter case, the EEC and Greece would each appoint one arbitrator, and these two arbitrators would then co-opt a third as umpire. The President of the European Court of Justice would act as umpire for the first five years, and thereafter the umpire would, in case of dispute, be appointed by the President of the International Court of Justice.

Escape clause. In the case of serious difficulties being encountered by any member of the association, the EEC member countries would have the right of recourse to Article 226 of the Treaty of Rome, while Greece would enjoy equal status as regards the application of this Article. This right, however, would remain in force only during the transition period of the Treaty of Rome and, in the case of the EEC countries, might only be applied after prior consultation with Greece. Moreover, in such a case it would not be possible for all the EEC member countries to take joint protective measures against Greece, and the member country in difficulties could not direct its own protective measures against Greece alone, but would have to apply them against all the other EEC member countries. Up to 1969, Greece would be entitled to resort to protective measures in the event of difficulties in any sector of her economy, and might resort to such measures unilaterally after prior consultation with the EEC.

Loans to Greece. A special protocol provided for loans to Greece of up to $125,000,000, to be used during the first five years of the Agreement. These loans would be for 25 years, and might be spent either in drachmas or foreign currencies. The Six would subsidize by up to 3 per cent per annum the rate of interest on loans representing two-thirds of the total financial support (i.e. on a maximum of approximately $83,000,000). They also agreed to consider within the first five years the provision of additional financial support, specifically through the recognition of Greece's need to apply for loans to the European Investment Bank.

Coal and Steel. Exports of coal and steel to Greece from EEC member countries were not covered by the Agreement but would be the subject of a further agreement to be concluded between Greece and the ECSC.

The principal developments up to the end of 1966 under the Association Agreement with Greece were:

Tariffs. In accordance with the provisions of the Association Agreement, the EEC extended to Greek products the internal tariff reductions introduced within the Six on Jan. 1, 1966, but a more favourable treatment was granted for the Greek key export products—raisins and tobacco. As to raisins, the remaining duty was fixed from Jan. 1, 1966, at 10 per cent. As regards the remaining duty on tobacco (already reduced by 70 per cent of the initial rates), the EEC decided on April 5, 1966, in accordance with a promise made at a meeting of the Association Council on March 23, to cut it by two further stages of 5 per cent each, viz. on July 1, 1966, and on Jan. 1, 1967, thereby reducing it as from the latter date to 20 per cent of the initial level.

Greece had reduced her customs duties on Nov. 1, 1965, for her imports from the EEC by 30 per cent for most products, and by 10 to 20 per cent for products subject to slower rates of dismantlement.

For imports from non-EEC countries Greece took the first step towards aligning her tariffs on the Community's common external tariff on Nov. 1, 1965.

The following table shows Greece's external trade in 1964–65 with the Six and the whole world (in $ million):

	Exports to:			Imports from:			Balance of trade:	
	Six	world	Six's %	Six	world	Six's %	with Six	with world
1961–2*	86	257	33.6	308	705	43.7	−222	−447
1961–3	86	274	31.4	313	763	41.1	−237	−489
1963–4	108	293	36.9	363	873	41.6	−255	−580
1964–5	129	351	36.8	455	1,098	41.4	−326	−747

*Year preceding association; years run from Nov. 1 to Oct. 31.

Harmonization of agricultural polices. At a meeting of the Council of Association held in Brussels on June 16, 1964, it was agreed that a plan to bring the Greek and EEC agricultural policies into harmony would have to be in two stages:

(i) The first stage would allow Greece the levies and other mechanisms of the common agricultural policy without, however, implementing the Common Market price structure; at the same time Greek agricultural produce would receive qualified preference on the EEC markets.

(ii) In the second stage Greece would progressively align her agricultural prices and protection levels on those prevailing in the EEC and would open her markets to Community farm exports, while US agricultural assistance would have to be discontinued.

The ministers, however, were unable to agree on a time-table for this plan, the Greek government asking for a longer period for the first stage when Dec. 31, 1967, was suggested as the ending date. These difficulties made it impossible to reach a decision on harmonization within the time-limit laid down in Article 35 of the Association Agreement, i.e. by Nov. 12, 1964. It was therefore decided that the provisional system applicable to trade in certain agricultural products should be extended to Nov. 12, 1965, and that a solution to the deadlock should be achieved by this date. As this proved impossible, however, the Council of the Association on Nov. 18, 1965, extended the provisional system until June 30, 1966, and at a further meeting held on June 24, 1966, the system was further extended until Dec. 31, 1966.

Following discussions in Athens on Oct. 4–7, 1966, the following communiqué was issued:

"The discussions concerned in general the problems of Greek agriculture in the framework of the common agricultural policy. Note was taken of the need to assure farmers of a fair and adequate income. There were exchanges of view more particularly on a common policy for tobacco, having regard to the great importance of this product to the Greek economy and the fact that this policy is currently under consideration. In this connexion the question of guaranteed prices to producers was first raised. The problems of trade with non-member countries was also examined in the light of certain special situations on the world market. Finally, note was taken that the question of financing should be examined when suitable solutions were being sought to the problems of harmonization of agricultural policies."

Development aid. The Association Agreement provided for loans of $125,000,000 over a period of five years. Loans of $13,800,000 were agreed in 1965 and a further $25,000,000 by July 1, 1966. Of this total, $33,000,000 was lent for infrastructure projects at reduced rates of interest and $3,500,000 at normal interest rates for industrial projects.

8.3 Suspension of Association Agreement during military regime 1967–74— Reactivation of Agreement in period prior to Greek accession to full membership

The Association Agreement was placed in virtual suspension from the time of the Greek military coup of April 21, 1967, until the restoration of a civilian regime in July 1974. During this period there was no progress on those aspects of the Agreement which set out a framework for further development of the Greek relationship with the EEC (including, most importantly, the harmonization of agricultural policies). Moreover, EEC lending to Greece was ended as of Oct. 31, 1967, the point of expiry of the time-limit for the use of the $125 million envisaged, at which date the uncommitted balance stood at $56 million.

As Greece's new civilian Prime Minister, Konstantinos Karamanlis led the liberal-conservative New Democracy party to victory in Greek general elections in November 1974, and immediately thereafter delivered on Nov. 26 an aide-mémoire to the Communities, stating that Greece wished to transform its association into full membership in the very near future, and that it would seek provision for a transitional period and certain special arrangements, as had been agreed for the UK, Denmark and Ireland.

Earlier, following a visit to Brussels by the then Greek Foreign Minister, George Mavros, on Sept. 10–12, 1974, the Council of Ministers had on Sept. 17 adopted a statement on the relationship of Greece with the Communities which said inter alia: "Having reviewed the situation in the association between the Community and Greece, the Council expresses its profound satisfaction with Greece's return to the ideals which inspired the negotiators of the Athens Agreement [of 1962]. It records its strongest determination to resume the process of developing the association immediately in order to facilitate Greece's subsequent accession to the Communities. The Council notes with pleasure that, in these new circumstances, the path is once more clear for the organs of the association to resume their normal functioning and, at a more general level, for the association to develop fully."

Subsequently, the first meeting of the EEC–Greece Association Council since the restoration of Greek democracy, held in Brussels on Dec. 2, 1974, formally reactivated the full machinery of the Association Agreement. Greece decided to resume negotiations on the harmonization of the agricultural sector, and to sign an Additional Protocol extending its association to include the three new EEC member states. (This latter process was completed in negotiations between Greece and the Commission ending on March 7, 1975; the resulting Protocol was signed in Athens on April 28 of the following year, with an interim agreement pending its entry into force, which took effect on July 1, 1978.)

Negotiations for a second financial protocol under the revived Association Agreement led to a Community offer on July 27, 1976, of 225 million EUA in loans and 55 million EUA in grants, this offer being incorporated in the protocol as signed in Brussels on Feb. 28, 1977. The protocol took effect from Aug. 1, 1978, and was designed to run until Oct. 31, 1981, but the total amount of funding had been committed by the end of 1980, for projects intended to help Greece adjust to full membership, and the association was itself superseded by full membership as from the beginning of 1981.

8.4 Negotiation and conclusion of Greek accession to full Community membership as from January 1981 (1975–79)

The Greek government submitted on June 12, 1975, its formal application for negotiations on transforming association into full membership. The European Council on June 24 requested the Commission to draft its Opinion in accordance with Article 237 of the Treaty of Rome, and this Opinion was delivered in January 1976. The Commission in its Opinion placed considerable emphasis on the economic problems which accession would entail for Greece and for the existing Community. It proposed that there should be a pre-accession period, of unspecified duration, for the implementation of economic reforms. The Greek government, reacting to the negative tone of the Opinion, renewed its approaches to the member governments of the Nine, with particular emphasis on the importance of confirming Greece's political stability and West European identity. The Commission's Opinion was rejected unanimously by the Community Council of Ministers in February 1976, and their political decision, in which the French government had taken the initiative, ensured that the negotiations on accession proper would begin. The formal opening of negotiations was marked by a ministerial-level conference in Brussels on July 27, 1976.

A series of four further ministerial-level meetings in 1977, and other meetings at deputy level, characterized the initial exploratory phase of negotiations, devoted to problem identification.

Memoranda were presented by the Greek side at these meetings setting out requests for transitional arrangements on customs union, external relations, regional policy, state aid, the budget, the ECSC, agriculture, social affairs, rights of establishment and capital movement, Euratom, and institutional matters. At the ministerial-level meeting on Dec. 19, 1977, the Commission announced that it would shortly be presenting to the Council its negotiating proposals on a sector-by-sector basis, enabling the substantive phase of the negotiations to proceed during 1978 at the agreed pace.

The negotiations with Greece overlapped with the beginning of talks with Portugal and Spain, which opened in March and July 1977 respectively [see 11.7 and 10.4]. Consideration of the three applications entailed for the existing Community of Nine a serious reappraisal of its balance as between northern and southern European economies.

Moreover, the Greek application gave rise to concern over Community relations with Turkey, which itself had an association agreement dating back to Dec. 1, 1964, and whose tense relations with Greece were dominated by the Cyprus and Aegean disputes. Turkey's concern about a Greek relationship closer than its own with the Nine led to Turkish suggestions for the establishment of "an antechamber" for both Greece and Turkey, stopping short of full membership for either. [See 8.13 for the Greek attitude, after Greek accession to EC membership in 1981, on the question of Turkey's relationship with the Communities.]

Negotiations with Greece were intensified in 1978 in accordance with a resolution of the Foreign Ministers of the Nine on Feb. 7, 1978, that they should be completed by the end of the year.

This resolution marked the success of Karamanlis's insistence that Greek accession should not be linked with that of Spain and Portugal in a "globalization" of the Community enlargement process. In a round of negotiations held in Brussels on Dec. 6, 1978, the Greek side rejected Council proposals that after the initial accession of Greece there should be transitional periods of eight years for agriculture and free movement of labour and of five years for industrial products, and reiterated the Greek demand for a maximum transitional period of five years for all areas.

However, further negotiations in Brussels, including the sixth ministerial-level meeting of the year held on Dec. 20, resulted in a compromise agreement on Dec. 21 under which there would be transitional periods of five years for most Greek agricultural exports and of seven years for free movement of labour; although certain aspects still remained to be settled, the Greek Foreign Minister, George Rallis, said that he expected that the Greek Treaty of Accession would be signed before June 1979 and that Greece would become a member of the Communities by Jan. 1, 1981, at the latest.

Negotiations were brought to a successful conclusion at a final ministerial meeting held in Luxembourg on April 3, 1979.

8.5 Terms of Accession Treaty
Under the Treaty of Accession as signed in Athens on May 28, 1979, at a ceremony in the Palace of Zappeion, Greece would become the 10th member state of the European Communities (i.e. the European Economic Community, the European Atomic Energy Community and the European Coal and Steel Community) as from Jan. 1, 1981, subject to ratification of the Treaty by all 10 countries concerned. The Treaties of Accession to the EEC and Euratom, the Act concerning the conditions of accession and the adjustments to the treaties, and the various protocols and annexes, were signed, on the Community side, by ministerial representatives of the nine existing member states and, on the Greek side, by Konstantinos Karamanlis (Prime Minister), George Rallis (Foreign Minister) and George Kontogeorgis

(Minister for Relations with the European Communities). Under Treaty of
Paris rules the instrument relating to Greek accession to the ECSC was not
signed.

The Accession Treaty provided for a general five-year transitional period (1981–85)
for Greek adaptation to Community membership, although seven-year transitional
periods were specified for the abolition of tariffs on a small number of agricultural
products and for free movement of labour. Details of these and other aspects of the
agreement are given below.

Customs union for industrial products. The Treaty specified a five-year transitional
period for the progressive elimination of residual customs duties on Greek imports of
Community goods and for the alignment of Greek tariff rates to the Communities'
common external tariff (CET). Both adaptations would be carried out in six stages,
beginning with two 10 per cent adjustments on Jan. 1, 1981, and Jan. 1, 1982, and
continuing with four further annual 20 per cent adjustments so that complete
elimination of duties and alignment to the CET were achieved on Jan. 1, 1986. (Under
the existing association arrangements the Community no longer applied customs
duties on incoming Greek industrial products with the exception of coal and steel,
while about two-thirds of the Communities' industrial exports to Greece were likewise
not subject to duty.)

Safeguard mechanism. The Treaty included a general and reciprocal safeguard
clause, in which connexion a special emergency procedure was agreed for implementation in cases of severe economic difficulty.

External relations. During the five-year transitional period Greece would be
allowed to maintain quantitative restrictions towards GATT and state-trading
countries for a small number of products, but would apply the Communities' generalized system of preferences for developing countries from accession subject to a five-
year transition for certain products. Subject to certain transitional arrangements
Greece would also apply the Communities' preferential trade agreements with third
countries and the 1977 Multifibre Arrangement and the accompanying bilateral
agreements concluded by the Communities.

Agriculture. The full application of the CAP would be subject to a five-year
transitional period, but a special seven-year period would apply to tomatoes and
peaches. The transitional measures related essentially to the progressive elimination of
residual custom duties and alignment of the Community's CET on the one hand and to
the alignment of Greek prices to those of the Communities on the other. During the
transitional period the differences between Greek and Community prices would be
compensated for by a system of accession compensation amounts, while a special
transitional compensatory mechanism was laid down for certain fresh fruit and
vegetables.

Freedom of movement. Freedom of movement of workers as between the Nine and
Greece would be achieved at the end of a seven-year transitional period, although in
the meantime priority would be given to Greek workers (as nationals of a member
state) where it proved necessary to recruit workers from outside the Community as
presently constituted. Workers already legally employed in the present member states
would progressively be able to bring in their families over the five-year transitional
period, and in cases where the family did not live in the same country as the Greek
worker family, allowances would be payable after three years (at which point Greek
workers would thus be receiving the same treatment as other Community workers).

Economic and monetary questions. The inclusion of the drachma in the EUA basket
of currencies would be achieved not later than the end of the five-year transitional
period, on the basis of the procedures laid down in the December 1978 agreement of
the European Council on the EMS. As regards capital movements, Greece would as a
general rule liberalize transactions from the date of accession, but would be able (i) to
defer until the end of the transitional period the liberalization of direct investments in

the present member states by persons resident in Greece and (ii) to defer until the end of 1983 the liberalization of the transfer of the proceeds of direct investments in Greece made before June 12, 1975, by persons resident in the Communities. Funds blocked in Greece belonging to residents of the present member states would be progressively released by equal annual instalments leading to full liberalization by Jan. 1, 1986. Current payments would be liberalized on accession.

Financial arrangements. From the date of accession Greece would apply in full the Communities' "own resources" budgetary system. However, in order to avoid Greece becoming a net contributor to the Community budget during the early years of the transitional period, certain special transitional mechanisms were established concerning Greece's participation in the gross national product/value added tax (GNP/VAT) element of the own resources system. Thus, although the amounts of duties accruing to own resources from VAT or from contributions based on GNP would be paid in full from the beginning of 1981, the Communities would refund a proportion of the amount paid as follows: 70 per cent in 1981, 50 per cent in 1982, 30 per cent in 1983, 20 per cent in 1984 and 10 per cent in 1985. As a result of these arrangements (and of the early implementation of certain agreements in the agricultural sector) the Commission calculated "that on the basis of a hypothetical 1979 budget Greece's net benefit from the Community budget will amount to about 80,000,000 EUA during the first year of the transitional period".

In the field of taxation Greece was granted a three-year delay in respect of the full implementation of the Communities' sixth directive of May 1977 establishing a common basis for the collection of a national VAT levy for the purposes of own resources.

Institutional arrangements. From the date of accession Greece would participate fully in all the Community institutions and other bodies in the same way as the present member states. Following the enlargement of the Communities (i) the Council of Ministers would be increased from nine to 10 members (i.e. one from each member state) and the presidency of the Council would rotate in the alphabetic order of member states as expressed in their respective languages (i.e. Belgium, Denmark, West Germany, Greece, France, Ireland, Italy, Luxembourg, Netherlands, United Kingdom), this order of precedence operating from Jan. 1, 1981, with the Netherlands in the chair; (ii) the European Commission would be increased from 13 to 14 members, with Greece nominating one member (George Kontogeorgis, who as Minister responsible for relations with the Communities had led the Greek side in the accession negotiations, took up this post as from Jan. 1, 1981, with charge of the Commission portfolios of Transport, Co-ordination of Tourism Questions, and Fisheries); (iii) Greece would have 24 seats in the European Parliament, the size of which would thus be increased from 410 to 434 members; (iv) the Communities' Economic and Social Committee would have 12 Greek members, its size thus being increased from 144 to 156 members; and (v) Greece would designate a representative to sit on the Board of Governors of the European Investment Bank, bringing the number of governors to 10.

When the enlarged Council of Ministers was required to act by a qualified majority the following adjustments would operate: *weighting of votes*—Greece's vote would be weighted by a factor of five (the total of weighted votes being thus increased from 58 to 63); *required qualified majority*—decisions would be valid (i) with the support of at least 45 votes (then at 41) on a Commission proposal, and (ii) with the support of at least 45 votes, including votes in favour from at least six member states, in other cases.

Coal and Steel Community. Tariff dismantlement between Greece and the ECSC would follow the same timetable as that applicable to EEC products. For the purpose of the progressive introduction of the ECSC unified tariff Greece would start aligning from Jan. 1, 1982, with a 20 per cent reduction of the difference between the Greek basic duty and the duty in the ECSC unified tariff, the difference to be further reduced by 20 per cent steps at the beginning of the following four years so that the full unified tariff would be applied by Greece on Jan. 1, 1986.

8.6 Ratification of Accession Treaty—Greek parliamentary debate
Ratification of the Accession Treaty was completed according to the various
national procedures during the remainder of 1979 and in the course of 1980.
The only significant opposition to ratification in the parliaments of the Nine
was that of socialists and particularly communists in France, where the vote in
the National Assembly was passed by 264 votes to 204 in December 1979 after a
debate in which concern had repeatedly been expressed about the impact of
Greek access to the Community market for Mediterranean agricultural produce.

The issue of ratifying the Accession Treaty was, however, particularly
controversial in Greece itself, where the left-wing opposition parties gave
expression to their hostility to Greek membership of the Communities by
boycotting the four- day parliamentary debate on June 25–28, 1979. At the
conclusion of the debate the principle of membership was approved by 193
votes to none with three abstentions and ratification of the treaty itself by 191
votes to two with three abstentions—the other 104 deputies in the 300-member
unicameral parliament being absent for each division.

In the first division on the principle of membership the 193 votes in favour were made
up as follows: New Democracy (the ruling party) 175, Party for Democratic Socialism
(KDS) 4, National Front 4, Union of Democratic Centre (EDHK) 2, United Demo-
cratic Left (EDA) 1, "interior" Communist Party (KKE) 1 and independents 6; the
abstentions came from the other three EDHK deputies, including the party leader,
Ioannis Zigdis. In the second division on ratification the voting pattern was as above
except that the KKE "interior" deputy and one independent voted against the treaty.
The 104 absentees from both divisions comprised deputies of the Pan-Hellenic Socialist
Movement (Pasok) led by Dr Papandreou and the pro-Moscow "exterior" Communist
Party (KKE).

Presenting the government's case during the debate, the then Prime Minister,
Konstantinos Karamanlis, said that the decision to seek membership of the European
Communities had been motivated by both economic and political considerations. The
latter were not simply the well-known national political advantages, he continued, but
included Greece's wish to participate in the efforts to create a unified democratic
Europe—a world power capable of facing the enormous problems of the present times.
The political considerations involved were of such significance that Greece should seek
accession even if there were no economic benefits to be gained; but it so happened that
membership of the Communities would facilitiate the country's economic and social
development and would result in a marked increase in living standards, particularly of
farmers but also of all working people.

Dealing with the objections to membership put forward by the left-wing opposition
parties, Karamanlis refuted Pasok's claim that Greece would be overrun by monopolistic
multinational companies by pointing to the anti-monopoly and free competition regulations of the Communities. He also dismissed Pasok's alternative proposal for an
industrial free trade agreement with the Communities of the type negotiated by Norway in
1972–73 [see 5.15], maintaining that such an arrangement would not provide a guaranteed
market or price support system for Greek agricultural products and would therefore
obviously be less advantageous for Greece. As regards Papandreou's call for a referendum
on Greek membership of the Communities, Karamanlis recalled that during the discussions
on the new Greek Constitution introduced in 1975 the Pasok leader had vigorously opposed
the article providing for the holding of referendums on the grounds that major issues could
not be resolved by such simplified means but only in the forum of parliament.

Of the organized pressure groups in Greece, the Confederation of Greek
Industries (SEV) favoured accession, as did the largest trade union confederation,
the General Confederation of Greek Workers (GSEE), and the largest farmers'

organization, the Greek Confederation of Agricultural Co-operatives (PASEGES), although other workers' and farmers' organizations affiliated to Pasok or KKE exterior followed the opposition line of their party leaders.

8.7 Greek participation in regional fund
Whereas most of the details of Greek participation in the Communities' institutions and established policy arrangements were laid down in the Accession Treaty, the percentage share of the European Regional Development Fund (ERDF) to which Greece became entitled from 1981 was not finally determined until Dec. 16, 1980. On that date the Communities' Council of (Foreign) Ministers reached agreement in Brussels that Greece would be allocated 13 per cent of ERDF payments and that the other nine member states' percentage quotas would be correspondingly reduced, as shown in the following table:

	New quotas per cent	Old quotas* per cent
Italy	35.49	39.39
United Kingdom	23.80	27.03
France	13.64	16.86
Greece	13.00	—
Irish Republic	5.94	6.46
West Germany	4.65	6.00
Netherlands	1.24	1.58
Belgium	1.11	1.39
Denmark	1.06	1.20
Luxembourg	0.07	0.09

*Operative for the period 1978–80

8.8 Accession (Jan. 1, 1981)
In a statement released on Jan. 1, 1981, the outgoing President of the European Commission, Roy Jenkins, said that the accession of Greece was "a great and historic day for Greece and for the European Community" and was "part of that gathering in of European civilization represented by the European idea".

The statement continued: "We could hardly be complete without the country where in the distant past so much that we now count as characteristically European had its origins. Not least of this is the very concept of democracy which is at the heart of the Community. This is the beginning of a new chapter, and our joint task will be to ensure that the participation of Greece in the Community is beneficial both to Greece and to the new Community of Ten. It will not be easy, and inevitably there will be problems of adjustment—on all sides. But I believe that Greece will from the beginning both contribute to and benefit from the Community. The Commission will certainly play its full role in helping to ensure this is the case. Greece joins the Community at a time of movement, for the Community is an organism in evolution. We face many challenges but even greater opportunities. What is important is that we use the sense of European purpose which motivated us all in creating and enlarging the Community for the greater advantage of all our peoples."

With the accession of the Hellenic Republic, Greek became the seventh official language of the Communities, together with Danish, Dutch, English, French, German and Italian.

In terms of population Greece became the seventh largest of the 10 member states (ahead of Denmark, the Irish Republic and Luxembourg), its

9,500,000 inhabitants increasing the Communities' aggregate population to
some 270,000,000. In terms of economic performance the main indicators
showed that Greece was below the average level of prosperity of the other
nine member states, although it compared well in many respects with the
two next least prosperous members, namely the Irish Republic and Italy.

According to statistics published by the European Commission in late 1980 (i) the
Greek per capita gross domestic product in 1978 was 2,628 European units of
account (EUA), compared with Irish and Italian levels of 2,899 EUA and 3,602
EUA respectively at the lower end of the range for the Nine and Danish and West
German levels of 8,601 EUA and 8,186 EUA respectively at the upper end (1 EUA
= £0.60 or $1.35 at the end of 1980); (ii) per capita private consumption in Greece in
1978 was 1,827 EUA compared with Irish and Italian levels of 1,842 EUA and 2,278
EUA respectively and West German and Danish levels of 4,882 EUA and 4,781
EUA respectively; and (iii) the agricultural sector accounted for 30.8 per cent of the
Greek working population in 1979, as against comparable proportions of 21 per cent
and 14.8 per cent in Ireland and Italy respectively and only 2.6 per cent in the UK.
   In the period 1973 to 1978 Greece achieved an average annual economic growth
rate of 3.6 per cent, higher than the comparable rates of the Nine with the exception
of Italy (4 per cent), but over the same period its average rate of price inflation (over
15 per cent a year) exceeded that of any other member state, as did its current level
of unemployment (15 per cent of the registered labour force). Moreover, the
economic development of Greece was accompanied by a growing trade deficit, which
in the case of exchanges with the Nine rose from 868,000,000 EUA in 1973 on
aggregate trade worth 2,400 million EUA to 1,872 million EUA in 1979 on aggregate
trade of 6,282 million EUA.

(The European currency unit (ECU) was introduced at the same time as
the creation of the European Monetary System (EMS) in March 1979, when
it replaced the identically valued European unit of account (EUA), except
that unlike the EUA changes could be made in the composition and balance
of the basket of currencies determining its value. The ECU finally replaced
the EUA as the unit of account used in the Community budget as from Jan.
1, 1981—see also pages 273–4.)

8.9 Greek elections to European Parliament (January and October 1981)
On Jan. 12, 1981, the 24 Greek members of the European Parliament took
their seats, bringing the total membership of that body to 434. The Greek
members were nominated by their national parliament on this occasion, but
it was envisaged that Greece would hold direct elections for the European
Parliament in 1984 on the expiry of the five-year term of the present
Parliament (which had been directly elected in the other nine member states
in June 1979).

Of the 24-strong Greek delegation, 14 were members of the ruling New Democracy and seven of the opposition Pasok, while one belonged to the "exterior" KKE,
one to the EDHK and one to the KDS.

In the event, the holding of national general elections in Greece on Oct.
18, 1981, was used as an earlier opportunity for concurrent direct elections
to the European Parliament on a conventional proportional representation
system.

The results of the Oct. 18 European Parliament elections (excluding parties which
failed to win representation) were as follows:

	Votes	Per cent	Seats
Pasok	2,280,793	40.17	10
New Democracy	1,779,923	31.35	8
KKE (exterior)	728,398	12.83	3
KKE (interior)	299,316	5.27	1
Democratic Unity	240,087	4.23	1
Progressive Party	110,857	1.95	1

It was noted (i) that Pasok, which had opposed Greece's entry into the European Communities, obtained a 7.89 per cent lower share of the vote in this election than in the general elections, and (ii) that there was a 7.41 per cent increase in the combined share of Democratic Unity and the KKE (interior), each of which supported Greece's membership of the Communities (although the latter party had voted against the actual terms of entry).

8.10 Criticism of membership terms by new Pasok government in Greece in 1981—Proposed holding of referendum—Greek memorandum (March 1982)

The Pasok victory in the general election in Greece on Oct. 18, 1981, was followed by a sustained period of criticism by the new Papandreou government of the terms on which Greece had acceded to Community membership. Dr Papandreou, in his policy statement prior to the three-day parliamentary debate on the government's programme on Nov. 22–24, said that these terms had exacerbated Greece's existing economic problems and created new ones. Pasok, he said, favoured the negotiation of a special relationship with the Communities which would "apply primarily to the industrial and agricultural sectors and will strengthen our national independence". The government would seek to hold a referendum on the continuation of Greece's full membership, and would in the meantime take every opportunity "to fight within the organizations of the Community to protect the interests of the Greek people". The government "would not hesitate to adopt the measures necessary to protect the workers and the producers and to develop goals independent of Community obligations".

Dr Papandreou repeated his intention of seeking a special status for Greece, when he outlined to the European Council on Nov. 26 his government's policy with regard to the Communities.

He could not be sure, he said, that it would be possible to take the measures necessary within the Communities to secure the special status which he sought. In his view the Communities' existing rules were better framed for the industrialized advanced economies of northern Europe, and did not suit countries like Greece which had not attained capitalist maturity.

The suggestion of holding a referendum posed a particular internal political problem, as it would be constitutionally necessary for such a referendum to be called by the President (an office held since May 1980 by the strongly pro-Community former Prime Minister Konstantinos Karamanlis). In the event the idea was not pursued by the Papandreou government, which concentrated instead on securing a response from the Communities to Greece's main grievances as expressed in the Greek memorandum of March 1982, which was worded as follows:

"(1) The economy of Greece differs markedly from that of the Community as regards both its level of development and its structures.

"The special features of the Greek economy hamper its smooth functioning within the Community framework, the more so because the Greek Accession Treaty ignored them.

"Community rules and mechanisms continue to be shaped and to operate to suit the central and developed economies for which they were of course originally conceived, whereas they have an adverse effect upon regional and less-developed economies.

"Because the enlargement of the Community did not go hand in hand with adjustment and differentiation of Community rules to take account of the special nature of the economy of Greece, the accession of Greece is either exacerbating some of our nation's problems or making their solution more difficult.

"The repercussions of accession upon the economy of Greece were of course aggravated because they appeared at a time of serious international crisis.

"Thus the economic problems which at present confront Greece principally spring from structural weaknesses, inequalities and imbalances within the economy, but their severity stems to some degree both from the international crisis and from the consequences of accession.

"(2) The Greek government feels that it must draw the attention of the Community both to the special nature of Greece's problems and to the policy which it has devised to deal with them, in the hope that the Community will effectively recognize the need for special arrangements permitting the development of the Greek economy and, more generally, of Greece's links with the Community, without dispute or conflict and to the advantage of both sides.

"The Greek government is ready to examine together with the Community the possibility of working out such special arrangements which would be consistent with Greek social and economic programmes and contribute to the attainment of its development objectives.

"In this context, 'special arrangements' should be taken to mean that, on the basis of consideration of the general interest and the necessary political resolve, a decision should be taken to introduce differentiation into the management of Community policies and to evolve new mechanisms which will make due allowance for the special nature of the economy of Greece.

"(3) The structural defects of the Greek economy are briefly the following: (i) an over-developed tertiary sector, a widespread black economy and a pronounced degree of parasitism; (ii) agricultural production accounts for only 17.2 per cent of GNP whereas the agricultural population is 30 per cent of the total population; (iii) the limited contribution (19.6 per cent) of processing industries to GNP.

"Weaknesses within each sector are as follows:

"*Industry*. (i) 85 per cent of companies employ fewer than five persons; (ii) Greece imports 80 per cent of its capital equipment (machines); (iii) investment in processing industries represents only 4 per cent of GNP.

"*Agriculture*. (i) underemployment of a large part of the active population which, under present circumstances, cannot be absorbed into other sectors of the economy, and certainly not in the workers' home areas; (ii) the extremely small size of agricultural holdings and their great fragmentation; (iii) the inadequacy of the infrastructure and organization for marketing and processing agricultural products.

"Lastly, a basic feature of the structure of the Greek economy is the existence of very great social and regional inequalities, and great disparities in incomes, along with the distorted overdevelopment of the Athens area.

"(4) The fact that the international economic crisis has hit an economy which, while suffering from structural inadequacies, has simultaneously to contend with the unsteadying effects of accession has led to a serious aggravation of its current problems.

"Between 1978 and 1981 the following developments may be noted: (i) the rate of inflation increased and hovered during those years around 25 per cent, more than double the rate of previous years and of the average for the Community; (ii) the rate of increase in GNP fell appreciably each year and in 1981 the figure was negative for the first time; (iii) the current trade deficit doubled and in 1981 rose to 6.5 per cent of GNP despite the continuing recession; (iv) the public sector deficit increased dramatically and in 1981 came to 17 per cent of GNP.

"(5) It became necessary to take urgent measures to reverse this negative trend so as to ensure the minimum level of economic balance and stability required to deal with structural weaknesses.

"The Greek government expects that the measures it has taken on financial, monetary and credit matters will have the following effects in 1982: (i) a slight increase in national income; (ii) a slight fall in the balance of payments deficit; (iii) a fall in the rate of inflation; and (iv) an appreciable decline in the public sector deficit, which it is estimated will be reduced from 17 per cent to 12 per cent of GNP despite the continuing imperative need to devote 5 per cent of GNP to defence expenditure.

"At the same time, as part of the more general incomes and social policy, the government took a series of measures for the redistribution of income in favour of the economically weakest classes who had suffered particularly in recent years; these measures are in fact the basis, in the first instance, of the awaited revival of the economy.

"The government's economic policy for 1982 is supplemented by certain institutional measures which, on the one hand, derive from the particular need—in view of the threatening dimensions of the phenomenon—to remedy the situation of undertakings which are overburdened by debt and, on the other hand, are designed to create incentives to investment.

"(6) The Greek government feels that financial, credit and monetary measures alone are not an adequate basis for a successful economic policy and that the need is for a decisive long-term political solution to structural inadequacies. The development of the Greek economy will be based on national programming, oriented towards solutions to sectoral problems and regional imbalances. The government is preparing a five-year programme for economic development and the restructuring of the Greek economy, the implementation of which will begin on Jan. 1, 1983. The programme provides for the modernization of the Greek economy to enable it to meet the demands imposed by international competition. This objective will, however, be fulfilled within the framework of basic and unswerving politico-economic options.

"The first option is the development of industry with a view particularly to boosting production, increasing added-value, developing strategic industries and advanced-technology industries and also supporting small and medium-sized undertakings.

"An equally crucial option, however, is keeping the population on the land, within the framework of increased administrative and economic decentralization.

"Essential prerequisites for this are: (i) support for agricultural incomes; (ii) substantial aid for the co-operative movement; (iii) the improvement of social and cultural infrastructures in the country.

"(7) The basic choice of objectives is first and foremost a problem and a responsibility for the Greeks themselves. At the same time, however, the harmonious development and convergence of the economies of the member states are basic aims of the Treaty establishing the Community.

"The Greek government believes that the development policy which it has forged does not merely correspond to Greece's own national interests.

"The Community has repeatedly declared the need for Community action to combat inequalities between its regions and members. These declarations have not, however, borne fruit either because suitable mechanisms have not yet been created or because existing policies and mechanisms fail to operate in accordance with the necessary criteria or in the right direction or do not operate effectively because the resources made available are inadequate.

"Particularly inadequate is the transfer of resources from the Community budget to the less-developed countries and especially to Greece. In order to have an entirely positive effect, such transfers would—and this never happens—have to offset the negative economic consequences deriving from the trend of trade whether at international level or between the internal market and imports, or from the unfair distribution of activities and the unfavourable terms of trade within the Community which adversely affect the least-developed members and particularly Greece. The result of this situation is the constant widening of imbalances within the EC. For Greece especially, these disparities are the result not only of the very particular structural inadequacies of the Greek economy but also of the unfavourable treatment by the Community of Mediterranean regions as compared with the others with regard to intervention prices, levels of support and the level of protection of Mediterranean products.

"To this should be added the fact that even within the Mediterranean area the Greek economy receives unfavourable treatment. Indeed, a number of regulations providing for greater intervention and participation by Community financial instruments in Mediterranean programmes and Mediterranean regions have not been extended to Greece.

"It should also be noted that the common organization of markets, which covers on average 95 per cent of the agricultural production of the other nine countries, only covers 75 per cent of that of Greece, which is in general less effectively covered.

"(8) The discussions in the framework of the mandate of May 30 [i.e. the May 1980 mandate for budgetary, agricultural, policy development and other reform proposals given to the Commission by the Council of Ministers] show that there is now awareness within the Community that its way of functioning is going to create unacceptable situations. In the opinion of the Greek government the most important of these is the widening of economic imbalances between the more and less-developed members. This problem is one of absolute priority for the cohesion of the Community.

"The mandate of May 30 traces out certain guidelines which show that the problem has been properly understood. However, the reforms envisaged are not such as to provide a thoroughgoing solution to regional imbalances as they do not afford the means of achieving the objectives set.

"(9) The Greek government believes that the peculiar problems of the Greek economy can be overcome through a series of new regulations different from those which govern present relations between Greece and the EEC.

"This new situation presupposes the extension and strengthening of the Community's financial instruments and at the same time the recognition by Community bodies of the possibility, in specific cases and for a reasonable period of time, of derogating from certain Community rules. In particular the following are necessary under the five-year development programme: (i) increased Community support for specific projects for the development of sectors, branches and regions, and (ii) the recognition by Community bodies for a sufficiently long period of the need for derogations from Community competition rules (granting of development incentives, provisional and regulated protection of newly created industries, granting of export aid for small and medium-sized undertakings, exemption from production limits).

"The Greek government believes that these arrangements can be based in part on the activation of Protocol No. 7 to the Act of Accession of Greece, which recognizes the need to settle special problems of concern to Greece and recommends that the Community institutions implement all the means and procedures laid down by the EEC Treaty, particularly by making adequate use of Community resources. It also recognizes in particular that, in the application of Articles 92 and 93 of the EEC Treaty, it will be necessary to take into account the objectives of economic expansion and the raising of the standard of living of the population.

"(10) With particular reference to the various Community financing instruments, we consider that: (i) the criteria must be reviewed so that the way in which resources are granted and used corresponds to the particular features of the social, economic and administrative situation in Greece; (ii) the resources available must be increased and the activities of the Funds co-ordinated; (iii) participation in the financing of projects must be considerably increased and expenditure on social infrastructure covered; (iv) a new Fund with special resources must be created for the development of the Mediterranean regions with its own resources; (v) there must be greater scope for financial resources to be procured by the New Community Instrument.

"(11) We attribute particular importance to the financing of special long-term programmes for the least-favoured regions of Greece (islands, frontier and mountain regions) to cover everything from small land-improvement projects to tourist development and the development of small industry, crafts and agro-industrial units. We feel that there must be combined intervention by the Community Funds and the financing mechanisms of the Community with the above development projects being financed up to 80 per cent.

"The specific geographical position of Greece (which has no land frontiers with the Community but an enormous island surface area) requires particular attention on the part of the Community bodies, given that transport costs, particularly from the Greek islands, are so high as to reduce even further the competitiveness of products from such regions.

"(12) The Greek government considers that Athens and Thessaloniki cannot be excluded from finance by the Community Funds. Living conditions in Athens, for example (environmental pollution, traffic congestion, total lack of town planning, absence of an efficient social infrastructure), constitute an enormous economic problem, the solution of which will require considerable financial resources to be made available. In the Athens and Thessaloniki regions both the projects carried out and the criteria which will be applied for financing them will of course be adapted to the problems involved, i.e. the aim will be infrastructure development to improve the quality of life, decentralizaton of industrial activity to the provinces, etc.

"(13) One point to be stressed is that Greek agriculture, having as it does to operate side by side with the developed and modernized agricultural systems of the other member states, faces acute problems under the CAP rules.

"In order to alleviate these problems, the Community must provide finance and technical aid for carrying out major land improvement projects, for developing certain sectors, such as fishing, by means of the efficient exploitation of Greek lagoons, for setting up and organizing agro-industrial complexes and for developing co-operatives.

"However, the immediate problem of income support for small farmers remains of vital importance. Given the high rate of inflation in Greece and until such time as it is brought down close to the Community average, the proposed Community increases will be useless for Greek farmers, particularly when it is borne in mind that, given the structure of the Greek economy, intervention prices constitute for them the decisive element in their relations with the commercial and industrial sectors.

"The problem of income support can only be dealt with by means of exceptional arrangements including direct and indirect aid for incomes, to be provided to a large extent by the Community. It must also be stressed that national aid to farmers is proportionally much higher than Community aid to this sector, and that per capita expenditure from national aid is greater in countries with a high per capita income.

"(14) The Greek government hopes that the Council of Ministers will recognize the particular nature of Greece's problems.

"This applies with respect both to direct measures of an urgent nature and to the general economic policy guidelines which, under a five-year programme for the restructuring of the Greek economy, will reflect fundamental economic policy options decided upon by the Greek government.

"As a concrete expression of such recognition, the Greek government would request the Council to instruct the Commission to study the problems referred to in this memorandum and to ask it to propose special arrangements to solve them.

"The Greek government will co-operate with the Commission and in the meantime will finalize its positions and proposals on certain individual sectors. Until special arrangements are decided upon, the Greek government hopes that the measures in

200 FROM THE SIX TO THE TWELVE

favour of other Mediterranean regions will be extended to Greece and that, in line with what has been stated above, a positive solution will be found for the vital problem of support prices for agricultural products and related forms of agricultural incomes support.

"The Greek government is also awaiting with understandable and considerable interest the further course of discussions currently taking place at various levels on proposals to which it attributes particular importance, and in particular those concerning new regulations for Mediterranean products, the provision of new Community resources for the implementation of comprehensive programmes in the Mediterranean regions and the reform and strengthening of Community Funds and financing bodies.

"The Greek government considers that recognition by the Community of the need to deal with the particular problems of Greece, in conjunction with progress towards a more general reform of Community policies, constitute the minimum possible for creating conditions for Greek membership of the European Communities which will not be in conflict with basic Greek national interests."

8.11 Community response to memorandum (1982–86)

The European Council at its 22nd meeting in Brussels on March 29–30, 1982, "noted a statement by the Greek Prime Minister" and promised that the Commission would study and report back on the memorandum.

According to estimates in *The Guardian* on June 16, 1983, Greece derived a net benefit of $500 million from Community membership in 1982. However, Greece's trade deficit with the Communities had by the end of 1982 risen to twice its 1980 level of $1,730 million. The Greek government requested on Jan. 13, 1983, the introduction of import quotas at 1980 levels on 22 products as part of the 15.5 per cent devaluation package of January 1983, but these were only accepted on 11 products in February. In October 1983 the Commission recommended to the Council of Ministers that the introduction of value added tax (VAT) in Greece be postponed from Jan. 1, 1984 to Jan. 1, 1986. After a further 12-month postponement, Greece officially announced the introduction of the VAT system (at rates ranging from 6 to 36 per cent) from Jan. 1, 1987, with the tax to take effect from Feb. 1.

Meanwhile, in response to the Greek memorandum, the Commission had produced a proposed package deal for Greece worth just under $3,000 million over four years. The European Council at its 26th meeting in Stuttgart on June 17–19, 1983, recognized "the special economic and social problems faced by Greece and the difficulties which these create in the process of integrating Greece into the European Communities". The Council agreed that "the Community should play its part in helping to overcome these difficulties"; its final communiqué continued as follows:

"It welcomes in this connexion the detailed and constructive examination of these problems undertaken by the Commission and the two communications which have resulted from this work. The communications clearly indicate that solutions can be found in the Community framework in order to permit the integration of Greece into the Community system in a harmonious and mutually beneficial manner.

"It welcomes the fact that the Commission intends shortly to submit specific proposals (including their financial aspects) in various sectors complementing its earlier proposals. It invites the Council to examine these proposals with a view to concrete decisions before the next European Council."

The rotating presidency of the Community Council of Ministers passed to Greece for the first time for the six months from July 1, 1983. Ioannis

Charalambopoulos, the Greek Foreign Minister, said in his statement to the European Parliament on July 5 that the Greek presidency would "devote particular attention to dealing with economic imbalances and regional inequalities".

Disputes principally over budgetary and agricultural policies meant that no agreement on finance, agriculture or other policy issues was reached at the Athens session of the European Council in December 1983, which thus represented a setback for the goal of "relaunching the Communities" as called for at the previous Council summit in Stuttgart. However, the problem of "regional inequalities" was subsequently tackled to the significant benefit of Greece in the context of the Integrated Mediterranean Programmes, eventually launched at the European Council summit meeting in Brussels on March 29–30, 1985. Dr Papandreou, who had effectively made Greek approval of the accession of Spain and Portugal conditional upon the Integrated Mediterranean Programmes, was thereafter able to base Pasok's successful campaign in the June 1985 general election largely on his government's success in obtaining favourable treatment for Greece in the Communities.

The conclusions of the presidency issued after the March 1985 Brussels summit contained the following passage on the Integrated Mediterranean Programmes:

"In accordance with the undertakings given at its meeting in Brussels on March 19–20, 1984, the European Council has decided to launch the Integrated Mediterranean Programmes in favour of the southern regions of the present Community within the framework of the proposals made by the Commission. These programmes will last seven years; their aim will be to improve the economic structures of those regions to enable them to adjust under the best conditions possible to the new situation created by enlargement.

"As far as financing arrangements and method are concerned, the European Council agrees with the broad outlines of the approach recommended by the Commission in its communication of Feb. 21, 1985, i.e.: (i) participation by the structural funds for an amount of 2,500 million ECU; (ii) an additional budget contribution amounting to 1,600 million ECU [as opposed to the 2,000 million ECU proposed by the Commission] which will permit the Commission to supply the additional funds for the implementation of the programmes approved by it; and (iii) loans of 2,500 million ECU contracted by the regions concerned with the EIB [European Investment Bank] and under the New Community Instrument. The two first categories of resources will benefit Greece for an amount of 2,000 million ECU. The European Council feels that these figures and the accompanying provisions in this text meet once and for all the commitments undertaken by the Community concerning the Integrated Mediterranean Programmes.

"The structural funds will continue to operate normally, on the basis of a Community-wide regional policy, in accordance with the regulations which have recently been revised. The increases in real terms which will apply to the Regional and Social Funds and the European Agricultural Fund Guidance Section over the next seven years will help to finance the IMPs, but without adversely affecting transfers from these funds to other less prosperous and priority regions of the Community. On this basis, the European Council agrees with the proposals of the Commission designed to achieve fully co-ordinated programmes for the Mediterranean regions most in need through the operation of the three structural funds.

"As regards resource allocation, which should be based on the criteria contained in the Commission proposal, the European Council would emphasize that the allocation criteria should take account, first and foremost, of the actual needs of the different regions and their situation as regards economic and social development. In particular, the European Council would draw attention to the special case of Greece, whose entire territory comes within the sphere of the Integrated Mediterranean Programmes, and to the legitimate expectations of the Greek government."

A further consensus was reached by the Council of (Foreign) Ministers meeting on June 25–26, 1985.

The bulk of the 2,000 million ECU due to go to Greece out of the 6,600 million ECU seven-year scheme would come from new funding of 1,600 million ECU, with the remainder coming from structural funds. (1.00 ECU = £0.59 = US$0.83 as at Sept. 30, 1985.) The proportional distribution of funds as between French and Italian regions was to be determined by the Commission rather than by fixed totals.

The first agreement under the Integrated Mediterranean Programmes was signed on Sept. 2, 1986, by the Greek Minister of National Economy, Costas Smitis, and the European Commission member responsible for the co-ordination of structural funds (and for consumer protection), Grigoris Varfis.

(Varfis had joined the Commission in 1985, succeeding Kontogeorgis as the Greek representative, and had taken on his current responsibilities in the reshuffle of portfolios which accompanied the appointment of the first Spanish and Portuguese Commissioners in January 1986. As a member of the Pasok government until January 1984, he had been regarded as one of its few pro-Community members, but after the failure of the December 1983 European Council summit in Athens he had resigned as Deputy Foreign Minister responsibe for European Affairs.)

The September 1986 agreement, on one of seven development plans put forward for consideration by the Greek government, involved the provision of funding amounting to 240 million ECU from the Community structural funds, using the extra financing made available for the IMPs. This funding would represent just over half of the total cost of a seven-year programme for the island of Crete, concentrating on industrial and infrastructure development as well as on agricultural diversification and the marketing of tourism. The programme would also attract EIB and New Community Instrument loans up to 130 million ECU.

8.12 Community links with other Mediterranean countries—Association and other agreements—The case of Turkey

The enlargement of the Communities to include Greece from 1981, and Spain and Portugal from 1986, shifted the "centre of balance" significantly towards the south, towards the Mediterranean basin.

In addition to its developing relationship with these three eventual new member countries, the EC had negotiated during the 1960s and early 1970s a series of individual agreements (drawn together from 1972 in the Community Mediterranean policy), including association agreements with Turkey (taking effect in 1964), Malta (concluded in 1970 and taking effect from April 1, 1971), and Cyprus (signed in December 1972 and taking effect from June 1, 1973), and commercial, industrial, technical and financial agreements with Algeria, Morocco and Tunisia (the Maghreb countries), Egypt, Jordan, Lebanon and Syria (the Mashraq countries), and Yugoslavia and Israel, although not with Libya or Albania.

(Morocco submitted in November 1984 a formal application for Community membership. No action was in effect taken on this, however, the main subject of discussions between Morocco and the EC in the subsequent period being the impact of Spanish and Portuguese accession on Morocco.)

It was intended that the Turkish, Maltese and Cypriot association agreements should lead progressively to customs union with the EC, although for various reasons the progress on the development of all three associations proved much slower than was originally anticipated. In the case of Turkey, it was further envisaged under the original association agreement that Turkey should ultimately become a full member country of the Communities, and that the Turkish government would make an application for such membership at an unspecified future date. As of late 1986, therefore, Turkey could be seen as representing the only unresolved Community enlargement issue (apart from the above-mentioned Moroccan application). This fact, and the problem of the relationship between Greek membership and the Community position on Turkey, makes it worthwhile to included here a brief treatment of the history of the Turkish Association Agreement.

8.13 Turkish association—Frozen relations after the 1980 coup—Turkey's continuing aspiration for membership—The position in late 1986

Turkey's first application for associate membership of the Communities, made on July 31, 1959, was shelved initially by the Gürsel regime when it came to power in May 1960, but the application was then taken up again under the Inönü government in 1961 and 1962. On July 25, 1962, the Council of Ministers of the EEC instructed the Commission to reopen the negotiations, which then proceeded to a successful conclusion over the following year. The Agreement, signed on Sept. 1, 1963, took effect from Dec. 1, 1964.

The first, preparatory, phase of the association (i.e. prior to what was designated the transitional stage) involved preferential treatment in the Community market for important Turkish agricultural exports (tobacco, raisins, dried figs and hazelnuts) and EIB loans for Turkish infrastructure projects (such as the Keban hydroelectric scheme) to a total value of some US$175 million.

The transitional stage of the association (towards full customs union over a 22-year period) was implemented according to a supplementary protocol agreed in July 1970 at a meeting of the EEC–Turkey Association Council and signed on Nov. 23, 1970. A delay until 1973 before this agreement was fully ratified by both sides (a requirement for its entry into force) made it necessary for certain of the provisions to be brought into operation (from September 1971) under an interim arrangement.

From this date, EEC tariffs and restrictions were lifted for Turkish industrial goods, except for certain categories of goods (machine-woven carpets, cotton yarn and cotton textiles) where the lifting of restrictions was to be phased in over 12 years. Turkey, for its part, was to abolish some duties over a 12-year period and others over 22 years, and would follow the same timetable in introducing the common Community external tariff. On agriculture, Turkey would adapt to Community policy over 22 years, during which time the EEC would grant preferences on about 90 per cent of its agricultural imports from Turkey.

Financial assistance would continue with the second and subsequent financial protocols; the second protocol, signed in June 1973, envisaged aid of some $195 million over 5½ years, with a further $25 million in EIB loans.

On the free movement of labour, the Community agreed to a phased process commencing in 1976 which would allow free movement of Turkish workers within the Community from Dec. 1, 1986.

Turkish concern grew during the 1970s not only over the potential impact of Greek accession on Turkey's own relations with the Communities, but also over the terms of operation of the Association Agreement.

Turkish criticism emphasized that tariff cuts were hampering the development of Turkish industry (although Turkey had in fact implemented only two phases of tariff reduction and had unilaterally refused to implement a 10 per cent cut in industrial import tariffs due on Jan. 1, 1978), that the value of agricultural preferences was undermined by the according of similar preferences in Community agreements with other Mediterranean countries, and that the level of Community aid was inadequate.

As Turkish Prime Minister, Bulent Ecevit on May 25, 1978, presented an outline plan for a revised Association Agreement, but his talks in Brussels with Community representatives resulted only in a declaration that "no efforts should be spared to revitalize" the existing Agreement. The Association Council on June 30–July 1, 1980, adopted a decision on the reactivation and development of the Agreement, but any development was forestalled by the effective freezing of relations after the Evren military coup in Turkey in September 1980.

Following the Evren régime's October 1981 decree on the dissolution of political parties, the Commission made clear in late October that it intended to delay implementation of the fourth financial protocol, a package of loans and grants worth 600 million ECU on which negotiations had been completed on June 19, because of the human rights situation and doubts about the value of Turkish assurances on the restoration of democracy. The release of Ecevit from prison in Turkey in February 1982 alleviated some of this Community criticism, but the mission to Turkey in March 1982 by Léo Tindemans, as Belgian Foreign Minister and president-in-office of the EC Council of Ministers, nevertheless produced a critical report to the March 1982 Brussels summit of Community heads of government. The report emphasized serious concern with regard to the position on human rights in Turkey, and stressed the need for restoration of democracy, the lifting of martial law and the release of those arrested for their beliefs or trade union activities. Meanwhile the European Parliament on Jan. 22, 1982, passed a resolution suspending the joint Community –Turkey parliamentary committee.

The Turkish military government under Gen. Kenan Evren, and the civilian government, with Evren as President, which was formed in December 1983 under Prime Minister Turgut Özal following elections in November 1983, continued to espouse the intention both of developing the association, and of applying for full Community membership, once "political and economic obstacles" had been overcome. On Jan. 24, 1984, Vahit Halefoglu, the new Turkish Foreign Minister, visited Brussels to express the new government's desire for normalization of relations with the Communities. Difficulties meanwhile continued over Turkey's human rights record, but also over three other main issues; Turkish textile exports to the Communities (agreements being reached only in December 1985 and April 1986 on import levels for various categories of products), the resumption of the financial aid blocked since 1981, and the issue of whether the Communities would allow free passage to Turkish workers from December 1986 as originally agreed.

On the last of these issues, concerns about guest worker numbers (notably in West Germany) were an important factor, but the matter was complicated by the further dimension of Greek opposition to the development of Community links with Turkey.

Although at the time of Greece's own accession the Greek government had accepted the terms of the EC Association Agreement with Turkey, the protocol formally extending this Agreement from the EC of nine to the EC of ten had remained unsigned. The Pasok government had placed two conditions on signing the protocol, firstly that Turkey rescind secret legislation (dating from 1964 but reissued in 1985) blocking the assets of Greek citizens in Istanbul, and secondly that Greece be allowed to exclude itself on security grounds from the proposed measure on free movement for Turkish workers. Greece also considered that there had not been sufficient progress on democratization in Turkey, and that there should be no normalization of EC relations with Turkey while Turkish troops continued to occupy the northern part of Cyprus (a country with its own association agreement with the EC).

On Feb. 17, 1986, the EC Foreign Ministers agreed to convene a special meeting of the EC–Turkey Association Council later in the year on Turkey's call for reactivation of the Association Agreement. Claude Cheysson, on a visit to Ankara in June as EC Commissioner responsible for Mediterranean policy and north-south relations, reportedly sought progress on the outstanding political and economic issues, while counselling against haste in Turkey applying for full Community membership.

The special meeting, held on Sept. 16, 1986, at Foreign Minister level, with Halefoglu leading the Turkish delegation, was officially described as the 31st meeting of the Association Council and as marking "the resumption of contacts at ministerial level between the Community and Turkey". The meeting was preceded, however, by Greek refusal on Sept. 15 to endorse a common Community position (which would have stressed the importance of normalizing relations, while attaching importance to the continuing process of democratization and restoration of human rights).

Sir Geoffrey Howe, the UK Foreign and Commonwealth Secretary and current president-in-office of the EC Council, said after the meeting that Turkey had been given the "green light" on normalizing relations, although in the absence of Greek agreement the reactivation of the association, and of aid under the fourth protocol, was referred to Community working groups and to the Commission. Halefoglu for his part stressed what he described as Turkey's "inalienable right" to apply for full integration, and on Dec. 9, 1986, Özal told the Turkish parliament that a Turkish formal application for full Community membership would be made in 1987.

8.14 Chronology of main events on Turkey's associate membership

Sept. 1, 1963   Signature of Association Agreement

Dec. 1, 1964   Entry into effect of Association Agreement

Nov. 23, 1970   Signature of supplementary protocol on move from pre-paratory to transitional stage of association

May 25, 1978   Presentation of Ecevit proposals for revised Agreement

September   Military coup in Turkey followed by effective freeze on de-
1980   velopment of Association Agreement

December   Formation of civilian government in Turkey
1983

Jan. 24, 1984   Halefoglu visit to Brussels stressing Turkish desire for normalization of relations with Communities

Sept. 16, 1986 Renewal of contacts at ministerial level at 31st Association Council meeting

Dec. 9, 1986   Turkish Prime Minister's announcement in Turkish parliament of intention to make formal application in 1987 for full Community membership

9: GREENLAND: WITHDRAWAL

9.1 Chronology of events

Jan. 1, 1973   Accession of Greenland to Communities as part of Denmark

May 1, 1979   Internal autonomy for Greenland

Feb. 23, 1982   Greenland referendum in favour of withdrawal

May 19, 1982   Danish government memorandum to Council of Ministers

Feb. 8, 1983   Commission paper

Feb. 20, 1984   Conclusion of negotiations on terms of withdrawal

March 10, 1984   *Landsting* approval of terms

March 13, 1984   Signature of documents on withdrawal

March 16, 1984   Fall of Motzfeldt government

June 8, 1984   General election leading to reappointment of Motzfeldt

Feb. 1, 1985   Withdrawal from Communities

9.2 Background—Greenland's transition to internal autonomy (May 1, 1979)—Attitudes in Greenland towards the Communities

As a dependency of Denmark, Greenland became part of the European Communities when Denmark acceded in 1973. After attaining internal autonomy under Danish sovereignty in May 1979, a vote in favour of withdrawal from the Communities was however, recorded in a referendum in February 1982. On Feb. 1, 1985, the island became the first territory ever to withdraw from the Communities, acquiring instead Overseas Countries and Territories (OCT) status.

Greenland had been a Danish colony from 1721 until it became an integral part of the Kingdom of Denmark under the 1953 Constitution of that country. However, after Danish proposals for Greenland home rule had been tabled in 1978 and approved in a consultative referendum on Jan. 17, 1979, Greenland achieved internal autonomy.

The existing *Landsraad* (council) was replaced by a *Landsting* (parliament) and *Landsstyre* (government), to which full control of local taxation, fisheries policy, planning, education, religious affairs, social welfare, labour, cultural affairs and nature conservation would be devolved by 1981. A Danish high commissioner would replace the present governor, and the Greenland Eskimo-based language would replace Danish as the "principal" language (Eskimos comprising 80 per cent of the island's population). The measures further provided (i) that by 1984 the Greenland government would take over the functions of the Royal Greenland Trade Department, which handled most of the island's trade; and (ii) that revenues from the exploitation of Greenland's mineral resources (which included lead, zinc, uranium and, potentially, hydrocarbons) would be used to offset a continuing Danish government subsidy of some $250,000,000 annually (representing 85 per cent of the island's national product), with any eventual surplus being the subject of negotiations between the two sides.

While the legislation stipulated that foreign affairs, defence and monetary policy would continue to be the sole responsibility of the metropolitan government (and also that the civil rights provisions of the Danish Constitution would continue to apply in Greenland), it was established that Greenland would have the right to opt out of full membership of the European Communities (which Denmark and thus Greenland had joined in 1973) with a view to attaining a status similar to that of the Faroe Islands, which had gained internal autonomy from Denmark in 1948 and which under the Danish Treaty of Accession participated only in the Communities' free trade arrangements [see 4.9]. In this context the Danish government undertook to seek special arrangements for Greenland from the European Communities which would (i) establish preferential rights for the island's fishermen in Greenland waters, (ii) exempt Greenland from automatic compliance with Community directives and (iii) restrict the right of free establishment in Greenland.

Of the two major political formations in Greenland (which both supported the internal autonomy proposals), the moderate *Atassut* (Feeling of Community) led by Lars Chemnitz (chairman of the *Landsraad*) was in favour of continued membership of the European Communities, whereas the socialist *Siumut* (Forward) led by Jonathan Motzfeldt (deputy chairman of the *Landsraad*) called for Greenland's withdrawal unless substantial special arrangements could be speedily negotiated.

In the Danish referendum on membership (held on Oct. 6, 1972, in Greenland) some 70 per cent of the Greenland voters expressed opposition to membership of the Communities.

9.3 Referendum in favour of withdrawal from Communities (Feb. 23, 1982)

Motzfeldt became the first Prime Minister of the newly formed *Landsstyre*, after preautonomy elections held on April 4, 1979, had given his *Siumut* party a majority of seats. He led a campaign for withdrawal from the Communities and on Aug. 20, 1981, obtained the consent of the Danish government to hold a referendum on the issue.

Within the Communities, Greenland's fishing industry (which accounted for 55 per cent of the country's exports) had been allowed exclusive fishing rights within a 12-mile coastal zone, with other countries (particularly West Germany) enjoying access within the remainder of Greenland's coastal waters up to 200 miles offshore. Although this arrangement was generally regarded as giving Greenland's fishermen rights over as much fish as their catch capacity required (82,000 tonnes in 1979), opponents of Community membership argued that withdrawal would give Greenland control over fishing rights within the whole 200-mile zone, and that access rights could then be sold to other countries, thereby helping to offset the financial consequences of losing Community aid funds. Grants to Greenland under the Communities' economic, regional and social funds had amounted to an estimated 645,000,000 Danish kroner since 1973 (about $88,000,000 at the end–1981 exchange rate), with a further 383,000,000 kroner in loans from the European Investment Bank (EIB) and 174,000,000 kroner in other project support. The Danish government made it clear that the loss of this aid would not automatically be made good by a commensurate increase in the substantial budgetary allocation made for Greenland by Denmark itself. During a visit in October 1981 to Nuuk (formerly called Godthaab, the capital of Greenland), Poul Dalsager the (Danish) European Commissioner with responsibility for Agriculture and Fisheries, had warned of the costs of withdrawal and that the Communities might not necessarily agree to external associate status for Greenland. However, it was understood that Denmark would accept, and act to implement, the views of the local population.

In the referendum, held on Feb. 23, 1982, with a 75 per cent turnout, 12,615 votes were cast in favour of withdrawal and 11,180 against, i.e. a 52 per cent majority in favour. The result was endorsed in late March by the *Landsting*, although the opposition *Atassut* party took the view that withdrawal was too important a step to be taken on the basis of such a narrow majority.

The conclusions of the Greenland government, which in formal terms were of an advisory nature only, were then referred for consideration by the Danish government, which would be responsible for bringing the matter before the appropriate Community bodies and conducting negotiations on the terms of Greenland's withdrawal. The results of the referendum had meanwhile been noted "with regret" by the Commission, according to a spokesman in Brussels.

9.4 Negotiation and conclusion of terms of Greenland's withdrawal (May 1982–March 1984)

The Danish government on May 19, 1982, sent a memorandum to the Council of Ministers proposing revision of the relevant treaties to bring about the withdrawal of Greenland from the Communities and its subsequent inclusion among the Overseas Countries and Territories (OCT) under Part IV of the Treaty of Rome.

Negotiations centred on the question of continued Community access to Greenland's waters for fishing (the territory's principal source of revenue) and the question of the potential exploitation of Greenland's extensive reserves of uranium, lead, zinc and oil.

A paper issued in February 1983 by the Commission of the European Communities followed a proposal by Richard Burke, the (Irish) member of the Commission charged with responsibility for the matter, and suggested OCT status for Greenland.

In practice this would mean little change in Greenland's relationship with the Communities other than institutional adjustments; Greenland would still have duty-free access to Community markets, and would continue to receive regional development and other aid, while the member countries of the Communities would retain their historic fishing rights in Greenland waters, but lose all rights to Greenland's mineral resources. Subsequently, on June 7, 1983, the European Parliament voted to respect the wishes of Greenland's population to withdraw from the Communities.

From the start of negotiations both the Danish government and the Commission had recommended that Greenland be accorded OCT status, but little progress was made at two Council of (Foreign) Ministers meetings held on May 24–25 and Nov. 29, 1983. In West Germany, where the fishing industry had strong interests in fishing rights in Greenland waters, there was particular concern over the possible implications if Greenland adopted a status similar to that of the Faroes, also a Danish dependency, which negotiated any fisheries agreements independently of the common fisheries policy. However, at a Council of (Foreign) Ministers meeting in Brussels on Dec. 19, ministers agreed to try and complete negotiations by the end of March 1984 so as to be able to respect Greenland's wishes to leave by January 1985.

A final decision on the terms of Greenland's withdrawal was adopted by the

Council of (Foreign) Ministers on Feb. 20, 1984, in Brussels. Representatives of the governments of the Community member countries (including Denmark), the local government of Greenland, and the Commission, signed the relevant documents on March 13, so that Greenland's withdrawal from the Communities could be effected by Jan. 1, 1985.

9.5 Terms of agreement

The terms agreed by the Council on Feb. 20, 1984, and signed on March 13, were based on detailed proposals presented by the Commission on Feb. 8, and provided for (i) the amendment of the EEC, ECSC and Euratom treaties to enable Greenland's withdrawal by Jan. 1, 1985; (ii) the granting of OCT status to Greenland which gave Greenland fisheries products duty-free access to Community markets; and (iii) a 10-year fisheries agreement which could automatically be renewed for periods of six years. Since a modification of the treaties was involved the agreement was subject to ratification by member countries' parliaments.

Under the fisheries agreement specific annual quotas for cod (23,500 tonnes), redfish (63,320 tonnes), halibut (5,800 tonnes), shrimps (4,350 tonnes), catfish (2,000 tonnes) and blue whiting (30,000 tonnes) were established for the initial five-year period to Dec. 31, 1989. Provisions were made for the reduction of quotas if scientific evidence found stocks were depleted, and for the guaranteed allocation to Community fishing fleets of a minimum of 20 per cent of any extra quotas. In return Greenland was guaranteed a minimum tonnage for its fish catch should overall quotas fall, and the Communities agreed to pay 26,500,000 ECU annually for the first five years, this being 8,000,000 ECU more than the amount recommended by the Commission. (1 ECU = £0.59 = US$0.80 as at June 25, 1984.) The sum was to be increased if quotas were increased but the Council made it clear that during the initial five-year period no other financial aid would be made available as a result of Greenland's OCT status.

9.6 Landsting approval of terms (March 10)—Elections following fall of
Greenland government (June 6, 1984)

The *Landsting* approved these terms on March 10, three days before the signing ceremony, by 24 votes to two. The two *Inuit Ataqatigiit* (Eskimo Movement) members voted against acceptance of the agreement, despite being the junior member of the coalition led by Motzfeldt which had come to power after a general election held on April 12, 1983. *Siumut* and the opposition *Atassut*, which each then held 12 seats in the *Landsting*, voted in favour of the agreement.

The governing coalition nevertheless lost its majority since *Inuit Ataqatigiit* on the same day proposed a vote of no confidence in the government. This led to Motzfeldt's resignation on March 16 and the calling of elections for June 6.

Chemnitz, the leader of the moderate pro-EC *Atassut*, resigned shortly after the March 10 vote, and declared that he would not stand for election to the new parliament. Otto Steenholt, who was also a member of the Danish parliament, agreed to stand as the *Atassut* leader. According to the *Neue Zürcher Zeitung* of March 18, *Atassut* hoped for a grand coaliton with *Siumut*, although the party was also critical of the fishing agreement, maintaining that the fishing rights bought by the EC were too comprehensive and that Motzfeldt had conducted negotiations with the EC without consulting the other Greenland parties.

The *Siumut* campaign centred on demands for unilateral control over the island's mineral resources, which along with the fisheries question had been the most complicated issue in the withdrawal negotiations. Mineral resources had previously been a joint matter between Greenland and Denmark, with each side retaining a veto in a joint commission. *Inuit Ataqatigiit* favoured withdrawal from the Communities, but was opposed to any subsequent ties with the EC and also stood for complete independence from Denmark.

Although the results of the election were inconclusive with the *Inuit Ataqatigiit* still holding the balance of power between the two larger parties and *Siumut* only polling 98 more votes than *Atassut*, the moderate-leftist coalition of *Siumut* and *Inuit Ataqatigiit* remained in power.

9.7 Withdrawal of Greenland from Communities

On Feb. 1, 1985, Greenland formally withdrew from the Communities, as agreed by the Council of (Foreign) Ministers in February 1984.

The island's withdrawal, the first ever withdrawal from the Communities, had originally been scheduled for Jan. 1, 1985, but was delayed by one month since the Irish parliament did not ratify the treaty (as required by the Treaty of Rome) until mid-January. Proposed provisional arrangements which would have enabled the terms of the withdrawal treaty to enter into force at the beginning of January, pending ratification by the Irish parliament, were rejected by the French government.

In the European Parliament the seat of Finn Lynge, previously the Greenland representative, was taken by John Iversen of the (Danish) Socialist People's Party, which belonged to the Communist group.

10: SPAIN: APPLICATION AND ACCESSION

10.1 Chronology of events

Feb. 9, 1962	Spanish government letter requesting negotiations on membership
June 29, 1970	Preferential trade agreement between EEC and Spain signed
Oct. 1, 1970	Preferential trade agreement between EEC and Spain comes into effect
Oct. 6, 1975	Negotiations on new trade agreement with Spain broken off
Nov. 20, 1975	Death of Franco
Jan. 20, 1976	Agreement on resumption of negotiations with Spain on new trade agreement
July 28, 1977	Spanish application for EC membership
Dec. 7, 1978	Multilateral free trade agreement initialled between Spain and EFTA
Dec. 29, 1978	Promulgation of nationally endorsed Constitution
Feb. 5, 1979	Opening of accession negotiations with Spain
March 1, 1979	First general elections under new Constitution
Feb. 23, 1981	Attempted coup in Madrid
Dec. 2, 1982	Accession to power of González Socialist government after general election on Oct. 28
Oct. 17–18, 1983	Community agreement on organization of fruit, vegetable and olive oil markets
March 29, 1985	Conclusion of enlargement negotiations with Spain and Portugal
June 12, 1985	Signature of Spanish and Portuguese Accession Treaties
Aug. 2, 1985	Promulgation of ratification by *Cortes* of Accession Treaty
Jan. 1, 1986	Accession
March 12, 1986	Referendum favouring continued membership of NATO

10.2 Outline of steps to membership

On June 12, 1985, the Treaty of Accession of Spain to the European Communities was signed at the Palais Royal in Madrid, the Spanish capital. The ceremony completed over six years of formal negotiations on membership which had been opened in February 1979 and concluded in March 1985. After the Accession Treaty was approved by the Spanish *Cortes* (parliament) and also by the Community member country parliaments, accession took place on Jan. 1, 1986.

Details of trade agreements existing before enlargement, of relations between Spain and the European Communities prior to accession, and of the progress of negotiations and ratification are given below.

10.3 Community preferential trade agreement with Spain

Agreement was reached on March 13, 1970, after 2½ years of negotiations, on a preferential agreement between Spain and the EEC, which was subsequently signed in Brussels on June 29 and came into force on Oct. 1, 1970.

The Spanish government of Gen. Franco had originally on Feb. 9, 1962, delivered a letter to the acting president of the Council of Ministers requesting that negotiations be opened with a view to examining the possibility of establishing an association with the EEC which would permit full membership at a suitable time in the future. This request was renewed by the government in a letter dated Feb. 14, 1964, and exploratory talks were held between December 1964 and July 1966. The negotiations which eventually led to the preferential trade agreement were opened in September 1967.

The 1970 agreement was designed to conform with GATT rules that preferential agreements must lead, in a reasonable time, to a customs union. About 95 per cent of EEC industrial imports from Spain subject to tariffs were covered by the agreement and 62 per cent of agricultural imports, while about 61 per cent of Spanish imports from the Communities were similarly affected.

The agreement provided for a first stage of at least six years, with the EEC reducing its tariffs on most industrial goods from Spain by 30 per cent initially; this reduction would rise to 50 per cent on Jan. 1, 1972, and 60 per cent on Jan. 1, 1973, and—subject to examination by the Communities—to 70 per cent on Jan. 1, 1974. For refined petroleum products the reductions would relate only to a quota of 1,200,000 tons a year and for certain cotton textiles to 1,800 tons a year. For Spanish agricultural exports the EEC would, inter alia, grant a 40 per cent tariff reduction for citrus fruit on certain conditions. Concessions would also be granted on imports of Spanish wines.

Spain for her part agreed to reduce her tariffs on three lists of EEC exports by six stages up to Jan. 1, 1977; for two lists the reductions would rise to 25 per cent and for the third to 60 per cent, but if EEC tariff reductions were raised to 70 per cent on Jan. 1, 1974, these Spanish reductions would be increased to 30 and 70 per cent respectively. Spain also agreed to abolish or reduce quantitative restrictions on EEC industrial products over the six-year period and to discontinue her 20 per cent import deposit scheme on Dec. 9, 1970.

Following the accession of Denmark, Ireland and the United Kingdom to the European Communities in January 1973, a temporary protocol covering Spain's trade relations with the three new European Community member countries was signed in Brussels on Jan. 29, 1973.

This protocol was designed to maintain the status quo pending negotiation of a new overall agreement establishing a free trade area and it provided initially for trade in industrial goods to continue on the same terms between Spain and the three acceding countries. Inconclusive negotiations on a new agreement were subsequently held in July, September and October 1973, in November 1974 and were to have resumed towards the end of 1975.

After a meeting of the Council of (Foreign) Ministers in Luxembourg on Oct. 6, 1975, these negotiations on a new agreement were, however, broken off in protest at the trial and execution in Spain of five men alleged to have killed policemen and civil guards. The executions which took place on Sept. 27, were, in the words of the foreign ministers' communiqué, "carried out after procedings violating the principles of the rule of law and in particular the rights of the defence" and in disregard of international demands for clemency for the accused.

Seven of the nine Community ambassadors in Madrid were temporarily recalled along with other European Ambassadors, while the European Parliament had already on Sept. 25 voted to freeze relations "until such time as freedom and democracy are established" in Spain. (The September 1975 executions were in contrast to an earlier trial in Burgos in the Basque country in December 1970 when partly as a result of international pressure from Community and other governments Franco decided to commute death sentences pronounced on two supporters of the Basque separatist organization *Euskadi Ta Askatasuna* or ETA.)

10.4 Return to democracy—Spain's application for European Community membership—Opening of accession negotiations

Gen. Franco died on Nov. 20, 1975, a month after the negotiations on a new trade agreement had been suspended. The new head of state, King Juan Carlos, committed himself at a swearing-in ceremony on Nov. 22 to "the peaceful establishment of democratic coexistence based on respect for the law as a manifestation of the sovereignty of the people". European Community foreign ministers subsequently agreed in principle on Jan. 20, 1976, to the resumption of trade negotiations in the light of the changed political situation in Spain.

Spain's first general elections since 1936 took place on June 15, 1977, after which the government of Adolfo Suárez González agreed to submit a formal application for full membership of the European Communities. Oreja Aguirre, the Spanish Foreign Minister, accordingly travelled to Brussels and presented his country's application on July 28.

With the appointment of Leopoldo Calvo Sotelo y Bustelo on Feb. 11, 1978, a new Ministry for Relations with the European Communities was also created to deal with all aspects of Spain's proposed entry to the Communities.

The Spanish application came after that of Portugal in March 1977 and was welcomed by the Council of (Foreign) Ministers' meeting on Sept. 20, 1977. On April 20, 1978, the Council received from the Commission three reports on the implications of enlargement which it had requested be drawn up at the September meeting. These dealt with general considerations, with the transitional period and institutional implications, and with economic and sectoral aspects. In the first of these the view was expressed that in seeking to join the Communities all three applicant countries (i.e. Greece, Portugal and Spain) were primarily motivated by political factors, in that they saw membership as a source of support in preserving their democratic institutions.

In the course of 1978 differences emerged within the Communities in that whereas the UK government strongly supported the enlargement of the Nine to include all three applicant countries, influential political circles in both France and Italy came out against Spanish and Portuguese membership because of the likely impact on the French and Italian agricultural sectors.

On Dec. 19 the Council of (Foreign) Ministers decided that a ceremony marking the marking the start of accession negotiations with Spain would be held in the first quarter of 1979; reportedly at the insistence of France, however, it also decided that substantive negotiations would not begin on the Spanish application until the two sides had agreed on a common negotiating basis.

Formal negotiations were opened at a ceremony in Brussels on Feb. 5, 1979, one month before the first general election to be held under Spain's new Constitution which had been promulgated in December 1978. Substantive negotiations did not start until the autumn after discussions with both parties had led the Council to adopt guidelines on a common negotiating basis on Sept. 18. (The subsequent sections on Spanish accession negotiations also cover in part parallel negotiations on Portugal's accession to the European Communities since both were interdependent.)

10.5 EFTA–Spain multilateral agreement on free trade

Spain, unlike Portugal, was not a member of the European Free Trade Association (EFTA). Given the then imminent Spanish application for full membership of the European Communities, it was decided by the EFTA ministerial council on May 12, 1977, to open immediate negotiations with Spain on the conclusion of a free trade agreement. These negotiations were accordingly opened the following month and on Dec. 7, 1978, at the EFTA Secretariat in Geneva, Switzerland, a multilateral free trade agreement between Spain and the seven member states of the European Free Trade Association—Austria, Finland (then an associate member), Iceland, Norway, Portugal, Sweden and Switzerland—was initialled.

The agreement provided principally for the application of the same rules for industrial trade between EFTA and Spain as already existed for industrial trade between the European Communities and Spain under the existing EEC-Spain association arrangements dating from October 1970.

When it entered into force in May 1980, it became the first multilateral agreement between EFTA and a non-member country (and also applied to Liechtenstein under that country's customs union with Switzerland).

Intended to eliminate the discriminations in EFTA-Spanish trade as compared with EEC-Spanish trade arising from the 1970 EEC-Spain agreement (in that EEC-Spanish trade enjoyed preferential tariff rates), the agreement provided (i) that the EFTA countries would reduce their import duties on almost all Spanish industrial products by 60 per cent (but only 30–40 per cent on certain sensitive items) and (ii) that Spain would reduce its import duties on a large number of EFTA industrial products by 25 per cent (and by 60 per cent on some others) and would also reduce its duties on some fish products from EFTA countries. The date for the first tariff cuts under the agreement remained to be fixed and certain special regulations concerning trade between Spain and Portugal also remained to be settled.

The final goal of negotiations between the EFTA countries and Spain was stated to be complete industrial free trade between the two sides such as had existed between EFTA and the European Communities since July 1, 1977. To this end it was agreed that any future concessions on industrial products given by Spain to the European Communities in the context of its negotiations for full accession would also be granted to the EFTA countries and that any given by the Communities to Spain would likewise be granted by the EFTA countries.

Parallel with the multilateral negotiations, bilateral agreements were also reached between Austria, Finland, Norway, Sweden and Switzerland on the one hand and Spain on the other to facilitate trade in agricultural products—such agreements being necessary in view of the wide disparity in agricultural conditions and policies as between the various EFTA member states.

10.6 Start of negotiations (1979)—French reservations (1980)

When negotiations with Spain and Portugal began in February 1979 and October 1978 respectively, both countries had hoped to achieve full Community membership as from the beginning of 1983. However, considerable doubt as to the feasibility of this target date was cast by President Valéry Giscard d'Estaing of France in a speech on June 5, 1980, in which he said that no further extension of the Communities should take place until the continuing problems arising from the previous enlargement in 1973 had been satisfactorily resolved.

Addressing French farmers' leaders in Paris, President Giscard d'Estaing said that recent discussions within the Communities had "demonstrated clearly that the integration of certain new members is still not complete" and continued: "It does not seem possible to me to compound the problems and uncertainties related to the prolongation of the first enlargement with those created by new accessions. That is why, bearing in mind the attitude of certain of our partners since the beginning of this year, it is necessary that the Community should give priority to completing the first enlargement before it can be in a position to undertake a second."

Although the French President did not mention any countries by name, his remarks were widely taken to refer to the dispute over Britain's contributions to the Community budget and to the fact that the May 1980 settlement of this dispute for the two years 1980 and 1981 incorporated a Community commitment to undertake a fundamental reform of its budgetary system with a view to introducing revised arrangements by 1982. The President's reservations concerning the timetable for new accessions (which a presidential spokesman said later applied to Portugal and Spain but not to Greece) were understood to reflect in part the serious concern expressed in many quarters in France that French agricultural interests would be seriously damaged by Portuguese and Spanish participation in the CAP.

The Portuguese and Spanish governments reacted strongly to President Giscard d'Estaing's remarks by deploring any suggestion that the accession negotiations should be unduly prolonged and by recalling that the Communities had entered into a unanimous commitment to accept Portugal and Spain as full members. The other existing Community member states for the most part effectively dissociated themselves from the French government's position by publicly reaffirming their support for Portuguese and Spanish membership, although the West German Federal Chancellor, Helmut Schmidt, said on June 9 that "without the indispensable adjustments to its agricultural policy and without a more balanced distribution of burdens the Community cannot finance the tasks which face it in its expansion southwards".

A statement issued by the Portuguese Foreign Ministry on June 6 said that the existing member states of the European Community, including France, "have approved clearly and without reservation the principle of enlarging the Community and have specifically accepted the idea of Portugal's accession", and continued: "The statement made by the French President does not call this into question. President Giscard d'Estaing merely came out in favour of the need for a pause in the process of enlarging the Community without expressing any opposition to the enlargement itself. . . . In the absence of a formal decision by the Community to the contrary, the negotiations with Portugal should continue in accordance with the procedure which has been adopted and in keeping with the timetable agreed upon. . . . If France's position came to be against the continuation of negotiations with Portugal, or against their conclusion as soon as possible, the Portuguese government could in no way agree with this and would act in such a way as to find—for our country and for our economy—the solutions likely best to defend the national interest."

A Spanish government statement, also issued on June 6, said that the "new attitude" expressed by the French President "appears to be shifting difficulties which have arisen in other member countries onto the candidate countries", and continued: "The government wishes to make known its conviction that neither the internal measures taken by the Community to tackle its own problems nor its economic or other circumstances should be grounds for interrupting the course of negotiations or affecting the political commitment given so many times to Spain by the governments of the Nine and especially by the President of the French Republic himself. Neither do they affect Spain's European vocation, which has been given unanimous approval in the *Cortes*, nor do they affect the right of Spaniards to become integrated into the Community within the period and under the reasonable conditions deriving from the negotiations themselves."

In both Portugal and Spain unofficial assessments in political circles and the media attributed the French President's remarks to electoral exigencies in the context of the presidential elections due to be held in May 1981. In particular it was noted that both the Gaullist *Rassemblement pour la république* (a member of the ruling French coalition) and the opposition Communist Party were laying great stress on the potentially harmful consequences which Portuguese and Spanish membership of the Communities implied vis-à-vis farmers in southern France.

Intensive diplomatic and ministerial contacts between Portuguese and Spanish representatives on the one hand and the Community member states on the other in the course of June and July included a visit to Paris on July 1 by the then Portuguese Prime Minister, Francisco Sá Carneiro, and a visit to Madrid on July 3 by the French Prime Minister, Raymond Barre. On both occasions the French side gave firm assurances of continued support for eventual Portuguese and Spanish accession but at the same time reiterated the need for a prior resolution of the Communities' existing budgetary and related problems.

Moreover, a meeting of EC Council of (Foreign) Ministers in Brussels on July 21–22 declined, principally in the light of French reservations, to endorse a Commission proposal that Jan. 1, 1983, should be the official target date for Portuguese and Spanish accession, although it promised "uninterrupted negotiations" to bring the two countries into the Communities "as soon as possible".

Meanwhile, an agreement was signed in Madrid on July 14, 1980, under which Spain would be linked with the programme of research into controlled thermonuclear fusion (the JET project) being undertaken by Euratom together with Sweden and Switzerland.

As signed by Guido Brunner (then European Commissioner responsible for energy policy) and Calvo Sotelo y Bustelo (then Spanish Minister for Relations with the European Community), the agreement provided for an exchange of scientists between the Commission and its associates and Spain so that Spain's fusion programme would be directed and developed along lines compatible with the Euratom programme and with a view to eventual fuller association.

10.7 Pre-accession financial co-operation (1981–84)

Although no agreement was worked out between Spain and the Communities similar to that on pre-accession aid signed by Portugal in December 1980 [see 11.8], the EIB board of governors decided on May 4, 1981, to authorize the EIB to grant loans from its own resources to finance capital projects in Spain. These were designed to facilitate Spain's economic integration into the Communities' economy.

The authorization was as recommended by the Council of Ministers on March 16 and followed a Spanish request of Oct. 15, 1980, for financial co-operation with the Communities. Initially 200,000,000 ECU was made available (although no more than 100,000,000 ECU was to be allocated in any one 12-month period).

On June 21, 1983, the Council agreed to make a further package of 100,000,000 ECU available to Spain for the period July 1, 1983, to June 30, 1984. Another package of 250,000,000 ECU was allocated for the period from July 1, 1984, to Dec. 31, 1985, as recommended by the Council of (Foreign) Ministers on June 18–19, 1984, and by the EIB board of governors on Aug. 10 [see also 11.11].

10.8 Continuing negotiations (1981)

The attempted military coup of Feb. 23, 1981, in Madrid, when armed Civil Guards led by Lt.-Col. Antonio Tejero Molina had taken the members of the lower house of parliament hostage whilst they were in session in the *Cortes* building, led to a renewed emphasis on the importance of Community membership in strengthening democratic institutions in Spain.

At its meeting in Maastricht, in the Netherlands, on March 23–24, 1981, the European Council of the Community heads of state and government stressed its commitment to Spanish accession and "expressed its great satisfaction at the reaction of the King, government and people of Spain in the face of the attacks recently made against the democratic system of their country. This reaction strengthens the political structures which will enable a democratic Spain to accede to the democratic community represented by the European Communities".

Gaston Thorn, the President of the European Commission, reportedly favoured some public affirmation by the governments of the Community member countries of their support for Spain's accession; however, it was noted that the Foreign Ministers, after a joint negotiating session with Spain on March 16, 1981, issued a declaration couched only in general terms, with a call for the "intensification" rather than the "acceleration" of the negotiations. Lorenzo Natali, the Vice-President of the Commission with responsibility for enlargement of the Communities, also declined to specify a target date for Spain's accession when he made an official visit to Madrid in May–June 1981, whereas a joint commission of the European Parliament and the Spanish *Cortes*, meeting in Madrid on June 1–3, 1981, issued a communiqué calling for the establishment of Jan. 1, 1984, as the date for Spain to accede.

At this latter meeting José Pedro Pérez-Llorca, the Foreign Minister of Spain (who was in addition responsible for relations with the Communities), said in his opening speech on June 1 that the Communities had so far given only superficial answers to Spain's proposals regarding the free movement of workers and the application of Community social policy, and he further suggested that Spain should be represented before its accession in internal Community discussions on agricultural and budget policy. This idea was rejected by Natali, who commented that obstacles to Spain's accession had also been raised by the Spanish, notably by their reluctance to introduce value added tax (VAT) for Community purposes from the date of accession; he also referred to "the negative effects of the lack of clarity in the Spanish fiscal system" (this remark being interpreted as a reference to indirect assistance for Spanish exports and protection of the domestic market).

Calvo Sotelo y Bustelo, the Spanish Prime Minister, had a meeting in Paris on June 25, 1981, with François Mitterrand, who had been elected President of France the previous month, after which it was reported that the Spanish were anticipating that discussions would begin shortly on agricultural aspects of accession. At ministerial-level discussions on July 13 the French continued to emphasize the need for prior resolution of the Communities' internal negotiations in this sphere, but agreement was reportedly reached at a meeting of the Council of (Foreign) Ministers on Sept. 14 on a more flexible Community approach. This would allow for a start to be made with negotiation of technical aspects of the agricultural arrangements, while the Communities would put forward their proposals on customs union at the same time as emphasizing the need for Spain to introduce VAT by the date of accession.

Edith Cresson, the French Minister of Agriculture, reportedly made certain remarks in a speech at Senas in southern France later in September 1981, to the effect that the support of the French Socialist Party in the European Parliament for Spanish accession to the Communities would be subject to satisfactory assurances that the interests of French farmers would not be damaged. Pérez-Llorca said on Sept. 22 that he was very surprised at these reported comments, and a communiqué issued on Sept. 24 by the Socialist Group in the European Parliament affirmed support for Spanish accession, provided that mechanisms were found to secure a smooth transition and to resolve complex problems existing especially in the agricultural sphere.

Meeting in London in the framework of the European Council, the heads of state and government of the Community member countries reiterated on Nov. 27, 1981, their political commitment to reaching a successful conclusion to the accession negotiations; the heads of state and government also stressed the importance of continuing progress and the need for good use to be made of the period before accession (although no timetable was indicated).

In the "conclusions of the presidency" issued at the end of their London meeting the European Council "recalled that the member states of the Community decided to open negotiations for the accession of Portugal and Spain in the knowledge that all the objectives of the Community, as set out in the preamble to the EEC Treaty, were shared by the democratic governments and by the peoples of the two countries concerned.
"The European Council confirmed the political commitment which was the basis for that decision and emphasized the determination of the Community to bring the negotiations to a successful conclusion and stressed the importance of continuing progress. It recalled the acceptance by the applicant countries that they will accede on the basis of the Community treaties and subordinate legislation in force on the date of accession, subject only to such transitional arrangements as may be agreed. It emphasized the need for both the Community and the acceding countries to make good use of the period until accession for careful preparations for the Community's further enlargement by introducing the necessary reforms so that the potential benefits for both sides can be realized. The Council agreed that, in the Community's deliberations on its internal development, regard would need to be paid to the importance of the accession of Portugal and Spain. It also agreed on the importance of the contacts established between the Ten and the applicant countries in the framework of political co-operation and confirmed that it is their intention to continue to keep Portugal and Spain closely

informed about developments in political co-operation. It looks forward to the day when the leaders of those two countries will take their places in the European Council as full and equal members".

Thorn paid an official visit to Madrid in late December 1981, and at a press conference on Dec. 29 he expressed the Commission's "unconditional support for Spain as a candidate for membership of the Community, in line with the statement adopted by the heads of state and government in London".

Thorn expressed his belief that there could be a resolution within a few weeks of the main outlines of the Communities' internal negotiations on agricultural matters; January 1984 could still be regarded as a target date for Spanish accession, he indicated, and he added that the Communities continued to regard it as desirable that Spain's accession should coincide with that of Portugal.

10.9 Internal Community problems hamper negotiations (1982–83)

Calvo Sotelo made a personal appeal for an acceleration of negotiations on Jan. 7, 1982, but fundamental problems within the Communities themselves began to come to a head and the question of finding solutions to these issues became increasingly to be regarded as a prerequisite for the conclusion of enlargement negotiations.

Problems over financing the Communities' activities, even as a 10-member grouping, became increasingly acute. The UK, which along with West Germany was a net contributer to the Community budget, insisted on rebates to offset its disproportionate contribution and on greater discipline in budgetary affairs to improve the efficient use of Community resources. The question of containing agricultural spending, which took up some two-thirds of total Community expenditure, also became increasingly important, since unless reform of the CAP was undertaken the inclusion of Spain and Portugal in the Communities was expected to extend the existing surpluses in such "north European" products as milk, grain and beef to "south European" products such as wine and olive oil.

As with the budgetary problems a start on reform of the Communities' common agricultural policy was not made until the European Council meeting in Stuttgart in June 1983. This planned a "relaunch" of the Communities and recognized that the CAP "must be adapted to the situation facing the Community in the foreseeable future, in order that it can fulfil its aim in a more coherent manner". The proposals requested by the Council which were presented by the Commission the following month however, received a mixed response and it was not until March 1984 that measures to limit dairy production in the Communities were initiated in the 1984–85 agreement on agricultural prices.

10.10 Limited progress in 1982

Against this background of continuing disagreement amongst Community member countries over internal Community issues, enlargement negotiations during 1982 and 1983 made progress on some issues but had to wait until a wider resolution of Community problems before a breakthrough could be achieved.

At ministerial level negotiations on March 22–23, 1982, progress was reportedly made with technical agreements concerning capital movements, regional policy, transport, rights of establishment and freedom to provide services. The Spanish government also agreed in early 1982 to implement VAT from accession.

Nevertheless at its meeting in Brussels on June 28–29, the European Council followed a French proposal by instructing the Commission to draw up a full list of outstanding issues, indicating how each country would be affected by enlargement and setting out proposals for solutions to the problems.

President Mitterrand said on June 29 that he was not opposed in principle to the enlargement of the Communities and that the admission of Portugal and Spain was politically desirable, but that problems must be resolved first to ensure that the balance of the Communities was not damaged. During an official visit to Spain the previous week, he had said (in a speech in Madrid on June 22) that he did not wish to see new tribulations added to the Communities' current ones and that Spanish accession under existing circumstances would mean an unfortunate state of anarchy, adding new pressures to those already facing the Communities. His comments on this occasion were widely reported as indicating a possible French veto against Spanish accession, following the adoption by the Foreign Ministers of the Community member countries on June 21 of what was regarded as a hard-line approach on certain aspects of the negotiations.

At its next meeting on Dec. 3–4, 1982, in Copenhagen the European Council again failed to fix a specific accession date. Instead the heads of state and government reaffirmed their "political commitment to the enlargement of the Community with Spain and Portugal" and called upon the Council of Ministers "to press ahead with the negotiations with both countries as rapidly as possible". The "inventory" requested in June 1982 and presented by the Commission in November was welcomed by the European Council as a "new impulse to the enlargement process".

According to the *Financial Times* of Nov. 17, this report called on Community member countries to reward Spain and Portugal with a definite date for joining the Communities if they took more drastic steps to cut back key crisis industries such as steel and shipbuilding. Whilst stressing "the importance of rapid progress within the Community on a number of important issues in order to facilitate a harmonious enlargement of the Community", the meeting in particular asked the Council of (Agriculture) Ministers "to complete urgently and before March 1983 the revision of existing rules for certain Mediterranean agricultural products on the basis of Commission proposals". However, agreement on this issue was not reached until October 1983 [see 10.11].

Agriculture was a crucial issue in negotiations with Spain and was seen as threatening the economies of southern France, Greece and Italy in particular. Spain's accession would increase the Communities' agricultural area by 30 per cent and its farm workforce by 25 per cent. Community production of vegetables, fresh fruit and olive oil would also be increased, by 25 per cent, 48 per cent and 59 per cent respectively, while Spanish wine represented nearly a quarter of Community output.

At the final ministerial level negotiating meeting in 1982, held on Dec. 13 (which followed two others on June 21 and Oct. 26) Fernando Morán, the Foreign Minister in the Spanish Socialist government of Felipe González which had taken office on Dec. 3, reportedly made a statement demanding membership within four years and "concrete proof" from the 10 Community member countries of their commitment to Spain's accession.

10.11 Attempted "relaunch" of the Communities in 1983

During 1983, ministerial-level meetings were held (i) on Feb. 22; (ii) on April 26 (when negotiations on quantitative restrictions on imports into Spain and on textiles were concluded); (iii) on June 21 (after which a deputy-level meeting on

July 15 managed to conclude agreements on the petroleum and tobacco monopolies in Spain, taxation and the approximation of laws); (iv) on Oct. 18 (when agreement was reached on the status of the north African enclaves of Ceuta and Melilla); and (v) on Dec. 19. At the Dec. 19 meeting, agreement was reached on various external issues, such as transitional arrangements regarding Japan, textiles and the duration of the transitional measures for quotas; certain ECSC matters were also agreed and negotiations were completed in all essentials for Spanish accession to Euratom.

Bilateral talks between Spain and France were held at various levels in 1983, in order particularly to find a solution to the question of transitional periods for the introduction of unlimited access to Community markets for Spanish agricultural produce. Any major concessions on this issue were vociferously opposed by French farmers. Other informal meetings held during the year included a visit to Bonn at the beginning of May by González, the Spanish Prime Minister, for talks with Dr Helmut Kohl, the West German Chancellor.

Meeting in Brussels on March 21–22, 1983, the Community heads of state and government declared their determination "that negotiations with Spain and Portugal should now make substantial progress" and called for a progress report to be made to their next meeting. The limited progress subsequently made on enlargement and other issues led the European Council at its June 17–19 meeting in Stuttgart to institute a programme of "broad action to ensure the relaunch of the European Community".

As stated in the declaration issued after the meeting: "The accession negotiations with Spain and Portugal will be pursued with the objective of concluding them, so that the accession treaties can be submitted for ratification when the result of the negotiation concerning the future financing of the Community is submitted."

Subsequently, after two years of negotiations, a meeting of the Council of (Agriculture) Ministers in Luxembourg on Oct. 17–18, 1983, approved rules for the organization of the Community fruit and vegetable and olive oil markets. The agreement helped improve the balance between CAP guarantees for Mediterranean products and those for "northern" products (such as wheat, dairy products, sugar, beef and sheepmeat). It also marked a breakthrough in negotiations for the enlargement of the Communities to include Spain and Portugal and was welcomed as a "positive development" by Morán. Furthermore, *The Times* reported on Oct. 19 that it was "probably not a complete coincidence" that this breakthrough had come after an informal "Socialist summit" meeting of five Socialist Prime Ministers (of France, Greece, Italy, Portugal and Spain) in Athens on Oct. 16–17, at which both González and Dr Mário Soares, the Portuguese Prime Minister, had expressed their discontent at the slow pace of negotiations.

Under the agreement provisions for fruit and vegetables were to be applied as soon as negotiations began with Spain and Portugal on these products, while on olive oil it was agreed that a decision should be taken in time for measures to be implemented at the start of the 1984–85 marketing year.

A month later González sent a letter to each of the 10 Community heads of government (as he did again on Oct. 15, 1984), formally asking them to declare where they stood on the question of Spain's membership of the Communities. Public opinion in Spain was reported to be becoming increasingly resentful towards what was seen as French obstruction of negotiations, and the Madrid newspaper *El País* on Nov. 17 published an article hinting at possible Spanish reprisals against French trade. This was denied by González on the same day, but he did say that the Spanish government would undoubtedly take into account "political criteria and not just economic ones, in international purchases".

The comprehensive programme embarked upon after Stuttgart did not however, result in the breakthrough hoped for by the time of the Athens summit on Dec. 3–4, 1983. Preparatory meetings failed to agree on substantive issues, which left the heads of state and government with a detailed agenda of reform proposals, and no agreement was reached on enlargement or on agricultural, financial and other policy issues, nor was a common communiqué issued.

10.12 Progress in 1984

By 1984 three major issues remained unresolved in Community negotiations with Spain: agriculture (including fruit and vegetables, olive oil and wine), fisheries, and the lowering of trade barriers for Spanish industrial goods. These issues dominated minsterial-level meetings on Feb. 21, April 10 (when agreement on patents and various external relations questions was reached), June 19, July 24, Sept. 3 and 18, Oct. 3 and 23, and Dec. 18–19.

For the first six months of the year the presidency of the European Council was held by France and a marked effort was made by the French government to speed up the negotiating process. In a speech on Feb. 7, President Mitterrand expressed his commitment to enlargement "without delay". Roland Dumas, then French Minister for European Affairs, visited Madrid on Jan. 30–31, and again on June 15, while Pierre Mauroy, then Prime Minister of France, visited Madrid on March 9 (two days after the fishing incident between the two countries—see 10.13). In a move described as marking a high point in bilateral relations between France and Spain, President Mitterrand flew to Madrid on June 29 shortly after the Fontainebleau summit in order to report to the Spanish government on the meeting.

Other Community heads of state or government who visited Madrid during 1984 to stress their commitment to enlargement were Dr Kohl, who had talks with González on May 17–18 following the latter's visit to Bonn in May 1983 [see 10.11], Bettino Craxi, the Italian Prime Minister (on May 24–25), Ruud Lubbers, the Dutch Prime Minister (on June 5), and Konstantinos Karamanlis, then Greek President (on Oct. 8–11).

In contrast to the Athens summit the Fontainebleau meeting of the European Council on June 25–26, 1984, succeeded in agreeing on a range of measures to enable a relaunch of the Communities. By fixing a 1984 UK budget rebate figure and a mechanism for future years, those at the meeting were able also to achieve a consensus on an increase in Community resources above the 1 per cent "ceiling", on agreements on budgetary and financial discipline and on new guidelines for the reactivation of European co-operation.

For the first time an offical date for accession of Jan. 1, 1986, was set, the relevant section of the "conclusions of the presidency" on increasing Community resources and on enlargement being worded as follows:

"The maximum rate of mobilization of VAT will be [increased from its existing 1 per cent 'ceiling' to] 1.4 per cent on Jan. 1, 1986; this maximum rate applies to every member state and will enter into force as soon as the ratification procedures are completed, and by

Jan. 1, 1986, at the latest. The maximum rate may be increased to 1.6 per cent on Jan. 1, 1988, by unanimous decision of the Council and after agreement has been given in accordance with national procedures.

"The European Council confirms that the negotiations for the accession of Spain and Portugal should be completed by Sept. 30, 1984, at the latest. Between now and then the Community will have to make every effort to create the right conditions for the success of this enlargement, both in the negotiations with Spain on fisheries to ensure the conservation of fish stocks and also by reforming the common organization of the wine market to ensure that the quantities of wine produced in the Community are controlled and by means of a fair balance between agricultural and industrial agreements."

10.13 Spanish fisheries question

Spain's fishing rights in Community waters were regulated according to an agreement which was signed on April 15, 1980, but had been applied de facto since the conclusion of a framework agreement in September 1978. This provided for decreasing Spanish quotas of hake (the country's most important commercial species) and related species, and for annual reductions in the number of licences for Spanish vessels to fish in Community waters.

The agreement for 1984 reached on March 5, 1984, provided for a hake quota of 7,900 tonnes, with a 15,000-tonne allowance for associated species. This compared with a hake quota of 8,300 tonnes for 1983.

Community member countries, having eventually reached agreement on a common fisheries policy in January 1983, were reluctant immediately to admit to Community waters the 17,000-strong Spanish fishing fleet, which was numerically larger than the entire Community fleet and equivalent to almost 70 per cent of the Community tonnage.

The Spanish fishing industry had suffered a marked decline since January 1977 with the international introduction of 200-mile national coastal limits. In 1983 the Spanish government had also been obliged to accept a 40 per cent reduction in its fishing rights off Morocco. Annual per capita fish consumption in Spain was 40 kg compared with the Community average of 15 kg.

French Navy patrol boats on March 7, 1984, fired on two Spanish fishing trawlers about 100 miles (160 km) off the south-western French coast in the Bay of Biscay. Nine fishermen were injured, although warning shots had been fired after the boats had ignored an order to stop for a licence check. The boats were reportedly outside French territorial waters but within the Communities' 200-mile economic zone; according to *The Times* of March 8, they had been fishing illegally in Community waters 10 or 12 times since the beginning of December 1983.

Protests were made to each country's respective ambassadors and during Mauroy's visit to Madrid on March 9. Fines of 122,200 French francs for each boat were imposed on March 15 for illegal fishing and resisting inspection, and were immediately paid by the Spanish government. (As at March 28, 1984, US$1.00 = F8.01.) Spanish fishermen burned over 30 foreign lorries in protests; in response, French and other lorry drivers mounted a blockade at the Spanish border until March 22 when they secured assurances from Spanish police that adequate protection would be given to convoys of foreign lorries.

Various incidents involving the apprehension of both Spanish and French fishing boats continued over subsequent months. On Oct. 20 a Spanish trawler sank in the

Irish Sea after the Irish Navy had fired nearly 600 rounds of cannon and small arms fireshot in an attempt to board the vessel. The boat, the crew of which was safely rescued, had been sighted off Wexford fishing within the 6-mile Irish zone and was one of more than 32 Spanish boats arrested during the year for illegally fishing in Irish waters.

The Spanish government having rejected on June 19, 1984, a proposal that existing limits on Spanish catches in Community waters should remain in force for at least 10 years, agreement on the fisheries issue was not reached until March 1985.

10.14 Negotiations on agricultural and other issues

Following agreement in October 1983 on the rules for a common organization of the Community fruit, vegetable and olive oil markets [see 10.11], Community Foreign Ministers managed to agree on Feb. 20, 1984, on terms for a 10-year integration period for Spanish fruit and vegetables (but not olive oil or wine); however, these were rejected as "insufficient" by Morán at the ministerial-level negotiating meeting the following day. Subsequently, a majority of the Council of (Foreign) Ministers agreed on May 14 that these rules should be applied from June 1, 1984, which meant that Spanish and Portuguese exports of fruit and vegetables would thereafter face Community tariff rises of between 3 and 20 percentage points.

An informal agreement on a basic 10-year transition period for agricultural goods was reached on June 20 after the ministerial-level meeting during discussions between Morán, Dumas and the Commission representative. However, by the next ministerial-level meeitng on July 24 it emerged that in the light of mounting opposition at home the Spanish government was seeking a general seven-year programme with total exemption from controls for the lucrative Spanish citrus crop. Agricultural issues dominated both formal and informal Council and negotiating meetings during subsequent months.

Meeting on Oct. 22–23 in Luxembourg, the Council of (Foreign) Ministers succeeded in establishing joint proposals regarding industrial tariffs, the volume of Community cars to be imported into Spain and Portugal, olive oil, steel (on which discussions were also held on Oct. 16 and Nov. 27), social issues (and in particular the free movement of labour for which a seven-year transition period was proposed), and sugar [see 11.10 on Portuguese negotiations].

Furthermore, at the ministerial-level meeting with Spain on Oct. 23 a statement was presented to Morán expressing the Communities' commitment to accession by Jan. 1, 1986. The conclusion of an Anglo-Spanish agreement on Gibraltar on Nov. 27, 1984, and the subsequent opening of the frontier between Gibraltar and Spain in February 1985 were also seen as lifting a major barrier to Spanish accession to the Communities. The key issues of agriculture (including in particular wine) and fisheries were, however, still on the agenda at the Dublin meeting of the European Council at the beginning of December.

The European Council summit session in Dublin on Dec. 3–4, 1984, in reaching agreement on curbing wine production and on positions as regards Spanish and Portuguese fish, fruit and vegetables, achieved what the *Financial Times* described as "a vital breakthrough towards completing the enlargement talks".

The agreement on Community wine production established three trigger mechanisms, which when activated would result in any surplus wine being compulsorily purchased at sharply reduced prices for distillation into industrial alcohol. This process was set in motion whenever (i) production exceeded consumption by 9 per cent; or (ii) the market price remained below 82 per cent of the official price for a representative period; or (iii) stocks exceeded four months' normal consumption. At Italian insistence, incentive payments were also to be made to wine growers who switched to other crops, while the West German government succeeded in safeguarding its growers' right to continue bringing their wine up to "quality" standard by adding sugar (although a report on this issue was to be prepared by the Commission by 1990).

A statement on these issues did not, however, feature in the final communiqué, since Dr Andreas Papandreou, the Greek Prime Minister, insisted that any agreement on wine or other Mediterranean products should be conditional upon Community leaders also agreeing by March 1985 a programme of financial support for the Greek economy (and for other Mediterranean economies already within the Communities).

Financial assistance of this sort had first been suggested by the Commission in June 1982. More detailed proposals for Integrated Mediterranean Programmes (IMPs) were presented to the Council in March 1983 and provided for some 6,628 million ECU in financial assistance over a six-year period from various sources. This was to be shared between Greece (38 per cent), Italy (44.5 per cent), and southern France (17.5 per cent) and was to help develop regional agriculture, tourism and small businesses.

At the time of the Dublin summit in December 1984, Margaret Thatcher, the UK Prime Minister, described the sums being demanded by Dr Papandreou (which were based on the Commission proposals as above) as "so far out of sight that they should never have been mentioned".

As part of the agreement on curbing wine production reached in Dublin, the question of establishing an effective mechanism to ensure the implementation of the restrictions was not agreed until the Council of (Agriculture) Ministers met on Feb. 25–26, 1985, in Brussels. Agreement was also finalized on March 11–13 on a five-year programme for structural aid to Community farmers.

Under the previously existing system of controlling wine production each country submitted in December estimates for projected wine production and consumption, after which the Commission was in theory able to assess and order the compulsory distillation of stocks (which at the end of the marketing year in August were expected to exceed five months' normal consumption). Excess stocks, which averaged 3,000 million litres more than annual consumption (of approximately 13,500 million litres), were intended to be purchased at only 60 per cent of the usual price, but estimates were often inaccurate and the compulsory purchase price had been allowed to rise steadily.

Under the agreement reached on Feb. 25–26 the Commission was empowered to make its own assessments of the market regardless of national estimates. It was to establish quantities of wine to be distilled, region by region, as based on previous years' production, with figures increasing progressively with yield, so that high-yielding vineyards would be most affected. A decision was postponed on the actual cost of compensation payments for viticulturalists who grubbed up, or did not replant, their vines.

10.15 Conclusion of enlargement negotiations in early 1985
After the Dublin summit, the Council of (Foreign) Ministers met on Dec. 17–18, Jan. 28, Feb. 18–20 and Feb. 28 to try and reach agreement on a common position on enlargement. Major outstanding issues—agriculture, fisheries, the rights of Spanish and Portuguese workers to find jobs in other Community countries, and the largely untouched question of Spain and Portugal's financial contributions—were nevertheless still unresolved at a final Council of (Foreign) Ministers meeting in Brussels on March 17–21.

The Council's failure to agree on these issues, even though a broad agreement had been worked out, was attributed in all the major Spanish newspapers to the French government's refusal to accept (i) the proposed quota of Spanish fishing boats to be allowed to fish in EC waters; and (ii) the proposed quantity of Spanish wine production to be permitted before obligatory distillation was required. However, the *International Herald Tribune* of March 23–24 reported that other countries also had objections, including Portugal which objected to the proposed financial arrangements whereby Portugal would receive a reimbursement on its VAT contributions for only one year (compared with reimbursements for six years as envisaged for Spain).

A further Council of (Foreign) Ministers meeting attended by Morán and Ernâni Lopes, the Portuguese Finance Minister, was therefore held on March 28–29, and it was announced early on the morning of March 29 that agreement had been reached in principle on all the issues concerning Spain and Portugal's accession (although the question of Community agreement on Dr Papandreou's demands for Greece had been carried over to the Brussels summit meeting on March 29–30). In order for Spain and Portugal to join the Communities as planned on Jan. 1, 1986, the final drafting of the accession treaties had still to be completed and signed by the European Council and ratified by the parliaments of the 10 member countries, as required by the Treaty of Rome.

González declared that the agreement was "an historic step forward", while Morán saw it as the recognition given to those nations (i.e. Greece, Spain and Portugal) which had re-established democracy.

10.16 Declaration on enlargement at Brussels meeting of European Council
The Community heads of state and government, at their meeting in Brussels on March 29–30, 1985, noted their great satisfaction over the settlement of the essential points in the accession talks. The following passage on enlargement was included in the "conclusions of the presidency":

"The European Council noted with great satisfaction that the essential points in the accession negotiations with Spain and Portugal have now been settled. as a result, in particular, of the considerable effort made by all parties in the week leading up to the European Council resulting in solutions to the key issues of fisheries, agriculture, social affairs and the own resources system. The European Council called upon the Community bodies, together with the applicant countries, to complete the drafting of the accession treaty as soon as possible so that actual enlargement of the Community could take place on Jan. 1, 1986, in accordance with the political resolve repeatedly expressed at the highest level."

The main agreement reached at this European Council meeting concerned the Integrated Mediterranean Programmes (IMPs), the consensus being based on Commission proposals presented on Feb. 21. Dr Papandreou's acceptance of the programmes removed a final obstacle before completion of the relevant legal documents for enlargement of the Communities could go ahead. Theodoros Pangalos, the Greek Secretary of State for European Affairs, described the IMP settlement as "not the agreement we hoped for, but . . . a successful solution".

As agreed these programmes were to last seven years and were intended to benefit the southern regions of the existing Communities by improving "the economic structures of those regions to enable them to adjust under the best conditions possible to the new situation created by enlargement". [For details of implementation of the IMPs see 8.11].

After the Brussels meeting Jacques Delors, the President of the Commission since January 1985, stated: "All the family quarrels have been sorted out. The family is now going to grow and we can think of the future." Mitterrand described the Brussels summit's programme as "enlargement and finalization of everything concerned with enlargement". He said that "at the next European Council in Milan, we will be considering what Europe will become".

10.17 Signature of Accession Treaty (June 12, 1985)

The signature ceremonies for the Treaty of Accession took place on June 12, 1985, at the Jerónimos Monastery in Lisbon, the Portuguese capital, and later on the same day at the Royal Palace in Madrid, the Spanish capital. Subject to the approval of the Treaty by the 10 existing member country parliaments and by the Spanish and Portuguese parliaments, accession was scheduled to take place on Jan. 1, 1986. [For bilateral agreement between Spain and Portugal concluded in April 1985 see 11.13.]

The treaty was signed by representatives of the European Commission, by the Prime Ministers of Belgium, Denmark, France, Ireland, Italy, and the Netherlands, and by the Foreign Ministers of the Federal Republic of Germany (West Germany), Greece, Luxembourg and the United Kingdom. On the Spanish side it was signed by González, the Prime Minister, Fernando Morán, then Foreign Minister, Manuel Marín, then Secretary of State with responsibility for relations with the European Communities, and Gabriel Ferrán de Alfaro, the Spanish Ambassador to the European Communities.

Three attacks attributed to the Basque separatist organization ETA were also committed on the same day.

Col. Vincente Romero, an Army lawyer, and his chauffeur were shot dead on a Madrid street by two men and a woman. A booby-trapped car was also left in the basement garage of a department store in central Madrid, from which 8,000 people were evacuated, but the car exploded before bomb disposal experts could neutralize it, killing one policeman and wounding eight others. José Millarengo, a naval petty officer, was shot dead in Portugalete near Bilbao in the Basque country.

At the time of the signing González declared: "I solemnly affirm that no-one through coercion or violence will upset our determination to co-operate in the building of Europe. . . . The events mean the abandonment of isolation and participation in a common destiny with the rest of the countries of Western Europe." Giulio Andreotti, the Italian Foreign Minister, whose country held the presidency of the Council's ministerial bodies for the first six months of 1985, said of both Portugal's and Spain's accession that "membership of the European Communities follows naturally from the restoration of the values inherent in a pluralist democracy".

10.18 Terms of accession

The accession document comprised 403 articles as compared with 161 for that of 1972 for Denmark, the Irish Republic and the UK; it ran to 1,300 pages including 36 annexes, 25 protocols and 47 declarations and joint declarations by the different member countries on issues not fully resolved.

After signature of the Treaty Spain and Portugal were permitted to send observers to all Community meetings affecting the two countries, while from September they were to be fully integrated into the Community Foreign Ministers' political co-operation meetings, at which member countries sought to co-ordinate their foreign policies.

Details of the terms of accession for both Spain and Portugal (including certain issues only resolved in the latter half of 1985) are given below. In general a seven-year transitional period was set up for the establishment of a common market in industrial and agricultural goods between the acceding countries and the Community of the Ten, although provision was made for longer periods in certain sectors.

Customs union for industrial goods. Both Spain and Portugal had hitherto applied a customs regime affording a high degree of protection to their economies. Customs duties were now to be dismantled in eight stages over a seven-year transitional period (with the first reductions on both sides beginning on March 1, two months after accession). By 1989 duties in both countries would be reduced by at least 50 per cent, and by 1993 they would be abolished. (Increased quotas at reduced tariff rates were established for Spanish car imports for 1986–88, after which the tariffs would be progressively phased out.)

As regards quantitative trade restrictions these were in general abolished from accession, although Spain was given between three and four years to phase out import quotas on such sensitive products as tractors, colour televisions, sewing machines and guns. Portugal had three years to abolish its existing system of import and export licences and two years to lift car import quotas. Trade restrictions in force as a result of the Spanish state petrol and tobacco monopolies and the Portuguese state petrol monopoly were to be phased out over six and seven years respectively for each country. In general the existing body of EC law on competition policy, the harmonization of laws, transport, environment and consumer protection policies applied from accession, although some temporary derogations were permitted.

In the textile sector, which was particularly sensitive for existing member countries, market access for some textile exports from both Portugal and Spain was made subject to a programme of double checking and statistical surveys of existing member countries' imports. Spain retained import quotas on four cotton products. On steel, access for Spanish and Portuguese exports was to be kept to a fixed volume over three years, while their steel industries were to be allowed to continue to receive national subsidies during that period for the purpose of restructuring the industry along EC lines.

Agriculture. Although in general a seven-year transitional period applied for the implementation of the CAP, a 10-year transitional period would apply for a range of sensitive products.

In Spain, transitional periods of 10 years applied (i) for oil-seeds and olive oil (where existing import controls were to remain for five years because of the danger of surpluses building up); (ii) for fruit and vegetables (where the complementary trade mechanism was also to apply and import controls were to remain largely as before enlargement for four years, after which Community prices were to apply); and (iii) for certain northern products such as milk and dairy products, beef and soft wheat, liable to cause problems for Spanish agriculture. Wine was subject to EC market management rules from accession [for EC agreements on wine sector see 10.14], although a "specific regulating amount" was allocated, to offset differences between Spanish and EC prices over a seven-year period, and a "complementary trade mechanism" was established, to set import guide levels and to establish an agreed and gradual transition from traditional trade patterns as markets were opened up. Production above a certain volume was to be obligatorily distilled.

In Portugal, the seven-year transitional period affected only 15 per cent of Portuguese production and most sectors had a 10-year transitional period, during the first part of which (for a maximum of five years) Portuguese marketing structures were to be set up or improved; the narrowing of price differences and opening of markets could take place in the second part of the transitional period. A complementary trade mechanism was agreed for sensitive products and special arrangements were made for Portuguese tomato and wine exports and sugar imports and for Community cereal exports to Portugal. Over the 10-year period some 700 million ECU were to be spent on developing Portuguese agriculture and assisting its integration into the CAP. (As at Dec. 31, 1985, 1.00 ECU=US$0.86=£0.62.)

Fisheries. The alignment of price differences and dismantling of customs duties were spread over seven years, except for sardines which were subject to a 10-year period, while specific regimes were set up for anchovy, tuna and mackerel products. The number of vessels allowed in specific fishing areas was laid down and during the transitional period licensing arrangements were to apply for Spanish fishing in Community waters beyond a 12-mile coastal economic zone, while restricted reciprocal access to Portuguese waters beyond but not within the 12-mile limit was also agreed. (At a meeting of the Council of Fisheries Ministers on Dec. 20, 1985, ministers failed to finalize such questions as the access of Community, and in particular French, vessels to Spanish waters.) The Iberian countries were to conform to EC rules on minimum fish sizes, fishing gear, catch limits and quotas (which for the key Spanish hake catch was more than doubled in 1986 to 18,000 tonnes). Spain received pre-accession aid amounting to 28,500,000 ECU for restructuring its fleet.

Social affairs. Most provisions for assistance through the European Social Fund (ESF) applied from the date of accession. Proposals put forward by the Commission in October 1985 identified all of Portugal and nine autonomous Spanish regions (Andalusia, the Canaries, Castilla-León, Castilla-La Mancha, Extremadura, Galicia, Murcia, and the enclaves of Ceuta and Melilla in North Africa) as "less-favoured" areas "characterized by especially serious and prolonged imbalance in employment", where programmes would therefore be able to qualify for increased ESF assistance.

Freedom of movement. A seven- to 10-year transitional period was to apply to the introduction of free movement of workers within the EC. Until the end of 1992 (or the end of 1995 in Luxembourg) existing member countries were permitted to require prior authorization for new immigrants seeking employment, with the situation being reviewed in 1991. Residence time limits could be imposed on members of families of established Spanish and Portuguese workers seeking work in EC countries, although these were to be phased out by 1992 and no restrictions could be placed on the families of workers already living in other EC countries when the treaty was signed in June 1985. At least until the end of 1988 family allowances would be restricted to the rates applied in the country of origin if the claimant's family were still resident there, although national rules already in force could not be made less favourable to Spanish and Portuguese workers on any of these issues.

External trade relations. Portugal's and Spain's external customs tariffs were gradually to be aligned with those of the EC over the seven-year transitional period. The preferential EC tariffs granted to Third World countries and especially those granted to the African, Caribbean and Pacific countries under the Lomé Convention and to the Mediterranean countries under co-operation agreements, were to apply from accession except for certain temporarily exempt products. The acceding countries' relations with the remaining EFTA countries (i.e. Austria, Finland, Iceland, Norway,

Sweden and Switzerland) were to be based on the special relations agreements reached with those countries [see also 6.13]. The treaty also provided for the opening of negotiations with the Mediterranean countries to modify existing agreements and to maintain trade patterns, and it mentioned the possibility of closer relations with the Spanish- and Portuguese-speaking countries of the American continent.

Monetary questions. Spanish and Portuguese participation in the exchange rate and intervention mechanisms of the European Monetary System (EMS) remained an open question (as was also the case for Greece and the UK). The question of the inclusion of the peseta and the escudo in the basket of currencies which formed the basis for the ECU was to be reconsidered in 1989.

Financial arrangements. The question of Portuguese and Spanish contributions to Community revenues (in the form of customs duties, agricultural levies and a percentage of the value added tax—VAT—levied in member countries), was regulated on the same principles as applied on the accession of Greece [see 8.5]. Over a six-year period the balance of Spanish contributions and receipts from the EC was to be neutral whereas Portugal was to be a net beneficiary. To ensure this, the EC was to refund to Spain and Portugal part of the payments due to the EC from VAT, starting at a rate of 87 per cent for 1986 and disappearing by 1992 (after which Portugal was permitted to keep its external agricultural levies for a further five years). Portugal was also to receive loans totalling 1,000 million ECU over six years to support its balance of payments, and ƃoth countries were able to apply for loans without individual limits within the resources of the EIB, the New Community Instrument, the ECSC and Euratom.

The board of governors of the EIB decided at its annual meeting on June 11, 1985, to double the bank's subscribed capital from 14,400 million ECU to 28,800 million ECU as from Jan. 1, 1986. (1 ECU = £0.57 = US$0.73, as at June 28, 1985.) The 10 existing members of the EC were to increase their subscriptions from 14,400 million ECU to 26,500 million ECU, while a further 2,300 million ECU were to come from Spain and Portugal. Since the formation of the EIB in 1958 as an independent, non-profit making institution within the terms of the 1957 Treaty of Rome, the board of governors (which comprised one government minister from each Community member country) had decided to increase the bank's subscribed capital on five occasions, most recently in 1981 (when Greece had also contributed to a small increase in the EIB's capital). As in 1981, the payment of the additional paid-in capital was in the proportion of 7.5 per cent of additional subscribed capital and was to be made in 12 equal half-yearly instalments, the first instalment being due on April 30, 1988. Total paid-in capital would be equivalent to 2,596 million ECU.

The Community member countries' percentage shares of the subscribed capital following the 1981 and 1985 decisions are given below.

	Percentage share following decision of June 1981	Percentage share following decision of June 1985
France	21.875	19.127
West Germany	21.875	19.127
Italy	17.5	19.127
United Kingdom......	21.875	19.127
Spain	–	7.031
Belgium	5.76	5.302
Netherlands...........	5.76	5.302
Denmark	2.925	2.684
Greece	1.563	1.438
Portugal	–	0.927
Ireland	0.729	0.671
Luxembourg	0.146	0.134

VAT was to be introduced from accession in Spain (where three rates were to apply—a reduced rate of 6 per cent, a standard rate of 12 per cent and a luxury rate of 33 per cent—and over 20 other taxes were to be removed) and from 1989 in Portugal, with Portugal's VAT contributions in the meantime being calculated as a proportion of its GNP.

Institutional arrangements. Portugal and Spain participated fully in all the EC institutions from accession (having already participated as observers after signing the treaty—see above). As a result of the enlargement membership of the Commission was increased by three to 17. [See 10.20 and 11.16 for appointment of new Commissioners.] Membership of the Council was increased by two to 12. In the weighted voting system used by the Council Spain would have eight votes and Portugal five, as compared with 10 votes each for France, West Germany, Italy and the UK, five each for Belgium, Greece and the Netherlands, three each for Denmark and Ireland and two for Luxembourg. Decisions made by qualified majority would require 54 of the 76 votes.

The European Parliament's membership was increased by 60 seats for Spain and 24 for Portugal, bringing the total to 518 seats [see 10.24 for first meeting of enlarged Parliament].

Membership of the Economic and Social Committee (Ecosoc), which comprised representatives of employers, workers and other interest groups, was increased from 156 to 189 members, including 21 from Spain and 12 from Portugal. The number of judges on the European Court of Justice was increased from 11 to 13 and the number of advocates-general was increased from five to six. Representation on the EIB's board of governors was increased to 12, and there were corresponding increases in the size of the various bodies of other Community institutions such as the Court of Auditors and the Coal and Steel Consultative Committee of the ECSC.

Regional assistance. The percentage share of assistance available to Spain and Portugal through the ERDF (or Feder according to its French acronym) was not agreed until a meeting of the Council of (Foreign) Ministers on Dec. 17, 1985. As had been the case since January 1985, ERDF funds were allocated between member countries within a percentage range.

	Percentage range for ERDF assistance as from 1986	Percentage range for ERDF assistance in 1985
Belgium	0.61– 0.82	0.90– 1.20
Denmark	0.34– 0.46	0.51– 0.67
France	7.48– 9.96	11.05–14.74
West Germany	2.55– 3.40	3.76– 4.81
Greece	8.36–10.64	12.35–15.74
Ireland	3.82– 4.61	5.64– 6.83
Italy	21.62–28.79	31.94–42.59
Luxembourg	0.04– 0.06	0.06– 0.08
Netherlands	0.68– 0.91	1.01– 1.34
Portugal	10.66–14.20	–
Spain	17.97–23.93	–
United Kingdom	14.50–19.31	21.42–28.56

As regards Gibraltar, *The Times* of June 27 reported that Spain and the United Kingdom had exchanged notes which "fully protected" Spain's position before the signing of the treaty. Both countries agreed that Spain's entry into the Communities would not affect the agreement reached in November 1984 under which the UK undertook to discuss the sovereignty of Gibraltar.

The question of the terms of entry for the Canary Islands, which had opted not to participate in the Communities' common agricultural policy nor in the customs union, had led to the fall of the government there on June 22.

10.19 Ratifications of the Accession Treaty (June–December 1985)
Both Spain and Portugal were quick to ratify the Accession Treaty, the
Spanish Congress of Deputies (lower house of parliament) passing the treaty
to general applause on June 26. After approval by the Senate (upper house)
the treaty was promulgated on Aug. 2.

Ratification procedures were completed by the member countries on July 15
(Belgium), on Oct. 17 (Luxembourg), on Nov. 5 (Greece), on Nov. 29 (Denmark), on
Dec. 2 (Ireland), on Dec. 11 (France), on Dec. 13 (West Germany), on Dec. 19 (the
Netherlands and UK) and on Dec. 20 (Italy).

On Sept. 11 the European Parliament also voted by 238 votes to 16 with 30
abstentions to ratify the Treaty. Those opposing Spain and Portugal's accession included Communists from Denmark, France, Greece and Italy, Danish anti-
marketeers, UK Socialists, and a member of the West German Green Party. Those
abstaining included French members of the group of the European Right, French and
Irish members of the European Democratic Alliance, Belgian and French members of
the Christian democratic European People's Party, and Belgian, Danish and Dutch
members of the Rainbow Group.

10.20 Nomination of Spanish Commissioners
Manuel Marín (36), who had been Secretary of State with responsibility for
relations with the European Communities in the Socialist government of
González and had been involved in many of the concluding negotiations on
enlargement, and Abel Matutes (44), a banker and deputy leader of Spain's
opposition Popular Alliance, were on Nov. 20, 1985, nominated as the two
Spanish members of the enlarged Commission. At the new Commission's first
sitting on Jan. 3, 1986, the two politicians were given the respective portfolios
of (i) Social Affairs, Employment, Education and Training and (ii) Credit and
Investment, Financial Instruments, Small and Medium Businesses.

Earlier, on Oct. 23, 1985, Pedros Solbes, who had previously been secretary general
at the Ministry of the Economy, had been appointed to take over Marín's post.

10.21 EC agreement on negotiating mandate for trade talks with
Mediterranean countries (Nov. 25, 1985)
The Council of (Foreign) Ministers agreed on Nov. 25, 1985, on a negotiating
mandate for talks with non-member Mediterranean countries on trading
relations following the accession of Spain and Portugal to the EC. The
mandate envisaged the progressive reduction of EC tariffs on agricultural
goods from non-EC Mediterranean countries, following a timetable similar to
that agreed for Portugal and Spain (i.e. a 10-year transitional period starting
on Jan. 1, 1986).

EC relations with the Maghreb countries (Algeria, Morocco and Tunisia) and with
the Mashraq countries (Egypt, Jordan, Lebanon and Syria) were regulated by trade
and co-operation agreements which had entered into force in November 1978 and by
two sets of five-year financial protocols, the first of which had covered the period until
Oct. 31, 1981, and the second of which had been concluded in June 1982 and was due
to expire at the end of October 1986. Agreements had also been reached with Cyprus,
Malta, Israel, Turkey and Yugoslavia. [See also 8.12.]

The agreed mandate proposed the use of quotas on specific products, with
a review in 1990 of the five most sensitive products (tomatoes, oranges,
clementines and mandarins, lemons and grapes). It envisaged increased aid

under the financial protocols, but no specific sum was approved by the ministers. Although the EC intended maintaining the volume of the Mediterranean countries' principal exports, the *Financial Times* of Nov. 26 claimed that "the plan would mean the non-member states [would lose] their advantage over Spain and Portugal".

Reports had earlier been presented by the Commission on March 30, 1984 and on July 17 and Sept. 25, 1985.

The March 1984 report was produced after the Council had instructed the Commission in early 1983 to conduct exploratory talks with all the Mediterranean countries which had co-operation agrements with the Communities. It found that "special importance should be given to the strengthening of the preferential relations of the Community to its partners in the Mediterranean regions", and suggested that greater adherence to the letter and spirit of the agreements as well as increased financial help was needed in order to win back the "unquestionably shattered trust" of the Mediterranean countries. In order to maintain the volume of the region's principal exports (i.e. citrus fruits, tomatoes, wine and olive oil) the Commission on July 17, 1985, proposed improving the preferential arrangements existing between the European Communities and the Mashraq and Maghreb countries and with Cyprus, Malta, Israel, Turkey and Yugoslavia. It was recommended that these improvements should run parallel with the opening of the Community market to Spanish goods. (Industrial products from the Mediterranean area already enjoyed free access to Community markets.) The third Commission document presented on Sept. 25 proposed greater Community investment in the non-member Mediterranean countries, particularly to increase their domestic food production.

10.22 Spanish visits to EC countries

The months preceding Spain's accession were marked by a series of visits by Spanish leaders to Community countries, during which agreements were signed with the French and UK governments in particular.

During a three-day official visit to France by King Juan Carlos and Queen Sofia, the Spanish Foreign Minister, Francisco Fernández Ordóñez, and his French counterpart, Dumas, on July 9 signed a joint declaration on friendship and co-operation, marking a new era of improved relations and providing for annual meetings between heads of government and regular formal contacts on terrorism and crime, defence, and economic and cultural issues.

On July 22 an extradition treaty was signed in London by the then UK Home Secretary, Leon Brittan, and the Spanish Minister of Justice, Fernando Ledesma. The agreement replaced a previous treaty which had expired in 1978 and covered terrorist offences and serious crime as well as fiscal and tax offences. Because Spanish law did not allow for legislation to be applied retroactively, wanted persons could only be arrested under its provisions if they left Spain and subsequently re-entered. (A new aliens law, however, which entered into force on July 24, 1985 provided for the expulsion of foreigners.)

González visited Bonn, the West German capital, for talks with Dr Kohl, on Sept. 30–Oct. 1, and Brussels on Dec. 10 for discussions with the Commission and Dr Wilfried Martens, the Belgian Prime Minister. On Jan. 20–21, 1986, he also met Craxi of Italy for a summit meeting in Taormina (Sicily), accompanied by government ministers from each country. The talks covered collaboration on military and industrial projects, and the threat of international terrorism.

10.23 Accession of Spain and Portugal (Jan. 1, 1986)

Spain and Portugal on Jan. 1, 1986, acceded to the European Communities, bringing to 12 the number of member countries in the EC.

With this third enlargement the Communities' population was increased from some 272,000,000 to over 320,000,000 and its surface area from 1,658,000 km^2 to 2,255,000 km^2. This latest enlargement (together with the earlier accession of Greece) increased the influence of the southern, less industrialized, "peripheral" countries within the EC and was expected to lead to pressure to improve the economic balance between the different regions of the Communities.

In Portugal and Spain the proportion of the population involved in agriculture (23 per cent and 18 per cent respectively) exceeded the average of 7 per cent of the Community of the Ten. Agriculture provided 8 per cent of Portugal's gross domestic product (GDP) and 6 per cent of Spain's as compared with an average of 3 per cent for the Community of the Ten. In terms of purchasing power parities (which took account of the different price structures in member countries) Spain's GDP per head in 1984 was 73 per cent of the EC average and that of Portugal was 46 per cent of the EC average.

Trade between the two Iberian countries and the EC was already substantial: in 1983, 48 per cent of all Spanish exports and 59 per cent of Portuguese exports went to the EC, while 32 per cent of Spain's imports and 39 per cent of Portugal's came from EC countries in that year. Trade between the two acceding countries was, however, much less developed: in 1984 trade with Spain amounted to 4 per cent of Portugal's exports and 7 per cent of its imports.

10.24 First meeting of enlarged European Parliament (Jan. 13, 1986)
The first meeting of the enlarged Parliament was held on Jan. 13, 1986, when 60 Spanish and 24 Portuguese delegates from their respective national parliaments attended the session pending the direct election of new members. The majority held by the right-wing parties in the Parliament was thereby reduced, although the Socialist Group was expanded considerably and remained the largest grouping with 172 seats.

The distribution of seats between the other political groupings was European People's Party (EPP or Christian Democrats)—118; European Democratic Group (EDG or Conservatives)—63; Communists and Allies Group—46; Liberal and Democratic Group—42; European Democratic Alliance—34; Rainbow Group—20; Group of the European Right—16; Non-attached—7.

Of the 60 Spanish delegates 36 members of the governing Socialist *Partido Socialista Obrero Español* (PSOE) went to the Socialist Group, 13 of the 17 members of the opposition *Coalición Popular* affiliated to the EDG while three went to the EPP and one joined the Non-attached Group; the two members of the Catalan Convergence and Union (*Convergéncia i Union*) went to the EPP and Liberals; the two members of the Basque Nationalist Party (*Partido Nacionalista Vasco*) went to the EPP and the remaining three members affiliated to the Rainbow Group, the Liberals and the EPP.

10.25 Agreement on additional trade protocols covering EFTA–Spanish and EFTA–Portuguese relations (Feb. 24, 1986)
With the accession of Spain to the EC the multilateral free trade agreement between Spain and the EFTA which had entered into force in May 1980 [see 10.5] expired on Dec. 31, 1985. Agreement on an alternative protocol covering EFTA–Spanish trade was not reached until Feb. 24, 1986.

Spain intitially insisted that its industrial exports be given immediate duty-free access to the markets of the six EFTA countries. The EFTA countries, however, had agreed to a seven-year transition period for the removal of Spanish duty on EFTA industrial exports to Spain. Since no agreement had been reached, the Swiss government on Dec. 16 decided to revoke its agreements with Spain and Portugal on trade in industrial products, and it was agreed to continue existing arrangements for the first two months of 1986 pending an agreement.

On Feb. 18, 1986, the Spanish government conceded that there should be reciprocal seven-year transitional periods, and EC–EFTA negotiations were concluded in Brussels on Feb. 24 (although the legal text of the agreement was not finalized before the first tariff reductions were due to take place on March 1).

On agricultural products the protocol extended to Spain (and also to Portugal—see 11.17) all current concessions enjoyed by the Community of the Ten in EFTA markets, while specific concessions were offered by the EC to individual EFTA member countries.

10.26 Referendum in favour of continued NATO membership

A referendum was held in Spain in March 12, 1986, on whether the country should remain in the Atlantic Alliance (NATO). In a 59.7 per cent turnout, 52.6 per cent voted in favour of staying, 39.8 per cent voted against and 7.6 per cent of the ballot papers were blank or invalid.

Spain had formally applied to join NATO on Dec. 2, 1981, as part of the process of "integrating Spain into the political, economic and defensive structures of the Western world", as stated in a resolution approved by the Spanish House of Deputies foreign affairs committee some months beforehand. The country became the 16th member of NATO on May 30, 1982, but negotiations on the completion of Spain's integration into the organization's military command structure were afterwards suspended until a referendum could be held as called for by González's government which came to power in November 1982.

Although González's Socialist Party had initially opposed Spain's continued membership of NATO, by the time of the referendum it had reversed its position and argued in favour on condition that (as stipulated in the referendum document) membership did not include incorporation into NATO's integrated military command structure, that the existing ban on installing, storing or introducing nuclear arms on Spanish territory be maintained, and that the 12,500-strong US military presence in Spain be progressively reduced. Before the referendum González affirmed his "trust in the common sense of the people who believe we are building peace with the rest of the democratic countries of Europe and who know we have broken down the barriers of two centuries of isolation".

During the campaign those calling for a withdrawal from NATO had often sought to draw on anti-US sentiment among the electorate, for whom the United States was not associated with liberation from dictatorship or economic reconstruction after the Second World War as elsewhere in Europe. The final vote was widely seen as a personal triumph for González and also as a vote confirming Spain's continued integration into Europe. As González himself stated in a party political broadcast shortly before the poll: "To vote against keeping Spain in NATO is to defend the existing link with the US and choose to be separated from Europe. To vote yes to the Atlantic Alliance is to maintain the link with Europe and to construct a joint policy for peace, security and development." (Of the 12 EC member countries, Ireland was not a member of NATO and France had withdrawn from the Nato military structure.)

11: PORTUGAL: APPLICATION AND ACCESSION

11.1 Chronology of events

Sept. 26, 1968	Appointment of Marcelo Caetano as Prime Minister following incapacitation of Salazar
July 27, 1970	Death of Salazar
July 22, 1972	Conclusion of Special Relations Agreements between EFTA countries (including Portugal) and European Communities
Jan. 1, 1973	Entry into force of Special Relations Agreement with Portugal and other EFTA countries not joining European Communities at that time
April 25, 1974	"Red Carnation" revolution. Overthrow of Caetano government by Movement of the Armed Forces
March 11, 1975	Attempted coup. Flight of former President Spínola and officers to Spain
April 25, 1975	Election of Constituent Assembly to draft Constitution
Nov. 25, 1975	Unsuccessful left-wing military putsch
April 2, 1976	Promulgation of new "socialist" Constitution
April 25, 1976	Elections to Legislative Assembly
June 27, 1976	Election of President Eanes
July 16, 1976	Swearing in of first Cabinet under new constitution with Mário Soares as Prime Minister
Sept. 20, 1976	Signature of additional protocol to Special Relations Agreement and of five-year EEC–Portugal financial protocol
March 28, 1977	Formal Portuguese application to join European Communities
Oct. 17, 1978	Opening of formal negotiations
Dec. 19, 1979	Signature of supplementary protocol revising provisions of Portuguese Special Relations Agreement
Dec. 3, 1980	Signature of agreement on further accession aid
Dec. 4, 1980	Death of Prime Minister Sá Carneiro in flying accident
Jan. 1, 1983	Entry into force of transitional protocol to 1972 trade agreement (as signed on Oct. 27, 1982)
June 9, 1983	Swearing in of centre-left Soares government
Jan. 1, 1984	Establishment of free trade in industrial goods between EFTA and European Communities

March 29, 1985   Conclusion of negotiations

April 29–30,   Agreement on bilateral relations between Spain and Portugal
1985

June 12, 1985   Signature in Lisbon of Accession Treaties

July 11, 1985   Ratification by Assembly of the Republic

Jan. 1, 1986   Accession

11.2 Background—Relations with EC and Spain

Under the dictatorship of António de Oliveira Salazar, which lasted from 1932 to 1968, and the reactionary régime of Dr Marcelo Caetano from 1968 to 1974, Portugal, like Spain under Franco, had little prospect of becoming a member of the European Communities. Instead a Special Relations Agreement was reached in 1972, which like similar agreements with other EFTA countries not joining the Communities, came into effect in January 1973. Only after the "Red Carnation Revolution" of April 1974, however, did significantly closer co-operation begin, backed by financial assistance for Portugal's economy.

The Portuguese government made its formal application to join the European Communities in March 1977, four months before Spain. Negotiations were generally admitted to be less complicated than those with Spain (not least because Portugal's relatively backward economy posed less of a threat to existing Community member country economies). Nevertheless negotiations were conducted largely in parallel despite considerable differences in economic strength, structure and activities between the two countries of the Iberian peninsular. This chapter should accordingly be read in conjunction with Chapter 10.

The question of Portugal's relations with Spain was in many ways more sensitive for Portugal than its relations with the Community countries, since Portugal's trade deficit with its neighbour was far greater than that with its principal Community trading partners. An agreement on this issue did not emerge until late April 1985.

11.3 Portuguese steps towards association with the Communities (June 1962, November 1970)

In the wake of the UK's first application to join the EEC in 1961, the Portuguese government on June 4, 1962, delivered an application to the EEC in Brussels, although without specifying what form of association or membership was sought. Negotiations were scheduled for Feb. 11, 1963, on the possible terms of Portuguese co-operation with the Communities, but these discussions were postponed following the breakdown of Community talks with the UK the previous month [see 1.10].

Discussions were not resumed until after the Hague summit of Community heads of state and government on Dec. 1–2, 1969, when the participants "reaffirmed their agreement on the principle of the enlargement of the Community" and undertook to reopen discussions with non-applicant EFTA countries [see 2.21]. As part of these discussions a meeting was held in Brussels on Nov. 24, 1970, between Portuguese representatives and the Council of Ministers.

At this meeting Dr Rui Patrício, the Minister for Foreign Affairs in Caetano's government, welcomed the Communities' undertaking in the Hague communiqué.

Portugal had, he said, been among the founder members of NATO, the OEEC (forerunner of the OECD) and EFTA, and had taken part in the liberalization of trade, services and capital movements over past years.

Emphasizing the importance of foreign trade to his country, the Minister pointed out that, as regards European Portugal, imports represented 26 per cent of gross national product and exports 17 per cent; 24 per cent of her exports and 40 per cent of her imports were exchanged with the six EC member states, and 72 and 69 per cent respectively with the combined EC and EFTA.

Turning to the position of the Portuguese economy, Dr Patrício said that there was a clear difference between per capita income in Portugal and in the Community member countries; industrial development had largely taken place only since the Second World War, and in future years it would be vital to establish new industries so that standards of living should approximate to those in the rest of Western Europe. Similarly, there were various difficulties connected with the low level of agricultural productivity, which could only be overcome slowly. Accordingly, Portugal would in certain cases seek special treatment in order to enable her to adapt to the new conditions of competition resulting from the negotia ions for both industry and agriculture.

Portugal's level of economic development and certain aspects of her constitutional principles would mean that she could not become a full member of the Communities; instead the government sought an "appropriate formula" to regulate relations between the European part of Portugal and the EC with the maximum content which the negotiations might show to be possible, consistent with Article XXIV of GATT —specifically in the form of an agreement of association. The position of Portugal's non-European provinces would require a different sort of treatment, having regard to their constitutional status and their own level of economic development.

Portugal accepted in principle the progressive abolition of customs duties on trade with the EC, although some products would require special transitional arrangements, and accepted also Community rules in agriculture, right of establishment, supply of services, capital movements, social policies, competition and transport—again subject to certain transitional measures.

Finally, Dr Patrício stressed his government's wish that negotiations should proceed in parallel with those between the Communities and the applicant countries, that liberalization of trade already achieved within EFTA should not be reduced, and that all agreements with EFTA countries should enter into force simultaneously.

11.4 Negotiation and conclusion of Special Relations Agreement (1971–July 1982)

After the November 1970 meeting detailed discussions between the Commission and Portugal began on Jan. 7, 1971, but it was not until November 1971 that the Council of Ministers agreed on a negotiating mandate [see also 6.10].

This took into account the special situation for Portuguese exports of agricultural products, but several important processed products, such as tinned tuna, sardines and mackerel, were not included in the concessions. Similarly, Rui Teixeira Guerra, leader of the Portuguese negotiating team, expressed disappointment with the Communities' insistence on minimum prices for Portuguese exports of tomato concentrate, which would be exempted from duty on entry to the Communities.

Only 38 per cent of total Portuguese exports would be covered by the general terms of the agreement, representing $157,000,000 in trade, compared with imports from the Communities representing 53 per cent of Portugal's total imports and valued at $410,000,000.

Dr Patrício said on April 19, 1972, after discussions with Ministers of Community member countries, that his own government was still insisting on consideration for processed agricultural products and for wines. In addition Dr Patrício said that the Portuguese negotiators were also asking for a slower rate of reduction of import tariffs on goods from the Community, although the EC had agreed to accept part of Annex G of the EFTA Stockholm Convention providing special conditions for Portugal until 1980. Portugal also hoped to extend these terms beyond 1980 and to gain protection for new industry.

Following a further round of talks with ministers of EFTA and EC countries, Dr Valentim Xavier Pintado, Portuguese Secretary of State for Commerce, declared in Lisbon on May 11: "In effect, unless these conditions are changed, more than a quarter of our exports destined for the enlarged Community will be subject to restrictions, and tariff barriers will again be erected in relation to about 40 per cent of our exports to the existing members of EFTA who are joining the Common Market where these barriers have been eliminated." Dr Pintado added that the terms were especially unfavourable to the textile industry, commenting that "it is difficult to justify discrimination against the industry because of its efficiency".

The Special Relations Agreement was eventually signed between the Communities and Portugal on July 22, 1972, along with those between the Communities and Austria, Finland, Iceland, Sweden and Switzerland, including Liechtenstein [see 6.13 for full details]. The Agreement, which entered into force on Jan. 1, 1973, contained a number of clauses concerning the economy of Portugal.

Special arrangements were made to take account of Portugal's relatively low level of industrial development, including provision for a longer transitional period extending to Jan. 1, 1980, for cuts on some products imported from the Communities and to Jan. 1, 1985, for a smaller number of goods, both sectors covering those products included in Annex G of the EFTA agreement with Portugal. The remaining industrial goods would be subject to the same schedule of tariff cuts as applied by the Communities, Ireland and the other five EFTA non-applicant countries.

In common with the other EFTA countries concerned, Portugal was to continue to trade freely with the UK, Norway and Denmark but was also permitted to maintain the same schedule of tariff cuts which had given her additional protection within EFTA, although a few reductions would be deferred in order to achieve parity of treatment for all members of the enlarged Communities by 1977.

Italy had been particularly concerned during the negotiations over the prospect of increased competition from Portuguese exports of tomato concentrate, canned fish and wine, but a compromise was eventually reached on July 19, 1972, under which Britain (the market for about half of all Portuguese tomato concentrate exports), Denmark, Norway and Ireland would pay a minimum price of 270 EUA per metric ton while the existing members of the Communities would pay a minimum of 345 EUA. In addition, Portugal undertook to export not more than 70,000 tons of concentrate, of which 20,000 tons would go to the six original members of the Communities and the remainder to the four new members.

On a quota of 350,000 hectolitres of port wine Portugal was granted tariff reductions of 60 per cent for bottled wine and of 50 per cent for wine in casks; other types of wine were granted a reduction of 30 per cent, with quotas of 15,000 hectolitres of Madeira and 3,000 hectolitres of Setubal muscatel.

Canned fish products were mostly granted a reduction of 40 per cent on existing tariff levels on condition that certain price criteria were respected, while other canned fish products, including tuna, were allowed a 30 per cent reduction.

Tariff reductions were also granted on some fish and molluscs, pine and conifer seeds, locust beans, some fish-liver oils, flours and meals of meat and fish, dehydrated vegetables (except onions) and, in certain months of the year, on new potatoes, fresh tomatoes, grapes and strawberries.

In addition a number of other Portuguese exports to the Communities were subject to indicative ceilings, including cork, cotton yarn and fabrics, fabrics of man-made fibre, jute fabrics, rope, and knitted and other garments.

Special arrangements were also made whereby Portugal could establish, increase or reintroduce ad valorem duties not exceeding 15 per cent (or in special cases 20 per cent) in order to protect new industries, although these duties could not cover more than 7.5 per cent of the value of Portuguese imports from the members of the enlarged Communities in 1970. It was also agreed that Portugal could impose or maintain quantitative restrictions on motor vehicles and a very few iron and steel products up to the end of 1979 and on some petroleum products up to the end of 1984.

[See 11.9 for transitional protocol to the 1972 agreement which was signed on Oct. 27, 1982.]

11.5 The "Red Carnation" revolution (1974–76)
The "Red Carnation" revolution of April 25, 1974, brought down Caetano's government, appointing instead Gen. António de Spínola as President with a junta of national salvation committed to free elections within a year. Although at first the revolution was widely welcomed internationally (by both democratic and authoritarian governments), the ensuing period of instability left foreign countries unwilling immediately to lend substantial support to the country.

After the revolution and just before being appointed Foreign Minister under the premiership of Adelino da Palma Carlos on May 16, 1974, Dr Mário Soares had discussions with members of the European Commission in Brussels. Da Palma Carlos and Dr Soares also visited Brussels on June 26, and at a meeting of the EEC–Portugal joint committee the following day the Portuguese delegation expressed its desire to extend co-operation, as provided for in the 1972 agreement, and to encourage financial assistance from the Community. The Community delegation indicated its intention of meeting Portugal's wishes on economic, financial and technical aid within the context of the country's stated desire to restore democracy.

The continuing instability in Portugal after April 1974, and uncertainty as to the ultimate outcome of the revolutionary process, nevertheless meant that substantive negotiations did not immediately take place.

A wave of strikes in mid-1974, rapid decolonization in Portugal's African colonies, the resignation of Gen. Spínola as President on Sept. 30, 1974, and his replacement by Gen. Francisco da Costa Gomes, the C.-in-C. of the Army, saw the country rapidly moving into a situation where it was increasingly difficult to ascertain where real authority lay. Following an abortive coup attempt on March 11, 1975, Gen. Spínola and 18 officers fled to Spain. The junta of national salvation set up by him was replaced by a supreme revolutionary council (CRS), whose members assumed the right to veto Cabinet decisions and to initiate legislation. Banks and other sectors of the economy were nationalized. Party leaders and the Armed Forces Movement (*Movimento das Forcas Armadas*—MFA) on April 11 signed a pact giving the MFA the right to veto decisions taken by a constitutional assembly (for which elections were held on April 24); the pact also stated that the President was to be an officer who could dissolve the assembly after consultation with the Cabinet and the CRS.

A succession of transitional governments and increasing divisions within the MFA and other organizations left the country without clear control and on Nov. 25, 1975, radical military elements attempted unsuccessfully to seize power. In April 1976 however, a "socialist" Constitution was ratified by the constitutional assembly; democratic, parliamentary elections were held on April 25 and presidential elections on June 27, 1976. The first government under the new Constitution was sworn in on July 16 with Dr Soares heading a minority Socialist Party Cabinet and with Gen. António Ramalho dos Santos Eanes as President.

Against the uncertain background of the turbulent first two years after the 1974 revolution, little progress was made on Portugal's links with the Communities.

Sir Christopher Soames, then EC Commissioner for External Affairs, visited Lisbon on Feb. 12–13, 1975. The European Council at its meeting on May 26 in Dublin, Ireland, called for the strengthening of links between the Communities and Portugal, and discussions were again held within the EEC–Portugal joint committee on May 28, but at the European Council meeting in Brussels on July 16–17, 1975, Community leaders while reaffirming "that the European Community is prepared to initiate discussions on closer economic and financial co-operation with Portugal", also pointed out that "in accordance with its historical and political traditions, the European Community can only give support to a democracy of a pluralist nature".

On the basis of this statement, the Foreign Ministers of the Nine on Oct. 6–7, 1975, held talks in Luxembourg with a delegation of the transitional Portuguese government of Admiral José Baptista Pinheiro de Azevedo formed the previous month, at which it was agreed that the Communities would make up to 150,000,000 EUA available to Portugal in emergency aid. However, although the Nine also announced (on Oct. 7) that substantive negotiations on improving the EEC–Portugal trade agreement would be put in hand before the end of the year, the Council of Ministers subsequently failed to agree on an appropriate negotiating mandate by that time.

11.6 Additional protocol to EEC–Portugal free trade agreement —Financial protocol (1976)

An additional protocol to the EEC–Portugal free trade agreement was not signed until Sept. 20, 1976, when Foreign Ministers of the Nine and José Medeiros Ferreira, then their Portuguese counterpart, also signed a five-year EEC–Portugal financial protocol in Brussels.

Designed to assist Portugal in overcoming some of the economic and social difficulties experienced since the 1974 revolution, the protocols provided respectively for (i) increased trade, industrial and agricultural co-operation between the two sides under an "evolutive" clause of the free trade agreement, and (ii) the implementation and extension to a maximum of 200,000,000 EUA of the emergency financial aid agreement reached by the two sides in October 1975.

Pending ratification of the additional protocol, its commercial provisions were to come into force immediately under an interim agreement also signed on Sept. 20, while the financial protocol was expected to come into effect on Jan. 1, 1978.

Although it was initially envisaged that this financial protocol would be implemented over a five-year period, the Council decided on Jan. 14–15, 1980, that the whole amount available would be placed at Portugal's disposal over a shortened three-year period.

11.7 Portugal's application for membership of the European Communities— Negotiations (1977–80)

Signature of these two protocols was understood to be regarded by the Portuguese government as a preliminary to the submission of a formal application to become a full member of the European Communities, and this was duly presented by the government of Dr Soares on March 28, 1977.

During the course of an EFTA heads of government meeting in Vienna on May 13, 1977, Dr Soares, then Portuguese Foreign Minister, explained that his government would not leave EFTA until it was able to join the European Communities. The other EFTA members at the meeting greeted the application "with understanding and sympathy". They noted "that this step is compatible with the preservation of the free trade established within EFTA and with the maintenance of close relations and co-operation with all EFTA countries" and recognized "the importance of supporting Portugal in its efforts to overcome its economic difficulties, thus contributing to the consolidation of Portuguese democratic institutions".

As far as the Communities were concerned the Commission on May 19 forwarded to the Council of Ministers an Opinion recommending (as it also did in an Opinion presented on Dec. 1, 1978, on the Spanish application) that the Council should agree promptly and unequivocally to the early opening of negotiations, although in the light of the complex economic, structural and administrative changes which needed to be agreed, no detailed timetable for the eventual accession of either Portugal or Spain was proposed.

Negotiations were accordingly officially opened in Luxembourg on Oct. 17, 1978, although substantive negotiations did not get under way until 1980 [see 10.6], when two ministerial meetings were held on Feb. 5 and July 22.

11.8 Signature of Community–Portugal supplementary protocol and pre-accession aid agreement (1979–80)

At ceremonies held in Brussels in December 1979 and December 1980 respectively, representatives of the European Communities and of the Portuguese government signed (i) a supplementary protocol revising the provisions of both the EEC–Portugal free trade agreement in force since Jan. 1, 1973, and the additional protocol to the agreement signed in September 1976, and (ii) an agreement concerning the provision to Portugal of pre-accession aid totalling 275,000,000 EUA.

The supplementary protocol, which was signed on Dec. 19, 1979, and which entered into force on Jan. 1, 1980, provided specifically for (i) the maintenance of the status quo reached in the dismantling of tariffs on industrial products under the existing agreement as revised in 1976, (ii) the extension of the period within which Portugal was required to make tariff reductions in certain sectors, with the aim of protecting Portuguese emergent industries, (iii) special Portuguese import arrangements for motor vehicles, again with the object of protecting that country's local motor industry, (iv) an increase in Community quotas for the import of certain paper products from Portugal and (v) improved concessions by the Community in respect of Portuguese agricultural exports, notably fish and wine. It was officially agreed by both sides that the December 1979 supplementary protocol should constitute the basis for conducting accession negotiations on the eventual achievement of a full customs union.

The pre-accession aid agreement with Portugal, which was signed on Dec. 3, 1980, marked a further important stage in the Communities' policy of providing financial support for Portugal's economic development as initiated under earlier agreements concluded in 1975–76. The actual amount to be provided under the new agreement was, however, considerably less than the original request of the Portuguese government that a total of 425,000,000 EUA should be made available mainly in the form of grants rather than EIB loans.

The pre-accession aid agreement entered into force on Jan. 1, 1981, after the completion of the necessary procedures by the two sides. It was intended to facilitate Portugal's eventual integration into the Communities by making Community aid available for the financing of specific operations undertaken by the Portuguese government in the pre-accession period with the aim of modernizing the country's economic structures.

Of the total Community aid of 275,000,000 EUA to be made available, 150,000,000 EUA would be in the form of loans from the EIB, of which 125,000,000 EUA would attract an interest rate subsidy of 3 per cent to be charged to the Community budget. These funds would be used for the financing in whole or in part of investment projects designed to increase productivity and to strengthen the Portuguese economy, with particular reference to the improvement of industrial structures, the modernization of Portuguese agriculture and fisheries, the development of infrastructures and the encouragement of regional development within Portugal.

The other 125,000,000 EUA would be in the form of grant aid to be charged to the Community budget, with 25,000,000 EUA being used to finance the aforementioned interest rate subsidy and 100,000,000 EUA being allocated for the financing in whole or in part of co-operation projects or programmes and of technical assistance operations. As regards the selection of projects or programmes which would attract Community aid, special attention would be given to those aimed at encouraging (i) the restructuring, modernization and development of small and medium-sized businesses, (ii) the improvement of production and marketing structures in agriculture and fisheries, (iii) the creation of infrastructures aimed at facilitating more balanced development between regions and (iv) the establishment of an integrated national vocational training policy based on a network of vocational training centres.

11.9 Progress in negotiations (1981–82)

Dr Francisco Pinto Balsemão, the Portuguese Prime Minister, said in Lisbon on April 13, 1981, that Portugal sought to accede to the Communities as soon as possible, but that the question of negotiating the right conditions for membership was more important than the actual date of accession.

Official Portuguese comments increasingly reflected an acceptance that the original target date of Jan. 1, 1983, was no longer realistic, and that detailed and serious negotiations would take some time to complete, notably regarding textile exports from Portugal to the Community, the free movement of workers, and agricultural issues.

Lorenzo Natali, then European Commissioner with responsibility for enlargement and Mediterranean affairs, visited Lisbon for talks in early May 1981, and later in that month the fourth ministerial-level joint negotiating meeting was held in Brussels (following those in October 1978 and February and July 1980), issuing a statement on May 18 which comprised a review of progress to date.

Agreement was reached on a traffic sector declaration, but not on the question of Portugal's textile exports to the Communities. The Commission had reportedly proposed that in the post-accession period there should be a mechanism under which consultations on voluntary restraint would be held when a given level of exports was reached, whereas representatives of some member states sought to limit Portuguese textile access, below the existing level, for a transitional period.

In October 1981 João Salgueiro, the Portuguese Minister of Finance, led a delegation which visited Luxembourg for talks with Commission officials, and presented the Portuguese proposals on a number of issues including capital transfers, freedom of labour movement, customs union and unrestricted textile access.

Dr Balsemão visited London on Dec. 9 for talks with Margaret Thatcher, the British Prime Minister, who reportedly agreed that the aim should be to end negotiations in 1982, so that ratification procedures could be completed in 1983 in time for Portuguese accession in January 1984; it was noted by the British side that there was no Community requirement that Portugal and Spain should necessarily accede simultaneously. Dr

Balsemão said at a press conference on Dec. 12 in Lisbon, at the end of a visit by President François Mitterrand of France and a high-level ministerial delegation, that Portugal was aiming for full Community membership by the beginning of 1984. He later reportedly agreed with Commission officials on a timetable for the remaining negotiations (during a visit to Brussels on Jan. 24–25, 1982, on which occasion he also had talks with Léo Tindemans, the Belgian Minister of Foreign Affairs and then President-in-office of the Communities' Council of Ministers).

Issues on which agreement was reached at a joint ministerial meeting in Brussels on Feb. 22, 1982, were capital movements, regional policy, transport, rights of establishment and freedom to provide services, nuclear co-operation and economic and financial questions. Another technical session was held in late April, at which the Portuguese side indicated willingness to introduce the Communities' system of VAT over a three-year rather than a five-year transitional period.

Within Portugal, where opposition to Community membership had hitherto been confined principally to the Communist Party, strong criticism was expressed on March 31, 1982, by Pedro Ferraz da Costa, the chairman of the Confederation of Portuguese Industry (CIP), over the government's handling of accession negotiations.

Da Costa spoke of the rush by Portuguese politicians to hasten entry to the Communities; he said that the CIP was against joining the Communities in a position of inferiority and would oppose membership on current terms "by all means possible". He made it clear that his criticisms were directed primarily at what he described as Portugal's ruinous economic structures, and at the apparent incapacity of politicians in contending with corruption, tax evasion and collective irresponsibility, and he called for urgent, firm and determined reform of the 1976 Constitution.

During a visit to Lisbon on April 14–16, 1982, Gaston Thorn was reportedly reluctant to give firm guarantees about the timing of Portugal's accession, and he warned of the amount of work still to be done on negotiating dossiers such as agriculture, fisheries, textiles and freedom of labour movement. Dr Balsemão emphasized on this occasion that, if Portugal were able to complete accession negotiations more rapidly than Spain, there would be no justification for delaying Portuguese accession for the sake of simultaneity with Spain, and he added that Portugal would in no circumstances accept linkage of the two sets of negotiations.

After the Feb. 22 meeting mentioned above, ministerial-level negotiating sessions, at which further appreciable progress was made, were held during 1982 on June 22, Sept. 21 and Nov. 22.

At the September meeting ministers resolved key questions regarding the textiles trade, ECSC, external relations, taxation and the right of establishment.

On the question of textiles (a major issue, since they represented 42 per cent of Portugal's industrial output and 33 per cent of its total exports, while production costs were 20–30 per cent below Community levels), Portugal accepted a three-year transition period on all products with an annual growth in shipments ranging from 7 per cent to 13 per cent according to product. Ministers also agreed on the implementation of VAT in Portugal and on a seven-year transition period after which foreign banks could be established in Portugal (agreement on the latter issue having eluded ministers on June 22). In the light of the progress made at this meeting, major issues still requiring agreement were agriculture, the free movement of labour and other social issues, regional policy and fisheries.

A transitional protocol to the 1972 trade agreement between Portugal and the Communities was also signed by both parties on Oct. 27 and adopted by the Council on Dec. 2, and entered into force on Jan. 1, 1983.

It was designed to allow Portugal to postpone further tariff dismantling for certain industrial products while simultaneously cutting tariffs generally vis-à-vis the EC, and was originally designed to apply until Dec. 31, 1984, or until Portugal joined the Communities. Proposals were subsequently made, in the light of progress on negotiations, to extend its validity to Dec. 31, 1985.

11.10 Community and Spanish problems hamper negotiations (1983–84)

During 1983 ministerial-level meetings were held on Jan. 25, March 15, May 25, July 18, and Nov. 29. At the May and November meetings Community proposals on fisheries and agriculture respectively were presented, while discussions were actually completed during the year on the environment, consumer protection, approximation of laws (except patents) and Euratom.

In June 1983, some months after Felipe González came to power at the head of a Socialist government in Spain, Dr Soares was sworn in as Prime Minister of a Socialist–Social Democratic coalition government which was able to provide a period of relative governmental stability. A series of austerity measures was also introduced and a loan agreement reached with the IMF in October 1983 enabling the country's substantial foreign debt problem to be brought under some control and beginning a process of restructuring of the economy in preparation for Portugal's accession to the Communities.

During the year Natali visited Lisbon on March 4–5 and again on Oct. 27–28. In a television interview given at the time of the latter visit Jaime Gama, Minister of Foreign Affairs in the Socialist government of Dr Soares, stated: "The Communities' internal problems, particularly those concerning its own resources, have led to an unacceptable delay in the treatment of the Portuguese dossiers. . . . Portugal must not be expected to accept willingly and silently the successive postponements, the vague decisions, the repeated excuses. . . ." Dr Soares visited Athens for talks with Dr Andreas Papandreou, the Greek Prime Minister, on July 18–19, and Paris for talks with President Mitterrand on Nov. 26, and sent a letter in November to all 10 member countries' governments asking for a commitment to enlargement by Jan. 1, 1986. [For failure of the European Communities to solve internal Community problems at this time see 10.11.]

During 1984, ministerial-level meetings were held on Jan. 23, March 13, May 15, June 18, July 23, Sept. 3 and 18, Oct. 3 and Dec. 18–19.

During the year Thorn, then President of the European Commission, and the following heads of state and government also made visits to Lisbon to emphasize their commitment to enlargement: Pierre Mauroy, then French Prime Minister, (Jan. 19–21), Margaret Thatcher, the UK Prime Minister (April 17–19), Bettino Craxi (May 3–4), Mitterrand (June 27, a visit followed by a similar visit to Madrid and immediately after the Fontainebleau summit meeting of June 25–26—see 10.12), Thorn (July 3) and Dr Garret FitzGerald, the Irish Prime Minister (Sept. 25–26). As well as his visit to Dublin on Oct. 24–25 [see below], Dr Soares visited London on Nov. 20–23.

At the May ministerial-level meeting the Community ministers presented another statement on fisheries, following an agreement reached at a Council of (Foreign) Ministers meeting the previous day, while agreement was reached on the question of zero-rating for VAT purposes, on direct investment in Portugal, and on certain agricultural questions.

Progress thereafter was hampered by the lack of success in parallel Spanish negotiations. Nevertheless, following the Council of (Foreign) Ministers meeting on Oct. 22–23, Portugal was informed of Community agreements on social policy, olive oil and the question of transition periods for Portugal's sugar imports for its refining industry. In response to a letter sent by Dr Soares on Oct. 19 to all 10 Community governments asking them for assurances that proposals would be produced enabling accession by 1986, Dr FitzGerald, who was President of the Council for the second half of 1984, signed a joint statement in Dublin with Dr Soares and Natali on Oct. 24, declaring the "irreversibility of the process of Portuguese integration into the European Communities", the determination of the parties involved "to reach mutually satisfactory negotiated conclusions in the very near future" and their commitment to accession by Jan. 1, 1986. (See 10.14 for similar statement also presented to Morán on Oct. 23.)

11.11 Funds under Community aid agreements with Spain and Portugal

Funds under the pre-accession aid agreements with both Spain and Portugal were increased in June 1984. Loans through the European Investment Bank (EIB) totalling 200,000,000 ECU and 150,000,000 ECU for Spain and Portugal respectively had been available since January 1981 and had already been increased by 100,000,000 ECU and 75,000,000 ECU respectively for the period from July 1, 1983, to June 30, 1984. (1.00 ECU = £0.59 = US$0.72 as at April 1, 1985.) The increased funds (which the Council of (Foreign) Ministers at its meeting in Luxembourg on June 18–19 recommended be made available) amounted to 250,000,000 ECU for Spain and 150,000,000 ECU for Portugal for the period from July 1, 1984, to Dec. 31, 1985.

A further 50,000,000 ECU in grants for Portugal (on top of the grant aid already available since 1981) was also agreed on March 13 by the Council, largely to implement structural improvements in Portugal's agriculture in advance of accession.

In addition the Portuguese government announced a detailed regional policy on July 4, 1984, as part of its three-year economic and financial recovery plan. The measures were designed to allow Portugal, which was in any case expected to become a participant in the Communities' common agricultural policy, to take full advantage of Community regional aid available through the ERDF and the European Social Fund.

11.12 Conclusion of negotiations (March 1985)

As with Spain, agreement on all major issues concerning enlargement was reached at the end of March 1985 [for full details see 10.15], and on March 29 a joint announcement on the conclusion of negotiations was made (after 27 ministerial negotiating sessions had been held between Portugal and the Communities as compared with 29 between Spain and the Communities).

After the announcement Dr Soares declared that "everything will change" and that "in five years Portugal will be a different country".

11.13 Bilateral agreement between Spain and Portugal (April 1985)

A bilateral agreement regulating relations between Spain and Portugal during the 10-year transition period after accession was also reached by Foreign Ministers Morán and Gama on April 29–30, 1985. This was seen as removing the only remaining major obstacle to the signing of the European Communities membership treaties in June.

Although relations between Spain and Portugal had cooled with Spain's cancellation of an annual November meeting in 1984, negotiations on the fisheries question in particular had been reopened in early March 1985 at the Commission's request.

Informal discussions were also held between González and Dr Soares on April 9 during a conference of the Confederation of Socialist Parties of the European Community in Madrid.

The April agreement covered both fisheries and customs union issues. The fisheries aspect replaced a contested 1969 agreement through which Spain had obtained "historic rights" to fish in Portugal's coastal waters. Under the new agreement both countries were barred from fishing in each other's 12-mile coastal waters except in a few common border areas. In the zone between 12 and 200 miles offshore, Spanish or Portuguese boats respectively were to be restricted by licence (as would be the case for other Community fishing boats in these waters). On bilateral trade, Spanish import duties and restrictions were to be abolished from January 1986 except for textiles, cork and some petrochemical products where quotas were to be kept for four or five years. Bilateral terms on tomato paste and fish conserves were left until terms with the Communities had been finalized.

The agreement marked a considerable improvement in relations between the two countries, while Dr Soares described a subsequent meeting between González and himself on May 25–26 in Alcántara (in Spain, near the border) as having "major importance" for both countries and for bilateral relations.

11.14 Signature and ratification of Accession Treaty (June 12 and July 11, 1985)—Fall of government

At the ceremonies for signing the Treaty of Accession held on June 12, 1985, in both Lisbon and Madrid [see 10.17, 10.18 for full details concerning the ceremony and terms] the Portuguese ministers to sign the treaty were Dr Soares, then Prime Minister, Rui Machete, then Deputy Prime Minister, Gama, then Foreign Minister, and Ernâni Lopes, then Minister for Finance and Planning.

Speaking on June 11, Dr Soares stated: "It has been a long journey and we know we will face many difficulties but in the end we have faith in the Community and its future." The following day he described the signing as "one of the most significant events in contemporary Portuguese history" which represented a "fundamental choice for a progressive and modern future". Alvaro Barreto, then Portuguese Agriculture Minister, conceded that the "modernization of our country is absolutely linked to accession to the Community", but he also expressed the apprehension of both the country's industry and its agriculture about the changes facing Portugal's backward economy when he said that he knew there would be a "tremendous shock".

However, one day after the ceremony the Social Democrats (*Partido Social Demócrata*—PSD), which had formed the coalition with the Socialists (*Partido Socialista Português*—PSP) under Dr Soares in June 1983, withdrew from the government, eventually obliging Dr Soares to resign on June 25 and precipitating a general election held on Oct. 6. The party's withdrawal followed months of instability within the PSD over its position towards government policy and towards the presidential elections due in December 1985.

The day before the dissolution of the Assembly of the Republic (parliament) to make way for the election, the Assembly on July 11 approved the Accession Treaty. All the delegates except the Communists, members of the Portuguese Democratic Movement (MDP) and the one Green deputy (who all sat together in the parliament) voted in favour of ratification.

11.15 Assembly and Presidential elections (Oct. 6, 1985, Jan. 26 and Feb. 16, 1986)

In the general election which followed on Oct. 6, 1985, the PSD became the largest single party in the Assembly and on Nov. 6, Aníbal Cavaço Silva, the

PSD leader since May 1985, was sworn in Prime Minister of a minority PSD government. This move towards the right was counterbalanced by the election, after two rounds held on Jan. 26 and Feb.16, 1986, of Dr Soares as the new Portuguese President in place of Gen. Eanes, who had served two terms and was debarred from standing again by the Constitution.

11.16 Nomination of Commissioner
António Cardoso e Cunha was on Dec. 2, 1985, nominated as the Portuguese representative on the EC Commission. He had been Agriculture and Fisheries Minister from January 1980 to August 1981 and at the new Commission's first sitting on Jan. 3, 1986, was given the Fisheries portfolio.

11.17 Withdrawal from EFTA—EC accession
Portugal continued to be an EFTA member until Dec. 31, 1985, after which trade relations were regulated by the Special Relations Agreements between the individual EFTA countries and the EC.

The few remaining obstacles to free trade in industrial goods were to be phased out over a seven-year period. On the question of Portuguese textile exports, Portugal agreed on Feb. 18, 1986, to the establishment of a system of "administrative co-operation" involving the exchange of statistical information to monitor textile sales in EFTA countries. (The Industrial Development Fund set up by EFTA in 1976 to finance new fixed investment in small and medium-sized businesses in Portugal was to continue to function until 2002 as originally planned.)

Portugal's accession to the EC took effect from Jan. 1, 1986.

11.18 First session of enlarged Parliament (Jan. 13, 1986)
At the first meeting of the enlarged European Parliament held on Jan. 13, 1986, the distribution of Portugal's 24 seats among the different Portuguese parties reflected the seat distribution in the National Assembly after the October 1985 general election, pending the direct election of delegates. The seat distribution among the different European Parliament groupings is given below.

The nine PSD delegates affiliated with the Liberal and Democratic Group; the six PSP members joined the Socialist Group; the four delegates from the Democratic Renewal Party (*Partido Renovador Democrático*, which had contested the National Assembly elections for the first time in October 1985) went to the European Democratic Alliance; the three Communist delegates affiliated with the Communist Group, and the two members of the Democratic Social Centre Party joined the European People's Party grouping.

[For full details of distribution of seats see 10.24.]

12: AFTER THE TWELVE: MEASURES TO REFORM THE COMMUNITIES

12.1 Chronology of events

January–September 1981	Genscher–Colombo initiative for a "European Act" on political co-operation
June 19, 1983	Signature of solemn declaration on European union by EC heads of state and government
Feb. 14, 1984	European Parliament's approval of plan for "treaty establishing the European union"
May 24, 1984	Mitterrand's speech to European Parliament calling for relaunch of EC
June 12 and Oct. 26–27, 1984	Revival of WEU as forum for European defence collaboration
June 25–26, 1984	Fontainebleau summit agreement on solutions to internal Community problems
March 19, 1985	Report of ad hoc committee on institutional affairs
June 19, 1985	Report of ad hoc committee on a people's Europe
June 28–29, 1985	Milan summit decision to hold intergovernmental conference on common foreign and security policy and on reform of the Treaty of Rome
September–December 1985	Sessions of intergovernmental conference
Dec. 2–3, 1985	Luxembourg summit agreement on provisional texts for Treaty of Rome amendments
Dec. 11, 1985, and Jan. 16, 1986	European Parliament's votes on reforms
Dec. 16, 1985	Foreign Ministers' agreement on reforms to Treaty of Rome
Feb. 17, 1986	Signature of reforms by nine Community member countries
Feb. 27, 1986	Danish referendum approving reforms
Feb. 28, 1986	Signature of reforms by Denmark, Greece and Italy

12.2 Beyond enlargement

The enlargement of the EC to a Community of Twelve highlighted the budgetary, agricultural, policy-development and decision-making problems of the Communities. It was not difficult to foresee greater problems in achieving consensus between 12 states than between 10, nine or six. Yet the accession of Spain and Portugal was also seen as marking the end of a difficult period in the Communities' development when member countries had been obliged to concentrate on solving problems of Community budget contributions and budgetary discipline as well as the enlargement negotiations. Almost immediately after the conclusion of these negotiations, discussions were broached, which led, as a first step, to an agreement on a "Single European Act" reforming the Treaty of Rome for the first time in the history of the Communities.

The enlargement thus provided both an opportunity for and the necessity of (i) a reform of existing policies, (ii) the development of new policies, and (iii) a streamlining of the decision-making process to enable these changes to take place.

In general terms, the third enlargement of the Communities (and the earlier accession of Greece) shifted the weight of the Communities' economies southwards and emphasized the differences between the industrialized north and the more rural south. The key to a reduction in north-south disparities was regarded partly as lying in the development of social and regional policies which favoured the less advantaged, peripheral sectors of the EC economy.

In specific terms, the third enlargement, which brought the prospect of surpluses of olive oil, wine and other Mediterranean products as well as those already existing in such northern products as wheat and milk, also necessitated a reform of the CAP, if its costs were not to increase seriously out of control. The negotiations on Integrated Mediterranean Programmes, on curbing wine production etc. described in the preceding chapters thus formed an integral part of an attempt to prepare the Communities for the impact of Spain and Portugal's accession.

Proposals for a reform of the Communities had these specific problems in mind, while often also supporting the wider, less tangible goal of laying "the foundations of an ever closer union among the peoples of Europe", as envisaged in the preamble to the Treaty of Rome.

12.3 Initiatives furthering European integration
Proposals envisaging closer European integration had been put forward on many occasions prior to the accession of Portugal and Spain. Many sought to increase the use of majority voting on policy-making decisions in the Council and to reduce the number of cases where member countries could apply the "Luxembourg compromise" of 1966, which had established the right of veto on decisions if a member country's "vital interests" were at stake.

Reforms proposed during the 1970s included the 1969 Barre plan and two reports drawn up in 1970 by Pierre Werner, then Prime Minister of Luxembourg and Minister of Finance, on economic and monetary union [see also 6.2]; the 1970 Davignon Report on political unification [ibid.]; the 1972 Vedel Report on increasing the European Parliament's decision-making powers; the Tindemans Report published in 1976 on ways and means of progressing towards European union, and the 1979 "Three Wise Men's Report" on the Communities' institutional structure and the prospective accession of Greece, Spain and Portugal.

More recent proposals included the so-called **Genscher–Colombo initiative** which was originally launched in January 1981 by Hans-Dietrich Genscher, the West German Foreign Minister and Free Democratic Party chairman, and was subsequently modified in the course of discussion within the West German Cabinet (on Sept. 18) and with Emilio Colombo, the Italian Foreign Minister.

It envisaged giving a new impetus to co-operation in the political sphere, notably by initiating co-ordination of members' security policy, by means of a solemn (but not legally binding) declaration—referred to as the "European Act". This declaration would also make explicit the role of Community bodies (most notably the European Council itself) which had grown up outside the institutional framework as laid down in the original treaties of Rome. The proposals emphasized the importance of strengthening the European Parliament's involvement in decision-making and policy review, and also suggested increased support staff to give continuity to the work of the rotating presidency of the European Council. Also proposed was the creation of machinery under which member countries could rapidly convene Community meetings to respond to crises and could liaise prior to the launching of individual initiatives in foreign policy. Another important feature of the proposal was that decision-making within the Community institutions should be improved by a return to greater reliance on majority voting, with member states being able to plead "vital interests" only in exceptional circumstances.

The provisions for co-ordination on security matters (hitherto not regarded as an area of Community competence) provoked particular concern on the part of Ireland, the only Community member state which was not also a member of NATO. Among other member states doubts were raised—particularly in the smaller countries—about the desirability of an explicit commitment to (and machinery for) furthering European union, while the French government submitted a memorandum on "Revitalization of the Community" which stressed the need to concentrate on the battle against unemployment and avoided specific reference to the development of greater co-ordination in the political field.

The initiative was welcomed by the European Parliament on Nov. 19, 1981, while the heads of state and government at their meeting in London on Nov. 26–27 "received" the proposals and "invited the Foreign Ministers in co-operation with the Commission to examine and clarify the German–Italian proposals and to report back to a future meeting of the European Council".

A "**solemn declaration on European union**" was eventually signed by the heads of government and the Foreign Ministers of the member countries on June 19, 1983, at the end of the European Council meeting held in Stuttgart, West Germany. The meeting also approved a plan for the "relaunch" of the European Communities "to tackle the most pressing problems facing the Community so as to provide a solid basis for the further dynamic development of the Community".

The declaration set out the implementation to date of each institution's potential as defined in the Treaty of Rome, and the further possibilities of increased co-ordination and development within and between Council, Parliament, Commission and Court of Justice, and listed the following objectives:

"To strengthen and continue the development of the Communities, which are the nucleus of European union, by reinforcing existing policies and elaborating new policies within the framework of the Treaties of Paris and Rome:

"To strengthen and develop European political co-operation through the elaboration and adoption of joint positions and joint action, on the basis of intensified consultations in the area of foreign policy, including the co-ordination of the positions of member states on the political and economic aspects of security, so as to promote and facilitate the progressive development of such positions and actions in a growing number of foreign policy fields;

"To promote, to the extent that these activities cannot be carried out within the framework of the Treaties, (i) closer co-operation on cultural matters, in order to affirm the awareness of a common cultural heritage as an element in the European identity; (ii) approximation of certain areas of the legislation of the member states in order to facilitate relationships between their nationals; and (iii) a common analysis and concerted action to deal with international problems of law and order, serious acts of violence, organized international crime and international lawlessness generally."

As compared with the original initiative, the declaration notably referred only to "consultations" and "co-ordination of . . . the economic and political aspects of security", rather than envisaging a new area of Community competence in co-ordinating security policy, while moreover the proposal for a return to the use of majority voting in the Council was replaced by a statement that "within the Council every possible means of facilitating the decision-making process will be used, including, in cases where unanimity is required, the possibility of abstaining from voting".

A formal plan for a **"treaty establishing the European union"** was approved by the European Parliament on Feb. 14, 1984, by 237 votes to 31 with 43 abstentions. The plan had originally been put forward by Altiero Spinelli, a former European Commissioner and a Communist member of the European Parliament, and sought to abolish the traditional national veto on policy making and to boost the powers of both Commission and Parliament vis-à-vis those of member governments.

In a key speech to the European Parliament on May 24, 1984, Mitterrand in his capacity as President of the European Council called for a relaunch of the Communities based on the Stuttgart declaration of June 1983 and incorporating a renegotiation of the 1957 Treaty of Rome to strengthen and widen its scope.

He stated that the French government would look closely at the plan for a treaty establishing a European Union, passed by the European Parliament in February 1984, and he proposed that the "unanimity rule" in the Council, which had been in use since the Luxembourg compromise of 1966, should be restricted to "specific cases". He proposed four areas for Community development and co-operation: the electronics sector, space (including the development of a permanently manned space station), transport (including the development of a high-speed railway network "to bring Europeans together") and communications (including the creation of a European television network to "defend European culture from a flood of words and pictures from outside"). He also insisted on the necessity of common defence policies, despite the "extreme difficulty" of trying to develop them, and he spoke of the possibility of a "two-speed Europe" and a "Europe of variable geometry", as well as of establishing a permanent secretariat of the Council to co-ordinate foreign policy.

In contrast, a set of UK proposals presented by Sir Geoffrey Howe at a Council of (Foreign) Ministers meeting in Luxembourg on June 19, 1984, called for "practical" rather than theoretical measures to improve the working of the Communities. The document (according to the *Financial Times* of June 20) called for a reduction in the size of the Commission with only one member for each country, for "more harmonious" work with the European Parliament on Community issues and for streamlined Community procedures and institutions which would stop "frivolous use of a nation's veto powers".

12.4 A "Europe of variable geometry"
President Mitterrand's concept of developing European policies if necessary at varying speeds depending on individual countries' differing levels of commitment, was evident in the revitalization in the latter half of 1984 of the Western European Union (WEU) as a forum for European co-operation on defence issues.

A memorandum on the revival of the WEU (which had itself been formed in 1954 following the collapse of attempts to set up a European Defence Community) was presented by the French government in February 1984. It was supported by Belgium and by the WEU Assembly of member country parliamentarians, which met in June and December each year. The initiative was seen as part of a shift in French defence policy which had become increasingly evident under President Mitterrand (who had been elected in May 1981) and enabled France to contribute to discussions on European security issues even though under President de Gaulle in 1966 the country had withdrawn from NATO's integrated military structure.

Moreover, the WEU did not include three of the 10 member countries of the EC, viz. Denmark and Greece, both of which were NATO countries, and the Republic of Ireland, a neutral state, which had repeatedly expressed concern at any extension of the Communities' competence to cover security issues.

As a result of the French initiative the Defence Ministers of the seven WEU countries (i.e. Belgium, France, West Germany, Italy, Luxembourg, the Netherlands and the UK) held a first meeting since 1973 in Paris on June 12, 1984, and discussed a report on strengthening the "European pillar" of NATO. A second meeting was held in Rome on Oct. 26–27 to commemorate the 30th anniversary of the signing of the Brussels Treaty in 1954. At this meeting ministers adopted a "Rome declaration" formally undertaking to reactivate the WEU and underlining the determination of the participants "to make better use of the WEU framework in order to increase co-operation between the member states in the field of security policy and to encourage consensus".

Similar areas of European co-operation on differing levels of commitment were to be found in other fields.

In the development of a European fighter aircraft, for instance, co-operation with France and Spain was eventually added to an initial agreement reached in August 1985 between West Germany, Italy and the UK (the three countries which had already collaborated in the mid-1970s on the development and production of the Tornado aircraft). Likewise, although the European Research Co-ordination Agency or "Eureka" project proposed by the French government in April 1985 was in part developed under European Community auspices, it also drew support from non-member countries. An initial conference held in Paris on July 17, 1985, was attended by the then 10 members of the EC and also by ministers and top-level officials from Portugal and Spain and from Austria, Finland, Norway, Sweden and Switzerland.

Other earlier programmes involving differing levels of co-operation by European countries included the Arianespace programme on space research, the Airbus project on the production of a European airliner, and the Joint European Torus or JET nuclear fusion project (in which Spain, Sweden and Switzerland participated as non-Community members—see also 10.6).

12.5 Fontainebleau summit (June 25–26, 1984)

An agreement on solutions to the Communities' immediate internal problems was reached at the Fontainebleau meeting of the European Council held on June 25–26, 1984, and was described by Dr Kohl as "a significant breakthrough with regard to the further development of the Communities".

At this meeting the Community heads of state and government succeeded in agreeing on a 1984 budgetary rebate for the UK and on a formula for the subsequent correction of imbalances in member countries' contributions. This made possible the adoption of agreements on budgetary and financial discipline, on new policies, on structural funds to reduce regional imbalances, on an increase in financial resources upon the accession of Spain and Portugal, and on a series of guidelines for the reactivation of European co-operation [see also 10.12 for further details].

As regards the development of new policies the conclusions of the presidency issued after the meeting stated: "With a view to the creation of a genuine economic union, the Council intends, through specific commitments, both externally and internally, to give the European economy an impetus comparable to that which it gained from the founding of the customs union in the early 1960s. The following priority objectives will be pursued: (i) convergence of economic policies and Community action, capable of promoting productive investment and thereby a vigorous and lasting economic recovery; (ii) development, in close consultation with the Community industries and bodies concerned, of Europe's scientific and technological potential; (iii) strengthening of the internal market so that European undertakings derive more benefit from the Community dimension; and (iv) protection and promotion of employment, which is a crucial factor in Community social policy, especially as regards young people.

The meeting also set up two ad hoc committees (i) on institutional affairs and (ii) on a people's Europe.

As far as the former was concerned: "The European Council decided to set up an ad hoc committee consisting of personal representatives of the heads of state or government, on the lines of the 'Spaak Committee' [the findings of which had formed the basis of the Treaty of Rome]. The committee's function will be to make suggestions for the improvement of the operation of European co-operation in both the Community field and that of political, or any other, co-operation. The President of the European Council will take the necessary steps to implement that decision."

On the question of a people's Europe the conclusions of the presidency declared: "The European Council considers it essential that the Community should respond to the expectations of the people of Europe by adopting measures to strengthen and promote its identity and its image both for its citizens and for the rest of the world. An ad hoc committee will be set up to prepare and co-ordinate this action. It will be composed of representatives of the heads of state or government of the member states.

"The committee will examine inter alia the following suggestions: (i) symbols of the Community's existence, such as a flag and an anthem; (ii) formation of European sports teams; (iii) streamlining procedures at frontier posts; and (iv) minting of a European coinage, namely the ECU. It would also like member states to take steps to encourage young people to participate in projects organized by the Community beyond its frontiers, and in particular to support the creation of national committees of European volunteers for development, bringing together young Europeans who wish to work on development projects in the Third World. The ad hoc committee will also examine the following suggestions: (i) measures to combat drug abuse; and (ii) the twinning of children's classes. The Commission will contribute to the proceedings of the committee within the limits of its powers."

12.6 Ad hoc committee on institutional affairs

The ad hoc committee on institutional affairs held its first meeting on Sept. 28, 1984, and produced an interim report in late November and its final report on March 19, 1985. Jim Dooge, a member of the Irish *Seanad Eireann* (Senate), was appointed to chair the meetings.

The final report called on member countries' heads of state and government to hold a conference to draft a treaty on European union, although this was opposed by the British, Danish and Greek members of the committee and was not supported at either the Dublin or the Brussels European Council meetings in December 1984 and March 1985. The report also called for a much wider use of qualified majority voting in the Council, a smaller Commission with only one member per country (instead of there being two members from France, West Germany, Italy and the UK and, after 1986, from Spain), and for increased powers for the European Parliament, whereby, for instance, Commission proposals would be sent first to the Parliament for debate and amendment before being passed on to the Council. The establishment of a permanent secretariat to co- ordinate political co-operation was proposed, and the March 1985 report envisaged a wider discussion of the nature of external threats and of such issues as weapons technology developments and strategic policy. Reservations on various sections of the report were expressed by all of the non-founding members of the Communities (i.e. Denmark, Greece, Ireland and the UK).

12.7 Ad hoc committee on a people's Europe

This committee was chaired by Pietro Adonnino and held its first meeting on Nov. 7, producing interim reports for the December and March European Council meetings in Dublin and Brussels. Its final report, on June 19, 1985, envisaged reforms relating to the special rights of citizens, culture and communication, information, youth, education, exchanges and sport, volunteer work in the Third World, health, social security and drugs, twinning of towns and universities etc., and the strengthening of the Communities' image and identity.

Among the measures proposed were the introduction of a uniform electoral system for elections to the European Parliament, the creation of a Community ombudsman, the simplification and systematic codification of Community law, the introduction of a European driving licence, the improvement of language training, school exchanges and youth work camps, increasing recognition of equivalent qualifications, the extension of Community sporting events, concerted action to avoid violence in stadiums, increased support for volunteer workers in developing countries, the introduction of a Community flag, emblem and anthem (the "Ode to Joy" from Beethoven's ninth symphony), the introduction of common postage stamps and the increase of tax-free allowances for travellers. Changes in the area of culture and communication were an important feature of the report and concentrated on television, science, technology and art. It was proposed that a European lottery should finance these particular projects, which included the declaration of 1988 as "European film and television year" and the creation of a European Academy of Science, Technology and Art.

12.8 European Council meeting in Milan (June 28–29, 1985)

The session of the European Council held on June 28–29, 1985, in the Castello Sforza in Milan, Italy, was dominated by discussions on a comprehensive institutional reform of the Communities. In an unprecedented vote, called for by Bettino Craxi, the Italian Prime Minister, who was in the chair, the six original Community members and Ireland voted in favour of an intergovernmental conference on reform, while Denmark, Greece and the UK opposed the move, although all three countries subsequently agreed to attend the conference.

The passage concerning these institutional questions in the conclusions of the presidency was as follows:

"The European Council held a wide-ranging discussion on the proposals of the ad hoc Committee for Institutional Affairs set up at Fontainebleau, and the draft mandate of the Italian presidency and in particular on the improvement of the Council's decision-making procedure, the enlargement of the European Parliament's role, the Commission's administrative powers and the strengthening of political co-operation in the general context of the transition to European union.

"It confirmed the need to improve the operation of the Community in order to give concrete form to the objectives it has set itself, in particular as regards the completion of the internal market by 1992 and measures to promote a technological Europe. The

European Council noted that the President of the Council would submit proposals for the improvement of the Council's decision-making procedure, the exercise of the Commission's administrative powers and the Parliament's powers with a view to their early adoption.

"The European Council discussed in detail the convening of a conference to work out the following with a view to achieving concrete progress on European union: (i) a treaty on a common foreign and security policy on the basis of the Franco-German and United Kingdom drafts [see 12.9]; (ii) the amendments to the EEC Treaty in accordance with Article 236 of that Treaty, required for the implementation of the institutional changes concerning the Council's decision-making procedure, the Commission's executive power and the powers of the European Parliament and the extension to new spheres of activity in accordance with the proposals of the Dooge Committee and the Adonnino Committee, as set out elsewhere [see 12.6, 12.7] and taking into account certain aspects of the Commission proposal concerning the freedom of movement of persons.

"The President noted that the required majority as laid down in Article 236 of the Treaty had been obtained for the convening of such a conference. The Portuguese and Spanish governments would be invited to take part in that conference. The Belgian, German, French, Irish, Italian, Luxembourg and Netherlands delegations were in favour of holding that conference. The presidency would consequently take the steps necessary to convene that conference with a view to submitting the results for a decision by the heads of state and of government at the European Council meeting in Luxembourg."

12.9 Proposals and preparations for intergovernmental conference

Various proposals on a broad reform of the Community institutions aimed at closer European union, and specifically on political co-operation on foreign policy issues, were tabled both before and after the Milan summit meeting by the UK, France and West Germany, the Netherlands, the Commission and Denmark, and by Italy at the first session of the intergovernmental conference on Sept. 9.

At one of the informal meetings of Community Foreign Ministers (held twice yearly) which took place on June 8–9, 1985, in Stresa on Lake Maggiore, Italy, discussion centred on institutional reform and in particular on a number of proposals outlined by Sir Geoffrey Howe, the UK Secretary of State for Foreign and Commonwealth Affairs. These and other measures were discussed at a formal Council of (Foreign) Ministers meeting on June 18 in Luxembourg.

The UK proposals envisaged (i) the formalization of existing co-operation on foreign policy issues by the establishment of a small secretariat in Brussels; (ii) a binding commitment by heads of government to consult one another before launching foreign policy initiatives; (iii) a commitment to vote the same way within the UN (or abstain); (iv) the extension of political co-operation to include more security issues; (v) more frequent use of majority voting or at least abstention; and (vi) the accelerated removal of the remaining barriers to the establishment of a full common internal market. These measures were put forward as practical alternatives to the lengthy process of amending the 1957 Treaty of Rome advocated by other member countries.

A report on European union by the UK House of Lords select committee on the European Communities published on July 31, found that "the essential steps to improve the functioning of the Community may not be possible without amendment of the treaties". The greatest obstacle to completion of the internal market was seen to be abuse of the Luxembourg compromise, while the UK's refusal to participate in the EMS would "inevitably delay" its completion too. The report proposed that invocation of a vital national interest blocking a Council decision should have to be justified at European Council level, that the Council of Ministers should become less involved in matters of detail and that the Commission "should be restored to the status envisaged for it in the treaties", but not that legislative powers should be given to the European Parliament.

A Franco-German plan for a "treaty on European union" was announced in the *Bundestag* (the lower house of the West German federal parliament) and confirmed by the French government on June 27, one day before the start of the Milan summit.

The 11-article document dealt exclusively with the issue of political co-operation on foreign policy and gave greater attention to the proposed structure of a foreign policy secretariat in Brussels than the British proposals. Co-operation on the political and economic aspects of security policy was not advocated, although recourse to the WEU was envisaged for those countries which wished to co-operate in this field [see also 12.4].

After the Milan meeting Dutch proposals were presented on July 23 by Willem van Eekelen, the Secretary of State for Foreign Affairs, who described them as more ambitious than the British proposals and more pragmatic than the Franco-German draft treaty on European union.

The Dutch proposals aimed to establish a common Community foreign policy rather than just a co-ordination of attitudes. They envisaged a strictly limited secretariat, and while including the political and economic aspects of security they specifically ruled out co-operation on military and arms procurement issues.

Meeting on July 22 in Brussels, the Council of (Foreign) Ministers agreed unanimously to hold an intergovernmental conference at Foreign Minister level on the institutional and political development of the European Communities. To this end two working parties were set up (i) to study possible amendments to the Treaty of Rome; and (ii) to establish by Oct. 15 at the latest the wording for a treaty on political co-operation on a common foreign and security policy, based on the UK and Franco-German proposals.

The Commission, setting out draft treaty articles in a submission to the first of these working parties in the third week of September, called for decision-making by qualified majority, a flexible framework for co-operation on technological and research issues, and specific Community obligations to protect the environment and human health.

Despite its earlier opposition to treaty changes the Danish government on Oct. 16 also presented a number of treaty amendments to the same working party. These covered such matters as technology, the environment and unemployment.

12.10 Sessions of intergovernmental conference on reform of the Communities (September–December 1985)

An initial session of the intergovernmental conference was held on Sept. 9 in Luxembourg and chaired by Jacques Poos, the Luxembourg Foreign Minister. This meeting was followed by others on Oct. 21–22 and on Nov. 11, 19 and 25–26, with a final "conclave" in Luxembourg on the two days preceding the Dec. 2–3 European Council summit [see 12.11]. During these sessions, which were in effect sessions of the Council of (Foreign) Ministers, discussions covered the establishment of a treaty on political co-operation on foreign and security policy and a whole range of possible reforms of the Treaty of Rome.

The possible reforms centred on measures (i) to establish a complete common internal market by 1992 with an increased use of majority voting in this area; (ii) to increase the powers of the European Parliament; (iii) to extend the Communities' competence under the Treaty to cover the environment, health, monetary development, research and technology and other issues; and (iv) to reduce the divergence between the economies of the northern and the southern member countries.

Among the proposals discussed at the Sept. 9 meeting were a series of Italian amendments to the UK and Franco-German proposals on external policy co-operation, presented by Giulio Andreotti, the Italian Foreign Minister. These envisaged the systematic implementation of a joint policy in which the European Parliament would also be involved; as regards security, the Italian proposals suggested joint meetings between the European Parliament and the WEU Parliamentary Assembly. If necessary decisions were to be taken on the basis of the majority consensus opinion.

Further proposals put forward by the Belgian government envisaged the inclusion in the Treaty of, among other things, a passage on human rights. Numerous proposals were also made by the Commission, which suggested on Oct. 28, for instance, that the EMS, set up in March 1979 following the Bremen declaration of July 1978, should be incorporated into the Treaty. In his presentation Jacques Delors, the President of the Commission, also proposed including a reference to the role of the ECU and establishing a procedure for creating a European Monetary Fund as envisaged in the Bremen declaration. Such changes were seen, however, as threatening the autonomy of central banks to control monetary policy, and as increasing the pressure on the UK and Greece to participate fully in the EMS.

French proposals published on Oct. 14 suggested that Council decisions covering the internal market should in principle be decided unanimously unless the European Parliament had itself approved the matter in question, in which case the Council would decide by a majority vote. The proposals published on Nov. 19 envisaged a single document under a general heading of "European union" (instead of the two areas for reform of the Communities established by the Council of Foreign Ministers on July 22—see 12.9), a new "super-secretariat" with a secretary-general independent of the Commission, and a separate secretariat to co-ordinate foreign policy co-operation.

12.11 Agreement on amendments to Treaty of Rome (December 1985)

The meeting of the European Council held on Dec. 2–3, 1985, in Luxembourg agreed on a series of changes to the Treaty of Rome, but their acceptance was made subject to a meeting of the Council of (Foreign) Ministers on Dec. 16. Furthermore, Denmark and Italy both placed reservations on their acceptance of the whole text, the former because the reforms were too far-reaching and the latter because they were not radical enough. Other countries also expressed reservations on certain aspects of the proposed treaty changes.

After the meeting Delors said in Brussels that the Commission had been "hoping for something better", but that the heads of state and government had "achieved a compromise and it is up to the Commission to make it dynamic". Pierre Pflimlin, the President of the European Parliament, expressed his "personal disappointment" that the decisions brought "no real improvement to the functioning of the institutions". Dr Kohl described the summit's achievements as "a small but decisive move forward", and on Dec. 5 in her report to the UK House of Commons Thatcher stressed that she still believed that most of the reforms agreed could have been achieved without revisions to the Treaty. Dr Papandreou described it as a "very good day", which had involved "real negotiation".

A summary of the provisional texts for amendment to the Treaty is given below:

Internal market. A deadline of Dec. 31, 1992, was set for the establishment of the internal market as "an area without frontiers in which the free movement of goods, persons, services and capital is ensured in accordance with the provisions of the Treaty".

Measures having "as their object the establishment and operation of the internal market" were in general to be decided by a qualified majority in the Council, instead of unanimously as previously. Exceptions were to be made, however, for "fiscal provisions", including measures harmonizing indirect taxes, and for measures "relating to the free movement of persons" and "to the rights and interests of employed persons". Measures affecting health, safety, environmental protection and consumer protection were to be "based on a high level of protection", and member countries could apply to the Commission for exemptions to harmonization provisions (Denmark and West Germany being anxious that their more stringent environmental and safety conditions should not be undermined by weaker provisions adopted by other countries). However, the Commission or any member state would be permitted to bring other member countries to the European Court of Justice for alleged abuse of such exemptions. The unanimity rule would remain for "measures constituting a step back with regard to liberalization of capital movements", and also, in accordance with West German demands, for matters concerning the Community-wide recognition of professional qualifications. At British and Irish insistence no steps to establish the internal market were to affect the right of member states to maintain border controls on "immigration from third countries and to combat terrorism, crime and the traffic in drugs". The French government was reportedly unwilling to allow decisions by majority vote on matters concerning the liberalization of air and sea transport. A statement was also made by Greece to the effect that steps towards the establishment of the internal market had to "take place in such a way as not to harm sensitive sectors of member states' economies".

Interim reports were to be prepared by the Commission before Dec. 31, 1988, and Dec. 31, 1990, on the progress made in establishing the internal market and a further report was to be drawn up in 1992 on areas still requiring harmonization.

Community monetary capacity. A new article was to be added stating that "in order to ensure the convergence of economic and monetary policy which is necessary for the further development of the Community, member states . . . shall take account of the experience acquired in co-operation in the framework of the EMS and in developing the ECU, and shall respect existing powers in this field". Reference was also to be made in the Treaty to the statement issued by heads of state and government in Paris in October 1972 approving "the objective of the progressive achievement of economic and monetary union", and to the statements made by the European Council meetings in Bremen in July 1978 and in Brussels in December 1978 on "the setting-up of the EMS and related questions". Further major reforms concerning monetary policy were to require formal treaty amendment and therefore approval by national parliaments.

The UK and West Germany had originally opposed any inclusion of monetary questions in the reform package but the *Financial Times* of Dec. 4 saw the changes as having "no appreciable effect on the control of monetary and exchange rate policy" and as possibly making "future development of the EMS even more difficult".

Economic and social cohesion. "In order to promote its harmonious development overall", the Community was to "develop and pursue its actions leading to strengthening its economic and social cohesion". In particular the Community was to aim to reduce the "disparities between the various regions and the backwardness of the least-favoured regions" (which at British insistence were to include "declining industrial regions"). Once the amended treaty entered into force the Commission was to present proposals for the improvement of the existing structural funds (i.e. the guidance section of the European Agricultural Guidance and Guarantee Fund, the European Social Fund, and the European Regional Development Fund), which were already considered to be "adequately financed so far as budgetary resources permit". The Council was required to act unanimously on these proposals within one year, with subsequent decisions being taken by a qualified majority.

European Parliament. The "institution of a procedure for co-operation with the European Parliament" was agreed. For decisions whose adoption required the co-operation of the Parliament, a common position reached by a qualified majority of the Council, based on a Commission proposal and an opinion of the European Parliament, had then to be sent to the Parliament. If within three months the Parliament had approved the Council's decision or had failed to take a decision the act would be adopted. Within that period the Parliament could by an absolute majority of its constituent members either propose amendments to the Council's common position or reject it outright. If a decision were rejected by the Parliament the Council would have to act unanimously on a second reading. Amendments proposed by the Parliament were to be re-examined by the Commission within one month, after which the Council had within three months either to accept the Commission's revised proposal by a qualified majority, or to amend it by unanimous decision. The heads of state and government did not agree on, and therefore instructed the Council of Ministers to clarify, the procedure to be adopted if the Parliament rejected the Council's common position at its second reading or if the Council failed to act within three months on a revised Commission proposal, although it was "agreed that the Council [would] have the last say".

Powers of the Commission. An obligation was to be incorporated into the Treaty for the Council to "confer on the Commission . . . powers for the implementation of the rules it lays down".

Research and technological development. The aim of the Communities was to be "to strengthen the scientific and technological basis of European industry and to encourage it to become more competitive at international level". In pursuing these objectives in co-ordination with the activities of member states the Communities were (i) to implement "research, demonstration and technological development programmes by promoting co-operation with undertakings, research centres and universities"; (ii) to promote "co-operation with third countries and international organizations"; (iii) to disseminate and optimize the "use of the results of Community activities"; and (iv) to stimulate "the training and mobility of researchers in the Community". A "multi-annual framework programme" and any structures established to execute Community research and development programmes were to be adopted unanimously by the Council, while detailed arrangements were to be approved by a qualified majority.

Environment. The objectives of action by the Communities relating to the environment were (i) "to preserve, protect and improve the quality of the environment; (ii) to contribute towards protecting human health; and (iii) to ensure the prudent and rational use of natural resources". Such action was to be based on the principles that preventive action should be taken, that environmental damage should as a priority be rectified at source and that the polluter should pay. In particular, as a result of West German and Danish insistence, measures adopted were not to prevent each member state "from maintaining and introducing more stringent protective measures compatible with the Treaty, and with the operation of the internal market in particular".

Social policy. Member states were to "pay particular attention to encouraging improvements, especially in the working environment, as regards the health and safety of workers", their objective being "the harmonization of conditions in this area, while maintaining the improvements". Measures gradually to implement this policy could be adopted by a qualified majority of the Council, but were not to prevent each member state from "introducing more stringent measures". The Commission was also to "endeavour to develop the dialogue between management and labour at European level, which could . . . lead to contractual relations". The UK government placed a reservation on this whole section.

"Draft treaty on European co-operation in the sphere of foreign policy". A provisional text was agreed which largely codified existing practice. Member states undertook "to inform and consult each other on any foreign policy matters of general interest so as to ensure that their combined influence is exercised as effectively as possible".

Such consultations, which were to take place at Foreign Minister level at least four times a year, were to "take full account of the positions of the other parties" and were to be consistent. "Common principles and objectives" were gradually to be "developed and defined". Member countries were to endeavour to adopt common positions in international institutions and at international conferences. "Political dialogue with third countries and regional groupings" was to be organized where necessary and liaison between member states' missions in third countries was to be intensified. The contracting parties to the treaty further considered that "closer co-operation on questions of European security would contribute in an essential way to the development of a European external identity", although "nothing [was to] stand in the way of closer co-operation in the field of security . . . in the framework of the WEU or the Atlantic Alliance". The European Parliament was to be "closely associated with political co-operation", with regular consultations being made and the Parliament's views being "duly taken into consideration". A secretariat was to be established in Brussels to assist the presidency (held by whichever member country held the presidency of the Council) in its co-ordination of Community foreign policy.

At the Dec. 16–17 meeting Andreotti (whose government had earlier taken the position that ratification of the reforms should be conditional upon their acceptability to the European Parliament), presented plans for increased parliamentary powers. In the event the Council finally agreed on two minor changes, (i) requiring any of Parliament's amendments to Community legislation to be presented to the full Council even if they were not endorsed by the Commission; and (ii) allowing for the extension by a further month, by agreement with Parliament, of the final three-month period for the Council to approve revised proposals (which would lapse without such approval).

On other issues, member countries dropped their reservations on various sections of the communiqué, except that Denmark maintained its overall reservation, Italy did not explicitly renew its condition of acceptance and the UK maintained its reservation on social legislation and the protection of the working environment. It was also agreed that the two sections of the reform package (covering economic co-operation and political or foreign policy co-operation) should be legally separate, although a preamble was to link the two.

The Danish reservation placed upon the whole document reflected the fact that Poul Schlüter's minority four-party government could not be sure of a parliamentary majority on foreign (and defence) policy issues. After the summit the four coalition parties and the opposition Social Democrats in the *Folketing* (parliament) confirmed in a vote on Dec. 10 their support for earlier Danish policy resolutions to the effect that "the basis of Denmark's membership of the EEC is the preservation of the veto right and the present division of competence between the Council, Commission and Parliament". The *Folketing* later decided to postpone a final decision on the proposed reforms until January 1986.

12.12 Votes by European Parliament on proposed changes

In an initial debate on the reforms on Dec. 11, members of the European Parliament voted by 243 votes to 47 that the Parliament "cannot accept the changes proposed in the EEC Treaty in their present state, especially what is proposed for the powers of the European Parliament". After the Council meeting on Dec. 16–17 a resolution was adopted on Jan. 16, 1986, by 208 votes to 63 with 40 abstentions. This resolution recalled the earlier vote but nevertheless undertook to "exploit all the possibilities" offered by the proposed changes with the aim of achieving a "genuine political and economic union". Earlier in the debate a vote rejecting the reforms was defeated by 220 votes to 76.

12.13 Signature of Single European Act by nine member countries (Feb. 17, 1986)

Nine of the 12 Community member countries on Feb. 17, 1986, signed the series of EC reforms agreed in December. Italy and Greece attended the ceremony in Luxembourg but refused to sign the "Single European Act", the former because the measures were still regarded as inadequate and the latter to convey a symbolic protest at the isolation of the third country which did not sign the document, Denmark [see 12.14 for referendum and subsequent signing of Act by all member countries].

Hans van den Broek, the Dutch Foreign Minister (whose country then held the Council presidency), described the reforms as the "absolute minimum we believe necessary for the survival of the Communities".

12.14 Danish referendum approving reforms (Feb. 27, 1986)

In Denmark the minority, non-socialist, four-party coalition government of Schlüter, which had been in power since 1982, was unable to sign the document since it had failed to win support in the *Folketing* in a debate held on Jan. 21.

In this debate an opposition resolution, which rejected the reforms and demanded a renegotiation of the package, was approved by 80 votes (Social Democrats, Radicals, Left Socialists and members of the Socialist People's Party) to 75 with 23 abstentions. Uffe Ellemann-Jensen, the Danish Foreign Minister, accordingly set out the following day on a tour of key EC capitals, but a possible renegotiation was ruled out by a majority of Community ministers (only the UK favouring such action).

A second debate was held in the *Folketing* on Jan. 28. On the previous day a Council of (Foreign) Ministers meeting in Brussels had given Ellemann-Jensen a further guarantee (in effect similar to that already in the reform document) of his country's right to use national measures to maintain the existing high standards in environmental and working conditions in Denmark, although these standards were not to serve as a hidden form of protectionism. This assurance failed to alter the opposition's stance and, as already proposed by Schlüter, a motion was passed (with the support of the four governing parties, Left Socialists and the majority of the Radicals and the abstention of the Social Democrats, three Radicals and members of the Socialist People's Party) calling upon the Cabinet to organize a national referendum on the issue.

In the referendum campaign the governing parties sought to portray the issue not only as a question of approving or rejecting the reform package but also as an endorsement or otherwise of Denmark's continued membership of the EC. Schlüter declared that a negative vote "would be playing Russian roulette with Denmark's whole future" and "would be interpreted as our first step towards leaving the European Common Market".

About half of all Danish exports went to the other Community member countries and a confidential government study leaked over the weekend of Feb. 8–9 maintained that withdrawal from the Communities would cost the country at least US$2,900 million each year.

The opposition Social Democrats led by Anker Joergensen focused on the reform measures themselves, particular concern being expressed about the *Folketing*'s loss of sovereignty if powers were transferred to the European Parliament and the danger of Danish environmental and work safety provisions being eroded by EC rules on free competition and common standards.

The Social Democrats were nevertheless still divided on attitudes towards the EC (as in the 1972 referendum on Community membership—see 4.12) with some former ministers openly campaigning for the reform package despite the official party stance. Opinion polls suggested that the Social Democrats had been losing support to left-wing rivals such as the anti-NATO, anti-EEC Socialist People's Party in what was described by the *Financial Times* of Jan. 16 as "a surge of anti-EEC feeling among the party's rank and file".

The referendum, held on Feb. 27 with a 74.8 per cent turnout, resulted in 1,629,824 votes (56.2 per cent of the votes cast) being cast in favour of the package of EC reforms, and 1,268,000 votes (43.8 per cent) against their acceptance.

The Social Democrats stressed that the result had produced a larger vote opposing the reforms than had originally been expected, but Ellemann-Jensen described the vote as "a clear signal that the people are in favour of Denmark's EC membership and wish Denmark to participate in the development of European co-operation". Jacques Delors expressed his confidence "that the future development enabled through the new provisions in the treaties will turn out to serve the interests of the Danish population as a whole".

The 1986 referendum was the second consultative referendum in Danish history after that of 1916, when the electorate had approved the sale of the Danish West Indies (Virgin Islands) to the USA for US$25,000,000. [See 4.13 for October 1972 referendum on EC membership when there was a 90.1 per cent turnout.]

12.15 Signature of Single European Act by Denmark, Greece and Italy (Feb. 28, 1986)—Ratification of Single European Act

Shortly after the referendum, Denmark, Greece and Italy all dropped their reservations on the reforms and on Feb. 28, the three countries' Foreign Ministers signed the document in The Hague, in the Netherlands. The Single European Act did not, however, enter into force as planned on Jan. 1, 1987, since one member country, Ireland, had not by that time deposited the instruments of ratification in Rome as required.

The 11 other member countries delivered the ratification documents on the following dates: Denmark (June 13), Belgium (Aug. 25), United Kingdom (Nov. 19), Luxembourg (Dec. 17), Spain (Dec. 18), the Netherlands (Dec. 24), France and West Germany (Dec. 29), Italy (Dec. 30), and Portugal and Greece (Dec. 31, although the Greek parliament did not in fact, because of the pressure of other legislation under consideration, complete full approval of the Act until Jan. 15, 1987, in a vote opposed only by 10 votes from the pro-Soviet Communist Party or KKE Exterior). During the process of ratification various politicians and groups within the EC (including the *Länder* (states) in West Germany which claimed that the Act reduced their regional powers as well as those of the federal government) expressed fears that the Act would result in a loss of sovereignty.

In Ireland the *Dáil* (lower house of parliament) approved the terms of the Single European Act on Dec. 11, after three opposition amendments had been defeated, while the *Seanad* (upper house) approved the legislation on Dec. 17. The instrument of ratification was signed by the President on Dec.

24. On that same day Mr Raymond Crotty, a 61-year-old farmer and lawyer, obtained an injunction in the Dublin High Court against ratification on the grounds that the Act contravened the Irish Constitution and had therefore to be put to a national referendum. The government lodged an appeal immediately afterwards and the hearing began in the High Court in Dublin on Jan. 15, 1987. The Act's reference to "closer co-operation on questions of European security" was seen as threatening the neutrality of the Republic, the only EC member country which was not also a member of NATO. Once the last instrument of ratification was deposited in Rome, the Act was to enter into force on the first day of the following month.

APPENDIX ONE:

INSTITUTIONAL CHANGES ARISING FROM ENLARGEMENT

Changes in the composition and structure of the various key Community bodies as a result of the successive enlargements of the EC are summarized below. Further details, such as the names of Commissioners appointed by acceding states, are to be found in the relevant chapters.

Country abbreviations used in the tables are as follows:

Belgium	B	Italy	I	
West Germany	D	Ireland	IRL	
Denmark	DK	Luxembourg	L	
Spain	E	Netherlands	NL	
France	F	Portugal	P	
Greece	GR	United Kingdom	UK	

Commission

Although appointed by the mutual agreement of member country governments, Commissioners are required to act independently of national governments in the interests of the Communities alone. They meet in Brussels where their work is supported by 20 directorates general.

Their numbers were increased progressively as follows:

		Before first enlargement	1973	1981	1986
Allocation of Commissioners per member country	B	1	(other member countries' allocation as before)		
	D	2			
	F	2			
	I	2			
	L	1			
	NL	1			
			plus DK 1	plus GR 1	plus E 2
			IRL 1		P 1
			UK 2		
Total members		9	13	14	17

Council

Community member countries are each represented by one delegated minister in the Council of Ministers, the key decision-making body of the Communities. With the successive enlargements of the EC, the size of the Council thus increased from six to nine (in 1973), to 10 (in 1981), and to 12 (in 1986).

The presidency of the Council rotates every six months according to the own-language alphabetical order of member countries and meets either in Brussels (where its secretariat is based) or in the member country holding the presidency. The committee of permanent representatives (COREPER), comprising member country ambassadors to the EC assisted by committees of national civil servants, helps prepare and co-ordinate the Council's work.

Each member country's votes are weighted according to the following table, which also gives the number of votes needed to reach decisions requiring only a qualified majority of votes rather than unanimity.

	Before first enlargement		1973		1981		1986	
Voting weighting	B	2	B	5				
	D	4	D	10	(other member countries'			
	F	4	F	10	voting weighting as before)			
	I	4	I	10				
	L	1	L	2				
	NL	2	NL	5				
			plus		plus		plus	
			DK	3	GR	5	E	8
			IRL	3			P	5
			UK	10				
Total number of votes	17		58		63		76	
Votes required for qualified majority decision	12		41		45		54	

European Council
The European Council comprises the heads of state and government of the Community member countries. It provides a forum for consultation at the highest level between member countries.

After the signing of the Treaty of Rome in 1957, summit meetings of the Six were held on six occasions, the participants being joined for the fifth and sixth meetings (in Paris and Copenhagen in October 1972 and December 1973 respectively) by the heads of government of the three countries about to accede to the Community membership. At the seventh summit meeting in Paris in December 1974 the heads of state and government recognized "the need for an overall approach to the internal problems in achieving European unity and the external problems facing Europe"; they agreed to meet three times a year "to ensure progress and overall consistency in the activities of the Communities and in the work on political co-operation". Under the Dutch presidency of the Council in the first half of 1986 it was agreed to hold these meetings twice a year only.

Parliament
Although at first members of the European Parliament (or European Assembly) were nominated by member countries' national parliaments, direct elections to the Parliament were held for the first time in June 1979, when the number of representatives was increased from 198 to 410.

Details of this change and other increases resulting from the three enlargements are given below, together with the seat allocation for each member country [for distribution of seats between the various political groupings following Spain and Portugal's accession see 10.24].

	Before first enlargement		1973	1979	1981	1986
Number of seats	142		198	410	434	518
Seat distribution per member country	B	14	B	14	24	(other member countries'
	D	36	D	36	81	seat distribution as before)
	F	36	DK	10	16	
	I	36	F	36	81	
	L	6	I	36	81	
	NL	14	IRL	10	15	
			L	6	6	
			NL	14	25	
			UK	36[1]	81	
					plus	plus
					GR 24	E 60
						P 24

[1] The UK Labour Party members did not at first take up the seats allocated to them, but only did so in 1975 after the referendum [see 7.11].

The work of the Parliament takes place in Strasbourg (where plenary sessions are held), in Luxembourg (where the secretariat is based) and in Brussels (where committee meetings are held).

Court of Justice
Before the first enlargement of the EC there were seven judges and two advocates general on the European Court of Justice, which is common to the EEC, ECSC and Euratom and is based in Luxembourg. Their number was increased to nine and four respectively in 1973 and a tenth judge was appointed upon the accession of Greece on Jan. 1, 1981. From March 30, 1981, a further increase to 11 judges and five advocates general came into effect, the additional judge coming from one of the larger member countries and being appointed in alphabetical order of country. With the accession of Spain and Portugal in January 1986 the number of judges was increased to 13 and a sixth advocate general was appointed.

European Investment Bank
Each country appointed one governor to the European Investment Bank's Board of Governors so that by 1986 the Board comprised 12 members (each of whom was normally the finance minister from the respective member country).

As from Jan. 1, 1986, the percentage shares of each member's subscription were as given in the table below. The change was made following a decision by the EIB Board of Governors on June 11, 1985, to double the Bank's subscribed capital (when for the first time since the establishment of the EIB, Italy's percentage share was aligned, at the Italian government's request, with the percentage shares of the other Community countries with relatively large gross national products).

F	19.127	NL	5.302
D	19.127	DK	2.684
I	19.127	GR	1.438
UK	19.127	P	0.927
E	7.031	IRL	0.671
B	5.302	L	0.134

The EIB's subscribed capital was doubled from 14,400 million ECU to 28,800 million ECU, with effect from Jan. 1, 1986. The Bank is based in Luxembourg.

Economic and Social Committee

The Economic and Social Committee (Ecosoc), which acts as a consultative body for EEC legislation proposed by the Commission and is based in Brussels, represents employers, trade unions and other interested groups. With the 1973 enlargement its membership was increased from 101 to 144.

The number of representatives from each country was then as follows:

B	12	IRL	9
D	24	L	6[1]
DK	9	NL	12
F	24	UK	24[2]
I	24		

[1] Previously 5.

[2] As was the case with the Labour Party members of the European Parliament, the trade union representatives from the UK did not take up their seats until after the 1975 referendum.

With the accession of Greece the number of Ecosoc representatives was increased by 12 to 156, and in 1986 it rose to 189 with 21 new members from Spain and 12 from Portugal.

The ECSC had its own separate and smaller but nevertheless similar Consultative Committee, while Euratom had its Scientific and Technical Committee.

APPENDIX TWO:

OTHER CHANGES ARISING FROM ENLARGEMENT

Community budget

Until 1970 the European Communities' revenues were dependent upon contributions from member countries which were determined by member countries' gross national product. From 1971 onwards the Commission was permitted to generate income from "own resources", comprising levies collected by member countries for the EC on imports of agricultural goods and customs duties on products covered by the common external tariff. A proportion of countries' revenue from the value added tax (VAT) levied on goods and services was also transferred to the Communities. This was not allowed to exceed 1 per cent until after the European Council meeting in June 1984, when member countries agreed to raise this ceiling to 1.4 per cent from January 1986 [see also 10.12].

European Monetary System and the European currency unit

The European Monetary System (EMS) came into effect on March 13, 1979, with the intention of increasing monetary co-operation and creating a zone of monetary stability in Europe.

All those countries which were members at that time, except for the UK joined the EMS. Greece did not join upon acceding to the EC in 1981; the Greek drachma was incorporated into the ECU from September 1984, although Greece did not participate in the exchange rate mechanism described below. Portugal and Spain did not join the EMS upon accession in January 1986 and the question of including the peseta and the escudo in the European currency unit (ECU) was only due to be considered in 1989.

The system works by fixing for each currency a central rate in the ECU, which is based on a "basket" of national currencies identical to those used to calculate the European unit of account (EUA). A reference rate in relation to other currencies is fixed for each currency with margins of permitted fluctuation (2.25 per cent for all participating currencies except the Italian lira which is allowed to fluctuate by 6 per cent) and Central Banks in member countries intervene when this agreed margin is likely to be exceeded. Each member places 20 per cent of its gold reserves and dollar reserves respectively into the European Monetary Co-operation Fund, which was set up in 1973 and keeps account of short-term borrowings to support currencies, and receives a supply of ECUs to regulate Central Bank interventions. Short- and medium-term credit facilities are also given to support the balance of payments of member countries. The EMS is put under strain by wide fluctuations in currencies not participating in the system and by disparities in developments among member countries, and this has resulted in 11 currency realignments between March 1979 and January 1987. The absence of the UK pound from the exchange rate mechanism is regarded by the Commission as hindering the EMS from realizing its potential.

In March 1979 a new monetary unit was also adopted. The ECU was identical in value and composition to the European unit of account (EUA) in use before that.

The ECU is a composite unit, in which the relative value of each currency is determined by the gross national product and the volume of trade in each country. The Greek drachma was incorporated in the ECU for the first time in September 1984, and the amounts of the other currencies were altered. The resulting composition of the ECU was therefore as given below (with previous amounts in brackets):

Belgian francs	3.71	(3.66)	Irish punt	0.00871	(0.00759)
Danish krone	0.219	(0.217)	Italian lire	140	(109)
French francs	1.31	(1.15)	Luxembourg franc	0.14	(0.14)
West German mark	0.719	(0.828)	Dutch guilder	0.256	(0.286)
Greek drachmae	1.15	—	UK pound	0.0878	(0.0885)

(The rate of the ECU in terms of any currency is equal to the sum of the equivalents in that currency of the amounts of each of the above currencies.)

From April 1979 onwards the ECU was used as the unit of account for the purposes of the common agricultural policy. In 1981 it replaced the EUA in the general budget of the EC and became the only unit of account used in the European Communities.

Foreign relations
Agreements between the Communities and third countries required ratification by the normal procedures of each member country. When a new member country or countries acceded to the Communities, the necessary modification of such agreements was established by means of additional protocols, similarly requiring ratification by the relevant national procedures. (Greece was not prepared to accept a protocol to cover Greek participation in the Community agreement with Turkey, unless certain conditions were met —see 8.13.)

Official languages of the Communities
With the accession of Spain and Portugal in 1986, the number of official Community languages (in which all official publications of the Communities were issued) rose to nine: Danish, Dutch, English, French, German, Greek, Italian, Portuguese and Spanish.

APPENDIX THREE:

TREATY OF PARIS

The Paris Treaty establishing the European Coal and Steel Community, signed in the French capital on April 18, 1951, entered into force on July 25, 1952, and the High Authority (created as the principal organ of the ECSC) began operations on Aug. 10, 1952. The main institutions of the ECSC, i.e. its High Authority and Council of Ministers, were merged with the EEC and Euratom from July 1, 1967.

The character, aims and functions of the ECSC are contained in Articles 1–6 of the Treaty as follows:

Art. 1. By the present Treaty the High Contracting Parties institute among themselves a European Coal and Steel Community, based on a common market, common objectives and common institutions.

Art. 2. The mission of the European Coal and Steel Community is to contribute to economic expansion, the development of employment and the improvement of the standard of living in the participating countries through the institution, in harmony with the general economy of the member states, of a common market as defined in Art. 4.

The Community must progressively establish conditions which will in themselves assure the most rational distribution of production at the highest possible level of productivity, while safeguarding the continuity of employment and avoiding the creation of fundamental and persistent disturbances in the economies of the member states.

Art. 3. Within the framework of their respective powers and responsibilities, the institutions of the Community should: (*a*) see that the common market is regularly supplied, taking account of the needs of third countries; (*b*) assure to all consumers in comparable positions within the common market equal access to the sources of production; (*c*) seek the establishment of the lowest prices which are possible without requiring any corresponding rise either in the prices charged by the same enterprises in other transactions or in the price-level as a whole in another period, while at the same time permitting necessary amortization and providing normal possibilities of re-muneration for capital invested; (*d*) see that conditions are maintained which will encourage enterprises to expand and improve their ability to produce and to promote a policy of rational development of natural resources, avoiding inconsiderate exhaustion of such resources; (*e*) promote the improvement of the living and working conditions of the labour force in each of the industries under its jurisdiction so as to make possible the equalization of such conditions in an upward direction; (*f*) further the development of international trade and see that equitable limits are observed in prices charged on external markets; (*g*) promote the regular expansion and the modernization of production, as well as the improvement of its quality, under conditions which preclude any protection against competing industries, except where justified by illegitimate action on the part of such industries or in their favour.

Art. 4. The following were recognized to be incompatible with the common market for coal and steel, and were therefore "abolished and prohibited" within the Community: (*a*) import and export duties, or charges with an equivalent effect, and quantitative restrictions on the movement of coal and steel; (*b*) measures or practices discriminating among producers, buyers or consumers, specifically as concerned prices, delivery terms and transportation rates, as well as measures or practices which hampered the buyer in the free choice of his supplier; (*c*) subsidies or state assistance, or special charges imposed by the state, in any form whatsoever; (*d*) restrictive practices tending towards the division of markets or the exploitation of the consumer.

Art. 5. The Community would accomplish its mission with "limited direct intervention," and to this end it would: "enlighten and facilitate the action of the interested parties" by collecting information, organizing consultations and defining general objectives, place financial means at the disposal of enterprises for their investments and participate in the expenses of readaptation; assure the establishment, maintenance and observance of normal conditions of competition, and take direct action with respect to production and the operation of the market only when circumstances made it absolutely necessary; publish the justifications for its action and take the necessary measures to ensure observance of the rules set forth in the Treaty. The institutions of the Community should carry out these activities with "as little administrative machinery as possible" and in close co-operation with the interested parties.

Art. 6 provided that the Community should have "juridical personality" and that it should enjoy, in its international relationships, "the juridical capacity necessary to the exercise of its functions and the attainment of its ends".

In addition:

Arts. 7–45 are concerned with the institutions of the Community—the High Authority, the Assembly, the Council and the Court—the functions of which have since been taken over by the European Commission, the European Parliament, the joint Council of Ministers and the European Court of Justice respectively.

Arts. 46–75 contain the technical details for the realization of the objectives of the Treaty. The remaining provisions are concerned, inter alia, with such general matters as the privileges and immunity of the Community on the territory of member states, settlement of disputes and relations with other international organizations.

Among the documents accompanying the Treaty was a Convention on Transitional Provisions, setting forth the measures necessary for the creation of the common market. These covered a five-year period from the creation of the common market for coal.

The Common Market between the six member countries of the ECSC was opened for coal, iron ore and scrap on Feb. 10, 1953; for steel on May 1, 1953; and for special steels on Aug. 1, 1954. The market came into full operation on Feb. 10, 1958, when the five-year transitional period of its formation came to an end.

APPENDIX FOUR:

TREATIES OF ROME

The Treaty establishing the European Economic Community, and that establishing the European Atomic Energy Community, were signed in Rome on March 25, 1957, and entered into force on Jan. 1, 1958.

The EEC Treaty, which was concluded for an unlimited period, consisted of 248 articles, 15 annexes, four "declarations of intention" and three protocols.

In the preamble to the Treaty, the six signatory countries declared their intention of establishing "the foundations of an enduring and closer union between European peoples" by gradually removing the economic effects of their political frontiers. A common market and a common external tariff (customs union) would be established for all goods; common policies would be devised for agriculture, transport, labour mobility, and important sectors of the economy; common institutions would be set up for economic development; and the overseas territories and possessions of member states would be associated with the new Community for an experimental five-year period. All these measures would have one "essential aim"—the steady improvement in the conditions of life and work of the peoples of the member countries.

The tasks of the Community were defined in Article 1 of the Treaty as the achievement of a harmonious development of the economy within the whole Community, a continuous and balanced economic expansion, increased economic stability, a more rapid improvement in living standards, and closer relations between the member countries.

Progressive implementation of Common Market and procedure during transitional period. One of the principal characteristics of the process of creating a Common Market would be its irrevocable character—i.e. once the process had been set in motion, the ultimate aim would have to be achieved. This constituted an important safeguard for the member countries inasmuch as their sacrifices in adjusting themselves to the new conditions would not be in vain, and would not involve a risk of a complete standstill and a subsequent return to the previous status after a number of years. The change from one stage to the next would thus in principle take place automatically.

The Common Market would be progressively established in three stages within a transitional period of 12 years, which might be extended to 15 years. Within the basic 12-year period there would be three stages, each lasting in principle four years. However, if at the end of the first four years the Council of Ministers and the Commission were not unanimously agreed that the objectives of that stage had been essentially accomplished, the stage would automatically be extended for one year. At the end of the fifth year there would be another one-year extension on the same condition, whilst at the end of the sixth year (when the decision of the Council of Ministers would no longer require unanimity but would be taken by a weighted majority) a further extension could be granted only if a request by a member state for such an extension was recognized as justified by an ad hoc arbitration tribunal of three members appointed by the Council of Ministers. In deciding whether the objectives of the respective stages had been essentially accomplished, and the obligations under the Treaty carried out, no member country could prevent a unanimous decision by basing its protest on non-compliance with its own obligations.

The second and third stages could either be prolonged or shortened by unanimous decision of the Council of Ministers, subject to the maximum limit of 15 years for the whole transitional period.

The member countries would co-ordinate their economic policy to the extent required for achieving the aims of the Treaty. The institutions of the Community would ensure that the internal and external financial stability of the member countries was not endangered. Any discrimination against nationals or companies of other member countries would be prohibited, except in the special cases expressly laid down in the Treaty.

The basis of the Economic Community. The European Economic Community would be based on a customs union covering the whole trade of member countries and entailing (*a*) a prohibition on imposing import or export duties or similar levies between member countries; (*b*) the introduction of a common tariff on imports from non-Community countries; (*c*) the abolition of all quantitative import and export restrictions and other similar measures between member countries. The free exchange of goods within the Community would apply not only to goods produced in the member countries but also to those which had been imported by a member country from outside the Community, and on which customs duties had been paid on entry. The only exception from the application of the common customs tariff vis-à-vis non-Community countries would be in the case of goods landed in a free trade zone where each member country could apply its own customs tariff.

Internal tariffs. Tariff restrictions on trade between member countries would have to be abolished entirely by the end of the transitional period at the latest. During the transitional period, national tariffs (those in force on Jan. 1, 1957, being taken as the basis for calculation in each case) would be reduced by 10 per cent three times in each of the first two stages, and by the remaining 40 per cent during the third stage. The first reduction would take effect a year after the Treaty came into force, and the next two would follow at intervals of 12 to 18 months.

Only the first tariff reduction, however, would be uniformly applied. Thereafter governments would have a certain discretion as to the incidence of the cuts on the various types of goods in the light of "their general economic situation and the conditions of the economic sector concerned", provided always (*a*) that the total amount of reductions made up the required percentage of 10 per cent of the total tariff proceeds on imports from the other member countries in 1956; (*b*) that no single reduction on any article was less than 5 per cent; and (*c*) that where the initial duty was more than 30 per cent, the reduction was at least 10 per cent. To prevent any excessive delay in the tariff reduction for certain goods, member countries would have to aim at achieving a reduction of at least 25 per cent for each item at the end of the first stage, and of at least 50 per cent at the end of the second stage.

Duties of a financial character on certain imported foodstuffs which constituted important revenue sources (e.g. coffee, tea, condiments) would be treated like other import duties. Member countries would be permitted, however, to replace them by internal consumption duties provided these would not discriminate between the home-produced product and that imported from another member country.

All export duties and similar levies on goods destined for other Community countries would be abolished not later than the end of the first stage.

External tariffs. A common tariff on imports from non-Community countries would be established in full not later than the end of the transitional period. As a general rule, the final tariff for each product would be the arithmetical average of the corresponding national tariffs in force on Jan. 1, 1957. National tariffs which varied initially by no more than 15 per cent from the average tariff would be replaced by the latter within four years; in other cases the gap would be reduced by 30 per cent after four years, by 60 per cent after eight years, and eliminated entirely by the end of the transitional period.

Certain exceptions to these general provisions were permitted: (*a*) on a certain number of commodities, fixed duties would replace the arithmetical average (some of these were laid down specifically in the Treaty, others would be settled by negotiation between the member countries during the first stage); (*b*) in the case of a wide range of raw materials, the common tariff would not exceed 3 per cent; (*c*) in the case of a wide range of semi-manufactured goods it would not exceed 10 per cent; (*d*) in the case of a range of inorganic chemical products, it would not exceed 15 per cent; (*e*) in the case of a range of organic chemical products, dyestuffs, and artificial fibres it would not exceed 25 per cent; (*f*) a member country finding itself in special difficulties could be authorized by the Commission to delay the reduction or increase of certain tariff items for a limited period, but this would only apply to items which represented not more than 5 per cent of the total value of that member country's imports from non-Community countries.

Member countries might be permitted by the Community to import at tariff rates below those of the common tariff, or duty free, certain goods up to a fixed quantity in the following cases: (*a*) if the supply of the member country concerned was traditionally dependent to a considerable extent on imports from non-Community countries, and if production within the Community was insufficient to cover that country's requirements; (*b*) if any change in the sources of supply, or an insufficient supply within the Community, involved serious disadvantage to the manufacturing industries of the member country concerned; (*c*) if the quantity of imports under this exemption was not so large as to cause the risk of a diversion of economic activities to the member country concerned (i.e. because of its lower tariffs) to the disadvantage of other member countries; (*d*) if, in the case of food products, such imports would not result in a serious disturbance of the market.

Rates in the common customs tariff could be altered or suspended either as a result of negotiations with non-Community countries in return for concessions by those countries, or because the Community considered such action necessary for reasons of its own economic policy. Decisions on this matter would require unanimity in the Council of Ministers. After the end of the transitional period, however, the Council could take decisions by qualified majority if the changes did not exceed 20 per cent of the duty on the tariff item in question, and if they were for a period of no more than six months—which might be prolonged once only.

Quantitative restrictions. All quantitative restrictions on trade within the Community would be progressively eliminated by a series of quota increases. This procedure differed from the one applied by the OEEC, which provides for the immediate complete removal of import quotas in respect of a growing range of individual products. (The OEEC —Organization for European Economic Co-operation—was the forerunner of the OECD—Organization for Economic Co-operation and Development.)

Thus, one year after the coming into force of the Treaty, the member states would convert all their existing bilateral import quotas into global quotas in favour of all other member countries, without any discrimination between them. All these global import quotas would then be increased annually by at least 20 per cent as regards their overall value, and by at least 10 per cent as regards each individual product; bigger increases would be made in the case of quotas amounting initially to less than three per cent of the domestic output of a given product. While governments would have a certain amount of discretion as to the incidence and timing of quota increases, they would nevertheless be required to work towards the ultimate objective—viz. that by the end of the tenth year each individual quota should be equivalent to at least 20 per cent of the national production of the article concerned.

Special provisions would regulate the position of those member countries which had already introduced high global import quotas on the coming into force of the Treaty, or which had gone beyond the obligations assumed within the OEEC as regards the liberalization of imports. If the Commission found that the imports of a certain commodity into a member country during two successive years had been below the respective import quota, the quota would be abolished altogether.

Quantitative restrictions on exports would have to be abolished by the end of the first stage at the latest.

Member countries were nevertheless permitted to impose import, export, or transit restrictions or prohibitions which were justified for reasons of public morality, public order, public security, or on similar grounds, provided there was no arbitrary discrimination or any concealed restriction of trade.

As regards certain state monopolies in the member countries which might lead to restrictions in inter-Community trade with effects similar to quota restrictions, the Treaty provided that all such monopolies would have to be gradually changed so that at the end of the transitional period any discrimination between nationals of member countries as regards both purchases and supplies would cease. If a certain product was subject to a commercial state monopoly in one or several member countries, the Commission could authorize the other member states to take certain protective measures.

Agriculture. Agricultural products would be included in the Common Market, although a special régime would apply in view of the different social structure of agriculture in the various member countries, which made it impossible to introduce a completely liberalized market.

(i) *Agricultural policy.* A common agricultural policy would be implemented in the course of the transitional period, aiming at increased agricultural productivity, safeguarding an adequate standard of living for the agricultural population, stabilization of agricultural markets, an assurance of adequate supplies, and fair prices for consumers. For this purpose a conference would be convened by the Commission within two years after the coming into force of the Treaty, one of its main tasks being to draw up a balance-sheet of agricultural needs and resources. In the light of the conclusions of this conference the Commission would draw up proposals and submit them to the Council of Ministers, which would take its decisions unanimously during the first two transitional stages and by a qualified majority thereafter.

(ii) *Agricultural markets.* A Joint Organization of agricultural markets would be created, but, because of the diversity of market conditions for individual products, this development would not take place under prearranged rules but through decisions of the organs of the Community, varying from case to case. The Joint Organization could accordingly be implemented by joint rules for competition, or by the obligatory co-ordination of differing national market rules, or by the introduction of European market rules. Measures which the Joint Organization might take to achieve the aims of a common agrarian policy might include price-fixing, subsidies, provisions for building up stocks and reserves, joint stabilization measures for imports and exports, and the setting-up of one or several support and guarantee funds for the latter purpose. National market policies would eventually be superseded by the Joint Organization, and by the abolition of all discriminatory measures between producers or consumers within the Community.

Decisions of the Council of Ministers in this sphere, based on proposals by the Commission, would be taken unanimously during the first two transitional stages and by a qualified majority thereafter. However, the latter voting procedure would only apply (*a*) if the proposed Joint Organization offered guarantees for the employment and the living standards of the producers concerned not inferior to those existing under national market regulations; and (*b*) if the Joint Organization created conditions for inter-Community trade which corresponds to those in the national markets concerned. The organs of the Community would decide how far the Treaty provisions concerning the regulation of competition should apply to agriculture.

(iii) *National minimum prices.* To facilitate the development of a common agricultural market, member countries would be permitted to fix minimum prices for imported agricultural products during the transitional period, provided these prices did not prevent the expansion of trade within the Community. Within four years after the Treaty came into force, the Commission would submit to the Council of Ministers a series of "objective criteria" concerning the fixing of such minimum prices. If the Council were unanimously agreed on these criteria, each country would fix its own minimum prices in the light thereof, but the Council and the Commission would retain certain powers of control to prevent abuses. If actual prices fell below the prescribed levels, the country concerned could temporarily suspend or reduce imports or admit them only at a higher price. At the end of the transitional period all the minimum prices then in force would be listed, and the Council of Ministers would decide by a simple weighted majority about the system to be applied in future under a joint agricultural policy.

(iv) *Long-term purchase agreements.* With a view to expanding the volume of trade within the Community steadily, a preferential purchase system would be set up amongst member states by means of multilateral long-term agreements and contracts which would exclude any discrimination between the producers of the various member countries concerned. Special provision was made in respect of agricultural production dependent upon the import of certain materials from non-Community countries.

Labour, settlement, services, and capital. The free circulation of labour, services, and capital, as well as the right to settle, work and trade anywhere in the Community, would be fully established by the end of the transitional period.

(i) *Labour.* As soon as the Treaty came into force, the Council of Ministers would decide by simple majority what measures were necessary to ensure complete mobility of labour within the Community, including (a) the abolition of all discriminatory measures between nationals of member countries; (b) the right to apply for jobs anywhere within the six countries, and—on terminating any employment—to stay on in the country concerned under conditions to be fixed by the Commission. Measures to be taken by the Council of Ministers would include provisions (a) for the dissemination of information about available jobs and labour, as well as other procedures to meet supply and demand under conditions which would avoid serious danger to the standard of living and employment in the various areas and industries; (b) for the removal of administrative difficulties; and (c) for close collaboration between national labour organizations. The Council of Ministers would also decide (by unanimous vote) on social security arrangements applicable to conditions of full mobility of labour.

(ii) *Right of settlement.* All restrictions on the right to settle freely in any member country, or the right of nationals of any member country to set up agencies, branches, or subsidiary companies in the territory of another, would be gradually removed during the transitional period. The right of settlement would include the right to engage in any economic activity and to establish or manage companies and other enterprises.

Before the end of the first stage of the transitional period the Council of Ministers would, by unanimous decision, work out a general programme to remove from existing restrictions every kind of activity, and to determine the various stages of implementation. All decisions relating to the execution of this general programme, or for the abolition of restrictions on specific activities, would be taken by the Council of Ministers by unanimous vote during the first stage and by a qualified majority thereafter.

The Council would also draw up rules for the mutual recognition of diplomas, certificates, and other qualifications, and for the co-ordination of existing regulations in the member countries concerning the practice of professions.

(iii) *Services.* All restrictions on the offering of services by insurance companies, banks, finance houses, the wholesale and retail trade, and by members of the professions would be gradually removed within the Community during the transitional period. Before the end of the first stage the Council of Ministers would (subject to unanimous approval) draw up a general programme to implement this principle. Any further Council decisions, either for implementing the general programme or, if none had been drawn up, for abolishing restrictions relating to specific services, would be taken by unanimous vote before the end of the first stage and by a qualified majority thereafter.

(iv) *Capital.* Existing restrictions on the movement of capital between the Community countries would be progressively removed. As far as was necessary for the proper working of the Common Market, restrictions on current payments relating to the movement of capital (e.g. interest, dividends, rents, premiums) would be completely abolished not later than the end of the first stage of the transitional period. Decisions of the Council of Ministers on the abolition of capital movement restrictions would be taken by unanimous vote during the first two stages, and by a qualified majority thereafter.

The only exceptions from the general rule of the eventual free movement of capital within the Community would apply in the following cases; (*a*) loans directly or indirectly intended to finance the government, public institutions, or organs of local government of one member country could be issued or sold in another member country only with that country's consent; (*b*) member countries, while generally forbidden to introduce any new restrictions concerning capital movements, would be entitled to take protective measures within certain limits if such movements were likely to disturb their economies—the application of these protective measures being, however, supervised by the Commission.

As regards capital movements between member countries and non-Community states, the Council of Ministers would lay down all the measures required for controlling such movements and the foreign exchange policies connected with them, with the aim of achieving the highest possible degree of liberalization. Council decisions in these matters would require unanimity. In the event of different degrees of liberalization of capital movements and foreign exchange policies between one member country and another leading to abuses of the regulations then existing, a member country affected by such abuses could take suitable measures to stop them after consulting with the other member countries and the Commission. Measures of this kind, however, might be subsequently amended or abolished altogether by decisions of the Council, taken by a qualified majority.

Transport. The Council of Ministers would establish a joint transport policy and common rules for international transport within or through the Community, covering rail, road, and inland water transport. It would also lay down the conditions under which transport undertakings of one member country would be permitted to operate in another. These decisions would have to be taken unanimously in the first two transitional stages and by a qualified majority thereafter, but unanimity would still be required after the second transitional stage whenever the Council's decisions related to principles of transport policy and might seriously impair the standard of living and employment in certain areas.

The extension of suitable common rules to sea and air transport, and the procedure applying in these cases, would be a matter for the Council to decide, such decisions requiring unanimity.

All freight rates which discriminated as to the national origin or destination of the goods transported would be suppressed by the end of the second stage of the transitional period, whilst all special rates or privileges granted by a member country for the purpose of helping or protecting specific undertakings or industries would have to be ended at the beginning of the second stage, unless specially authorized by the Commission. Within two years after the coming into force of the Treaty, and after hearing the views of the Economic and Social Committee, the Council would, by a qualified majority, issue general regulations under which the Commission would take the necessary individual decisions after hearing the views of all the member countries concerned.

In taking its decisions, the Commission would take into account not only the requirements of an adequate location of industry but also the needs of less developed areas; the problems of areas which had suffered greatly through political conditions; and the effects of the various rates and tariffs on the competitive position between various kinds of transport. West Germany was authorized, notwithstanding the provisions of the Treaty, to take any measures required to compensate the areas affected for economic disadvantages arising from the political division of Germany.

A consultative committee of experts appointed by member governments would be set up to advise the Commission on all transport questions.

To ensure free and equal competition within the Community, common rules and policies would be introduced in the member countries as summarized below.

Cartels and monopolies. Any agreement or association preventing, restraining, or distorting competition within the Community would be forbidden—e.g. agreements or associations directly or indirectly fixing prices; regulating or controlling production, investment, or technical development; sharing markets; requiring the acceptance of additional goods besides those needed by the customer; or providing for discriminatory conditions of supply. Exceptions would only be permissible if such agreements contributed to production, distribution, or technical or economic progress, and if (i) an adequate share of the benefits arising therefrom was passed on to the consumer; (ii) the restrictive effect was not greater than was necessary for the purpose; (iii) the agreements would not open the way to monopolistic practices. The abuse by any or a number of enterprises enjoying a dominant position in a given market within the Community would also be forbidden.

During the early period anti-monopoly rules would be enforced nationally on the basis of detailed reports by the Commission to member governments. Within three years, however, international rules and directives having the force of law throughout the Community would be issued by the Council of Ministers; these decisions would require a unanimous vote. If no such rules and directives had been issued by the Council within the three-year period, it would be able to make them thereafter by a qualified majority, on a proposal of the Commission and after consulting the Assembly.

Although the member countries themselves would initially enforce anti-cartel and anti-monopoly regulations, the Commission would have certain supervisory functions immediately after the coming into force of the Treaty. Specifically, the Commission could note violations of anti-cartel or anti-monopoly rules and could authorize a member country whose interests were affected to take the necessary protective measures.

The above principles would apply not only to private industry but also to public enterprises, as well as to enterprises enjoying special or exclusive rights and privileges. State monopolies of a fiscal character and similar undertakings would, in principle, also come under the Treaty.

Dumping. Dumping practices by any member country within the Common Market would be prohibited. If, during the transitional period, the Commission found that a member state had engaged in such practices, it would make "suitable recommendations" to the country concerned with a view to ending them. If the country concerned nevertheless continued such practices, the Commission might authorize the other member country or countries affected to take the necessary protective measures, details of which would be laid down by the Commission.

State subsidies. Unless otherwise provided by the Treaty, state subsidies (of whatever kind) which distorted or threatened to distort competition would be prohibited. Nevertheless, certain subsidies would be permissible, notably subsidies of a social character: relief after natural catastrophes; subsidies given to certain areas in West Germany as compensation for the economic disadvantages caused by the division of Germany; special aid for under-developed areas or for projects of common European importance; and aid for the development of certain branches of the economy, provided it did not affect trade conditions in a manner detrimental to the common interest. The Council, taking its decisions by a qualified majority on proposals of the Commission, might also determine other kinds of subsidies which could be regarded as compatible with the Common Market.

On the entry into force of the Treaty, the Commission would examine all existing subsidies falling under this provision, in co-operation with the member countries. If it found that they were incompatible with the principles laid down in the Treaty, or were abused, it could order their abolition or amendment. If the country concerned did not carry out the Commission's decision within the stipulated period, the Commission itself or any other member country affected could immediately appeal to the Court of Justice.

All member countries would be obliged to inform the Commission in advance of any proposed introduction or amendment of such subsidies: if the Commission considered these measures impermissible it would apply the above-mentioned procedure.

Fiscal policy. While the fiscal autonomy of member countries would in principle not be affected, certain restrictions essential for the working of the Common Market were laid down in the Treaty. These prohibited any discrimination by means of fiscal policy, as well as concealed subsidies for exports to other member countries.

Adjustment of national legislation. By unanimous vote, the Council of Ministers could issue rules for the co-ordination of existing legislation in member countries which directly affected the setting-up or working of the Common Market.

Member countries would harmonize their general economic, foreign exchange, and foreign trade policies.

General economic policy. The general economic policies of member countries would be regarded as a matter of joint interest, and the countries concerned would consult each other as well as the Commission on the measures which should be taken to meet changing circumstances. Such measures might be laid down by a unanimous vote of the Council of Ministers.

Balance of payments. Although each member country would remain autonomous in currency matters and would have sole responsibility for the maintenance of equilibrium in its balance of payments, combined with the maintenance of a high degree of employment and stable prices, all members would co-ordinate their general economic and foreign exchange policies to the extent necessary for the efficient working of the Common Market. This co-ordination would include co-operation between their Economic Ministries and Central Banks. A Monetary Committee would be set up with the task of supervising the exchange and financial positions of member countries and of making regular reports to the organs of the Community.

Each member country would conduct its foreign exchange policy in harmony with the common interest. All payments relating to the exchange of goods and services and the movement of capital, as well as the transfer of interest, dividends, rents, wages, salaries, etc., to other member countries, would be permitted as far as such transactions were liberalized under the Treaty. While the European Payments Union (EPU) would be used for the time being as a multilateral clearing-house for such payments and transfers, member countries would consult each other on an alternative payments mechanism if the EPU came to an end—unless by that time all their currencies had become freely convertible. Restrictions on other "invisible" transactions outside the above-mentioned categories would be gradually removed. (The "EPU unit" was the accounting unit under a European Payments Union to be superseded at the end of 1958 by a further agreement; this unit was equivalent to one US dollar at the then existing parity, and also to the unit of account subsequently used within the EEC.)

If a member state were threatened with serious balance-of-payments difficulties the Commission would be required to conduct an inquiry without delay. It could then propose to the Council of Ministers measures whereby the rest of the Community might help the member state concerned, such "mutual help" including the provision of limited credits by the other member countries. If the latter refused to give such aid, however, the organs of the Community would permit certain protective measures in favour of the country affected. Member countries would nevertheless be able to take the necessary protective measures on their own initiative, and without waiting for the Commission's decision, if they were threatened by a sudden balance-of-payments crisis; in such eventualities the Council might, however, subsequently demand (by a qualified majority decision) that the country concerned should amend, suspend, or abolish the measures in question.

A special protocol annexed to the Treaty dealt with French export subsidies and special import duties [see below].

External trade policy. A common external trade policy would be established by the end of the transitional period; pending this, member countries would be required to co-ordinate their trade relations with non-Community countries. The Commission would work out proposals for the procedure to be applied during the transitional period with a view to the eventual unification of external trade policies, and would submit these proposals to the Council of Ministers for the latter's approval; the Council's decisions would be taken by a unanimous vote during the first two transitional stages and by a qualified majority thereafter. In harmonizing their trade policies during the transitional period, member countries would endeavour to unify their liberalization lists vis-à-vis non-Community countries at the highest possible level, on the basis of recommendations by the Commission. As an important aspect of this process of co-ordination, the export subsidy policies of the member states would be harmonized before the end of the second transitional period.

The common external trade policy after the end of the transitional period would cover the application of a common customs tariff; the joint conclusion of trade and customs agreements; the unification of trade liberalization measures; the working-out of common export policies; and the joint application of protective measures, e.g. against dumping or subsidies by non-Community countries. The Council of Ministers would take the necessary decisions by a qualified majority on proposals by the Commission.

In future trade and customs negotiations with non-Community countries it would be the task of the Commission to initiate discussions with the consent of the Council of Ministers, and to conduct negotiations on the basis of any instructions issued by the Council. During the negotiations the Commission would be in continuous consultation with a special committee appointed by the Council for this purpose; any agreements reached would need confirmation by the Council, which would be the organ for officially concluding agreements on behalf of the Community. The Council's decisions would be taken unanimously during the first two transitional stages, and by a qualified majority thereafter. The above-mentioned procedure would apply to all customs negotiations from the coming into force of the Treaty, and to all trade negotiations from the end of the transitional period.

During the transitional period member countries would consult each other in all matters relating to international economic organizations, with a view to harmonizing their actions, and would pursue a common policy as far as possible. Thereafter they would act in agreement throughout.

In formulating their joint trade policy, member countries would take into account the favourable results which the abolition of customs duties within the Community were expected to produce in increasing the competitive power of their industries.

The Commission would promote the co-ordination of the social policies of member countries, with particular reference to employment, labour legislation, conditions of work, vocational training, social security, prevention of industrial accidents and occupational diseases, health protection, trade union rights, and collective bargaining between employers and employed.

The Commission would carry out this task by means of inquiries, recommendations, and consultations, and would deal with both internal problems and questions raised by international organizations. Before making any recommendations, the Commission would hear the Economic and Social Committee. The Commission would also report on social developments within the Community in its annual report to the Assembly. The latter body might request the Commission to make reports on special problems of a social nature.

Wages and social insurance contributions. The principle of equal pay for equal work would be generally applied during the first transitional stage. A special protocol annexed to the Treaty dealt with social security contributions in France.

European Social Fund. A European Social Fund would be established to facilitate employment and the mobility of labour within the Community. This Fund would refund to any member country 50 per cent of the cost incurred by that country, or its public bodies, for the following purposes: (a) retraining workers who had become unemployed as a result of the Common Market for another occupation, provided they had worked at least six months in their new jobs; (b) moving workers who had been compelled to change their residence (as a result of the setting-up of the Common Market) to other localities, provided they had been employed at their new places of residence for at least six months; (c) special subsidies paid to workers who were temporarily forced to work short time, or who had been temporarily thrown out of work, through changes in production by the undertaking employing them, and which had been paid to enable the workers concerned to maintain their standard of living pending the restoration of their full employment. The 50 per cent refund would be dependent on (i) the workers affected having been fully employed again by the undertaking concerned for at least six months, and (ii) the government concerned having previously submitted an approved reorganization scheme to the Commission.

The Fund would be administered by the Commission, assisted by a Committee consisting of representatives of member governments and trade unions. The Fund's budget would be part of the Community's general budget, and would be prepared by the Commission and approved by the Council of Ministers. All regulations for the working of the European Social Fund, and for laying down in detail the terms on which it would aid member countries, would be issued by the Council of Ministers (deciding by a qualified majority) on proposals of the Commission, and after consulting the Economic and Social Committee and the Assembly. The Council of Ministers would also lay down general principles for a joint policy in vocational training, designed to contribute to a harmonious economic development both in the individual member countries and in the Common Market as a whole.

A European Investment Bank would be set up as an independent legal entity, its members consisting of the countries signatory to the Treaty. The Bank would promote a common investment policy within the Community and would, on a non-profit basis, grant loans or guarantees for (i) projects in under-developed regions; (ii) the modernization, reorganization, or extension of industries which were difficult to finance on a purely national basis; and (iii) new industries of joint interest to several member countries which, because of their size or special character, would be difficult to finance by a single member country.

The Bank's capital would be 1,000,000,000 units of account ($1,000,000,000), of which France and West Germany would each contribute $300,000,000, Italy $240,000,000, Belgium $86,500,000, the Netherlands $71,500,000, and Luxembourg $2,000,000. Member countries would be required to pay in 25 per cent of their capital shares, in five equal instalments, within 2½ years after the Treaty entered into force; of each payment, 25 per cent would be in gold and the remainder in the national currency. [See appendix 1 for contributions shares as from January 1986.]

The Bank could also borrow in the capital market, but if this were not possible on reasonable terms it could request member countries to grant it special loans for financing specified projects. Such requests could only be made, at the earliest, four years after the Treaty came into force, and the loans might not exceed a total of $400,000,000, or $100,000,000 borrowed in any one year. They would bear 4 per cent interest per annum unless the Board of Governors fixed another rate.

The Bank—the statutes of which were annexed to the Treaty—would have (a) a Board of Governors, consisting of the members of the Council of Ministers; (b) a Board of Directors, comprising 12 members and 12 alternate members who would be appointed by the Board of Governors for five years. The Board of Directors would be independent of the member governments and would comprise three members and three alternate members nominated by France, three each by Germany, three each by Italy, two each by the Benelux countries jointly, and one each by the Commission. There would also be a Steering Committee consisting of a chairman and two vice-chairmen, appointed by the Board of Governors on the recommendation of the Board of Directors.

The overseas territories of Belgium, France, Italy, and the Netherlands would be associated with the Community. A special convention annexed to the Treaty laid down the details of this association for the initial five-year period.

Territories. The territories concerned were: *France*—French West Africa (including Senegal, French Sudan, French Guinea, the Ivory Coast, Dahomey, Mauretania, the Niger, and Upper Volta); French Equatorial Africa (including Chad, Gaboon, the Middle Congo, and Ubangi-Shari); St Pierre and Miquelon; the Comoro Islands; Madagascar; French Somaliland; New Caledonia; the French Settlements in Oceania; the Republic of (French) Togoland; and the Trust territory of the French Cameroons; *Belgium*—Belgian Congo and the Trust territory of Ruanda-Urundi; *Italy*—the Trust territory of Italian Somaliland; *Netherlands*—Dutch New Guinea.

Principles of association. The products of the overseas territories would enter the Community on equal terms with those of the member states, and each territory would extend to all the other member countries any concessions applying to the country with which it was specially connected. Whilst customs duties between the overseas territories and member countries would, in general, be gradually removed under the five-year convention, and quantitative import restrictions progressively abolished, the overseas territories would nevertheless be allowed to continue to impose customs duties required for the development of their industries and the financing of their public expenditure. Such duties, however, would be progressively reduced vis-à-vis other member countries to the same level applicable to goods imported by the territory concerned from the member country with which it was specially connected—thus abolishing any discrimination against the other member countries.

As regards existing individual import quotas of the overseas territories, these would be converted into global quotas for the benefit of all those member countries (and their overseas territories) with whom the territory in question was not specially connected. (Thus, in a French overseas territory there would be a global import quota for imports from, e.g., Belgium, Germany, Italy, and the Netherlands, in place of previously existing individual import quotas from each of these countries.)

Overseas Development Fund. The five-year convention provided for the setting-up of a special Development Fund for the overseas territories, with a total of 581,250,000 EPU units ($581,250,000). Of this sum, France and West Germany would each contribute $200,000,000, Belgium and the Netherlands each $70,000,000, Italy $40,000,000, and Luxembourg $1,250,000. The Fund would be allocated to the overseas territories of the four member countries concerned as follows: France $511,250,000; Netherlands $35,000,000; Belgium $30,000,000; and Italy $5,000,000.

Applications for the financing of projects out of the Development Fund would be made by the responsible authorities of the member countries and overseas territories concerned. The Commission would then draw up annually the general programme of proposed investments on which the Council of Ministers (by a qualified majority vote) would make the final decisions, on the principle of a rational geographical distribution of the projects to be financed. These projects would comprise, in particular, hospitals, technical training and research institutions, institutions to increase employment, and investment projects connected with productive development.

Within six months after the Treaty came into force, the Council (by a qualified majority vote) would also lay down the procedure for calling in contributions and paying out allocations, and for administering the Fund.

The qualified majority in this case would be one of 67 votes, "weighted" as follows: France and West Germany 33 each, Belgium, Italy, and the Netherlands 11 each, and Luxembourg one vote.

Participation in overseas projects. The measures to expand the volume of trade between the member countries and the overseas territories in question would be accompanied by decisions facilitating the settlement of nationals of all member countries in the overseas territories, as well as the participation of enterprises of all member countries in projects to be financed by the Development Fund.

Conventions for subsequent periods. Before the end of the initial five-year period the Council of Ministers would lay down rules for the next period on the basis of the results achieved, the Council's decision requiring a unanimous vote. It was, however, laid down that in any case customs tariffs would continue to be reduced in accordance with the general principles, and that the introduction of a common tariff applying both to the member countries and to their overseas territories would be proceeded with. (Certain exceptions were permitted in respect of commodities the import of which was of special importance to the member country concerned.)

Mobility of labour. Subsequent conventions (requiring unanimous acceptance by all the member countries) would regulate the mobility of labour between the member countries and the overseas territories, and vice versa.

Association of other countries. It was provided that member countries might offer participation in the Community to certain independent countries such as Morocco, Tunisia, and Libya, and to the autonomous territories of the Netherlands Antilles and Surinam.

The member states would contribute to the Community budget in the following proportions: France, Italy, and West Germany, each 28 per cent; Belgium and the Netherlands, each 7.9 per cent; Luxembourg 0.2 per cent.

The budget would be prepared by the Commission, which would also investigate the possibility of replacing the contributions of member countries by independent resources, notably receipts from the common tariff. The budget would be submitted for approval first to the Council of Ministers and thereafter to the Assembly. In the case of any modifications proposed by the Assembly, the Council of Ministers, in consultation with the Commission, would make the final decision.

With the consent of the Commission, member countries would be able during a limited period to deviate from the provisions of the Treaty in order to meet special difficulties which might be caused to some of their industries during the gradual introduction of the Common Market.

A member country which was in serious and persistent difficulties would be entitled during the transitional period to take special steps to safeguard its economy or the economy of certain areas; in such a case the Commission would decide without delay about the measures which it considered necessary, and would at the same time lay down the conditions of their implementation.

Member states would also be allowed to take special measures for the protection of their interests in the sphere of defence or in the event of war.

The treaty would apply to Algeria and the French Overseas Departments under special conditions.

Any other European country could apply for membership of the Community; the terms of its admission, and any consequential amendments of the Treaty which might become necessary, would be agreed between the original member countries and the applicant country.

Agreements might also be concluded with another country or group of countries for their association with the Community, based on certain mutual rights and obligations, joint action, and special procedures. Similar agreements of association might be entered into with international organizations.

In a special "declaration of intent" annexed to the Treaty, the member countries expressed their interest in bringing about an association between the Community and the European Free Trade Association as proposed by the OEEC.

The following protocols were annexed to the Treaty:

(1) A protocol containing the statutes of the European Investment Bank.

(2) A protocol sanctioning the continuation of trade between West and East Germany as a German internal matter. It laid down that each member country would inform both the other members and the Commission of any agreements relating to its trade with East Germany; that member countries would ensure that the implementation of such agreements were not contrary to the principles of the Common Market: and that they would accordingly take suitable measures to avoid any damage to the economies of the other member countries. It was also laid down that member countries would be permitted to take suitable measures to prevent difficulties for themselves arising from the trade of another member country with East Germany.

(3) A protocol allowing France to maintain for the time being the system of export subsidies and import duties in the franc area. This system would, however, be reviewed annually by the Commission and the Council of Ministers. If the Council found that it worked to the disadvantage of the industries of the other member countries, it might (by a qualified majority vote) request the French government to take certain measures; if the French government failed to carry out this request, the Council might (by the same majority) authorize the other member countries to take certain protective measures. The Council, by qualified majority vote, could demand the total abolition of the system if the franc area's balance of payments had been in equilibrium for more than a year and if its exchange reserves had reached a satisfactory level.

The protocol also dealt with the situation concerning overtime pay at the end of the first transitional stage. If the level of overtime pay in the other member countries had by then not reached the average level prevailing in France in 1956, the French government would be authorized to take certain protective measures to maintain French prices at a competitive level, unless the average rise of the general wage-level in the same branches of industry in the other member countries exceeded the average rise in the French general wage-level.

(4) A protocol stipulating that the Italian 10-year plan for industrial expansion (the "Vanoni Plan") would be taken into account in the policy of the Community.

(5) A protocol providing for certain protective measures for the agriculture of Luxembourg.

(6) A protocol allowing the continuation of special tariffs for imports by member countries from certain other countries with which they maintained particularly close political or economic relations—e.g. imports into the Benelux countries from Surinam and the Netherlands Antilles; imports into France from Morocco, Tunisia, and the Indo-Chinese States (Cambodia, Laos, and Vietnam); and imports into Italy from Libya and Italian Somaliland.

(7) A protocol providing that tariffs for imports from the other member countries into Algeria and the French overseas Departments would be regulated in due course.

(8) A protocol on oil products allowing member countries to maintain their customs duties on such products vis-à-vis other member countries for a period of six years.

(9) A protocol confirming that the Netherlands would ratify the Treaty only in respect of its European territory and Dutch New Guinea.

(10) A protocol allowing West Germany to import certain quantities of bananas below the common customs tariff.

(11) A protocol containing special provisions for the import of coffee into Italy and the Benelux countries.

(12) A special declaration on Berlin was annexed to the Treaty, reading as follows: "The governments of Belgium, the German Federal Republic, France, Italy, Luxembourg, and the Netherlands, having regard to the special position of Berlin and the need for the free world to support it, and wishing to reaffirm their association with the population of Berlin, will support within the Community all measures required to

ease the economic and social situation of the city, to further its reconstruction, and to secure its economic stability."

(13) Seven lists covering the items for which special maximum levels would be provided in the common customs tariff [see above] were also annexed to the Treaty, together with a list dealing with agricultural products.

Among the subsidiary conventions and protocols also signed at Rome on March 25, 1957, was an agreement laying down: (a) that there should be one Assembly common to the three European Communities (i.e. the Economic, Atomic Energy, and Coal and Steel Communities) and replacing the Common Assembly of the ECSC; (b) that there should be a common Court of Justice, also replacing the existing institution of the Coal and Steel Community; and (c) that the two new Communities should share a single Economic and Social Committee.

Treaty establishing the European Atomic Energy Community (Euratom)

The Euratom Treaty, which is valid for an unlimited period contains 222 Articles, an annex, and three lists of nuclear and other materials and products.

The aims of the Community were defined in the preamble as the raising of living standards in the member countries and the promotion of trade with non-Community countries. The tasks of Euratom were defined in Article 1 of the Treaty as the creation within a short period of the technical and industrial conditions necessary to utilize nuclear discoveries, and especially to produce nuclear energy on a large scale. This result would be achieved by joint measures of the member countries and through the activities of the institutions of the Community.

Provisions of the Treaty on nuclear development (Articles 4–106) were divided into sections dealing respectively with the development of nuclear research, dissemination of nuclear information, protection of health, investments, Community undertakings, supplies of nuclear materials, security measures, ownership of fissile material, and external relations.

The remaining principal provisions of the Treaty included the following subjects.

Finance. Estimates of all the Community's revenue and expenditure (apart from those of the Commercial Agency, which was to be established to regulate the supply of ores, raw materials and special fissile matter, and the joint undertakings) would be drawn up for each financial year and entered either in the operational budget or the research and investment budget. The revenue and expenditure of the Agency, which would operate on commercial lines, would be estimated separately. The preliminary draft budgets of the various Community institutions under the aegis of the Commission would have to be submitted to the Council of Ministers not later than Sept. 30 of each year (the financial year being Jan. 1–Dec. 31). The Council would be entitled to propose amendments but would be required, in its turn, to submit the budgets to the Assembly by Oct. 21 at the latest. If the Assembly either signified its approval or expressed no opinion within a month, the draft budgets would be deemed to be finally adopted. If the Assembly proposed amendments, the final decision would lie with the Council of Ministers. The Council's decisions would be taken by a qualified majority. For the adoption of the operational budget this would be the normal qualified majority—i.e. at least 12 out of 17 votes. For the adoption of the research and investment budget, however, the votes of the Council members would be weighted as follows: France 30, West Germany 30, Italy 23, Belgium 9, the Netherlands 7, and Luxembourg 1. A qualified majority in this case would require at least 67 votes.

Overseas Territories. Unless otherwise provided, the Treaty would apply to non-European territories under the jurisdiction of member states.

Amendment of the Treaty. The Commission or any member state would be entitled to submit proposals for amending the Treaty to the Council of Ministers, which could then decide to convene a conference of the member states to consider such proposals.

Admission of new members. Any European state could apply to become a member of the Community, and could be admitted by unanimous vote of the Council of Ministers. In the case of a successful application, the conditions of admission and the resultant changes in the Treaty would be set out in an agreement between the member states and the applicant state.

An Annex to the Treaty outlined the first five-year research programme of the Community, costing US $215,000,000.

INDEX